Get the eBook FREE!

(PDF, ePub, Kindle, and liveBook all included)

We believe that once you buy a book from us, you should be able to read it in any format we have available. To get electronic versions of this book at no additional cost to you, purchase and then register this book at the Manning website.

Go to https://www.manning.com/freebook and follow the instructions to complete your pBook registration.

That's it!
Thanks from Manning!

Tiny CSS Projects

Tiny CSS Projects

MARTINE DOWDEN
MICHAEL GEARON

MANNING
SHELTER ISLAND

For online information and ordering of this and other Manning books, please visit
www.manning.com. The publisher offers discounts on this book when ordered in quantity.
For more information, please contact

Special Sales Department
Manning Publications Co.
20 Baldwin Road
PO Box 761
Shelter Island, NY 11964
Email: orders@manning.com

Manning Publications Co.
20 Baldwin Road
PO Box 761
Shelter Island, NY 11964

Development editor:	Elesha Hyde
Technical Development editor:	Arthur Zubarev
Review editor:	Adriana Sabo
Production editor:	Andy Marinkovich
Copy editor:	Keir Simpson
Proofreader:	Katie Tennant
Technical proofreader:	Louis Lazaris
Typesetter:	Dennis Dalinnik
Cover designer:	Marija Tudor

ISBN: 9781633439832
Printed in the United States of America

brief contents

contents

preface

One of the hard parts of learning a new language or skill is extrapolating the individual skills learned into the thing we're trying to build. Although we may know the mechanics of grid or understand how flex works, learning which to choose and when (or how) to achieve a specific end that we're envisioning can be challenging. Rather than start with the theory and then apply it to our projects, in this book we took the opposite approach. We started with the project and then looked at which skills and techniques are necessary to achieve our end.

But why talk about CSS? We can write an entire application using nothing but browser-provided defaults, but it wouldn't have much personality, now, would it? With CSS, we can achieve a lot for both our users and our business needs. For everything from brand recognition to guiding users with consistent styles and design paradigms to making the project eye-catching, CSS is an important tool in our toolbox.

Regardless of libraries, preprocessors, or frameworks, the underlying technology that drives how our applications and websites look is CSS. With that in mind, so as not to get sidetracked by the individual quirks and functionality of libraries and frameworks, we chose to go back to the basics, writing this book in plain old vanilla CSS because, if we understand CSS, applying it to any other tech stack or environment becomes much easier down the line.

acknowledgments

We, Martine and Michael, thank Andrew Waldron, acquisitions editor, and Ian Hough, assistant acquisitions editor, for all their support and enthusiasm about getting the book off the ground and during the development process. We thank Elesha Hyde, development editor, who was a huge source of support from start to finish, providing professional guidance, editing, and encouragement. Louis Lazaris, technical proofreader, and Arthur Zubarev, technical development editor, provided thoughtful, useful technical feedback and code reviews. Thank you both for all your input. Finally, we send a huge thank-you to all the early-access readers and reviewers throughout the process, whose input helped shape and develop this book.

We thank all the reviewers: Abhijith Nayak, Al Norman, Alain Couniot, Aldo Solis Zenteno, Andy Robinson, Anil Radhakrishna, Anton Rich, Aryan Maurya, Ashley Eatly, Beardsley Ruml, Bruno Sonnino, Carla Butler, Charles Lam, Danilo Zeković, Derick Hitchcock, Francesco Argese, Hiroyuki Musha, Humberto A. Sanchez II, James Alonso, James Carella, Jereme Allen, Jeremy Chen, Joel Clermont, Joel Holmes, Jon Riddle, Jonathan Reeves, Jonny Nisbet, Josh Cohen, Kelum Senanayake, Lee Harding, Lin Zhang, Lucian Enache, Marco Carnini, Marc-Oliver Scheele, Margret "Pax" Williams, Matt Deimel, Mladen Đurić, Neil Croll, Nick McGinness, Nitin Ainani, Pavel Šimon, Ranjit Sahai, Ricardo Marotti, Rodney Weis, Steffen Gläser, Stephan Max, Steve Grey-Wilson, and Vincent Delcoigne. Your suggestions helped make this book better.

MARTINE DOWDEN: I thank my family, friends, and coworkers at Andromeda Galactic Solutions for their unwavering support and encouragement through my career and the writing of this book.

I'd also like to recognize the Mozilla Foundation and the countless individual contributors to the MDN docs for their tireless efforts in providing the developer community documentation for web languages such as CSS. Finally, I'd like to thank the creators, Lennart Schoors and Alexis Deveria, and all the contributors to Caniuse, for making it easy to know which browsers will support which CSS features.

MICHAEL GEARON: This being my first book, producing it has been a fun and challenging process. I'd like to thank all my family members for their support, especially my wife, Amy Smith, who has been there through the whole process. I must also say a special thank-you to my cats, Puffin and Porg, who tried (and failed) to get the odd word in the book.

about this book

Tiny CSS Projects enables designers and developers to learn CSS through a series of 12 projects.

Who should read this book?

Tiny CSS Projects is for readers who know the basics of HTML and frontend development. No experience in CSS is required. Both beginners and experienced coders will develop a deeper understanding of CSS through this book. Rather than present a theoretical view of CSS, each chapter applies a different part of CSS to a project to demonstrate in practice how CSS works.

How this book is organized: A roadmap

The book has 12 chapters, each of which is a self-contained project:

- Chapter 1, "CSS introduction"—This chapter's project walks readers through the basics of CSS, examining cascade, specificity, and selectors.
- Chapter 2, "Designing a layout using CSS grids"—This chapter explores CSS grids by designing a layout for an article while, in the process, looking at concepts such as grid tracks, minmax(), repeat functions, and the fractions unit.
- Chapter 3, "Creating a responsive animated loading screen"—This project uses CSS to create a responsive animated loading screen, using scalable vector graphics and animation to style an HTML progress bar.
- Chapter 4, "Creating a responsive web newspaper layout"—This chapter is about designing a multicolumn responsive web newspaper layout. It explores

the CSS Multi-column Layout Module, counter styles, and broken images, as well as how to adapt the layout by using media queries.

- Chapter 5, "Summary cards with hover interactions"—This project creates a series of cards using background images, transitions to reveal content on hover, and media queries to check capabilities and browser window size.
- Chapter 6, "Creating a profile card"—This chapter's project creates a profile card and explores custom properties and background gradients, as well as setting image sizes and using Flexbox for layout.
- Chapter 7, "Harnessing the full power of float"—This chapter shows the power of CSS floats to position images, shape content around CSS shapes, and even create a drop cap.
- Chapter 8, "Designing a checkout cart"—This chapter is about designing a checkout cart, which involves styling responsive tables, using a CSS grid for layout, formatting numbers, and setting CSS conditionally based on viewport size by using media queries.
- Chapter 9, "Creating a virtual credit card"—This chapter focuses on creating a virtual credit card and achieving a 3D effect by flipping the card over on hover.
- Chapter 10, "Styling forms"—This chapter looks at designing forms, including radio buttons, inputs, and drop-down menus, as well as promoting accessibility.
- Chapter 11, "Animated social media share links"—This project employs CSS transitions to animate social media share links and examines CSS architecture options such as OOCSS, SMACSS, and BEM.
- Chapter 12, "Using preprocessors"—The final chapter demonstrates how we can use preprocessors when writing CSS and presents the Sass syntax.

About the code

This book contains many examples of source code, both in numbered listings and inline with normal text. In both cases, source code is formatted in a `fixed-width font` `like this` to separate it from ordinary text. Sometimes code is also **in bold** to highlight changes from previous steps in the chapter, such as when a new feature adds to an existing line of code.

In many cases, the original source code has been reformatted; we've added line breaks and reworked indentation to accommodate the available page space in the book. In some cases, even this was not enough, and listings include line-continuation markers (➥). Code annotations accompany many of the listings, highlighting important concepts.

You can get executable snippets of code from the liveBook (online) version of this book at https://livebook.manning.com/book/tiny-css-projects. The complete code for the examples in the book is available for download from the Manning website at https://www.manning.com and from GitHub at https://github.com/michaelgearon/Tiny-CSS-Projects.

liveBook discussion forum

Purchase of *Tiny CSS Projects* includes free access to liveBook, Manning's online reading platform. Using liveBook's exclusive discussion features, you can attach comments to the book globally or to specific sections or paragraphs. It's a snap to make notes for yourself, ask and answer technical questions, and receive help from the authors and other users. To access the forum, go to https://livebook.manning.com/book/tiny-css-projects/discussion. You can also learn more about Manning's forums and the rules of conduct at https://livebook.manning.com/discussion.

Manning's commitment to our readers is to provide a venue where a meaningful dialogue between individual readers and between readers and authors can take place. It is not a commitment to any specific amount of participation on the part of the authors, whose contributions to the forum remain voluntary (and unpaid). We suggest that you try asking them some challenging questions lest their interest stray! The forum and the archives of previous discussions will be accessible from the publisher's website for as long as the book is in print.

Other online resources

Often, we can't remember how a property works or what values are available to us. One great resource for looking up how a particular property, function, or value works is the MDN docs (https://developer.mozilla.org/en-US).

Although any given aspect of CSS functionality may be defined in the CSS specification, that doesn't mean all browsers support it yet. We often find ourselves needing to understand which browsers support what and whether we should create a fallback or use alternative methods to achieve our goal. Caniuse (https://caniuse.com) is a great resource that allows us to check a particular property or function to see how well supported it is in browsers by version.

Finally, to make sure that everyone can access and use our websites and applications, we can't forget the importance of accessibility. The documents provided by the World Wide Web Consortium's Web Accessibility Initiative are great places to start, and they link to many other resources, including Web Content Accessibility Guidelines (https://www.w3.org/WAI/fundamentals).

about the authors

MARTINE DOWDEN is an author, international speaker, and award-winning chief technology officer of Andromeda Galactic Solutions. Her expertise includes psychology, design, art, accessibility, education, consulting, and software development. *Tiny CSS Projects* is her fourth book about web technologies and draws on 15 years of experience in building web interfaces that are beautiful, functional, and accessible. For her community contributions, Martine has been named a Microsoft MVP in Developer Technologies and a Google Developer Expert in Web Technologies and Angular.

MICHAEL GEARON is a user experience designer and frontend developer from Wales, UK. He earned a BS in Media Technology at the University of South Wales while practicing coding and design. Since then, Mike has worked with well-known UK brands, including Go.Compare and Ageas. He now works in the Civil Service, previously for Companies House and currently at Government Digital Service.

about the cover illustration

The figure on the cover of *Tiny CSS Projects* is captioned "M'de. de bouquets à Vienne," or "Flower seller from Vienna," and is taken from a collection by Jacques Grasset de Saint-Sauveur, published in 1797. Each illustration is finely drawn and colored by hand.

In those days, it was easy to identify where people lived and what their trade or station in life was just by their dress. Manning celebrates the inventiveness and initiative of the computer business with book covers based on the rich diversity of regional culture centuries ago, brought back to life by pictures from collections such as this one.

CSS introduction

Cascading Style Sheets (CSS) is used to control the appearance of the elements of a web page. CSS uses style rules to instruct the browser to select certain elements and apply styles and effects to them.

Chapter 1 is a good place to start if you're new to CSS or in need of a refresher. We'll start with a brief history of CSS and swiftly move on to getting started with CSS, looking at ways to link CSS with HTML.

When we have our CSS up and running, we'll look at the structure of CSS by creating a static, single-column article page with basic media components such as headings, content, and imagery to see how everything works together.

1.1 Overview of CSS

Håkon Wium Lie proposed the idea of CSS in 1994, a few years after Tim Berners-Lee created HTML in 1990. CSS was introduced to separate styling from the content of the web page through the options of colors, layout, and typography.

1.1.1 Separation of Concerns

This separation of content and presentation is based on the design principle Separation of Concerns (SoC). The idea behind this principle is that a computer program or application should be broken into individual, distinct sections segregated by purpose. The benefits of keeping good SoC include

- Decreased code duplication and, therefore, easier maintainability
- Extendibility, because it requires elements to focus on a single purpose
- Stability, because code is easier to maintain and test

With this principle in mind, HTML serves as the structure and content of a web page, CSS is the presentation, and JavaScript (JS) provides additional functionality. Together, they form the web pages. Figure 1.1 displays a diagram of this process.

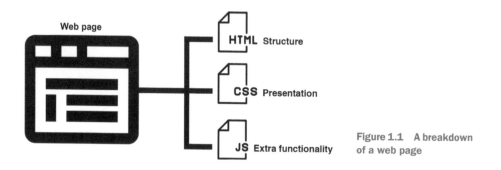

Figure 1.1   A breakdown of a web page

Since the introduction of smartphones in the mid-2000s, the web has expanded to mobile websites (often using m. subdomains, such as m.mywebsite.com), which tend to have fewer features than the desktop versions, and to responsive and adaptive designs. There are benefits and drawbacks to creating responsive/adaptive or mobile-specific websites.

The difference between responsive and adaptive designs

Responsive design uses a single fluid layout that can change based on factors such as screen size, orientation, and device preferences. *Adaptive design* can also change based on these factors. But instead of having a single fluid layout, we can create multiple fixed layouts, which gives us greater control of each one—at the cost of taking more time than a singular responsive layout. In practice, we can use both methods in conjunction with one another.

In general, responsive and adaptive designs are the way the industry is moving, especially as CSS expands, giving us more ability to apply CSS based on window sizes and media types (such as screen or print). Since the announcement of CSS in 1994, there have been three overall releases:

- 1996—First World Wide Web Consortium (W3C) recommendation of CSS
- 1997—First working draft of CSS2
- 1999—First three CSS3 drafts (color profiles, multicolumn layouts, and paged media; https://www.w3.org/Style/CSS20)

After 1999, the release strategy was changed to allow for faster, more frequent releases of new features. Now CSS is divided into modules, with numbered levels starting at 1 and incrementing upward as features and functionality evolve and expand.

A CSS level-1 module is something that's brand new to CSS, such as a property that hasn't existed as an official standard before. Modules that have gone through a few versions—such as media queries, color, fonts, and cascading and inheritance modules—have higher-level numbers.

The benefit of breaking CSS into modules is that each part can move independently, without requiring large sweeping changes to the language as a whole. There have been some discussions about the need for someone to declare the current stage as CSS4, even if only to acknowledge that CSS has changed a lot since 1999. This idea hasn't gained any traction so far, however.

1.1.2 What is CSS?

CSS is a declarative programming language: the code tells the browser what needs to be done rather than how to do it. Our code says we want a certain heading to be red, for example, and the browser determines how it's going to apply the style. This is useful because if we want to increase the line height of a paragraph to improve the reading experience, it's up to the browser to determine the layout, sizing, and formatting of that new line height, which reduces effort for the developer.

> ### Domain-specific language
> CSS is a *domain-specific language* (DSL)—a specialized language created to solve a specific problem. DSLs are generally less complex than general-purpose languages (GPLs) such as Java and C#. CSS's specific purpose is to style web content. Languages such as SQL, HTML, and XPath are also DSLs.

CSS has come a long way since 1994. Now we have ways to animate and transition elements, create motion paths to animate Scalable Vector Graphics (SVG) images, and conditionally apply styles based on viewport size. This type of functionality used to be possible only through JavaScript or Adobe Flash (now retired). We can look at CSS Zen Garden (www.csszengarden.com) for a glimpse of the possibilities; by looking at the first versus last designs, we can observe CSS's progression over time (https://www.w3.org/Style/CSS20).

In the past, design choices such as the use of transparency, rounded corners, masking, and blending were possible but required unconventional CSS techniques and hacks. As CSS evolved, properties were added to replace these hacks with standard, documented features.

> **CSS preprocessors**
>
> The evolution of CSS also led to the creation of CSS preprocessors and the introduction of Syntactically Awesome Style Sheets (Sass), released in 2006. They were created to facilitate writing code that's easier to read and maintain, as well as to provide added functionality that's not available in CSS alone. We'll use a preprocessor to style a page in chapter 12.

It could be said that CSS is in a golden age. With the continual development of the language, opportunities for new and creative experiences are virtually endless.

1.2   Getting started with CSS by creating an article layout

In our first project, we'll explore a common use case on the web: creating a single-column article. This chapter focuses on how to link CSS to HTML and explores the selectors we can use to style our HTML.

The first thing we need to understand is how to tie our CSS to our HTML and how to select an element. Then we can worry about what properties and values we want to apply. Let's start by going over some basics.

If you're new to coding, you can often find free tools to use for these projects. You have the option of coding online, or you can do the work on your computer, using a code editor such as Sublime Text (https://www.sublimetext.com), Brackets (https://brackets.io), or Visual Studio Code (https://code.visualstudio.com). Alternatively, you can use a basic text editor such as TextEdit for Mac (http://mng.bz/rd9x), Windows Notepad (http://mng.bz/VpAN), or gedit for Linux (https://wiki.gnome.org/Apps/Gedit).

The downside to using a basic text editor instead of a code editor or integrated development environment (IDE) is that it lacks syntax highlighting. This highlighting displays text in different colors and fonts according to its purpose in the code, which helps readability.

You can also use a free online development editor such as CodePen (https://codepen.io). Online development editors are great ways to test ideas; they provide quick, easy access for frontend projects. CodePen provides a paid pro option that allows you to host assets such as images, which you'll need in later chapters. Another option is to link to the GitHub location where the images are stored, as all assets that are uploaded to GitHub are stored in the raw.githubusercontent.com domain.

When you have a code editor installed on your computer or have chosen an online editor and created an account, you'll need to get the starter code for the chapter. We created a code repository in GitHub (https://github.com/michaelgearon/Tiny-CSS-Projects) containing all the code you'll need to follow along with each chapter. Figure 1.2 shows a screenshot of the repository.

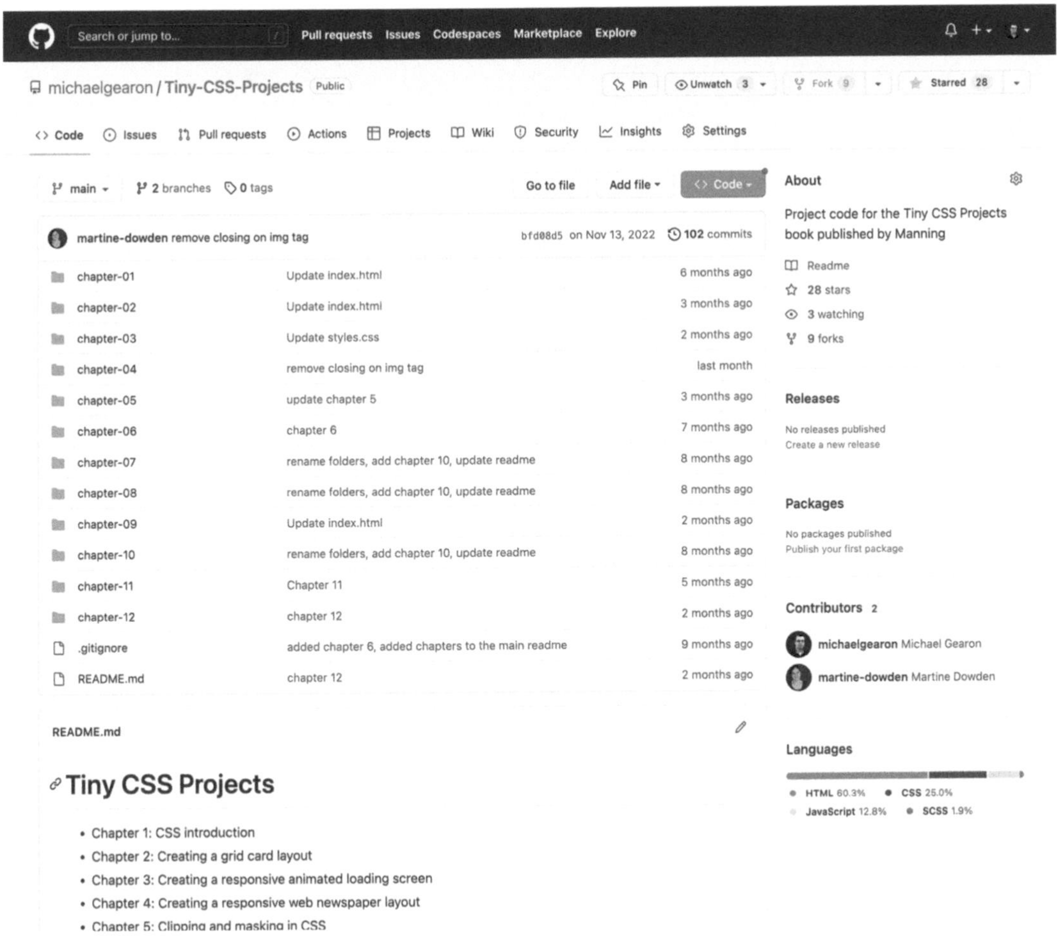

Figure 1.2   Tiny-CSS-Projects repository in GitHub

The code is organized in folders by chapter. Inside each chapter folder are two versions of the code:

- `before`—Contains the starter code for the project. You'll want this version if you're coding along with the chapter.
- `after`—Contains the completed project as it is at the end of the chapter with the presented CSS applied.

Download (or, if you're familiar with Git, clone) the project, using the Code dropdown menu at the top of the screen. If you're coding along with the chapter, grab the files from the `before` folder for chapter 1 and copy them to your project folder or pen. You should see an HTML file with some starter code and an empty CSS file. If you open the HTML file in a web browser or copy the contents of the `<body>` tag into

CodePen, you'll see that the content is unstyled except for the defaults provided by your browser (figure 1.3). Now you're ready to start styling the content with CSS, as shown in listing 1.1.

Title of our article (heading 1)

Posted on May 16 by Lisa.

Lorem ipsum dolor sit amet, consectetur adipiscing elit. Pellentesque tincidunt dapibus eleifend. Nam eu urna ipsum. Etiam consequat ac dolor et dapibus. Duis eros arcu, interdum eu volutpat ac, lacinia a tortor. Vivamus justo tortor, porttitor in arcu nec, pretium viverra ipsum. Nam sit amet nibh magna. Sed ut imperdiet orci, id finibus justo. Maecenas magna mauris, tempor nec tempor id, aliquam et nibh. Nunc elementum ut purus id eleifend. Phasellus pulvinar dui orci, sed eleifend magna ullamcorper sit amet. Proin iaculis lacus congue aliquam sodales.

1. List item 1
   - Nested item 1
   - Nested item 2
2. List item 2
3. List item 3
4. List item 4

Curabitur id augue nulla. Aliquam purus urna, aliquam eu ornare id, maximus et tellus. Aliquam eleifend sem vitae urna blandit, non bibendum tellus dignissim. Aliquam imperdiet imperdiet sapien sit amet consectetur. Nam convallis turpis felis, sedvulputate lacus eleifend a. Mauris pharetra imperdiet lacinia. Sed sit amet feugiat lectus, in consectetur magna. Vestibulum accumsan porta enim at ultricies. Vestibulum vitae massa quis massa dignissim imperdiet.

Nunc eleifend nulla lobortis porta rhoncus. Vivamus feugiat, sem vitae feugiat aliquam, orci nulla venenatis libero, vitae rhoncus nibh neque ac velit.

Etiam tempor vulputate varius. Duis at metus ut eros ultrices facilisis. Donec ut est finibus, egestas nisl eu, placerat neque. Pellentesque cursus, turpis nec sollicitudin sodales, nis tellus ultrices lectus, nec facilisis purus neque vitae diam. Nunc eleifend nulla lobortis porta rhoncus. Vivamus feugiat, sem vitae feugiat aliquam, orci nulla venenatis libero, vita rhoncus nibh neque ac velit. Donec non fringilla magna. Vivamus eleifend ligula libero, fermentum imperdiet arcu viverra in. Vivamus pellentesque odio interdum mauris aliquam scelerisque.

Heading 2

In ac euismod tortor. Vivamus vitae velit efficitur, mattis turpis quis, tincidunt elit. In eleifend in dolor id aliquet. Vivamus pellentesque erat a magna ultricies rhoncus. Vestibulun at mattis purus, non lobortis risus. Mauris porta ullamcorper mollis. Sed et placerat nisi, quis porttitor lacus. Curabitur sagittis nisl egestas ipsum tristique, eu semper erat gravida. Vestibulum sagittis quam sit amet tristique ultricies.

In id lobortis leo. Nullam commodo tortor eu neque tempus accumsan. Vivamus molestie, felis consequat consequat iaculis, justo massa porttitor tellus, ac suscipit urna erat eu erat. Nunc malesuada eleifend erat nec pharetra. Sed eu magna iaculis, elementum dui ac, sagittis augue. Nam sit amet risus dapibus massa rutrum faucibus. Sed rhoncus finibus magna, vel tristique sem bibendum nec.

Heading 3

Mauris sit amet tempor ex. Morbi eu semper velit. Nullam hendrerit urna pellentesque, interdum lectus volutpat, gravida odio. Sed vulputate eget ante vel vehicula. Curabitur ac velit sed magna malesuada hendrerit. Vestibulum ante ipsum primis in faucibus orci luctus et ultrices posuere cubilia curae; Ut volutpat nisi purus. Morbi venenatis fermentum commodo. Nam accumsan mollis neque non interdum. Aenean cursus metus ac est gravida, placerat interdum justo pellentesque. Duis nec scelerisque lacus, elementum tincidunt est. Maecenas et leo justo. Nam porta risus porttitor vulputate laoreet. Nulla sodales sagittis nulla, non viverra erat consectetur et.

Figure 1.3   Starter HTML for our article

NOTE   CodePen handles the information in the <head> tag for you automatically. Therefore, if you're following along in CodePen or a similar online editor, you need to copy only the code within the <body> tag.

Listing 1.1   Starting HTML

```html
<!doctype html>
<html lang="en">
<head>
  <meta charset="utf-8">
  <meta name="viewport" content="width=device-width, initial-scale=1">
  <title>Chapter 1 - CSS introduction</title>
  <link rel="stylesheet" href="styles.css">
</head>
<body>
  <img src="sample-image.svg" width="100" height="75" alt="">
  <article>
    <header>
      <h1>Title of our article (heading 1)</h1>
      <p>
        Posted on
        <time datetime="2015-05-16 19:00">May 16</time>
        by Lisa.
      </p>
    </header>
    <p>Lorem ipsum dolor sit amet, …</p>
    <ol class="ordered-list">
      <li>List item 1
        <ul>
          <li>Nested item 1</li>
          <li>Nested item 2</li>
        </ul>
      </li>
      <li>List item 2</li>
      <li>List item 3</li>
      <li>List item 4</li>
    </ol>
    <img src="sample-image.svg" width="200" height="150" alt="">
    <p>Curabitur id augue nulla ...</p>
    <blockquote id="quote-by-author">
     Nunc eleifend nulla lobortis ...
    </blockquote>
    <p>Etiam tempor vulputate varius ...</p>
    <h2>Heading 2</h2>
    <p>
      In ac euismod tortor ...
      <a target="_blank" href="#">In eleifend in dolor id aliquet</a>
      ...
    </p>
    <p>In id lobortis leo ...</p>
    <img src="sample-image.svg" width="200" height="150" alt="">
    <h3>Heading 3</h3>
    <p>
      Mauris sit amet tempor ex ...
```

```
    <a href="#">Sed vulputate eget ante vel vehicula</a>.
    Curabitur ac velit sed ...
  </p>
  <p>Quisque vel erat et ...</p>
  <h4 class="small-heading">Heading 4</h4>
  <p>Aliquam porttitor, ex ...
    <a href="#">Cras sed finibus libero</a>
    Duis lobortis, ipsum ut consectetur …
  </p>
  <h2>Heading 2</h2>
  <h3>Heading 3</h3>
  <svg xmlns="http://www.w3.org/2000/svg" width="300" height="150">
    <circle cx="70" cy="70" r="50"></circle>
    <rect y="80" x="200" width="50" height="50" />
  </svg>
  <h4>Heading 4</h4>
  <h5 class="small-heading">Heading 5</h5>
  <p>In finibus ultrices nulla ut rhoncus …</p>
  <h6 class="small-heading">Heading 6</h6>
  <p lang="it">Questo paragrafo è definito in italiano.</p>
  <ul class="list">
    <li>List item 1
      <ul>
        <li>Nested item 1</li>
        <li>Nested item 2</li>
      </ul>
    </li>
    <li>List item 2</li>
    <li>List item 3</li>
    <li>List item 4</li>
  </ul>
  <footer>
    <p>Footer text</p>
  </footer>
</article>
<p>Nam rutrum nunc at lectus …</p>
</body>
</html>
```

1.3   Adding CSS to our HTML

When we're styling with CSS, we have three ways to apply CSS to our HTML:

- Inline
- Embedded
- External

1.3.1   Inline CSS

We can inline the CSS by adding a `style` attribute to an element. This method has us add the CSS to the element directly in the HTML.

Attributes are always specified in the opening tag and typically consist of the name of the attribute—in this case, `style`. The attribute is sometimes followed by an equal sign (=) and its value in quotes. All the CSS goes inside the opening and closing quotation marks.

As an example, let's set the color of our heading to crimson: <h1 style="color: crimson"> Title of our article (heading 1) </h1>. If we save our HTML and view it in a browser, we'll see that it's crimson. If we're using a code editor rather than a web client (CodePen), we need to refresh the browser page to view our changes. Figure 1.4 shows the output. Notice that the only element affected is the <h1> to which we applied the style.

Title of our article (heading 1)

Posted on May 16 by Lisa.

Lorem ipsum dolor sit amet, consectetur adipiscing elit. Pellentesque tincidunt dapibus eleifend. Nam eu urna ipsum. Etiam consequat ac dolor et dapibus. Duis eros arcu, interdum eu volutpat ac, lacinia a tortor. Vivamus justo tortor, porttitor in arcu nec, pretium viverra ipsum. Nam sit amet nibh magna. Sed ut imperdiet orci, id finibus justo. Maecenas magna mauris, tempor nec tempor id, aliquam et nibh. Nunc elementum ut purus id eleifend. Phasellus pulvinar dui orci, sed eleifend magna ullamcorper sit amet. Proin iaculis lacus congue aliquam sodales.

  1. List item 1
       ○ Nested item 1
       ○ Nested item 2
  2. List item 2
  3. List item 3
  4. List item 4

Curabitur id augue nulla. Aliquam purus urna, aliquam eu ornare id, maximus et tellus. Aliquam eleifend sem vitae urna blandit, non bibendum tellus dignissim. Aliquam imperdiet imperdiet sapien sit amet consectetur. Nam convallis turpis felis, sedvulputate lacus eleifend a. Mauris pharetra imperdiet lacinia. Sed sit amet feugiat lectus, in consectetur magna. Vestibulum accumsan porta enim at ultricies. Vestibulum vitae massa quis massa dignissim imperdiet.

   Nunc eleifend nulla lobortis porta rhoncus. Vivamus feugiat, sem vitae feugiat aliquam, orci nulla venenatis libero, vitae rhoncus nibh neque ac velit.

Etiam tempor vulputate varius. Duis at metus ut eros ultrices facilisis. Donec ut est finibus, egestas nisl eu, placerat neque. Pellentesque cursus, turpis nec sollicitudin sodales, nisi tellus ultrices lectus, nec facilisis purus neque vitae diam. Nunc eleifend nulla lobortis porta rhoncus. Vivamus feugiat, sem vitae feugiat aliquam, orci nulla venenatis libero, vitae rhoncus nibh neque ac velit. Donec non fringilla magna. Vivamus eleifend ligula libero, fermentum imperdiet arcu viverra in. Vivamus pellentesque odio interdum mauris aliquam scelerisque.

Heading 2

In ac euismod tortor. Vivamus vitae velit efficitur, mattis turpis quis, tincidunt elit. In eleifend in dolor id aliquet. Vivamus pellentesque erat a magna ultricies rhoncus. Vestibulum at mattis purus, non lobortis risus. Mauris porta ullamcorper mollis. Sed et placerat nisi, quis porttitor lacus. Curabitur sagittis nisl egestas ipsum tristique, eu semper erat gravida.

Figure 1.4   Crimson header

One downside of inline CSS is that it takes the highest specificity in CSS, which we'll look at in more detail soon. Another major downside to inline CSS is that it can become unmanageable quickly. Suppose that we have 20 paragraphs within an HTML document. We would need to apply the same style attributes with the same CSS properties 20 times to make sure that all our paragraphs look the same. This case involves two problems:

- Our concerns are no longer separated. Our HTML, which is responsible for the content, and our CSS, which is responsible for styling, are now in the same place and tightly coupled.
- We're repeating the code in many places, which makes it extremely difficult to maintain and keep our styles consistent.

The benefit of inline CSS is page-load performance. The browser loads the HTML file first and then loads any other files it needs to render the page. When the CSS is already in the HTML file, the browser doesn't need to wait for it to load from a separate location. Let's undo the style we added to the `<h1>` and look at a different technique that has the same benefits as inline but fewer drawbacks.

1.3.2 Embedded CSS

To resolve the problem of repeating code, we can add our CSS within an embedded (sometimes referred to as internal) `<style>` element. The `<style>` element must be placed between the opening and closing `<head>` tags. To color all our heading elements crimson, we can use the snippet of code in the following listing.

Listing 1.2   Embedded CSS

```
<!DOCTYPE html>
<html lang="en">
 <head>
   ...
  <style>
   h1, h2, h3, h4, h5, h6 {
    color: crimson;
   }
  </style>
 </head>
 <body>
   ...
 </body>
</html>
```

The benefit of this approach is that now we're grouping all our CSS together, and the CSS will be applied to the whole HTML document. In our example, all headings (`<h1>`, `<h2>`, `<h3>`, `<h4>`, `<h5>`, and `<h6>`) within that web page will be crimson, as we can observe in figure 1.5.

We also see a difference in how the embedded CSS is written compared with inline CSS. When we're writing embedded CSS, we create what are known as *rulesets*, which are composed of the parts shown in figure 1.6.

The part of the rule that defines which elements to apply the styles to is called the *selector*. The rule in figure 1.6 will be applied to all `<h1>` elements; its selector is `h1`.

To apply multiple selectors, we write them as a comma-delimited list before the opening curly brace. To select all `<h1>` and `<h2>` elements, for example, we would write `h1,h2 { … }`.

Title of our article (heading 1)

Posted on May 16 by Lisa.

Lorem ipsum dolor sit amet, consectetur adipiscing elit. Pellentesque tincidunt dapibus eleifend. Nam eu urna ipsum. Etiam consequat ac dolor et dapibus. Duis eros arcu, interdum eu volutpat ac, lacinia a tortor. Vivamus justo tortor, porttitor in arcu nec, pretium viverra ipsum. Nam sit amet nibh magna. Sed ut imperdiet orci, id finibus justo. Maecenas magna mauris, tempor nec tempor id, aliquam et nibh. Nunc elementum ut purus id eleifend. Phasellus pulvinar dui orci, sed eleifend magna ullamcorper sit amet. Proin iaculis lacus congue aliquam sodales.

1. List item 1
   - Nested item 1
   - Nested item 2
2. List item 2
3. List item 3
4. List item 4

Curabitur id augue nulla. Aliquam purus urna, aliquam eu ornare id, maximus et tellus. Aliquam eleifend sem vitae urna blandit, non bibendum tellus dignissim. Aliquam imperdiet imperdiet sapien sit amet consectetur. Nam convallis turpis felis, sedvulputate lacus eleifend a. Mauris pharetra imperdiet lacinia. Sed sit amet feugiat lectus, in consectetur magna. Vestibulum accumsan porta enim at ultricies. Vestibulum vitae massa quis massa dignissim imperdiet.

Nunc eleifend nulla lobortis porta rhoncus. Vivamus feugiat, sem vitae feugiat aliquam, orci nulla venenatis libero, vitae rhoncus nibh neque ac velit.

Etiam tempor vulputate varius. Duis at metus ut eros ultrices facilisis. Donec ut est finibus, egestas nisl eu, placerat neque. Pellentesque cursus, turpis nec sollicitudin sodales, nisi tellus ultrices lectus, nec facilisis purus neque vitae diam. Nunc eleifend nulla lobortis porta rhoncus. Vivamus feugiat, sem vitae feugiat aliquam, orci nulla venenatis libero, vitae rhoncus nibh neque ac velit. Donec non fringilla magna. Vivamus eleifend ligula libero, fermentum imperdiet arcu viverra in. Vivamus pellentesque odio interdum mauris aliquam scelerisque.

Heading 2

In ac euismod tortor. Vivamus vitae velit efficitur, mattis turpis quis, tincidunt elit. In eleifend in dolor id aliquet. Vivamus pellentesque erat a magna ultricies rhoncus. Vestibulum at mattis purus, non lobortis risus. Mauris porta ullamcorper mollis. Sed et placerat nisi, quis porttitor lacus. Curabitur sagittis nisl egestas ipsum tristique, eu semper erat gravida. Vestibulum sagittis quam sit amet tristique ultricies.

In id lobortis leo. Nullam commodo tortor eu neque tempus accumsan. Vivamus molestie, felis consequat consequat iaculis, justo massa porttitor tellus, ac suscipit urna erat eu erat. Nunc malesuada eleifend erat nec pharetra. Sed eu magna iaculis, elementum dui ac, sagittis augue. Nam sit amet risus dapibus massa rutrum faucibus. Sed rhoncus finibus magna, vel tristique sem bibendum nec.

Heading 3

Mauris sit amet tempor ex. Morbi eu semper velit. Nullam hendrerit urna pellentesque, interdum lectus volutpat, gravida odio. Sed vulputate eget ante vel vehicula. Curabitur ac velit sed magna malesuada hendrerit. Vestibulum ante ipsum primis in faucibus orci luctus et ultrices posuere cubilia curae; Ut volutpat nisi purus. Morbi venenatis fermentum commodo. Nam accumsan mollis neque non interdum. Aenean cursus metus ac est gravida, placerat interdum justo pellentesque. Duis nec scelerisque lacus, elementum tincidunt est. Maecenas et leo justo. Nam porta risus porttitor vulputate laoreet. Nulla sodales sagittis nulla, non viverra erat consectetur et.

Figure 1.5   Styles applied to all headings

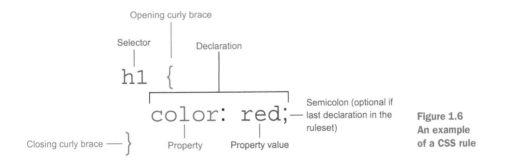

**Figure 1.6
An example
of a CSS rule**

The declaration is made up of the property—in this case, `color`–followed by a colon and then the property value (`red`). The declaration defines how the element selected will be styled. Both properties and values must be written in American English. Spelling variations such as *colour* and *capitalise* aren't supported and won't be recognized by the browser. When a browser comes across invalid CSS, it ignores it. If a rule has an invalid declaration inside it, valid declarations will still be applied; only those that are invalid will be ignored.

Embedded CSS works well for one-off web pages in which the styles are specific to that page. It groups CSS nicely, allowing us to write rules that are applied across elements, preventing us from having to copy and paste the same styles in multiple places. It also has the same performance benefits as inline styles, in that the browser has immediate access to the CSS; it doesn't have to wait for the CSS to be fetched from a different location.

The downside of having our CSS within our HTML document is that the CSS will work for only that document. So if our website has multiple pages, which is often the case, we'd need to copy that CSS into each HTML document. Unless these styles are being generated by a template of backend language (such as PHP), this task will become unmaintainable quickly, especially for large applications such as blogs and e-commerce websites. Next, let's undo the changes to our project one last time and look at a third technique.

1.3.3   *External CSS*

Like embedded CSS, the external CSS approach keeps our styles grouped together, but it places the CSS in a separate `.css` file. By separating our HTML and CSS, we can effectively separate our concerns: content and style.

We link the stylesheet to the HTML by using the `<link>` HTML tag. The link element needs two attributes for stylesheets: the `rel` attribute, which describes the relationship between the HTML document and the thing being linked to, and the `href` attribute, which stands for *hypertext reference* and indicates where to find the document that we want to include. The following listing shows how we link our stylesheet to our HTML for our project.

> **Listing 1.3   Applying external CSS to HTML**

```
<!DOCTYPE html>
<html>
<head>
   <link rel="stylesheet" href="styles.css">
 </head>
 <body>
   <h1>Inline CSS</h1>
 </body>
</html>
```

Most of the time, this approach is the one we see across the web, so it's the approach we'll use throughout this book. The benefit of external stylesheets is that our CSS is in one single document that can be modified once to apply the changes across all of our HTML pages. The downside to this approach is that it takes an extra request from the browser to retrieve that document, losing the performance benefit provided by putting the CSS directly inside the HTML.

1.4   The cascade of CSS

One fundamental feature of CSS that we need to understand is the cascade. When CSS was created, it was developed around the concept of *cascading*, which allows styles to overwrite or inherit from one another. This concept paved the way for multiple stylesheets that compete over the presentation of the web page.

For this reason, while inspecting an element with the browser's developer tools, we sometimes see multiple CSS values fighting to be the one rendered by the browser. The browser decides which CSS property values to apply to an element through specificity. Specificity allows the browser (or the user agent) to determine which declarations are relevant to the HTML and apply the styling to that element.

One aspect in which specificity is calculated is the order in which stylesheets are applied. When multiple stylesheets are applied, the styles in a later stylesheet will override styles provided by the preceding stylesheet. In other words, assuming that the same selector is used, the last one declared wins. CSS has three different stylesheet origins:

- User-agent stylesheets
- Author stylesheets
- User stylesheets

1.4.1   User-agent stylesheets

The first origin is the browser's default styles. When we opened the project, before we added any styles to it, our elements didn't all look the same. Our headers are bigger and bolder than our text, for example. This formatting is defined by *user-agent* (UA) *stylesheets*. These stylesheets have the lowest priority of the three types, and we find that different browsers present HTML properties slightly differently.

Most of the time, UA stylesheets set the font size, border styles, and some basic layout for form elements such as the text input and progress bar, which can be useful if the user stylesheet can't be found or a file-loading error occurs. The UA stylesheet provides some fallback styling, which makes the page more readable and maintains visual differentiation between element types.

1.4.2   Author stylesheets

The stylesheets that we developers write are known as *author stylesheets*, which typically have the second-highest priority in terms of the styles that the browser displays. When we create a web page, the CSS we write (embedded, external, or inline) and apply to our web pages consists of author stylesheets.

1.4.3   User stylesheets

A user who is accessing our web page can use their own stylesheet to override both author and UA styles. This option can improve their experience, especially for disabled users.

Users may use their own stylesheets for a variety of reasons, such as to set a minimum font size, choose a custom font, improve contrast, or increase the spacing between elements. Any user can apply a user stylesheet to a web page. How these stylesheets are applied to the web page depends on the browser, usually through browser settings or a plugin.

The user stylesheet is applied only for the user who added it, and only in the browser in which they applied it. Whether the change is carried over from one device to another depends on the browser itself and its ability to sync user settings and installed plugins across multiple devices.

1.4.4 CSS reset

Default styles provided by the browser aren't consistent. Each browser has its own stylesheet. Default styles are different in Google Chrome from the way they are in Apple's Safari, for example. This difference can create some challenges if we want our applications to look the same across all browsers.

Luckily, two options are available: CSS resets and CSS normalizers (such as Normalize.css; https://github.com/necolas/normalize.css). Although both can be used to solve cross-browser styling problems, they work in radically different ways.

By using a CSS reset, we undo the browser's default styles; we're telling the browser we don't want any defaults at all. Without any author styles applied, all elements, regardless of what they are, look like plain text (figure 1.7).

Title of our article (heading 1)
Posted on May 16 by Lisa.
Lorem ipsum dolor sit amet, consectetur adipiscing elit. Pellentesque tincidunt dapibus eleifend. Nam eu urna ipsum. Etiam consequat ac dolor et dapibus. Duis eros arcu, interdum eu volutpat ac, lacinia a tortor. Vivamus justo tortor porttitor in arcu nec, pretium viverra ipsum. Nam sit amet nibh magna. Sed ut imperdiet orci, id finibus justo. Maecenas magna mauris, tempor nec tempor id, aliquam et nibh. Nunc elementum ut purus id eleifend. Phasellus pulvinar dui orci, sed eleifend magna ullamcorper sit amet. Proin iaculis lacus congue aliquam sodales.
List item 1
Nested item 1
Nested item 2
List item 2
List item 3
List item 4

Curabitur id augue nulla. Aliquam purus urna, aliquam eu ornare id, maximus et tellus. Aliquam eleifend sem vitae urna blandit, non bibendum tellus dignissim. Aliquam imperdiet imperdiet sapien sit amet consectetur. Nam convallis turpis felis, sedvulputate lacus eleifend a. Mauris pharetra imperdiet lacinia. Sed sit amet feugiat lectus, in consectetur magna. Vestibulum accumsan porta enim at ultricies. Vestibulum vitae massa quis massa dignissim imperdiet.
Nunc eleifend nulla lobortis porta rhoncus. Vivamus feugiat, sem vitae feugiat aliquam, orci nulla venenatis libero, vitae rhoncus nibh neque ac velit.
Etiam tempor vulputate varius. Duis at metus ut eros ultrices facilisis. Donec ut est finibus, egestas nisi eu, placerat neque. Pellentesque cursus, turpis nec sollicitudin sodales, nisi tellus ultrices lectus, nec facilisis purus neque vitae diam. Nunc eleifend nulla lobortis porta rhoncus. Vivamus feugiat, sem vitae feugiat aliquam, orci nulla venenatis libero, vitae rhoncus nibh neque ac velit. Donec non fringilla magna. Vivamus eleifend ligula libero, fermentum imperdiet arcu viverra in. Vivamus pellentesque odio interdum mauris aliquam scelerisque.
Heading 2
In ac euismod tortor. Vivamus vitae velit efficitur, mattis turpis quis, tincidunt elit. In eleifend in dolor id aliquet. Vivamus pellentesque erat a magna ultricies rhoncus. Vestibulum at mattis purus, non lobortis risus. Mauris porta ullamcorper mollis. Sed et placerat nisi, quis porttitor lacus. Curabitur sagittis nisl egestas ipsum tristique, eu semper erat gravida. Vestibulum sagittis quam sit amet tristique ultricies.
In id lobortis leo. Nullam commodo tortor eu neque tempus accumsan. Vivamus molestie, felis consequat consequat iaculis, justo massa porttitor tellus, ac suscipit urna erat eu erat. Nunc malesuada eleifend erat nec pharetra. Sed eu magna iaculis, elementum dui ac, sagittis augue. Nam sit amet risus dapibus massa rutrum faucibus. Sed rhoncus finibus magna, vel tristique sem bibendum nec.

Heading 3
Mauris sit amet tempor ex. Morbi eu semper velit. Nullam hendrerit urna pellentesque, interdum lectus volutpat, gravida odio. Sed vulputate eget ante vel vehicula. Curabitur ac velit sed magna malesuada hendrerit. Vestibulum ante ipsum primis in faucibus orci luctus et ultrices posuere cubilia curae; Ut volutpat nisl purus. Morbi venenatis fermentum commodo. Nam accumsan mollis neque non interdum. Aenean cursus metus ac est gravida, placerat interdum justo pellentesque. Duis nec scelerisque lacus, elementum tincidunt est. Maecenas et leo justo. Nam porta risus porttitor vulputate laoreet. Nulla sodales sagittis nulla, non viverra erat consectetur et.
Quisque vel erat et leo efficitur sollicitudin. Donec id ipsum eget lacus pellentesque consequat. Praesent id justo tellus. Maecenas convallis magna ut diam euismod, et porta lacus lacinia. Sed a placerat justo. Quisque dictum augue quis dapibus posuere. Sed rutrum sed leo eget pretium. Donec fermentum varius vestibulum. Nam ultrices ornare risus, vel malesuada sapien volutpat ac. Duis sit amet leo ut metus dignissim sollicitudin nec eget diam. Nullam tortor erat, tincidunt ut venenatis at, lacinia in libero. Mauris feugiat commodo lectus eget hendrerit. Curabitur pharetra cursus eleifend.
Heading 4
Aliquam porttitor, ex sed suscipit scelerisque, arcu urna rhoncus lacus, eget aliquam enim quam ut lacus. Cras sed finibus libero. Duis lobortis, ipsum ut consectetur eleifend, libero magna ullamcorper ex, eget eleifend mi risus in erat. Ut consequat nunc diam, et convallis orci efficitur id. Etiam finibus metus a bibendum lobortis. Sed est turpis, maximus id magna vitae, lobortis faucibus turpis. Maecenas in ipsum ut nibh dignissim venenatis. Aenean laoreet, arcu a ornare feugiat, augue enim bibendum leo, in dapibus tortor ipsum nec massa. Pellentesque mollis massa magna, imperdiet elementum justo sodales vitae.
Heading 2
Heading 3

Figure 1.7   CSS reset applied

To apply a CSS reset to our project, first we create a reset stylesheet to add to our project. In our project folder, we create a file called `reset.css`. Then we copy the reset CSS into the file. Many reset options exist; one commonly used option is available at https://meyerweb.com/eric/tools/css/reset.

Finally, we need to link our stylesheet to our HTML. Because order matters, we want to make sure to include the reset CSS *before* our author styles in our <head>. Our HTML, therefore, will look like listing 1.4.

Page-load performance

For readability, having the reset and our styles in separate files is a lot nicer than having everything in one file. This approach isn't ideal for page-load performance, however.

In a production environment, we'd want to do one of the following things:

- Place the reset CSS at the beginning of the same file we have our own styles in so that we load only one stylesheet. We could do this manually or as part of a build process.
- Load the reset code from a content delivery network (CDN) before our own styles. By loading it from a CDN, we increase the likelihood that our users will have the code already cached on their machines.

Listing 1.4   Adding a CSS reset

```
<head>
  ...
  <link rel="stylesheet" href="reset.css">        ⟵  Resets
  <link rel="stylesheet" href="styles.css">       ⟵  stylesheet
</head>                                                Author
                                                      stylesheet
```

The benefit of the CSS reset is that we have a blank slate to start from. As shown in figure 1.7, all our elements look like plain text now. The downside is that we need to define basic styles for all elements, including adding bullets to lists and differentiating header levels. Furthermore, each version of CSS reset will be slightly different, based on the version and the developer who authored it.

Our other option is using a normalizer. Instead of resetting the styles, a normalizer specifically targets elements that have differences across browsers and applies rules to standardize them.

1.4.5   Normalizer

Like a CSS reset, a normalizer styles things slightly differently depending on the version and author. One commonly used CSS normalizer is available at https://necolas .github.io/normalize.css. We can apply it to our project in much the same way that we did the CSS reset code: create a file, copy the code into the file, and link it to our HTML. Note that the same performance consideration holds true here.

When the normalizer is applied (figure 1.8), our HTML looks the same as it did originally, as most of the discrepancies it handles are on elements that aren't being used in this particular project. Depending on the browser we're using, we may notice a difference in the size of the `<h1>`s.

Title of our article (heading 1)

Posted on May 16 by Lisa.

Lorem ipsum dolor sit amet, consectetur adipiscing elit. Pellentesque tincidunt dapibus eleifend. Nam eu urna ipsum. Etiam consequat ac dolor et dapibus. Duis eros arcu, interdum eu volutpat ac, lacinia a tortor. Vivamus justo tortor, porttitor in arcu nec, pretium viverra ipsum. Nam sit amet nibh magna. Sed ut imperdiet orci, id finibus justo. Maecenas magna mauris, tempor nec tempor id, aliquam et nibh. Nunc elementum ut purus id eleifend. Phasellus pulvinar dui orci, sed eleifend magna ullamcorper sit amet. Proin iaculis lacus congue aliquam sodales.

1. List item 1
     ◦ Nested item 1
     ◦ Nested item 2
2. List item 2
3. List item 3
4. List item 4

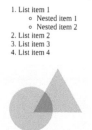

Curabitur id augue nulla. Aliquam purus urna, aliquam eu ornare id, maximus et tellus. Aliquam eleifend sem vitae urna blandit, non bibendum tellus dignissim. Aliquam imperdiet imperdiet sapien sit amet consectetur. Nam convallis turpis felis, sedvulputate lacus eleifend a. Mauris pharetra imperdiet lacinia. Sed sit amet feugiat lectus, in consectetur magna. Vestibulum accumsan porta enim at ultricies. Vestibulum vitae massa quis massa dignissim imperdiet.

Nunc eleifend nulla lobortis porta rhoncus. Vivamus feugiat, sem vitae feugiat aliquam, orci nulla venenatis libero, vitae rhoncus nibh neque ac velit.

Etiam tempor vulputate varius. Duis at metus ut eros ultrices facilisis. Donec ut est finibus, egestas nisl eu, placerat neque. Pellentesque cursus, turpis nec sollicitudin sodales, nis tellus ultrices lectus, nec facilisis purus neque vitae diam. Nunc eleifend nulla lobortis porta rhoncus. Vivamus feugiat, sem vitae feugiat aliquam, orci nulla venenatis libero, vitae rhoncus nibh neque ac velit. Donec non fringilla magna. Vivamus eleifend ligula libero, fermentum imperdiet arcu viverra in. Vivamus pellentesque odio interdum mauris aliquam scelerisque.

Heading 2

In ac euismod tortor. Vivamus vitae velit efficitur, mattis turpis quis, tincidunt elit. In eleifend in dolor id aliquet. Vivamus pellentesque erat a magna ultricies rhoncus. Vestibulun at mattis purus, non lobortis risus. Mauris porta ullamcorper mollis. Sed et placerat nisi, quis porttitor lacus. Curabitur sagittis nisl egestas ipsum tristique, eu semper erat gravida. Vestibulum sagittis quam sit amet tristique ultricies.

In id lobortis leo. Nullam commodo tortor eu neque tempus accumsan. Vivamus molestie, felis consequat consequat iaculis, justo massa porttitor tellus, ac suscipit urna erat eu erat. Nunc malesuada eleifend erat nec pharetra. Sed eu magna iaculis, elementum dui ac, sagittis augue. Nam sit amet risus dapibus massa rutrum faucibus. Sed rhoncus finibus magna, vel tristique sem bibendum nec.

Heading 3

Mauris sit amet tempor ex. Morbi eu semper velit. Nullam hendrerit urna pellentesque, interdum lectus volutpat, gravida odio. Sed vulputate eget ante vel vehicula. Curabitur ac velit sed magna malesuada hendrerit. Vestibulum ante ipsum primis in faucibus orci luctus et ultrices posuere cubilia curae; Ut volutpat nisi purus. Morbi venenatis fermentum commodo. Nam accumsan mollis neque non interdum. Aenean cursus metus ac est gravida, placerat interdum justo pellentesque. Duis nec scelerisque lacus, elementum tincidunt est. Maecenas et leo justo. Nam porta risus porttitor vulputate laoreet. Nulla sodales sagittis nulla, non viverra erat consectetur et.

Figure 1.8   A normalizer applied to our project

The good news is that UA stylesheet differences are far less problematic than they were more than 10 years ago. Today, browsers are more consistent in styling, so using a CSS reset or a normalizer is more a personal choice than a necessity.

Some differences still exist, however. Whether or not we use a CSS reset or a normalizer, we should be testing our code across a variety of devices and browsers.

1.4.6 The !important annotation

The !important annotation is one you may have seen in some stylesheets. Often used as a last resort when all else fails, it's a way to override the specificity and declare that a particular value is the most important thing. With great power, however, comes great responsibility. The !important annotation was originally created as an accessibility feature.

Remember that we talked about users being able to apply their own styles to have a better user experience? This annotation was created to help users define their own styles without having to worry about specificity. Because it overrides any other styles, it ensures that a user's styles always have the highest importance and therefore are the ones applied.

Using !important is considered to be bad practice, so we should generally avoid using it in our author stylesheets. Also, this annotation breaks the natural cascade of the CSS and can make it harder to manage the stylesheet going forward.

1.5 Specificity in CSS

When multiple property values are being applied to an element, one will win over the others. We determine the winner through a multistep process. We'll ignore !important (section 1.4.6) for the time being, as it breaks the normal flow; we'll come back to it later.

First, we look at where the value comes from. Anything explicitly defined in a rule will override inherited values. In listings 1.5 and 1.6, for example, if we set the font color to red on the <body> element, the elements inside <body> will have red text.

The font color is inherited by child elements. If we specifically set a different color on a paragraph inside the body, the inherited red value would be overridden by the more specific blue value set on the paragraph. Therefore, that paragraph's text color would be blue.

Listing 1.5 Example of inheritance (HTML)

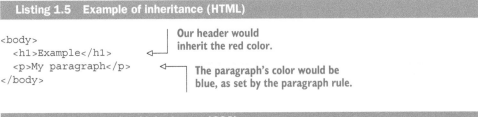

```
<body>
  <h1>Example</h1>
  <p>My paragraph</p>
</body>
```

Our header would inherit the red color.

The paragraph's color would be blue, as set by the paragraph rule.

Listing 1.6 Example of inheritance (CSS)

```
body { color: red }
p { color: blue }
```

Not all property values will be inherited. Theme-related styles such as color and font size will generally be inherited; layout considerations generally are not. This guideline is a loose one, with definite exceptions, but it's a good place to start. We'll cover exceptions on a case-by-case basis throughout the projects.

If the property value isn't being inherited, the browser looks at the type of selector that was used and mathematically calculates the specificity value. We'll get into more detail about what each selector type is in section 1.6, but first let's look at how the math is applied.

The browser looks at the selector, categorizes the types of selectors being used by the rule, and applies the type value. Then it adds all the values and gets a final specificity value. Figure 1.9 diagrams the process. The biggest number wins, so rule 1 in the diagram would win over rule 2.

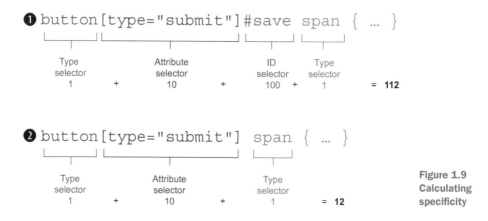

Figure 1.9 Calculating specificity

Specificity values by selector type are as follows:

- `100`—ID selectors
- `10`—Class selectors, attribute selectors, and pseudo-classes
- `1`—Type selectors and pseudo-elements
- `0`—Universal selectors

If we still have a tie, the browser looks at which stylesheet the style originated from. If both values come from the same stylesheet, the one later in the document wins. If the values come from different stylesheets, the order is as follows:

1. User stylesheet
2. Author stylesheets (in the order in which they're being imported; the last one wins)
3. UA stylesheet

We set `!important` to the side earlier. Now that we understand the normal flow, let's add it back into the mix. When a value has the `!important` annotation, the process is short-circuited, and the value with the annotation automatically wins.

If both values have the !important annotation, the browser follows the normal flow. Figure 1.10 shows the flow through the stylesheets, including !important declarations.

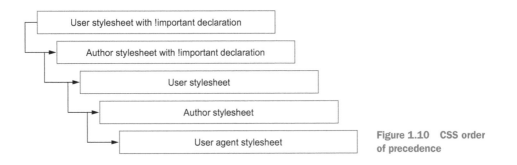

Figure 1.10   CSS order of precedence

We've established that the type of selector will affect specificity. Let's take a closer look at the selectors and use them in our project.

1.6   CSS selectors

The selector sets what HTML elements we want to target. In CSS, we have seven ways to target the HTML elements we want to style, as discussed in the following sections.

1.6.1   Basic selectors

The most common method of applying styles to HTML elements is selecting them based on name, ID, or class name. These are used most often because of their one-to-one mapping to the HTML element itself or attributes set on the element.

TYPE SELECTOR

The *type selector* targets the HTML element by name. The benefit of using the type selector is that when we read through our CSS, we can quickly work out which HTML elements would be affected if we made changes in the rule. This selector doesn't require us to add any particular markup to the HTML to target the element.

Let's use a type selector to target all our headings (<h1> through <h6>) and change their color to crimson. Our CSS would be h1, h2, h3, h4, h5, h6 { color: crimson; }. Figure 1.11 shows that our headers have changed colors.

CLASS SELECTORS

We can use class selectors on as many different elements as we want. By applying a class name to elements, we're grouping multiple HTML elements so that when we apply styles, they'll roll out to any element with that class name.

To add classes to HTML, we use the class attribute. Within the class attribute, we can add as many values (or classes) as we want, separating each with a space.

Title of our article (heading 1)

Posted on May 16 by Lisa.

Lorem ipsum dolor sit amet, consectetur adipiscing elit. Pellentesque tincidunt dapibus eleifend. Nam eu urna ipsum. Etiam consequat ac dolor et dapibus. Duis eros arcu, interdum eu volutpat ac, lacinia a tortor. Vivamus justo tortor, porttitor in arcu nec, pretium viverra ipsum. Nam sit amet nibh magna. Sed ut imperdiet orci, id finibus justo. Maecenas magna mauris, tempor nec tempor id, aliquam et nibh. Nunc elementum ut purus id eleifend. Phasellus pulvinar dui orci, sed eleifend magna ullamcorper sit amet. Proin iaculis lacus congue aliquam sodales.

1. List item 1
   - Nested item 1
   - Nested item 2
2. List item 2
3. List item 3
4. List item 4

Curabitur id augue nulla. Aliquam purus urna, aliquam eu ornare id, maximus et tellus. Aliquam eleifend sem vitae urna blandit, non bibendum tellus dignissim. Aliquam imperdiet imperdiet sapien sit amet consectetur. Nam convallis turpis felis, sedvulputate lacus eleifend a. Mauris pharetra imperdiet lacinia. Sed sit amet feugiat lectus, in consectetur magna. Vestibulum accumsan porta enim at ultricies. Vestibulum vitae massa quis massa dignissim imperdiet.

Nunc eleifend nulla lobortis porta rhoncus. Vivamus feugiat, sem vitae feugiat aliquam, orci nulla venenatis libero, vitae rhoncus nibh neque ac velit.

Etiam tempor vulputate varius. Duis at metus ut eros ultrices facilisis. Donec ut est finibus, egestas nisi eu, placerat neque. Pellentesque cursus, turpis nec sollicitudin sodales, nisi tellus ultrices lectus, nec facilisis purus neque vitae diam. Nunc eleifend nulla lobortis porta rhoncus. Vivamus feugiat, sem vitae feugiat aliquam, orci nulla venenatis libero, vitae rhoncus nibh neque ac velit. Donec non fringilla magna. Vivamus eleifend ligula libero, fermentum imperdiet arcu viverra in. Vivamus pellentesque odio interdum mauris aliquam scelerisque.

Heading 2

In ac euismod tortor. Vivamus vitae velit efficitur, mattis turpis quis, tincidunt elit. In eleifend in dolor id aliquet. Vivamus pellentesque erat a magna ultricies rhoncus. Vestibulum at mattis purus, non lobortis risus. Mauris porta ullamcorper mollis. Sed et placerat nisi, quis porttitor lacus. Curabitur sagittis nisi egestas ipsum tristique, eu semper erat gravida. Vestibulum sagittis quam sit amet tristique ultricies.

In id lobortis leo. Nullam commodo tortor eu neque tempus accumsan. Vivamus molestie, felis consequat consequat iaculis, justo massa porttitor tellus, ac suscipit urna erat eu erat. Nunc malesuada eleifend erat nec pharetra. Sed eu magna iaculis, elementum dui ac, sagittis augue. Nam sit amet risus dapibus massa rutrum faucibus. Sed rhoncus finibus magna, vel tristique sem bibendum nec.

Heading 3

Mauris sit amet tempor ex. Morbi eu semper velit. Nullam hendrerit urna pellentesque, interdum lectus volutpat, gravida odio. Sed vulputate eget ante vel vehicula. Curabitur ac velit sed magna malesuada hendrerit. Vestibulum ante ipsum primis in faucibus orci luctus et ultrices posuere cubilia curae; Ut volutpat nisi purus. Morbi venenatis fermentum commodo. Nam accumsan mollis neque non interdum. Aenean cursus metus ac est gravida, placerat interdum justo pellentesque. Duis nec scelerisque lacus, elementum tincidunt est. Maecenas et leo justo. Nam porta risus porttitor vulputate laoreet. Nulla sodales sagittis nulla, non viverra erat consectetur et.

Quisque vel erat et leo efficitur sollicitudin. Donec id ipsum eget lacus pellentesque consequat. Praesent id justo tellus. Maecenas convallis magna ut diam euismod, et porta lacus lacinia. Sed a placerat justo. Quisque dictum augue quis dapibus posuere. Sed rutrum sed leo eget pretium. Donec fermentum varius vestibulum. Nam ultrices ornare risus, vel malesuada sapien volutpat ac. Duis sit amet leo ut metus dignissim sollicitudin nec eget diam. Nullam tortor erat, tincidunt ut venenatis at, lacinia in libero. Mauris feugiat commodo lectus eget hendrerit. Curabitur pharetra cursus eleifend.

Heading 4

Aliquam porttitor, ex sed suscipit scelerisque, arcu urna rhoncus lacus, eget aliquam enim quam ut lacus. Cras sed finibus libero. Duis lobortis, ipsum ut consectetur eleifend, libero magna ullamcorper ex, eget eleifend mi risus in erat. Ut consequat nunc diam, et convallis orci dictum id. Etiam finibus metus a bibendum lobortis. Sed est turpis, maximus id magna vitae, lobortis faucibus turpis. Maecenas in ipsum ut nibh dignissim venenatis. Aenean laoreet, arcu a ornare feugiat, augue enim bibendum leo, in dapibus tortor ipsum nec massa. Pellentesque mollis massa magna, imperdiet elementum justo sodales vitae.

Heading 2

Heading 3

Heading 4

Heading 5

In finibus ultrices nulla ut rhoncus. Suspendisse potenti. Phasellus id tortor nec elit aliquet ullamcorper ut ut tortor. Morbi vehicula massa sit amet luctus posuere. Nullam eu lacinia tortor. Aenean eget pulvinar nulla, sit amet accumsan tortor. Praesent augue nunc, luctus ornare consequat id, ultricies vel tellus. Nullam gravida tellus a nisi elementum interdum. In scelerisque turpis vitae sem convallis venenatis. Donec aliquam, nibh sit amet placerat posuere, neque metus ultricies risus, at luctus leo arcu a augue. Class aptent taciti sociosqu ad litora torquent per conubia nostra, per inceptos himenaeos. Sed congue lectus quis velit fringilla, a ultricies dui vestibulum. Vestibulum ornare leo augue, vel pretium ipsum vehicula et. Nulla vel efficitur risus. Proin malesuada lobortis orci sit amet scelerisque. Sed tincidunt felis vel aliquet tristique.

Heading 6

Questo paragrafo è definito in italiano.

- List item 1
  - Nested item 1
  - Nested item 2
- List item 2
- List item 3
- List item 4

Nam rutrum nunc at lectus egestas porta. Ut molestie posuere faucibus. Pellentesque habitant morbi tristique senectus et netus et malesuada fames ac turpis egestas. Phasellus fermentum auctor arcu ultricies tincidunt. Quisque urna magna, congue et condimentum ut, varius sed arcu. Morbi hendrerit justo eget porta venenatis. Donec id ligula accumsan, congue mauris at, ornare sem. Aenean lobortis est ac nisl consequat venenatis.

Footer text

Figure 1.11   Header color change

We have many ways and methods to write our class names, such as Block, Element, Modifier (BEM) methodology (https://en.bem.info) and Scalable and Modular Architecture for CSS (SMACSS; http://smacss.com), which are style guides for writing consistent stylesheets.

The main point is to write class names that make sense to everyone. Adding the class name `text` to paragraph elements, for example, would be highly confusing. Other elements, such as our headings, can also be thought of as text, so it may not be clear which specific element we're referring to.

Applying class names based on a specific style, such as a `color`, can also be dangerous. Giving an element the class name `blue` might work immediately, but if the design changes and the color applied is now red, our class name will no longer make sense.

In our HTML, we find that some of our headings have a class of `small-heading`. We're going to create a rule that selects `small-heading` and changes the text of the elements to uppercase.

To select the `small-heading` class name, in the CSS we first type dot (`.`) followed by the class name `small-heading`. Then our styles go into curly braces as follows: `.small-heading { text-transform: uppercase }`. Figure 1.12 shows our uppercased headings. Notice that the other headings aren't affected—only those to which the class was applied.

Quisque vel erat et leo efficitur sollicitudin. Donec id ipsum eget lacus pellentesque consequat. Praesent id justo tellus. Maecenas convallis magna ut diam euismod, et porta lacus lacinia. Sed a placerat justo. Quisque dictum augue quis dapibus posuere. Sed rutrum sed leo eget pretium. Donec fermentum varius vestibulum. Nam ultrices ornare risus, vel malesuada sapien volutpat ac. Duis sit amet leo ut metus dignissim sollicitudin nec eget diam. Nullam tortor erat, tincidunt ut venenatis at, lacinia in libero. Mauris feugiat commodo lectus eget hendrerit. Curabitur pharetra cursus eleifend.

HEADING 4 ◄————————— **Has a class of small-heading**

Aliquam porttitor, ex sed suscipit scelerisque, arcu urna rhoncus lacus, eget aliquam enim quam ut lacus. Cras sed finibus libero. Duis lobortis, ipsum ut consectetur eleifend, libero magna ullamcorper ex, eget eleifend mi risus in erat. Ut consequat nunc diam, et convallis orci efficitur id. Etiam finibus metus a bibendum lobortis. Sed est turpis, maximus id magna vitae, lobortis faucibus turpis. Maecenas in ipsum ut nibh dignissim venenatis. Aenean laoreet, arcu a ornare feugiat, augue enim bibendum leo, in dapibus tortor ipsum nec massa. Pellentesque mollis massa magna, imperdiet elementum justo sodales vitae.

Heading 2

Heading 3

Heading 4 ◄————————— **Does not have a class of small-heading**

HEADING 5

In finibus ultrices nulla ut rhoncus. Suspendisse potenti. Phasellus id tortor nec elit aliquet ullamcorper ut ut tortor. Morbi vehicula massa sit amet luctus posuere. Nullam eu lacinia tortor. Aenean eget pulvinar nulla, sit amet accumsan tortor. Praesent augue nunc, luctus ornare consequat id, ultricies vel tellus. Nullam gravida tellus a nisi elementum interdum. In scelerisque turpis vitae sem convallis venenatis. Donec aliquam, nibh sit amet placerat posuere, neque metus ultricies risus, at luctus leo arcu a augue. Class aptent taciti sociosqu ad litora torquent per conubia nostra, per inceptos himenaeos. Sed congue lectus quis velit fringilla, a ultricies dui vestibulum. Vestibulum ornare leo augue, vel pretium ipsum vehicula et. Nulla vel efficitur risus. Proin malesuada lobortis orci sit amet scelerisque. Sed tincidunt felis vel aliquet tristique.

HEADING 6

Questo paragrafo è definito in italiano.

• List item 1

Figure 1.12   Class selector applied to elements that have the class name `small-heading`

ID SELECTOR

In HTML, IDs are unique. Any given ID should be used only once on a web page. If an ID is repeated, our code is considered to be invalid HTML.

Generally we should avoid using ID selectors; because they need to be unique in the HTML, rules constructed against the ID aren't easy to reuse. Furthermore, an ID selector is one of the most specific selectors available, making the styles applied with an ID selector difficult to override. Unless the uniqueness of the element is key, avoid using ID attributes.

Our example article contains a `blockquote` with an ID attribute containing the value `quote-by-author`. In our CSS, to select the `blockquote` we use a hash (#), followed immediately by the ID we want to target. Then we have curly braces, inside which we place our declarations, as shown in the following listing.

Listing 1.7   ID selector

```
#quote-by-author {
  background: lightgrey;
  padding: 10px;
  line-height: 1.75;
}
```

Figure 1.13 shows the code applied to our project.

Curabitur id augue nulla. Aliquam purus urna, aliquam eu ornare id, maximus et tellus. Aliquam eleifend sem vitae urna blandit, non bibendum tellus dignissim. Aliquam imperdiet imperdiet sapien sit amet consectetur. Nam convallis turpis felis, sedvulputate lacus eleifend a. Mauris pharetra imperdiet lacinia. Sed sit amet feugiat lectus, in consectetur magna. Vestibulum accumsan porta enim at ultricies. Vestibulum vitae massa quis massa dignissim imperdiet.

Nunc eleifend nulla lobortis porta rhoncus. Vivamus feugiat, sem vitae feugiat aliquam, orci nulla venenatis libero, vitae rhoncus nibh neque ac velit.

Etiam tempor vulputate varius. Duis at metus ut eros ultrices facilisis. Donec ut est finibus, egestas nisl eu, placerat neque. Pellentesque cursus, turpis nec sollicitudin sodales, nisi tellus ultrices lectus, nec facilisis purus neque vitae diam. Nunc eleifend nulla lobortis porta rhoncus. Vivamus feugiat, sem vitae feugiat aliquam, orci nulla venenatis libero, vitae rhoncus nibh neque ac velit. Donec non fringilla magna. Vivamus eleifend ligula libero, fermentum imperdiet arcu viverra in. Vivamus pellentesque odio interdum mauris aliquam scelerisque.

Heading 2

In ac euismod tortor. Vivamus vitae velit efficitur, mattis turpis quis, tincidunt elit. In eleifend in dolor id aliquet. Vivamus pellentesque erat a magna ultricies rhoncus. Vestibulum at mattis purus, non lobortis risus. Mauris porta ullamcorper mollis. Sed et placerat nisi, quis porttitor lacus. Curabitur sagittis nisl egestas ipsum tristique, eu semper erat gravida. Vestibulum sagittis quam sit amet tristique ultricies.

Figure 1.13   Styles applied by `#quote-by-author`

1.6.2   *Combinators*

Another way to write CSS is through *combinators,* which allow for more complex CSS without overusing `class` or ID names. There are four combinators:

- Descendant combinator (`space`)
- Child combinator (`>`)

- Adjacent sibling combinator (+)
- General sibling combinator (~)

One important concept to understand is the relationships between elements. In the next couple of examples, we'll look at how we can use the relationships between elements to target different HTML elements to style our article. Figure 1.14 introduces the types of relationships we're going to examine.

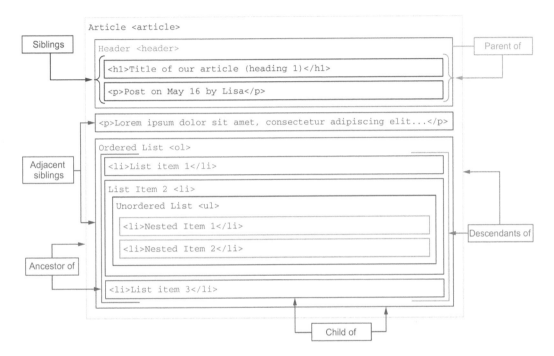

Figure 1.14 The relationships between elements in HTML

DESCENDANT COMBINATOR (SPACE)

Selectors that use descendant combinators select all the HTML elements within a parent. A selector that uses a descendant combinator is made up of three parts. The first part is the parent, which in this case is the article element. The parent is followed by a space and then by any element we want to select. Figure 1.15 diagrams the syntax.

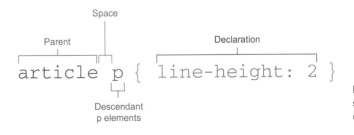

Figure 1.15 An example of a selector using a descendant combinator

In this example, the browser would find any `<article>` element, target all descendant paragraphs (`<p>`) in the parent `<article>` element, and make the text double-spaced. When this selector is applied, our article looks like figure 1.16.

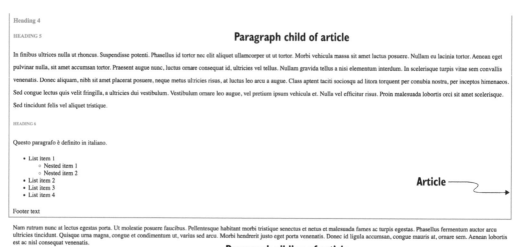

Figure 1.16   **Child paragraphs are double-spaced**

CHILD COMBINATOR (>)

The child combinator allows us to target the immediate child elements of a particular selector. This combinator is different from a selector that uses a descendant combinator because in the case of a child combinator, the targeted element must be an immediate child. A selector that uses a descendant combinator can select any descendent (child, grandchild, great-grandchild, and so on).

In our project, we'll style the list items in the article. As listing 1.8 shows, we have an unordered list (`<ul>`) with list items (`<li>`). That first child element has its own nested items, which would be grandchildren and great-grandchildren.

Listing 1.8   HTML list items

```
<ul class="list">
  <li>List item 1
    <ul>
      <li>Nested item 1</li>
      <li>Nested item 2</li>
    </ul>
  </li>
  <li>List item 2</li>
  <li>List item 3</li>
  <li>List item 4</li>
</ul>
```

Children of .list

Grandchild of .list

Great-grandchildren of .list

Parent item (.list)

We're going to style only the first-level list items—or immediate children of the <ul> with a class attribute value containing list—in a crimson color, without affecting the nested list items (the great-grandchildren). So the browser will find elements containing the list class, target only their immediate children that are list items (<li>), and change color to crimson. We'll use the following CSS:

```
.list > li { color: crimson; }
```

With this CSS, the entire list becomes crimson, not just the top-level list items. The color is applied to the <li> element and all of its descendants. Even though we select the immediate child, because color is inherited, the children also turn crimson.

To select only the top-level elements, we therefore need to add a second rule

```
.list > li ul { color: initial }
```

which returns the nested list items to their initial color, as shown in figure 1.17.

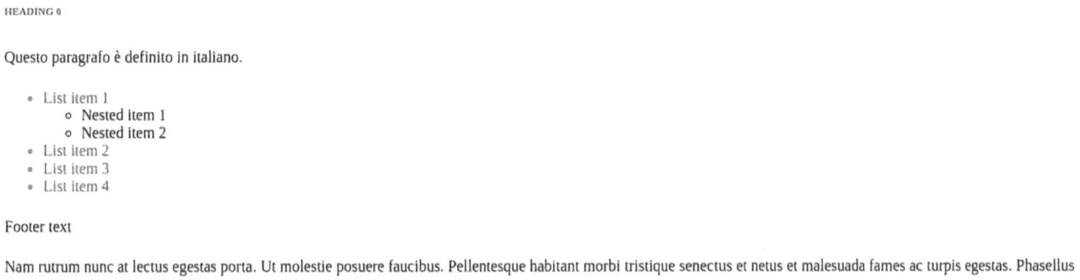

HEADING 6

Questo paragrafo è definito in italiano.

- List item 1
    - Nested item 1
    - Nested item 2
- List item 2
- List item 3
- List item 4

Footer text

Nam rutrum nunc at lectus egestas porta. Ut molestie posuere faucibus. Pellentesque habitant morbi tristique senectus et netus et malesuada fames ac turpis egestas. Phasellus

Figure 1.17   Child combinator applied to list **items**

We can perform this operation in reverse and select the parent of the child element, right? The short answer is no, as the following example wouldn't work: article < p { color: blue; }. If we want to select the parent or ancestor of an element, we need to use the has() pseudo-class—article:has(p) { color: blue; }—covered in section 1.6.3.

ADJACENT SIBLING COMBINATOR (+)

When we need to style an element that's at the same level as another, the way your brother or sister is on the same level of the family tree as you, we can use the adjacent sibling combinator. If we want to target the element that's directly after another, we can use a selector that uses an adjacent sibling combinator.

In listing 1.9, the browser will find any uses of the <header> element, target the first paragraph (<p>) immediately after (or adjacent to) the <header> element, and change the font-size to 1.5rem and the font-weight to bold. Figure 1.18 shows the code applied to our article.

Listing 1.9   Adjacent sibling combinator

```
header + p {
  font-size: 1.25rem;
  font-weight: bold;
}
```

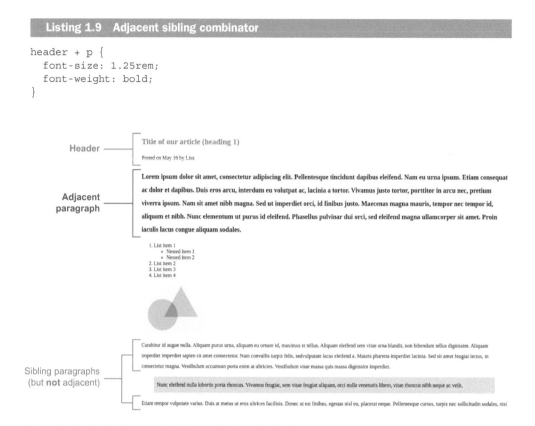

Figure 1.18   Styling the paragraph immediately after the header

This approach could be useful if we're trying to style the first element differently from the others to make it stand out. We might see this effect in a newspaper. The first paragraph of an article might be made to look more prominent than the rest to catch our attention.

Another use case is for error handling in forms. Adjacent sibling combinators allow us to display an error message to the user immediately following an invalid value in a form control.

GENERAL SIBLING COMBINATOR (~)

The general sibling combinator is more open-ended than the other methods, as it allows us to target all elements that are siblings after the element targeted by the selector.

In our example, we'll style all images that come after the element `<header>`. Notice that we have three placeholder images. The first image is small (it could be a logo or an author photo) and resides above the `<header>`. We don't want to style it. The other two images are farther down in the article. We want to apply a border around them to keep the color theme consistent with the rest of the article.

Our rule will be as follows: `header ~ img { border: 4px solid crimson; }`. The browser will find the `<header>` element; target all the sibling images (`<img>`) after that element; and add a `border` that's `4px` in thickness, that's a `solid` line (as opposed to a `dotted`, `dashed`, or `double` line), and that's colored `crimson`. We can see the code applied to our article in figure 1.19.

Title of our article (heading 1)

Posted on May 16 by Lisa.

Lorem ipsum dolor sit amet, consectetur adipiscing elit. Pellentesque tincidunt dapibus eleifend. Nam eu urna ipsum. Etiam consequat ac dolor et dapibus. Duis eros arcu, interdum eu volutpat ac, lacinia a tortor. Vivamus justo tortor, porttitor in arcu nec, pretium viverra ipsum. Nam sit amet nibh magna. Sed ut imperdiet orci, id finibus justo. Maecenas magna mauris, tempor nec tempor id, aliquam et nibh. Nunc elementum ut purus id eleifend. Phasellus pulvinar dui orci, sed eleifend magna ullamcorper sit amet. Proin iaculis lacus congue aliquam sodales.

1. List item 1
   - Nested item 1
   - Nested item 2
2. List item 2
3. List item 3
4. List item 4

Curabitur id augue nulla. Aliquam purus urna, aliquam eu ornare id, maximus et tellus. Aliquam eleifend sem vitae urna blandit, non bibendum tellus dignissim. Aliquam imperdiet imperdiet sapien sit amet consectetur. Nam convallis turpis felis, sedvulputate lacus eleifend a. Mauris pharetra imperdiet lacinia. Sed sit amet feugiat lectus, in consectetur magna. Vestibulum accumsan porta enim at ultricies. Vestibulum vitae massa quis massa dignissim imperdiet.

> Nunc eleifend nulla lobortis porta rhoncus. Vivamus feugiat, sem vitae feugiat aliquam, orci nulla venenatis libero, vitae rhoncus nibh neque ac velit.

Etiam tempor vulputate varius. Duis at metus ut eros ultrices facilisis. Donec ut est finibus, egestas nisl eu, placerat neque. Pellentesque cursus, turpis nec sollicitudin sodales, nisi tellus ultrices lectus, nec facilisis purus neque vitae diam. Nunc eleifend nulla lobortis porta rhoncus. Vivamus feugiat, sem vitae feugiat aliquam, orci nulla venenatis libero, vitae rhoncus nibh neque ac velit. Donec non fringilla magna. Vivamus eleifend ligula libero, fermentum imperdiet arcu viverra in. Vivamus pellentesque odio interdum mauris aliquam scelerisque.

Heading 2

In ac euismod tortor. Vivamus vitae velit efficitur, mattis turpis quis, tincidunt elit. In eleifend in dolor id aliquet. Vivamus pellentesque erat a magna ultricies rhoncus. Vestibulum at mattis purus, non lobortis risus. Mauris porta ullamcorper mollis. Sed et placerat nisi, quis porttitor lacus. Curabitur sagittis nisl egestas ipsum tristique, eu semper erat gravida. Vestibulum sagittis quam sit amet tristique

Figure 1.19 General sibling combinator targeting sibling images of header

1.6.3 *Pseudo-class and pseudo-element selectors*

CSS has selectors called *pseudo-classes* and *pseudo-elements.* You may wonder where the names come from. *Pseudo* means "not genuine, false, or pretend." This definition makes sense because, technically, we're targeting a state or parts of an element that may not exist yet. We're simply pretending.

Not all pseudo-elements and pseudo-classes work on all HTML elements. Throughout this book, we'll look at where we can use pseudo-classes and with which HTML elements.

PSEUDO-CLASS

A *pseudo-class* is added to a selector to target a specific state of the element. Pseudo-classes are especially useful for elements that the user will interact with, such as links, buttons, and form fields. Pseudo-classes use a single colon (:) followed by the state of the element.

Our article contains a few links. We haven't styled the links in any way; therefore, their styles will come from the UA stylesheet. Most browsers underline links and display them in a color based on whether the link was previously visited—that is, whether the URL appears in the browser's history.

With links, we have a few states to consider. The most common are

- `link`—An anchor tag (`<a>`) contains an `href` attribute and a URL that doesn't appear in the user's browser history.
- `visited`—An anchor (`<a>`) element contains an `href` attribute and a URL that does appear in the user's browser history.
- `hover`—The user has the cursor over the element but hasn't clicked it.
- `active`—The user is clicking and holding the element.
- `focus`—A *focused element* is an element that receives keyboard events by default. When a user clicks a focusable element, it automatically gains focus (unless some JavaScript alters this behavior). Using the keyboard to navigate among form fields, links, and buttons also changes the element that is in focus.
- `focus-within`—When `focus-within` is applied to a parent element and the child of the parent has focus, `focus-within` styles will be applied.
- `focus-visible`—When elements are selected using `focus-visible`, styles are applied only when focus has been gained via keyboard navigation or the user is interacting with the element via the keyboard.

We mentioned `:has()` earlier. Also a pseudo-class but not specific to links, `:has()` applies when the element has at least one descendent that meets the selector specified inside the parentheses. When we wrote this book, `:has()` had not yet been implemented in all major browsers.

In our current article project, we'll create an `a:link` rule to change the color of anchor tags that contain an `href` attribute and haven't been visited to light blue, using the hex color code `#1D70B8`. The `:visited` state should be different from the `:link` state because it should indicate to the user that they haven't visited that page before (that is, the URL isn't present in their browser history). Often, websites don't differentiate between the two states, but discerning them can provide a better user experience. In our example, we'll change the `:visited` state to a purple `color`, using the hex code value `#4C2C92`.

Then we'll handle the `:hover` state. This state doesn't apply to mobile users, as there's no way to recognize a user hovering over a link on a mobile device. In our article, we'll change the :hover state text color to a dark blue, using the hex code value #003078.

Finally, we'll handle the :focus state. We can use this state on any focusable elements. Links, buttons, and form fields are focusable by default (unless disabled), but we can make any element focusable by using a positive-numbered tabindex, in which case focus-based styles could be applied. The :focus state is shown when the user clicks or taps an element. When the element is focused, we add a 1-pixel crimson outline to the element. All put together, our link rules appear as shown in the following listing.

Listing 1.10   Styling links using pseudo-elements

```
a:link {
  color: #1D70B8;
}
a:visited {
  color: #4C2C92;
}
a:hover {
  color: #003078;
}
a:focus {
 outline: solid 1px crimson;
}
```

Note that the order in which these rulesets are written matters, as they have the same level of specificity. The condition that's farthest down in the stylesheet will win if multiple conditions apply. In our example, if a link has been visited but is being hovered over, the link will take the color assigned to it by the a:hover {} rule because it comes after the a:visited {} rule in our stylesheet.

Although developer tools vary in features and how those features are accessed, in most browsers, we can view the different element states by going into our browser, right-clicking, and choosing Inspect from the contextual menu. Typically, we get a view of the HTML with the CSS on the side. By clicking the :hov button in the Styles section, we see a panel that may say something like *force element state*, and then we can toggle different pseudo-classes on and off. Figure 1.20 shows the Chrome developer tools with the :hov panel open.

Developer tools in browsers

All major browsers have developer tools that allow developers to modify, debug, and optimize websites. For this book, we will use developer tools to examine our code. We will also examine the compiled code in the browser tools to understand how the browser is processing our CSS. For more information about developer tools and how to access them, see the appendix.

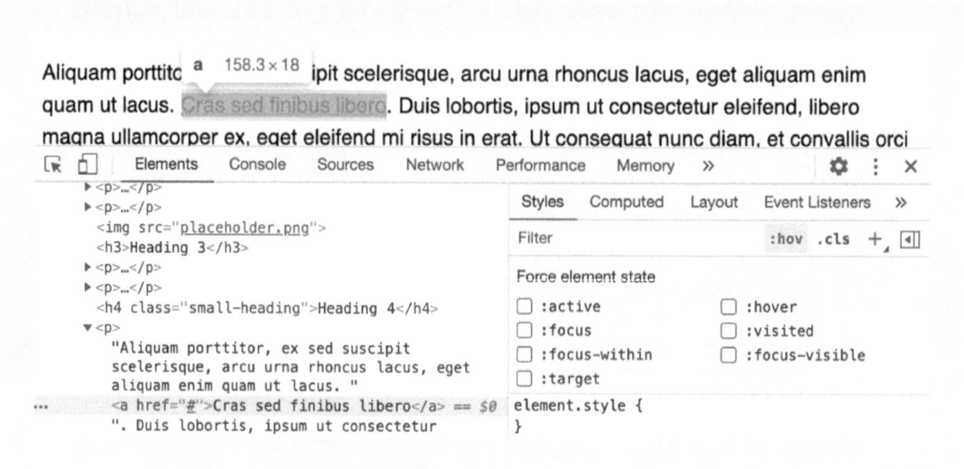

Figure 1.20   **Viewing different element states by using the browser's developer tools**

Pseudo-elements use a double colon (::). The purpose of pseudo-elements is to allow us to style a specific part of an element. Sometimes, pseudo-elements are written with a single colon, although using two is strongly recommended. The ability to ignore the second colon is for backward compatibility; the two-colon syntax was introduced as part of CSS3 to better differentiate between pseudo-classes and pseudo-elements.

Using the ::first-letter pseudo-element, we can target the first letter of a paragraph rather than wrap the letter in something like a span element, which would break the word apart and clutter our HTML. This approach allows us to create complex CSS without complicating the HTML.

In our article, we used the adjacent sibling combinator to make our first paragraph bold and in a larger font size than the rest. Now we're going to change the color of the first letter of that first paragraph and change the font style to italic.

First, we target the header element; then, we target the first letter (::first-letter) of the paragraph (<p>). With our selector created, we add our declarations. Our CSS will look like the following listing.

Listing 1.11   Selecting the first letter

```
header + p::first-letter {
  color: crimson;
  font-style: italic;
}
```

When this code is applied, the first letter is red and italicized (figure 1.21).

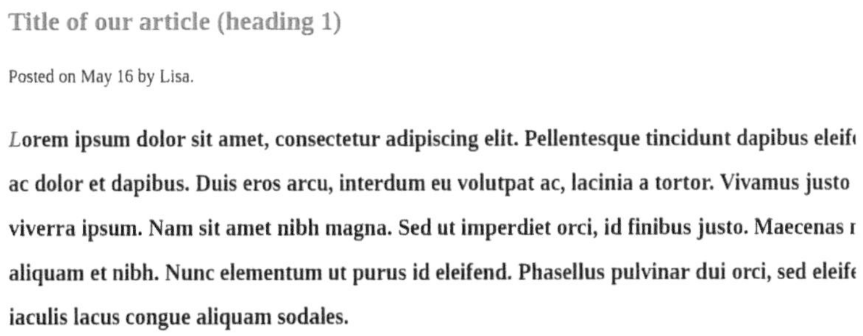

Title of our article (heading 1)

Posted on May 16 by Lisa.

Lorem ipsum dolor sit amet, consectetur adipiscing elit. Pellentesque tincidunt dapibus eleife

ac dolor et dapibus. Duis eros arcu, interdum eu volutpat ac, lacinia a tortor. Vivamus justo

viverra ipsum. Nam sit amet nibh magna. Sed ut imperdiet orci, id finibus justo. Maecenas i

aliquam et nibh. Nunc elementum ut purus id eleifend. Phasellus pulvinar dui orci, sed eleife

iaculis lacus congue aliquam sodales.

Figure 1.21   Pseudo-element targeting the first letter of the first paragraph
immediately after the header

1.6.4   *Attribute value selectors*

Commonly used for styling links and form elements, the attribute selector styles
HTML elements that include a specified attribute. The attribute value selector looks
for a specific attribute with the same value.

In our article, we have some content in Italian. The language of the paragraph is
specified by the `lang` attribute, as shown in the following listing.

Listing 1.12   Specifying Italian content

```
<p lang="it">Questo paragrafo è definito in italiano.</p>
```

To hint to users that this content is in Italian, we'll use CSS to add the Italian-flag
emoji. The browser will find the language (`lang`) attribute with the value of Italian
(`it`) and then add an Italian-flag emoji `before` it. Listing 1.13 uses a `::before` pseudo-
element as well. We can use multiple types of selectors to target the exact part of the
HTML we want to style.

Listing 1.13   Using multiple types of selectors to add a flag before Italian content

```
[lang="it"]::before {
  content: "🇮🇹"
}
```

When this code is applied, our Italian content has an emoji flag before it (figure 1.22).

Emoji differences across devices and applications
If you're coding along with this chapter, your output may differ from figure 1.22. Emojis present differently depending on the device, operating system, and application
being used. Sites such as Emojipedia (https://emojipedia.org) show how a particular
emoji would look across applications and devices. You can find details on the Italian
flag at https://emojipedia.org/flag-italy.

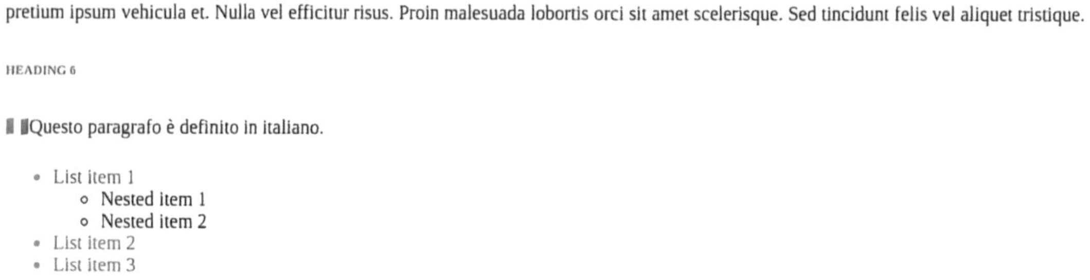

pretium ipsum vehicula et. Nulla vel efficitur risus. Proin malesuada lobortis orci sit amet scelerisque. Sed tincidunt felis vel aliquet tristique.

HEADING 6

▌ ▌Questo paragrafo è definito in italiano.

- List item 1
    - Nested item 1
    - Nested item 2
- List item 2
- List item 3

Figure 1.22   **Italian flag applied by the attribute selector and a pseudo-element**

1.6.5   *Universal selector*

The broadest type of selector is the universal selector, which uses the asterisk symbol (*). Any declarations made with the universal selector will be applied to all the HTML elements.

Sometimes, this selector can be used to reset CSS, but in terms of specificity, it has a specificity value of 0, which means that it can be overridden easily if necessary. This is important because it targets every element. The universal selector can also be used to target any and all descendants of a particular selector, as in .foo * { background: yellow; }, in which any and all descendants of an element with the class foo would be given a yellow background.

In our example project, we'll use a universal selector (*) to set the font-family to sans-serif so that the font will be sans-serif consistently throughout the article, as shown in the following listing.

> **Listing 1.14   Making our font-family consistent**

```
* { font-family: sans-serif; }
```

When this code is applied, all the text in our document uses a sans-serif font regardless of element type (figure 1.23).

1.7   *Different ways to write CSS*

CSS allows flexibility in the way we write our rules and formatting. In this section, we'll look at shorthand properties (which we will keep coming back to throughout the book) and ways to format CSS.

1.7.1   *Shorthand*

Shorthand replaces writing multiple CSS properties with merging all the values into one property. We can do this with a few properties such as padding, margin, and animation, all of which are covered at various points throughout this book. The benefit of writing shorthand is that it reduces the size of our stylesheet, which improves readability, performance, and memory use.

Title of our article (heading 1)

Posted on May 16 by Lisa.

*L*orem ipsum dolor sit amet, consectetur adipiscing elit. Pellentesque tincidunt dapibus eleifend. Nam eu urna ipsum. Etiam consequat ac dolor et dapibus. Duis eros arcu, interdum eu volutpat ac, lacinia a tortor. Vivamus justo tortor, porttitor in arcu nec, pretium viverra ipsum. Nam sit amet nibh magna. Sed ut imperdiet orci, id finibus justo. Maecenas magna mauris, tempor nec tempor id, aliquam et nibh. Nunc elementum ut purus id eleifend. Phasellus pulvinar dui orci, sed eleifend magna ullamcorper sit amet. Proin iaculis lacus congue aliquam sodales.

1. List item 1
   - Nested item 1
   - Nested item 2
2. List item 2
3. List item 3
4. List item 4

Curabitur id augue nulla. Aliquam purus urna, aliquam eu ornare id, maximus et tellus. Aliquam eleifend sem vitae urna blandit, non bibendum tellus dignissim. Aliquam imperdiet imperdiet sapien sit amet consectetur. Nam convallis turpis felis, sedvulputate lacus eleifend a. Mauris pharetra imperdiet lacinia. Sed sit amet feugiat lectus, in consectetur magna. Vestibulum accumsan porta enim at ultricies. Vestibulum vitae massa quis massa dignissim imperdiet.

Nunc eleifend nulla lobortis porta rhoncus. Vivamus feugiat, sem vitae feugiat aliquam, orci nulla venenatis libero, vitae rhoncus nibh neque ac velit.

Etiam tempor vulputate varius. Duis at metus ut eros ultrices facilisis. Donec ut est finibus, egestas nisl eu, placerat neque. Pellentesque cursus, turpis nec sollicitudin sodales, nisi tellus ultrices lectus, nec facilisis purus neque vitae diam. Nunc eleifend nulla lobortis porta rhoncus. Vivamus feugiat, sem vitae feugiat aliquam, orci nulla venenatis libero, vitae

Figure 1.23   Using the universal selector to change the font type on all elements

Each shorthand property takes different values. Let's explore the one we used in our project. We have a `blockquote` in our article. When we styled it, we used the `padding` property and declared our padding as follows: `padding: 10px`. In doing so, we used shorthand. Instead, we could have written the code as shown in the following listing.

Listing 1.15   Padding expanded

```
padding-top: 10px;
padding-right: 10px;
padding-bottom: 10px;
padding-left: 10px;
```

It's completely fine to write each declaration separately, but doing that is expensive in terms of computing performance, especially because all the property values are the same. Instead, we can use the `padding` property and put all four values on the same line. The order is `top`, `right`, `bottom`, and `left`. We can also combine `right`/`left` and `top`/`bottom` values if they're identical, as depicted in figure 1.24.

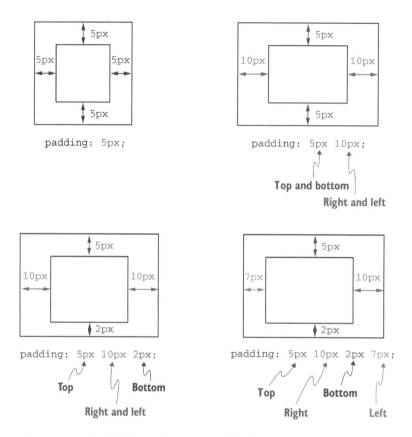

Figure 1.24   Padding shorthand property explained

As shown in the figure, we can declare all four values to define the top, right, bottom, and left values. But if we say that right and left are the same and top and bottom are different, we can specify three values, in the order top, right & left, bottom.

If two values are declared, we're saying the first value is what the top and bottom should be; then the second value sets the right and left. Finally, if only one value is declared, the value sets all four sides.

1.7.2   Formatting

We can write CSS in a few ways, and often when we view other people's code, we see different formats. This section shows a few examples.

The multiline format shown in listing 1.16 is likely the most popular choice for formatting. Each declaration is on its own line and indented by means of tabs or spaces.

Listing 1.16　Multiline format

```
h1 {
  color: red;
  font-size: 16px;
  font-family: sans-serif
}
```

A variation on the multiline format, shown in listing 1.17, places the opening curly brace on its own line. This example is something we might see in the PHP language. It could be considered unnecessary to place the opening brace on its own line.

Listing 1.17　A variation on multiline format

```
h1
{
  color: red;
  font-size: 16px;
  font-family: sans-serif
}
```

The single-line format shown in listing 1.18 makes a lot of sense; it's compact, and we can scan a file knowing that the first part is the selector. The downside is that it can be difficult to read if a rule contains many declarations.

Listing 1.18　Single-line format

```
h1 { color: red; font-size: 16px; font-family: sans-serif }
```

All these options have positives and negatives, but the projects in this book use a combination of options one and three. The main thing to know is that there's no right or wrong method; the choice generally comes down to what works best for you and/or your team. As long as the code is easy to understand, that's all that matters.

Those with an eagle eye will notice that in listings 1.16, 1.17, and 1.18, there's no semicolon (;) at the end of the last declaration of the rules. This semicolon is optional. One of the best aspects of CSS is that we can write it in the way that's most comfortable for us.

Summary

- CSS is a well-established coding language, and each part of CSS is made up of modules.
- Modules replaced large releases such as CSS3.
- Inline CSS can take the highest priority and has good performance, but it's repetitive and hard to maintain.
- External CSS keeps our CSS separate from our HTML, maintaining SoC.
- Along with our own CSS, the browser applies default styling.

- The user may also apply their own CSS, which can override the author and UA stylesheets.
- Using !important is considered to be bad practice.
- A CSS rule consists of a selector and one or more declarations.
- We can create rules for many types of selectors, and each rule can have its own level of specificity.

Designing a layout using CSS Grid

This chapter covers

- Exploring grid tracks and arranging our grids
- Using the `minmax` and `repeat` functions in CSS Grid
- Working with the fraction unit, which is unique to CSS Grid
- Creating template areas and placing items in the areas
- Considering accessibility when using grids
- Creating gutters between columns and rows within grids

Now that we have a basic understanding of how CSS works, we can begin exploring our options for laying out HTML content. In this chapter, we'll focus on layout with grids.

2.1   CSS Grid

A *grid*, in this sense, is a network of lines that cross to form a series of squares or rectangles. Now supported by all major browsers, CSS Grid has become a popular layout technique.

Essentially, a grid is made up of columns and rows. We'll create our grid and then assign positions to our items much as we place boats on a grid when playing the board game Battleship.

Although grid layouts are sometimes compared with tables, they have different uses and fulfill different needs. Grids are for layouts, whereas tables are for tabular data. If the content being styled is appropriate for a Microsoft Excel sheet, it's tabular data and should be placed in a table.

In the mid-2000s, we used tables for layouts, and sometimes we still need to. (Emails, for example, sometimes require the use of tables for layout, as they support only a subset of CSS styles.) On the web, however, this technique is considered to be bad practice because it leads to poor accessibility and lack of semantics. Now we can use a grid instead.

CSS Grid empowers us to be creative, to produce a range of layouts, and to adapt those layouts for different conditions in conjunction with media queries. We'll use a grid to style our project, and by the end of the chapter, our layout will look like figure 2.1.

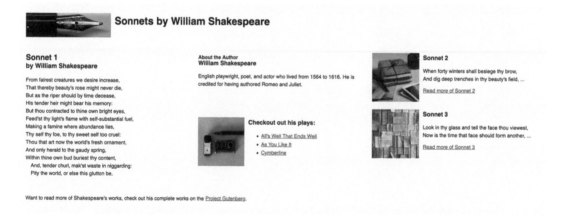

Figure 2.1   Final output

Our starting HTML, in the chapter-02 folder of the GitHub repository (https:// github.com/michaelgearon/Tiny-CSS-Projects) or in CodePen (https://codepen.io/ michaelgearon/pen/eYRKXqv), looks like the following listing.

Listing 2.1   Project HTML

```
<body>
  <main>              ◁──┤ The container for
                          our project
───▷ <header>
       <img src="./img/logo.jpg" alt="">
       <h1>Sonnets by William Shakespeare</h1>
     </header>
───▷ <article>
       <h2>
         Sonnet 1
         <br><small>by William Shakespeare</small>
       </h2>
       <p>
         <span>From fairest creatures we desire increase,</span>
         ...
       </p>
     </article>
───▷ <aside>
       <section>
         <img src="./img/image-1.jpg" alt="">
         <h3>Sonnet 2</h3>
         <p>
           When forty winters shall besiege thy brow,
           <br>And dig deep trenches in thy beauty's field, ...
         </p>
         <a href="">Read more of Sonnet 2</a>
       </section>
       <section>
         <img src="./img/image-2.jpg" alt="">
         <h3>Sonnet 3</h3>
         <p>
           Look in thy glass and tell the face thou viewest,
           <br>Now is the time that face should form another, ...
         </p>
         <a href="">Read more of Sonnet 3</a>
       </section>
     </aside>
───▷ <section class="author-details">
       <h3>
         <small>About the Author</small>
         <br>William Shakespeare
       </h3>
       <p>English playwright, poet, ...</p>
     </section>
───▷ <section class="plays">
       <img src="./img/play.jpg" alt="">
       <h3>Checkout out his plays:</h3>
       <ul>
         <li><a href="">All's Well That Ends Well</a></li>
         ...
       </ul>
     </section>
───▷ <footer>
       <p>Want to read more ...</p>
```

The child items within our container

```
    </footer>
  </main>
</body>
```

We also have some starting CSS (listing 2.2) to guide us as we start to place our HTML elements in a grid format. We won't worry about these preset styles (such as margin, padding, colors, typography, and borders) in this chapter. Those concepts are covered in other parts of the book because we want to focus on the layout for this project.

Listing 2.2   Starting CSS

```
body {
  margin: 0;
  padding: 0;
  background: #fff9e8;
  min-height: 100vh;          ◁─── The background covers
  font-family: sans-serif;         the whole page even
  color: #151412                   when the window is
}                                   longer than the content.
main { margin: 24px }
img {                           Allows text to
  float: left;                  wrap around
  margin: 12px 12px 12px 0  ◁── the image
}
main > * {                      Asterisk and child combinator
  border: solid 1px #bfbfbf; ◁── selects any and all immediate
  padding: 12px;                  children of main.
}
                            ◁── border points out sections
main > *, section { display: flow-root }   to be positioned via a grid.
p, ul { line-height: 1.5 }
article p span { display: block; }   ◁── Prevents images
article p span:last-of-type,              from bleeding out
article p span:nth-last-child(2) {        of their containers
  text-indent: 16px                 Indents the
}                                    last two lines
.plays ul { margin-left: 162px }  ◁── of the sonnet
```

Indents the list; otherwise,
bullets are right up
against the image.

We change the font from serif to sans-serif, and we increase the margin between the boundary of the browser window and the container by using margin. We also float images to the left and adjust the line heights, typography, and padding.

Note that we added a border and some padding to the immediate children of the main element to help us define our layout. We'll remove those elements later in the project. Our starting point looks like figure 2.2.

CSS grids are a way to place items on a 2D layout: horizontal (x-axis) and vertical (y-axis). By contrast, the flexbox (covered in chapter 6) is single-axis-oriented. It operates only on the x- or y-axis, depending on its configuration.

 **Sonnets by William Shakespeare**

Sonnet 1
by William Shakespeare

From fairest creatures we desire increase,
That thereby beauty's rose might never die,
But as the riper should by time decease,
His tender heir might bear his memory:
But thou contracted to thine own bright eyes,
Feed'st thy light's flame with self-substantial fuel,
Making a famine where abundance lies,
Thy self thy foe, to thy sweet self too cruel:
Thou that art now the world's fresh ornament,
And only herald to the gaudy spring,
Within thine own bud buriest thy content,
  And, tender churl, mak'st waste in niggarding:
  Pity the world, or else this glutton be,

 Sonnet 2

When forty winters shall besiege thy brow,
And dig deep trenches in thy beauty's field, ...

Read more of Sonnet 2

 Sonnet 3

Look in thy glass and tell the face thou viewest,
Now is the time that face should form another, ...

Read more of Sonnet 3

About the Author
William Shakespeare

English playwright, poet, and actor who lived from 1564 to 1616. He is credited for having authored Romeo and Juliet.

 Checkout out his plays:

- All's Well That Ends Well
- As You Like It
- Cymberline

Want to read more of Shakespeare's works, check out his complete works on the Project Gutenberg.

Figure 2.2   Starting point

We can use both CSS Flexbox and CSS Grid to align and lay out items on a web page. But as we go through the chapter, we'll find that one of the benefits of Grid over Flexbox is that it allows us to divide a page into regions and create complex layouts with relative ease.

First, we'll set up our grid. Then we'll look at ways to alter how our grid behaves based on window size.

2.2   Display grid

The first part of arranging a grid is setting the `display` value to `grid` on the parent container item. When creating a grid layout, we can use one of two values:

- `grid`—Used when we want the browser to display the grid in a block-level box. The grid takes the full width of the container and sets itself on a new line.
- `inline-grid`—Used when we want the grid to be an inline-level box. The grid sets itself inline with the previous content, much like a `<span>`.

We'll use the value `grid` for our layout, as shown in listing 2.3.

> **Difference between block-level and inline-level box**
> In HTML, every element is a box. A block-level box says that an element's box should use the entire horizontal space of its parent element, therefore preventing any other element from being on the same horizontal line by default. By contrast, inline elements can allow other inline elements to be on the same horizontal line, depending on the remaining space.

Listing 2.3   Setting the display to `grid`

```
main {
  display: grid;
}
```

If we preview this code in the browser, we notice that nothing has changed visually because the browser by default displays the direct child items in one column. Then the browser generates enough rows for all of the child elements.

Using the developer tools in our browser (figure 2.3), we see that, programmatically, the grid has been created even though the layout has not changed visually. To view the underlying grid in most browsers, we can right-click the web page and choose Inspect from the contextual menu. In the Inspect window in Mozilla Firefox, when we select the parent container, we see two things to indicate the layout is now a grid:

- Purple lines around each direct child item.
- In the HTML, an icon called grid in the `<main>` element. When we click the grid icon next to `<main>`, the layout panel shows us our grid structure.

We can follow similar steps in Google Chrome or Apple's Safari.

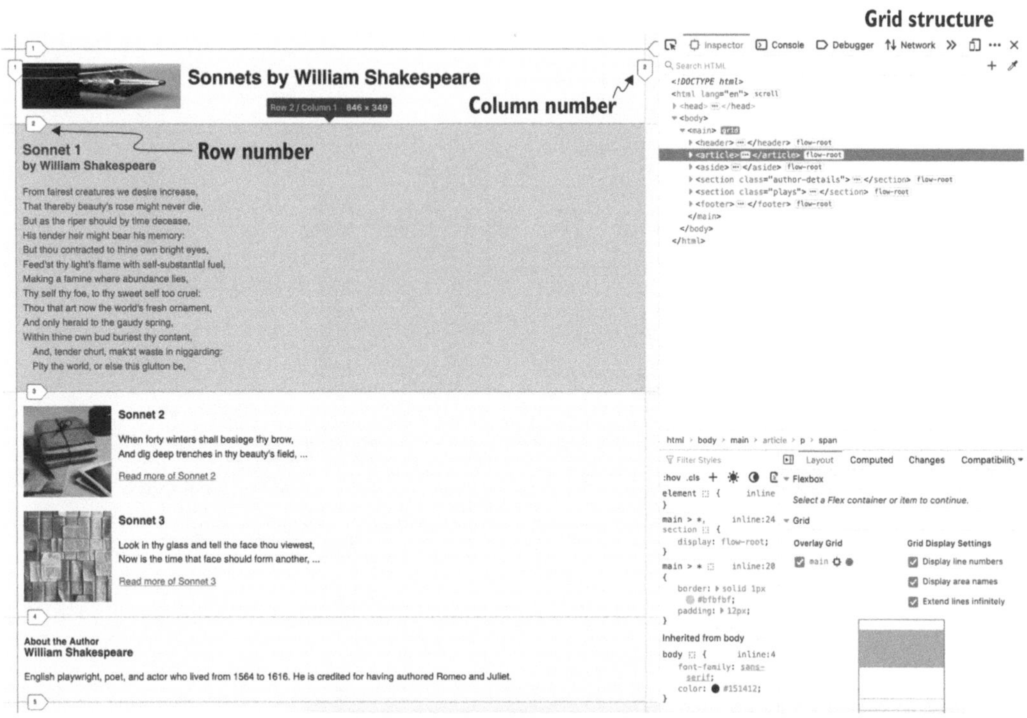

Figure 2.3   Development tools in Firefox

2.3   *Grid tracks and lines*

When the CSS Grid Layout Module was introduced, it brought in new terminology to describe laying out items. The first of those terms is *grid lines*. Lines run horizontally and vertically, and they're numbered starting from 1 in the top-left corner. On the opposite side to the positive numbers are the negative numbers.

Writing mode and script direction

The number assigned to each line depends on the writing mode (whether lines of text are laid out horizontally or vertically) and the script direction of the component. If the writing mode is English, for example, the first line on the left is numbered 1. If the language direction is set to right-to-left because of the language, for example, Arabic (which is written from right to left), line 1 would be the farthest line to the right.

The spaces between the grid lines are known as *grid tracks,* and they're made up of columns and rows. Columns go from left to right, and rows go from top to bottom. A *track* is the space between any two lines on a grid. In figure 2.4, the highlighted track is the first row track in our grid. A column track would be the space between two vertical lines.

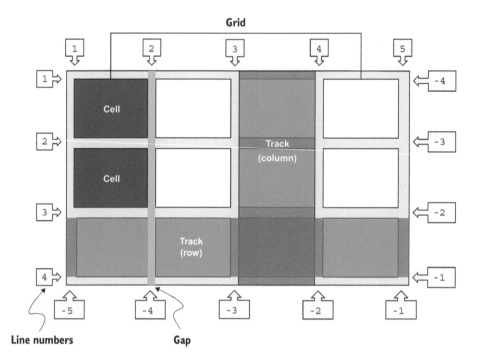

Figure 2.4   Grid structure based on English as the writing mode, with the direction set to left-to-right

Within each track are grid cells. A *cell* is the intersection of a grid row and a grid column.

We can use the grid-template-columns and grid-template-rows properties to lay out our grid. These properties specify, as a space-separated track list, the line names and track sizing functions of the grid. The grid-template-columns property specifies the track list for the grid's columns, and grid-template-rows specifies the track list for the grid's rows.

Before we set our columns, we need to understand a few concepts that are specific to CSS Grid.

2.3.1   Repeating columns

To save repetition in your code, you can use the repeat() function to specify how many columns or rows you need.

> **DEFINITION**   A *function* is a self-contained, reusable piece of code that has a specific role. Functions exist in other programming languages, such as Java-Script. Sometimes, we can pass one or more values to the function; these values are referred to as *parameters*. To pass values to a function, we place them in parentheses. We can't create our own functions in CSS; instead, we use the built-in functions that CSS offers.

The `repeat()` function needs two values that are comma-separated. The first value indicates how many columns or rows to create. The second value is the sizing of each column or row.

For our project, we'll specify that we want two columns, and for the sizing of each column, we'll use the `minmax()` function. Our column definition, therefore, will be `grid-template-columns: repeat(2, minmax(auto, 1fr)) 250px;`. If we were defining the height of our rows, we'd use `repeat()` with `grid-template-rows`.

This declaration produces three columns, two of equal width using the fraction unit and one of 250 pixels. Let's look at this declaration a bit further. Notice that inside the `repeat()` function, we use the `minmax()` function.

2.3.2 The minmax() function

The `minmax(min, max)` function is made up of two arguments: the minimum and maximum range of the grid track. The World Wide Web Consortium (W3C) specification states that the `minmax` function "defines a size range greater than or equal to `min` and less than or equal to `max`" (https://www.w3.org/TR/css-grid-2).

> **NOTE** To make the function valid, the `min` value (the first argument) needs to be smaller than the `max` value. Otherwise, the browser ignores `max`, and the function relies only on the `min` value.

For our project, we set the `min` value to `auto` and the `max` value to 2. Let's look at what `auto` means.

2.3.3 The auto keyword

The `auto` keyword can be used for either the minimum or maximum value within the function. When the keyword `auto` is used for the maximum value, it's treated the same as the `max-content` keyword. The row's or column's dimensions will be equal to the amount of room that the content within the row or column requires.

Although we don't use it in our project, a common use case for the `auto` keyword is making layouts that include fixed headers and footers. When we assign overflow to the area for which `auto` was set, the area shrinks and grows with the window size, as shown in figure 2.5.

For our use case, in the statement `grid-template-columns: repeat(2, minmax(auto, 1fr)) 250px;`, the `auto` keyword dictates that for our first two columns, the column should be, at minimum, as wide as the element it contains. Let's take a look at the flexible length unit (`fr`) used to set our maximum width.

2.3.4 The fractions (fr) unit

The fractions (`fr`) unit was introduced in the CSS Grid Layout Module. The `fr` unit, which is unique to Grid, tells the browser how much room an HTML element should have compared with other elements by distributing the leftover space after the minimums have been applied. CSS distributes the available space equally among the `fr`

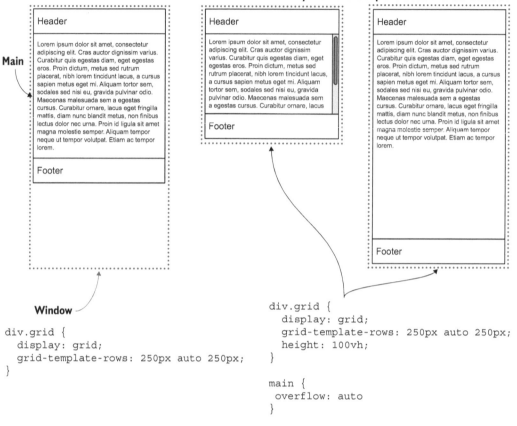

Header and footer stay fixed to the top and bottom of the window.

```
div.grid {
  display: grid;
  grid-template-rows: 250px auto 250px;
}
```

```
div.grid {
  display: grid;
  grid-template-rows: 250px auto 250px;
  height: 100vh;
}

main {
  overflow: auto
}
```

Figure 2.5   **Examples of using the** auto **keyword**

units, so the value of 1fr is equal to the available space divided by the total number of fr units specified.

Let's explore what a fraction is through the tasty cake diagrams shown in figure 2.6. (Sorry if this figure makes you crave a slice of cake.)

If you had a whole cake, it would equal 100%. From a CSS perspective, if we decided to eat all the cake, that would be 1 fraction. In our CSS, that would be the same as grid-template-columns: 1fr, which would be 100% of the column.

But we're friendly, so we decide to give some of our cake to four friends. We need to determine how many slices of our cake each person is going to have.

If we're fair, we can say that our cake can be divided into four equal slices. In our CSS, this would be the same as grid-template-columns: 1fr 1fr 1fr 1fr. We're telling the browser to give each HTML element an equal slice of the whole thing.

But what if we decided to be sneaky and keep a larger slice for ourselves? After all, we baked the cake. We decide to take half of the cake for ourselves and divide the

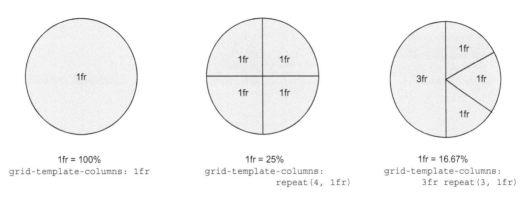

1fr = 100%
grid-template-columns: 1fr

1fr = 25%
grid-template-columns:
          repeat(4, 1fr)

1fr = 16.67%
grid-template-columns:
      3fr repeat(3, 1fr)

Figure 2.6   Fractions values

remaining half into three slices. To do this, we need six fractions: three fractions for our 50% of the cake and then one fraction three times to divide the other 50% of the cake.

Our CSS would be `grid-template-columns: 3fr 1fr 1fr 1fr`. So we're saying that there are six fractions total; the first column gets three of them (or 50% of the total), and then the remaining 50% should be divided equally among the other three columns. We can use the `fr` unit with the `repeat()` function to make this value easier to read, which would be `grid-template-columns: 3fr repeat(3, 1fr)`.

For our project we'll create our grid lines for the columns by adding the code in the following listing to our `main` rule.

Listing 2.4   Setting the amount of columns

```
main {
  display: grid;
  grid-template-columns: repeat(2, minmax(auto, 1fr)) 250px;
}
```

When previewed in the browser (figure 2.7), we see that now our grid has numbers set across each line. What we can do with this information is explicitly choose where to place our HTML elements within the grid based on the grid line number.

We also notice that the browser assumed that we want to place our HTML elements within each grid cell. Rather than stacking the elements vertically, the browser filled each column cell until it ran out, created a new row, and filled in those columns. The automatic creation of extra grid cells is also known as *an implicit grid*.

At this juncture, we've created a grid containing three columns. Two of those columns use `minmax()`, and our third column has a fixed value of `250px`. These settings give us a three-column layout. We want to distribute the main content in the first two columns and use the third one for less important content, which is why we give it less visual real estate. (On most screens, the third column will be narrower than the first two columns.)

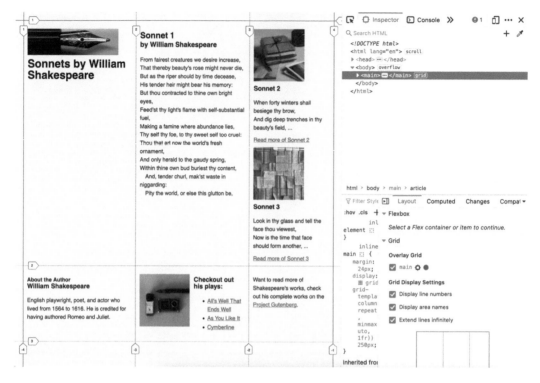

Figure 2.7   Firefox browser preview showing the grid lines and associated numbers for each line

Explicit versus implicit grid

When we use `grid-template-columns` or `grid-template-rows`, we're creating an explicit grid. We're clearly stating to the browser the exact amount of columns and rows this grid should have.

The implicit parts (for both rows and columns) are those that the browser creates automatically, which can happen when there are more child items than grid cells. In this case, the browser implicitly adds cells to our grid to make sure that all elements have a grid cell.

We can control implicit behavior through `grid-auto-flow`, `grid-auto-columns`, and `grid-auto-rows`.

2.4   Grid template areas

If we want to set an element explicitly on a particular row and column of our grid, we have two options. First, we can use the line numbers and dictate the position of the child as follows: `grid-column: 1 / 4`. In this syntax, the first number represents where the element starts, and the second represents where it ends (figure 2.8). This example places the element in the first column, spanning the second and third. If only one number is provided, the element spans only one row or column.

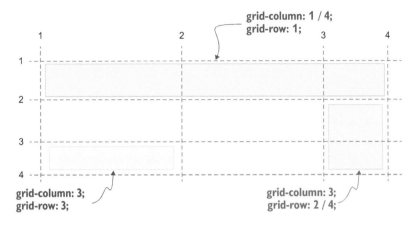

Figure 2.8 **Example** grid-column **and** grid-row **syntax**

To define the row, we would use the same syntax as for columns with the grid-row property. To place an element so that it starts on the third row and spans two rows, we would write grid-row: 3 / 5. The grid-column and grid-row properties are shorthand for grid-column-start, grid-column-end, grid-row-start, and grid-row-end.

Rather than deal with numbers, we can use named areas to be referenced when we explicitly place elements on the grid. To do this, we use the grid-template-areas property, which allows us to define how we want the web page to be laid out.

The grid-template-areas property takes multiple strings, each composed of the names of the areas they describe. Each string represents a row in the layout, as shown in figure 2.8. Each name represents a column within the row. If two adjacent cells have the same name (horizontally or vertically), the two cells are treated as one area. A grid area can be a single cell, such as the area defined as plays in figure 2.9, but if it's more than one cell, the cells must create a rectangular shape with all cells of the same name being adjacent. You wouldn't be able to make an L shape, for example.

The benefit of named areas is in the visualization of the final outcome. We'll define our grid-template-areas as shown in listing 2.5. Notice the dot (.) in the fourth row in figure 2.9. The dot is used to define a cell that we intend to keep empty. Because that cell doesn't have a name, content can't be assigned to it.

Listing 2.5 Creating our template areas

```
main {
  display: grid;
  grid-template-columns: repeat(2, minmax(auto, 1fr)) 250px;
  grid-template-areas:
  "header  header   header"
  "content content author"
  "content content aside "
  "plays       .    aside "
  "footer  footer   footer";
}
```

```
grid-template-areas:
  "header   header   header"
  "content  content  author"
  "content  content  aside "
  "plays    .        aside "
  "footer   footer   footer";
```

header	header	header
content	content	author
content	content	aside
plays	.	aside
footer	footer	footer

Figure 2.9   Syntax of the `grid-template-areas` **property**

Although we've defined areas, the content still implicitly positions itself in each available cell, ignoring the areas we defined (figure 2.10). We need to assign our content to each of these areas.

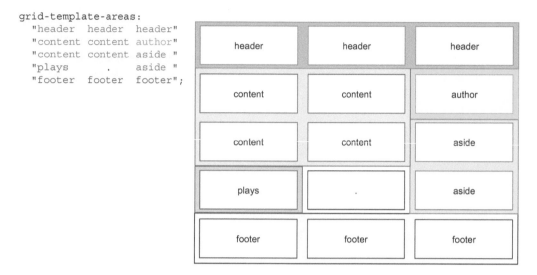

Figure 2.10   Defined grid areas shown in Firefox

2.4.1   The grid-area property

To place an element in a defined area, we use the `grid-area` property. Its value is the name we assigned in the `grid-template-areas` property. If we want the `<header>` element to be placed inside the area we defined as `header`, for example, we would define `header { grid-area: header; }`. For our project, we set our elements on our grid as shown in the following listing.

Listing 2.6   Assigning content to the grid area

```
header { grid-area: header }
article { grid-area: content }
aside { grid-area: aside }
.author-details { grid-area: author }
.plays { grid-area: plays }
footer { grid-area: footer }
```

Now that we've explicitly defined where the content should go, the content falls into place (figure 2.11).

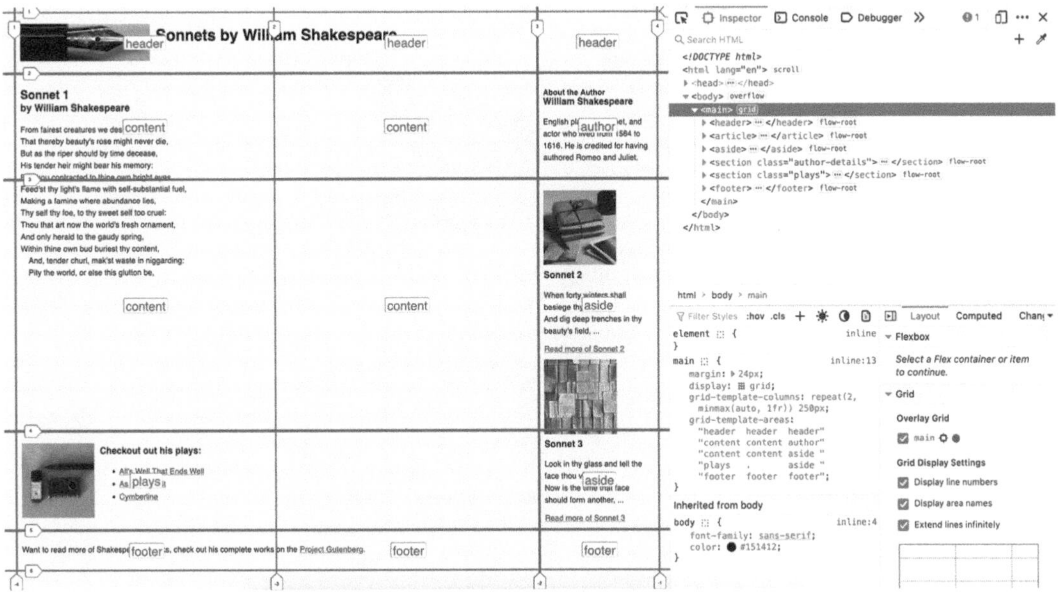

Figure 2.11   Content explicitly placed on the grid

With the layout setup, let's remove some of the styles we added for the purpose of understanding what our layout was doing. As shown in the following listing, we remove the padding and borders of our content sections.

Listing 2.7   Removing debugging styles

```
main > * {
  border: solid 1px #bfbfbf;
  padding: 12px;
}
```

With those styles removed and the screen width narrowed (figure 2.12), the content in adjacent columns or rows appears to be closer together.

Sonnets by William Shakespeare

Sonnet 1
by William Shakespeare

From fairest creatures we desire increase,
That thereby beauty's rose might never die,
But as the riper should by time decease,
His tender heir might bear his memory:
But thou contracted to thine own bright eyes,
Feed'st thy light's flame with self-substantial fuel,
Making a famine where abundance lies,
Thy self thy foe, to thy sweet self too cruel:
Thou that art now the world's fresh ornament,
And only herald to the gaudy spring,
Within thine own bud buriest thy content,
    And, tender churl, mak'st waste in niggarding:
    Pity the world, or else this glutton be,

About the Author
William Shakespeare

English playwright, poet, and actor who lived from 1564 to 1616. He is credited for having authored Romeo and Juliet.

Sonnet 2

When forty winters shall besiege thy brow,
And dig deep trenches in thy beauty's field, ...

Read more of Sonnet 2

Checkout out his plays:

- All's Well That Ends Well
- As You Like It
- Cymberline

Sonnet 3

Look in thy glass and tell the face thou viewest,
Now is the time that face should form another, ...

Read more of Sonnet 3

Figure 2.12   Narrow screen width

Let's add space between the areas. To accomplish this task, we will use the gap property.

2.4.2   The gap property

The gap property is shorthand for the row-gap and column-gap properties. By setting the row and column gaps, we're defining the gutters between rows and columns. *Gutters* is a term from print design, defining the gap between columns. By default, the gap between columns and rows is the keyword normal. This value equates to 0px in all contexts except when it's used with the CSS Multi-Column Module, which equates it to 1em.

When we use the gap property, the extra space applies only between the tracks of the grid. No gutters are applied before the first track or after the last track. To set space around the grid, we use padding and margin properties.

> **gap vs. grid-gap**
> As CSS Grid was being defined, the specification for this property was called the grid-gap property, but now gap is recommended. We may see grid-gap in older projects.

The gap property can have up to two positive values. The first value sets the row-gap, and the second is for the column-gap. If only one value is declared, it's applied to both the row-gap and column-gap properties.

For our project, we'll set a 20px gap between our rows and columns by adding gap: 20px to our main rule. Figure 2.13 shows the gaps added to our layout. With the gaps added, let's switch our focus to adjusting our layout based on screen size.

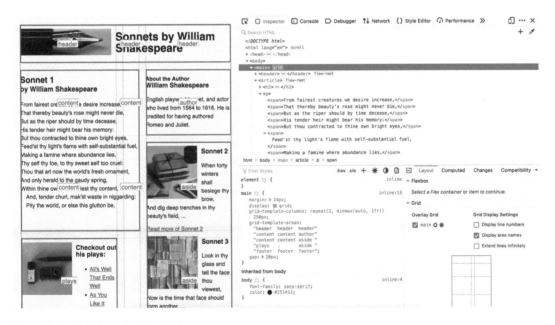

Figure 2.13   Grid layout with added gap

2.5   *Media queries*

CSS allows us to apply styles to our layout conditionally. One type of condition is screen size. Media queries are *at-rules*: they start with the at (@) symbol and define the condition under which the styles they contain should be applied. If we look at our current layout on a wide screen (figure 2.14), we notice a large amount of space in the center of the page that could be put to better use.

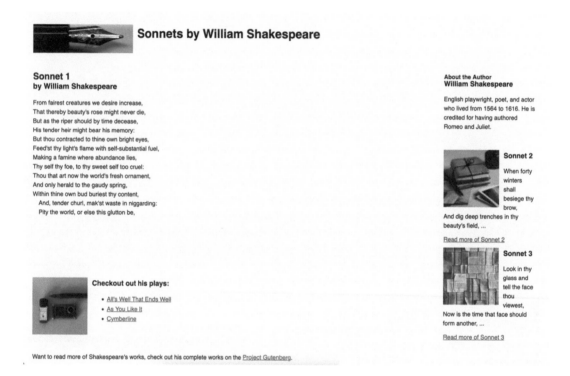

Figure 2.14   **Our layout on a wide screen**

Let's create a media query that targets screens wider than 955px. The query is @media (min-width: 955px) { }. All the rules we place inside the curly braces ({}) will be applied only if the screen size is greater than or equal to 955px.

Listing 2.8 shows our media query. We redefine our grid-template-areas to have a different configuration if the media-query condition is met. We also update the column sizes so that the columns have equal widths.

> Listing 2.8   **Creating our template areas with media queries**

```
@media (min-width: 955px) {      ◁────┤  The at-rule along
  main {                                with media feature
```

```
    grid-template-columns: repeat(3, 1fr);      ◁────   Redefines
    grid-template-areas:                                the column
    "header  header  header"            Reconfigures    sizes
    "content author aside"              where the content
    "content plays aside "              should be placed
    "footer  footer  footer";
  }
}
```

Now our layout looks like figure 2.15 and figure 2.16.

Sonnets by William Shakespeare

Sonnet 1
by William Shakespeare

From fairest creatures we desire increase,
That thereby beauty's rose might never die,
But as the riper should by time decease,
His tender heir might bear his memory:
But thou contracted to thine own bright eyes,
Feed'st thy light's flame with self-substantial fuel,
Making a famine where abundance lies,
Thy self thy foe, to thy sweet self too cruel:
Thou that art now the world's fresh ornament,
And only herald to the gaudy spring,
Within thine own bud buriest thy content,
    And, tender churl, mak'st waste in niggarding:
    Pity the world, or else this glutton be,

About the Author
William Shakespeare

English playwright, poet, and actor
who lived from 1564 to 1616. He is
credited for having authored
Romeo and Juliet.

Sonnet 2

When forty
winters
shall
besiege thy
brow,
And dig deep trenches in thy
beauty's field, ...

Read more of Sonnet 2

**Checkout out
his plays:**

- All's Well
  That Ends
  Well
- As You
  Like It
- Cymberline

Sonnet 3

Look in thy
glass and
tell the face
thou
viewest,
Now is the time that face should
form another, ...

Read more of Sonnet 3

Want to read more of Shakespeare's works, check out his complete works on the Project
Gutenberg.

Figure 2.15   Narrow screen uses the original layout.

Sonnets by William Shakespeare

Sonnet 1
by William Shakespeare

From fairest creatures we desire increase,
That thereby beauty's rose might never die,
But as the riper should by time decease,
His tender heir might bear his memory:
But thou contracted to thine own bright eyes,
Feed'st thy light's flame with self-substantial fuel,
Making a famine where abundance lies,
Thy self thy foe, to thy sweet self too cruel:
Thou that art now the world's fresh ornament,
And only herald to the gaudy spring,
Within thine own bud buriest thy content,
  And, tender churl, mak'st waste in niggarding:
  Pity the world, or else this glutton be,

About the Author
William Shakespeare

English playwright, poet, and actor who lived from
1564 to 1616. He is credited for having authored
Romeo and Juliet.

Checkout out his plays:

- All's Well That Ends Well
- As You Like It
- Cymberline

Sonnet 2

When forty winters shall
besiege thy brow,
And dig deep trenches in thy
beauty's field, ...

Read more of Sonnet 2

Sonnet 3

Look in thy glass and tell the
face thou viewest,
Now is the time that face
should form another, ...

Read more of Sonnet 3

Want to read more of Shakespeare's works, check out his complete works on the Project Gutenberg.

Figure 2.16   Wide screen uses the layout from the media query.

Using `grid-template-areas` in conjunction with media queries allows us to reconfigure our layout with minimal code. But we must avoid some accessibility pitfalls.

2.6   *Accessibility considerations*

When we placed our items in the grid area, we mostly kept the elements in the order in which they appeared in the HTML: the header stayed at the top, footer remained at the bottom, and the content was in a logical visual order. But what if the HTML order and the visual display order were different?

If a user is following along with a screen reader or navigating the page via the keyboard, and the programmatic order doesn't match what's being displayed, the behavior will seem to be random. This randomness will make it difficult for the user to navigate the page and to comprehend what's going on with it. Visually changing the location of a piece of content by using a grid won't affect the order in which assistive technology presents the information to the user. The W3 Grid Layout Module Recommendations states the following about this case (http://mng.bz/xdD7):

> Authors must use order and the `grid-placement` properties only for visual, not logical, reordering of content. Style sheets that use these features to perform logical reordering are non-conforming.

The solution is to keep the source code and the visual experience the same, or at least in a sensible order. This approach gives you both the most accessible web document and a good structure to work from. For English, this means that content and HTML should follow the same order, from top left to bottom right.

After assigning our elements to their respective areas of the grid, we should always test our page to ensure that regardless of how the user accesses the page, the order will be logical. One way to do this is to visit our page with a screen reader and tab through the elements to make sure that the tab order still works.

Some tools and extensions can help with visualizing tab order. In Firefox DevTools, for example, we can select the Accessibility tab and check the Show Tabbing Order check box, which outlines and numbers focusable elements as shown in figure 2.17. We can see that our tab order is logical and unlikely to confuse the user, so we're good to go.

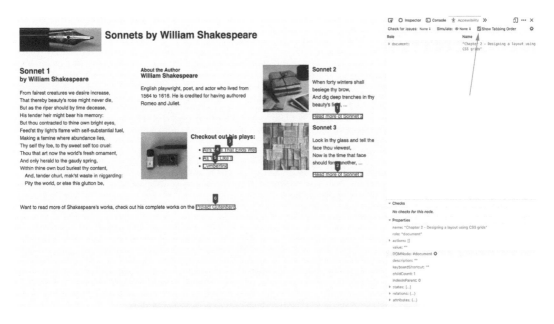

Figure 2.17 Tabbing order of HTML exposed in Firefox DevTools

Now our project is complete (figure 2.18).

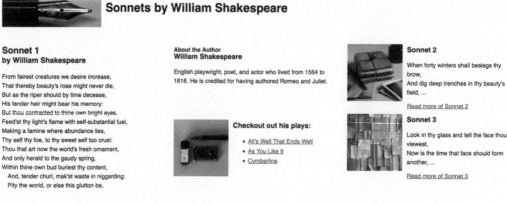

Figure 2.18   Final product on wide screen

Future of Grid

In this chapter, we used the CSS Grid Layout Module to create a layout that's responsive depending on the browser width. Many aspects of the grid are still being developed and iterated, most notably subgrids, which would allow for grids within grids.

Although you can set a grid within a grid now, subgrids have the benefit of being more closely related to their parent grid. To keep an eye on future enhancements and development, check out the grid specification at https://www.w3.org/TR/css-grid.

Summary

- A grid is a network of lines that cross to form a series of squares or rectangles.
- The display property with a value of grid allows us to place items on a grid layout.
- The display property is applied to the parent item that contains the child elements that are to be placed on the grid.
- The grid-template-columns and grid-template-rows properties are used to explicitly define the quantity and size of the columns and rows the grid should contain.
- The flexible length (fr) unit is a unit of measurement that was formed as part of CSS Grid as an alternative way to set the dimension of items.
- We can use the repeat() function to improve code efficiency where one or more rows or columns are the same size.
- The minmax() function allows us to set two arguments: the minimum width a column should be and the maximum width a column should be.

- The `grid-template-areas` property allows us to define what each grid area is called. Then we can use the `grid-area` property on the child items to assign them to those named locations.
- The `gap` property adds spacing (creates gutters) between grid cells.
- The source code and the visual experience need to stay in the same logical order. When in doubt, we can use browser developer tools to check the tabbing order.

Creating a responsive
animated loading screen

This chapter covers

- Creating basic shapes using Scalable Vector Graphics (SVGs)
- Finding out the difference between viewboxes and viewports in SVGs
- Understanding keyframes and animating SVGs
- Using animation properties
- Styling SVGs with CSS
- Styling an HTML progress bar element with appearance properties

We see loaders in most applications today. These loaders communicate to the user that something is loading, uploading, or waiting. They give the user confidence that something is happening.

Without some sort of indicator to tell the user that something is happening, they may try reloading, click the link again, or give up and leave. We should be using some sort of progress indicator when an action takes longer than 1 second, which is when users tend to lose focus and question whether there's a problem. As well as having a graphic showing that something is happening, the loader should be accompanied by text that tells the user what is happening to improve the accessibility of the web page for screen readers and other assistive technologies.

For our animation, we'll be looking into the CSS Animation Module, understanding the animation property, keyframes, and transitions, as well as accessibility and respect for user preferences.

3.1   Setup

In this project, we'll be creating rectangles within an SVG. We'll see what SVGs offer and understand the slight differences between styling HTML elements and SVG elements.

We'll also create a progress bar, which shows the user how much of the task has been completed and how much is left to go. We'll use the HTML `<progress>` element and then look at how we can edit the browser's default styles and apply our own. Overall, we want to create a consistent, responsive loader that works across devices. Figure 3.1 shows the result.

Figure 3.1   Goal for this chapter

The code for this project is in the GitHub repository (https://github.com/michael gearon/Tiny-CSS-Projects) in the chapter 3 folder. You can find a demonstration of the completed project on CodePen at https://codepen.io/michaelgearon/pen/eYvVVre.

3.2   SVG basics

SVG stands for *Scalable Vector Graphics*. SVGs are written in an XML-based markup language and consist of vectors on a Cartesian plane. Vector graphics can be coded from scratch but often are created in a graphics program such as Adobe Illustrator, Figma, or Sketch. Then they're exported in the SVG file format and can then be opened in a code text editor.

A *vector* is a mathematical formula that defines a geometric primitive. Lines, polygons, curves, circles, and rectangles are all examples of geometric primitives.

A *Cartesian coordinate system* in a plane is a grid-based system that defines a point by using a pair of numerical coordinates based on the point's distance from two perpendicular axes. The location where these two axes cross is the *origin*, which has a coordinate value of (0, 0). Think back to math class; when you were asked to plot lines on a graph, you were using a Cartesian coordinate system. Essentially, SVGs are shapes on a coordinate plane written in XML.

By contrast, PNGs, JPEGs, and GIFs are *raster images*, which are created by using a grid of pixels. Figure 3.2 illustrates the difference between raster and vector graphics.

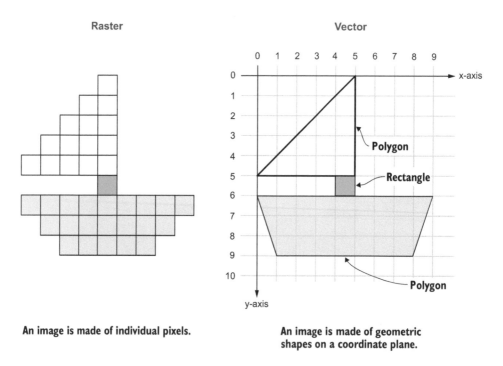

Figure 3.2   Raster versus vector graphics

SVGs have many advantages over raster images, including being infinitely scalable. We can shrink or enlarge the image as much as we want without losing quality. We can't enlarge raster images without seeing *pixelation*, which results from enlarging the grid of pixels that renders the individual squares of the grid visible. By contrast, when we enlarge an SVG, we're setting shapes and lines on a coordinate plane programmatically; the paths between points are redrawn, and the quality doesn't degrade.

Because SVGs are written in XML, we can place SVG code directly in our HTML and access, manipulate, and edit it in much the same way that we do our other HTML elements. SVGs are to graphics as HTML is to web pages.

Rasters, however, are a better choice for dealing with images that are highly complex, such as photos. It's possible to create a photorealistic image by using an SVG, but it wouldn't be practical. The file size and, therefore, load performance are significantly larger for vector graphics than for raster images.

The most common use case for SVGs are logos, icons, and loaders. We use them for logos because logos are often simple images that need to be crisp regardless of the size or medium. Furthermore, it's not uncommon for a company or product to have several versions of a logo for use on a dark background versus a light background. Recoloring, simplicity, and scaling are other reasons why we use SVGs for icons.

We use SVGs for loaders because unlike their raster counterparts, they allow us to add animations inside the image itself. We can isolate an individual element inside the graphic and apply CSS or JavaScript to that individual piece—an exercise that isn't possible with rasters.

Earlier, we mentioned that SVGs are based on a Cartesian plane (a 2D coordinate plane). Let's look into what that means and how it works.

3.2.1 Positions of SVG elements

When we're working with SVG elements, the way to think about positioning is to imagine that we're placing elements on a grid. Everything starts at (0,0) (the origin) which is the top-left corner of the SVG document. The higher the x or y value is, the farther it is from the top-left corner. Figure 3.3 expands on the example of the boat in figure 3.2, adding the origin and the coordinate values for each shape.

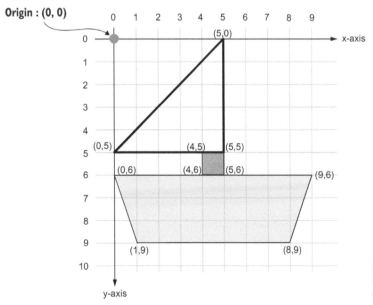

Figure 3.3
Positioning elements
on a coordinate plane

The loader in our project is composed of a series of 11 rectangles. To place them, we need to think of their positions on a coordinate plane, taking both their widths and the gaps between them into consideration.

3.2.2   Viewport

The *viewport* is the area in which the user can see the SVG. It's set by two attributes: width and height. Think of the viewport as being a picture frame: it sets the size of the frame but doesn't affect the size of the graphic it contains. If we place an image inside a picture frame that's larger than the frame, however, we have overflow. The same thing happens to our SVG. As in CSS positioning, viewport measurements have their origin in the top-left corner of the SVG (figure 3.4).

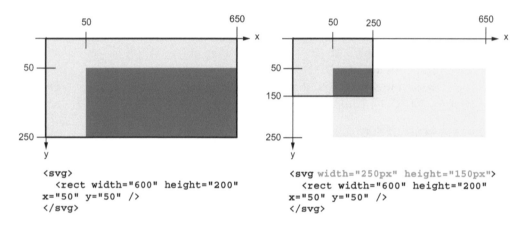

```
<svg>                            <svg width="250px" height="150px">
  <rect width="600" height="200"   <rect width="600" height="200"
x="50" y="50" />                 x="50" y="50" />
</svg>                           </svg>
```

Figure 3.4   SVGs with and without a defined viewport

The viewport for our loader will be

```
<svg width="100%" height="300px"> <!--SVG code --> </svg>
```

The width is set at 100%, but 100% of what? We're dictating that the loader will take 100% of the available space it's given by its parent item.

The following listing shows our starting HTML. We see that our loader is nested inside a section; therefore, our loader will be the same width as that section.

Listing 3.1   **Starting HTML**

```
<body>
  <section>
    <svg width="100%" height="300px"></svg>        ⟵  Loader with added
    <h1>Scanning channels</h1>                         viewport of 100% width
    <p>This may take a few minutes</p>                 by 300-pixel height
    <progress value="32" max="100">32%</progress>  ⟵  The progress bar,
  </section>                                           which we address
</body>                                                later in the chapter
```

We have some starting CSS as well (listing 3.2). The background (`<body>`), `<section>`, header (`<h1>`), and paragraph (`<p>`) have been prestyled to focus on the loader, progress bar, and animations.

Listing 3.2   Starting CSS

Margin written using the shorthand property: top and bottom, 40px margin; left and right, auto

Start of rule styling the loader's container

```
body { background: rgb(0 28 47); }
section {
  display: flex;
  flex-direction: column;
  justify-content: space-between;
  align-items: center;
  max-width: 800px;
  margin: 40px auto;
  font: 300 100% 'Roboto', sans-serif;
  text-align: center;
  color: rgb(255 255 255);
}
h1 {
  font-size: 4.5vw;
  margin: 40px 0 12px;
}

p {
  font-size: 2.8vw;
  margin-top: 0;
}
```

Layout using flexbox to set the child items in the column direction, centering horizontally and setting equal spaces between elements

Typography setting the font weight to light, in the Roboto font, with a fallback of sans-serif and centering the text

Sets the color to white using RGB

End of rule styling the loader's container

We see that our section has its width capped at 800 pixels. `<section>` is a block-level element, so by default, it will take up the full width available to it. `<body>` and `<html>` are also block-level elements.

Because we don't specify a width, padding, or margin on `<body>` or `<html>`, they will take the full width of the window. `<section>` will take the full width of the `<body>`. But because we assigned a maximum width to the `<section>`, when the window reaches 800 pixels wide, the section will stop growing with the `<body>` and remain 800 pixels wide. Because the section element has a top and bottom margin of `40px`, it will slightly increase the gap between the browser window and the element.

Our loader is contained within the section. The section will take the full width of the body until it reaches 800 pixels; therefore, our loader will do the same. Figure 3.5 shows how the width of the loader will be affected by the screen size.

With the viewport set, let's set the viewbox so that the contents of the SVG can scale with its container. Remember that up to now, we've dealt only with the frame, not its innards.

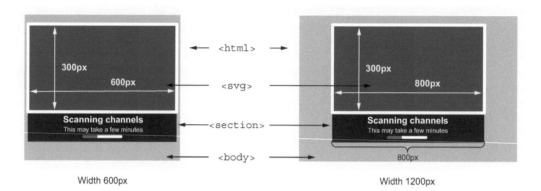

Figure 3.5 **Window-width effect on SVG width when using** `max-width`

3.2.3 *Viewbox*

The *viewbox* sets the position, height, and width of the graphic within the viewport. Earlier, we likened the viewport to a picture frame. The viewbox allows us to adjust the image to fit our frame. It can position the image and also scale the graphic so that it fits inside the frame. We can think of the viewbox as being our pan and zoom tools. To set the viewbox, we apply the `viewBox` attribute to the SVG with the following four values and syntax: `viewBox="min-x min-y width height"`. Listing 3.3 shows `viewBox` applied to our loader.

Dissecting the numbers in order, we start with `min-x` and `min-y`, both of which are set to `0`. We want the top-left corner of the graphic to be in the top-left corner of our frame. `min-x` and `min-y` allow us to adjust the position of the graphic in its frame; it's the pan tool. Because we want it to be exactly in the top-left corner, we set the values to `0`.

Next, we apply the width, which is set to `710` because our loader has 11 total bars, each created with a width of `60`. `60 × 11 = 660`, and we have 10 gaps. The gap width between each bar is `5 × 10 = 50`; therefore, our loader's width will be `660 + 50 = 710`.

We'll base the height of the `viewBox` on the height of the bars in our loader. The bars have a height value of `300`, so we also set the viewport height to `300`. Our loader will fit exactly inside its viewport. The next listing shows the `viewBox` applied to the SVG.

Listing 3.3 **Declaring the viewbox**

```
<svg viewBox="0 0 710 300" width="100%" height="300px">
 <!--SVG code-->
</svg>
```

Notice that both our viewbox and viewport heights equal `300`. This is how we zoom. If the viewbox figures are less than the viewport figures, we're effectively zooming out of the frame, and the graphic will be smaller. If the viewbox figures are more than the viewport figures, we're zooming in. Because we have equal viewport and viewbox heights, however, we're not zooming.

Now that we've defined the space we'll be working in, we can start adding shapes to the loader.

3.2.4 Shapes in SVG

There are a few standard SVG shapes and elements:

- rect (rectangle)
- circle
- ellipse
- line
- polyline
- polygon

If we want to create an irregular shape, we can also use path, but we won't need it for this loader. Most often, paths are what we see when we look at the XML behind logos, icons, and complex animation graphics. For our project, we'll use the basic rectangle shape to create the wave.

To define our rectangles, which will create the bars in our loader, we'll use the `<rect>` element and add four properties: height, width, x, and y. The x and y attributes determine the position of the top-left corner of the rectangle relative to the top-left corner of the SVG.

We want to create 11 rectangles (listing 3.4) that have a width of 60 and a height of 300, and we'll use the x attribute to move the rectangles across the graphic. We start at 0 and increase the value by the width of our bar (60) plus an additional gap of 5. Each rectangle's x value will be 65 more than the previous one. Our 11th rectangle should have an x value of 650.

Listing 3.4 Eleven rectangles

```
<svg viewBox="0 0 710 300" width="100%" height="300">
    <rect width="60" height="300" x="0" />
    <rect width="60" height="300" x="65" />
    <rect width="60" height="300" x="130" />
    <rect width="60" height="300" x="195"/>
    <rect width="60" height="300" x="260"/>
    <rect width="60" height="300" x="325"/>
    <rect width="60" height="300" x="390"/>
    <rect width="60" height="300" x="455"/>
    <rect width="60" height="300" x="520"/>
    <rect width="60" height="300" x="585"/>
    <rect width="60" height="300" x="650"/>
</svg>
```

Now we have our rectangles positioned inside our viewport, and they're resized correctly as we increase and decrease the window size by our viewBox. Figure 3.6 shows our SVG in different window sizes. (We added a white border to the SVG and bars to make them more visible in the screenshots.) The contents shrink and grow within

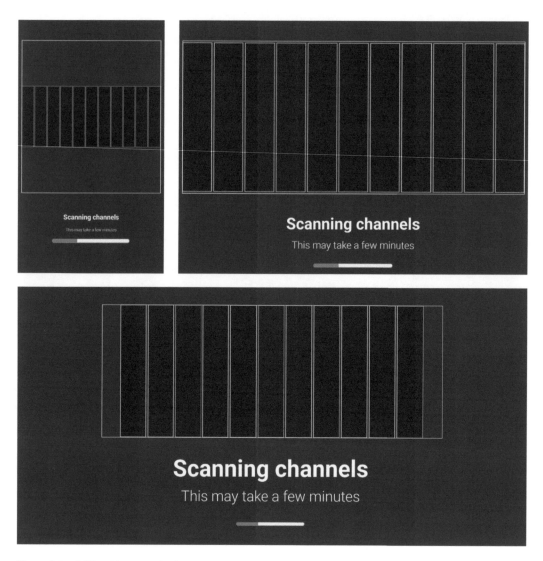

Figure 3.6   Adding 11 rectangles inside an SVG

their available space without skewing the rectangles that they contain as the width-to-height ratio changes with the resizing of the window.

Notice that our rectangles are black. Our next order of business is to style them.

3.3   *Applying styles to SVGs*

We can apply styles to SVG elements in much the same way that we do in HTML: inline, internally in a `<style>` tag, or in a separate stylesheet. Some minor differences exist, however. First and foremost, how the SVG is imported into our HTML affects where the styles need to live to affect the elements.

The easiest way to add a vector graphic to a web page is to use an image tag. We reference the image file the same way that we would any other image: `<img src="myImage.svg" alt="">`. We can also add it as a `background-image` inside our CSS: `background-image: url("myImage.svg");`.

In both of these cases, our HTML and styles can affect the SVG but not the elements within it. We can affect the size of the image, for example, but we can't change the color of a particular shape inside the SVG. The image is essentially a black box that we can't penetrate to make changes. To manipulate elements within the image, we'd have to place the styles inside the SVG itself.

Our third option—the one we'll use in this chapter—is to place the SVG's XML inline, directly in our HTML rather than in an external file, preventing the black-box issue we'd encounter if the code were in an external file. The drawback is that our concerns aren't as well separated because now our image code is mixed in with our HTML.

When our SVG is placed inline in our HTML, the standard ways to apply CSS to any other HTML element apply. Therefore, we can place the styles we want to apply to our SVG inside our CSS as though the SVG were any other HTML element.

> **SVG presentation attributes**
>
> In HTML, when we apply styles inline, we need to include a style attribute, such as `<p style="background: blue">`. SVGs, however, have styles that we can add directly to the element as attributes. These styles are called *presentation attributes*.
>
> The `fill` attribute (the SVG equivalent of `background-color`), for example, can be applied directly to the element without a style tag: `<rect fill="blue">`. These properties don't have to be applied inline directly on the element. They can be added inside a style tag or stylesheet the same way that we apply any other CSS style: `rect { fill: blue: }`.
>
> You can find a comprehensive list of SVG presentation attributes at http://mng .bz/Alee.

Although the techniques for applying styles to our SVG elements remain the same as those for HTML (except for the aforementioned SVG presentation attributes when applied inline), some of the properties we'll use to style our elements will be different. Let's take a closer look at one we'll be using for this project.

To set the background color of the loader bars, instead of using `background-color`, we'll use the `fill` property, as the `background-color` property doesn't work for SVG elements. The `fill` property supports the same values as `background-color`, such as color name, RGB(a), HSL(a) and hex. So instead of `rect { background-color: blue; }`, we'd write `rect { fill: blue; }`. If no `fill` value is assigned to a particular shape, the `fill` will default to black, which is why our rectangles are black.

Let's add a fill color to our rectangles. Because not all the rectangles are the same color (they have varying colors of blue and green to give the loader a bit of a gradient effect), rather than give each element a class, we'll use the pseudo-class `nth-of-child(n)`, which matches elements based on their positions within the parent. We'll look for the nth rectangle, to which we'll apply the fill. Therefore, `section rect:nth-of-type(3)` would find the third rectangle of the section container. Listing 3.5 shows the fill color applied to each of our rectangles.

> NOTE A pseudo-class targets the state of an element—in this case, its position relative to the positions of its siblings.

Listing 3.5 Adding a fill color to our rectangles

```
rect:nth-child(1)  { fill: #1a9f8c }
rect:nth-child(2)  { fill: #1eab8d }
rect:nth-child(3)  { fill: #20b38e }
rect:nth-child(4)  { fill: #22b78d }
rect:nth-child(5)  { fill: #22b88e }
rect:nth-child(6)  { fill: #21b48d }
rect:nth-child(7)  { fill: #1eaf8e }
rect:nth-child(8)  { fill: #1ca48d }
rect:nth-child(9)  { fill: #17968b }
rect:nth-child(10) { fill: #128688 }
rect:nth-child(11) { fill: #128688 }
```

Figure 3.7 shows our output. We can see that the bars in the loader are no longer black; color has been applied to them.

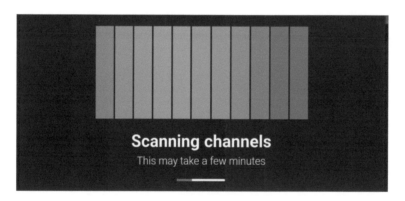

Figure 3.7 Fill applied to loader rectangles

The downside to our declarations is that if another SVG graphic had rectangles, our code could style the wrong graphic. To avoid this issue, we can add a class name to our SVG graphic as an identifier to specify the rectangle we want to style. But because we have only one SVG in our project, we won't need to worry about that.

3.4 Animating elements in CSS

The CSS Animation Module allows us to animate properties using keyframes, which we'll look at in section 3.4.1. We can control aspects of the animation such as how long it lasts and how many times it animates. CSS provides several properties we can use to define our animations' behavior, including the following:

- `animation-delay`—How long to wait before the animation starts
- `animation-direction`—Whether the animation is played forward or backward
- `animation-duration`—How long it should take for the animation to run once
- `animation-fill-mode`—How the element being animated should be styled when the animation is done executing
- `animation-iteration-count`—How many times the animation should run
- `animation-name`—Name of the keyframes being applied
- `animation-play-state`—Whether the animation is running or paused
- `animation-timing-function`—How the animation progresses through the styles over time

For our animation, we'll focus on four of these properties:

- `animation-name`
- `animation-duration`
- `animation-iteration-count`
- `animation-delay`

The effect we want to create is the rectangles shrinking and growing, but not in sync. At any given point in time, we want the heights of the elements to be slightly different. When the rectangles are shrinking and growing, we want the tops and bottoms of the rectangle to move toward the center and then expand back to full height. Essentially, we'll be creating a squeezing effect, going from large to small and back to large.

Although we'll apply the same animation to all the rectangles, to stagger their sizes we'll apply a slightly different delay to the start of the animation of each rectangle. As each rectangle starts animating at a different time, each one will be in a different stage of expanding and shrinking, creating a ripple effect.

First, we'll create the animation itself. Then, we'll apply it to the rectangles. Finally, we'll add the individual delays to stagger the size at any given point in time. To create the animation, we'll use keyframes. The `animation` property will reference the keyframes and dictate the duration, the delay, and how many times we want the animation to run.

3.4.1 Keyframe and animation-name

When we create a keyframe, we need to give it a name. The `animation-name` declaration value matches the keyframe name to join the two. With the `animation-name` property, we can list multiple animations separated by commas.

Origins of keyframes

Keyframes come to us from the animation and motion-picture industry. When companies used to do animation by hand, artists composed many individual pictures, with a change within each picture or frame. Over time, they made changes in each frame and gradually got to the end frame. A simple example of this technique is flipbook animation. The more frames you have and the more subtle the tweak is over a short period, the more fluid the animation is.

A keyframe represents the most important (key) changes in your animation (the frame). Then the browser works out the changes over time between defined frames. This process is known as *in-betweening*. Allowing the hardware to do the work, the browser can quickly fill the gaps between the keyframes, creating a smooth transition between one state and another. The in-betweening process is illustrated in figure 3.8.

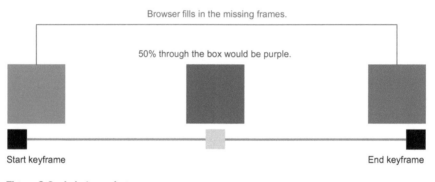

Browser fills in the missing frames.

50% through the box would be purple.

Start keyframe   End keyframe

Figure 3.8   In-betweening

In CSS, keyframes are defined using an at-rule called `@keyframes`, which controls the steps within an animation sequence. *At-rules* are CSS statements that dictate how our styles should behave and/or when they should be applied. They begin with an at (`@`) symbol followed by an identifier (in our case, keyframes). We used an at-rule in chapter 2 to create our media query; here, we'll use one to create our keyframes. The syntax is `@keyframes animation-name { … }`. The code inside the curly braces defines the animation's behavior. Each keyframe inside the `@keyframes` at-rule block is defined by a percentage (percentage of time passed in the animation) and the styles applied when we reach that point in time.

Before we dive into applying animations to our project, let's look at a simpler scenario to get a feel for the syntax (listing 3.6). You can also find this example on Code-Pen at https://codepen.io/michaelgearon/pen/oNyvbWX, where you can see the animation run (figure 3.9).

Listing 3.6 Example animation

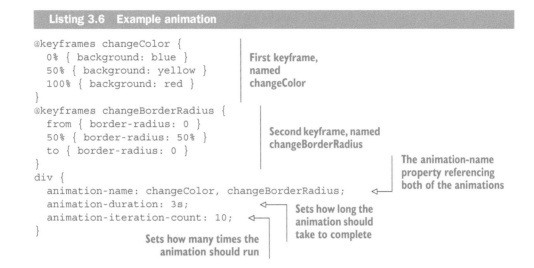

```
@keyframes changeColor {
  0% { background: blue }
  50% { background: yellow }
  100% { background: red }
}
@keyframes changeBorderRadius {
  from { border-radius: 0 }
  50% { border-radius: 50% }
  to { border-radius: 0 }
}
div {
  animation-name: changeColor, changeBorderRadius;
  animation-duration: 3s;
  animation-iteration-count: 10;
}
```

First keyframe, named changeColor

Second keyframe, named changeBorderRadius

The animation-name property referencing both of the animations

Sets how long the animation should take to complete

Sets how many times the animation should run

Figure 3.9 Simple animation scenario in CodePen

The example has two sets of keyframes: one named changeColor and one named
changeBorderRadius. We apply both of the animations to a div. Then we define
how long the animation should take to run (3 seconds) and how many times it
should run (10 times). Inside each set of keyframes is code specifying what styles

should be applied to the elements. So we have two different types of notation, we have keywords, and we have percentages. Let's break down what we're defining in the first set of keyframes.

We assert that when the animation begins (0%), we want to set the background color of the <div> to blue. By the time we reach 50% of our animation (half of 3 seconds, or 1.5 seconds), our background will be yellow. And when the animation ends (100%, or at 3 seconds), our background will be red. In between the keyframes. the color changes smoothly from one state to the next.

In the second set of keyframes, changeBorderRadius, instead of percentages we use the keywords from and to. from is the equivalent of 0%, and to is equivalent to 100%. We can mix the notation we want to use within the same set of keyframes.

When we apply the animation to the div ruleset, we also set a duration and iteration count. Notice that these two values are being applied to both of the animations.

Before we take a closer look at these two properties and how they work, let's create the animations for our loader. For our loader, we want to grow and shrink—or *scale*—our rectangles over time. Therefore, we'll call our keyframe doScale. Our at-rule will be @keyframes doScale { }.

Inside the at-rule, we define the keyframes for the animation. We'll start with the rectangle having its full height. Halfway through the animation, we want the height of the rectangle to be 20 percent of its original height. When the animation terminates, we want the rectangle's height to be back to full size. So we have three steps to define: from (or 0%), 50%, and to (or 100%).

To change the size of the rectangle, we'll use the transform property, which allows us to change the appearance of an element (rotate, scale, distorted, move, and so on) without affecting the elements around it. If we were to reduce the height of an element by using the height property, the content below it would move up to fill the newly available space. With transform, the amount of space and the location of the element in terms of the page flow don't change—only the visible aspect. Using the same scenario, if we were to decrease the height of that same element using transform, the content below it wouldn't move up. We'd have a blank space.

To affect the element, the transform property takes a transform() function. We'll use scaleY(). (You can find a full list of available functions at http://mng.bz/Zo1N.)

The scaleY() function resizes an element vertically without affecting its width or squishing or stretching it. To define how much an element should be scrunched or stretched, we pass the function a percentage or a number value. The number value maps to the decimal value of its percentage equivalent; therefore, scaleY(.5) and scaleY(50%) achieve the same result, decreasing the element's height to 50% of its original value. Values above 100% increase the size of the element, and values between 0% and 100% shrink it.

Negative values applied to scaleY() flip the element vertically, so scaleY(-0.5) would flip the element upside down and shrink its height by 50%. scaleY(-1.5) flips the element upside down and makes the height 1.5 times the original value.

For our loader bars, we want our rectangles to be full height at the beginning and the end of the animation, and 20% of the original height halfway through the animation. Our completed keyframe with transforms applied looks like the following listing.

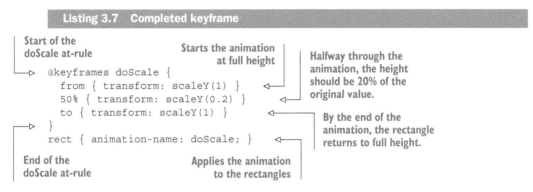

Listing 3.7 Completed keyframe

Start of the doScale at-rule

Starts the animation at full height

Halfway through the animation, the height should be 20% of the original value.

```
@keyframes doScale {
    from { transform: scaleY(1) }
    50% { transform: scaleY(0.2) }
    to { transform: scaleY(1) }
}
rect { animation-name: doScale; }
```

By the end of the animation, the rectangle returns to full height.

End of the doScale at-rule

Applies the animation to the rectangles

If we run the code, we notice that nothing has changed; our rectangles aren't growing and shrinking yet, even though we applied the keyframe to our rectangles. We still need to define the duration and iteration count. Let's dig into those properties a bit further.

3.4.2 *The duration property*

The duration property sets how long we want the animation to happen from start to finish. The duration can be set in seconds (s) or milliseconds (ms). The longer the duration, the more slowly the animation completes. With accessibility in mind, we want to consider users who are sensitive to motion (section 3.4) and choose a duration that is reasonable.

> **Animations, seizures, and flash rate**
> The World Wide Web Consortium (W3C) recommends that to prevent inducing seizures in photosensitive users, we need to make sure that our animations don't contain anything that flashes more than three times in any 1-second period (http://mng .bz/RldR).

A lot goes into choosing appropriate animation timing. An animation that's too fast can create changes that are imperceptible or cause seizures, depending on its nature. An animation that's too slow can make our application look laggy. Most microanimations are short and transitional; they animate the change of an element from one state to another, such as flipping an arrow from pointing up to pointing down. A generally accepted duration for this type of animation is around 250 milliseconds.

If the animation is larger or more complex, such as opening and closing a large panel or menu, we can increase the duration to around 500 milliseconds. A loader is a bit different, though. It's not a quick change in response to a user's action; it's a large visual element that the user will focus on for some time.

Most often when determining the "correct" timing for a loader, we use trial and error to find the speed that works best with our graphic. For our project, we want to set the animation to happen over 2.2 seconds. To apply the amount of time the animation should take, we add the `animation-duration` property to our rectangles, as shown in the following listing.

Listing 3.8   Added animation duration

```
rect {
  animation-name: doScale;
  animation-duration: 2.2s;
}
```

When we run the code, our loader animates once and then never animates again unless we reload the browser window. We also notice that all the bars increase and decrease in size at the same time. First, let's make our loader continue to animate over time; then we'll stagger the animation across our rectangles so that they appear to be different heights.

3.4.3   *The iteration-count property*

To make our animation restart after it has completed, we use the `iteration-count` property, which sets the number of times the animation should repeat. By default, its value is 1. Because we haven't set a value yet, the browser assumes that we want the animation to run once and be done. We want our animation to repeat continuously, so we'll use the `infinite` keyword value.

By applying this value, we're declaring that the animation should keep playing forever. If we wanted to run a specific number of times, we'd use an integer value. After we add our iteration count, our code looks like the following listing.

Listing 3.9   Added animation iteration count

```
rect {
  animation-name: doScale;
  animation-duration: 2.2s;
  animation-iteration-count: infinite;
}
```

When we run the code, we see that all the rectangles grow and shrink in sync, starting from the top, and that the animation restarts after it completes. We still have some work to do to set the animation to start in the middle of the rectangle rather than at the top, as well as to stagger the animation between our elements. First, though, let's take a quick pause to look at the animation shorthand property.

3.4.4   *The animation shorthand property*

We currently have three declarations that define our animation: `animation-name`, `animation-duration`, and `animation-iteration-count`. We can simplify our code by combining all three declarations in the `animation` shorthand property, which allows us to define our animation's behavior with a single property. In this property, we can define the values for any of the properties listed in section 3.3. We don't need to provide values for all the properties. If properties aren't defined as part of the shorthand property or individually, they use their default values.

As mentioned earlier, we're defining three properties: `animation-name`, `animation-duration`, and `animation-iteration-count`. Refactored to use the animation shorthand property, our declaration looks like figure 3.10.

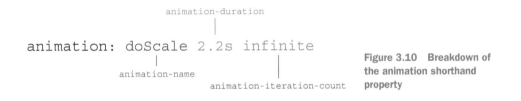

Figure 3.10   Breakdown of the animation shorthand property

This code is functionally identical to the code that currently applies to our rectangle. Using shorthand properties makes our code more concise and can make it easier to read. But if you find that writing out each property is easier for you, either method is perfectly valid. Do what works best for you.

When we use the animation shorthand property, our updated CSS looks like the following listing. After making the change to our code, we notice that our animation hasn't changed.

Listing 3.10   Refactoring to use the shorthand property

```
rect {
  animation-name: doScale;
  animation-duration: 2.2s;
  animation-iteration-count: infinite;
  animation: doScale 2.2s infinite;
}
```

Next, let's address the staggering of heights for each of our rectangles.

3.4.5   *The animation-delay property*

The `animation-delay` property does what its name implies: it allows us to delay an animation on an element. The delay applies to the start of the animation. When the animation starts, it loops normally. As with the `duration` property, we can use seconds (s) or milliseconds (ms) to set the delay's duration value. The default value is `0`. By default, an animation doesn't have a delay.

To create the staggered effect in our animation, we'll assign different delay values to each of our rectangles, as shown in listing 3.11. The first rectangle's animation will start immediately. We give it a delay of 0. We could omit this declaration, because 0 is the default value for animation-delay; we added it here for clarity in explaining the code.

The second rectangle gets a 200ms delay, and we continue to increment the delay by 200ms for every rectangle thereafter. Notice that on the sixth rectangle, we switch to using seconds instead of milliseconds. We do this to make the code more readable because either second or millisecond values are acceptable.

Listing 3.11   Added animation iteration count

```
rect:nth-child(1) {
  fill: #1a9f8c;
  animation-delay: 0;
}
rect:nth-child(2) {
  fill: #1eab8d;
  animation-delay: 200ms;
}
rect:nth-child(3) {
  fill: #20b38e;
  animation-delay: 400ms;
}

rect:nth-child(4) {
  fill: #22b78d;
  animation-delay: 600ms;
}
rect:nth-child(5) {
  fill: #22b88e;
  animation-delay: 800ms;
}
rect:nth-child(6) {
  fill: #21b48d;
  animation-delay: 1s;
}
rect:nth-child(7) {
  fill: #1eaf8e;
  animation-delay: 1.2s;
}
rect:nth-child(8) {
  fill: #1ca48d;
  animation-delay: 1.4s;
}
rect:nth-child(9) {
  fill: #17968b;
  animation-delay: 1.6s;
}
rect:nth-child(10) {
  fill: #128688;
  animation-delay: 1.8s;
}
```

```
rect:nth-child(11) {
  fill: #128688;
  animation-delay: 2s;
}
```

After adding the delay, we see that we achieved our staggered effect (figure 3.11). But the elements are growing and shrinking from the top rather than from the center.

Figure 3.11   Animated rectangles with height change emanating from the top

To say where we want the element to grow and shrink from, we need to tell the browser where on the rectangle the animation should originate. To address this problem, we'll use the `transform-origin` property.

3.4.6   *The transform-origin property*

The `transform-origin` property sets the origin, or point, for an element's transformations. If we were to rotate the object, the `transform-origin` property would set where on the element we want to rotate from. In our case, we'll use this property to set the position the animation should start from (the point of origin).

If the transform is happening in three dimensions (3D), the value can be up to three values (x, y, and z); if the transform is in two dimensions (2D), we can have up to two values (x and y). The first value is the horizontal position, or the x-axis; the second value is the vertical position, or the y-axis. When we're working in 3D, the third value would be forward and backward, or the z-axis.

We can declare the value of the `transform-origin` property in three ways:

- Length
- Percentage
- Keywords
  - `top`
  - `right`

  – bottom
  – left
  – center

In HTML, the initial value for this property is `50% 50% 0`, which is `center`, `center`, `flat`. For SVG elements, however, the initial value is `0 0 0`, which places it in the top-left corner.

For our animation, we want the rectangle's transform origin to be at the center. We want the top and bottom of the rectangles to shrink rather than having the top fixed and the rectangles expanding and contracting from that point. To do this, we can either apply the keyword value `center` or assign a value of `50%` to the `transform-origin` property for our rectangles. Either way, we're saying that we want the point of origin to be the center of the rectangle. For our project, we'll use the keyword value `center`. Listing 3.12 shows our updated `rect` rule.

We mentioned earlier that when working with 2D animations, the property takes two values, but we passed only one. When only one value is passed, it is applied to both the vertical and horizontal positions; therefore, `transform-origin: center;` is equivalent to `transform-origin: center center;`.

> **Listing 3.12 Updated `rect` rule with `transform-origin` property**

```
rect {
  animation: doScale 2.2s infinite;
  transform-origin: center;
}
```

We've finished our loader animation (figure 3.12). But we still need to consider how accessible our design is. Section 3.4 dives into some ways we can provide a positive experience for all our users.

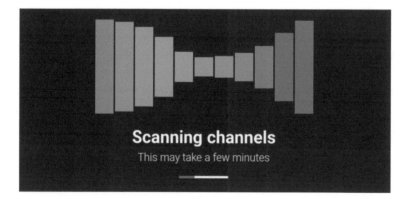

Figure 3.12 Finished loader animation

3.5 *Accessibility and the prefers-reduced-motion media query*

The use of motion, parallax (an effect in which the background moves slower than the foreground), and animations on the web has increased as these effects have become easier to implement and browser support has improved. By using these techniques, we can create richer user interfaces that are interactive and provide richer user experiences.

The use of these techniques comes at a cost, however. For some users, especially those who have vestibular disorders, movement on the screen can cause headaches, dizziness, and nausea. As we mentioned earlier, animations can also cause seizures, especially if they contain elements that flash.

In many operating systems, users can disable animations on their devices. In our applications, we need to make sure that we respect those preferences. To check user settings the level-5 Media Queries Module has introduced the `prefers-reduced-motion` media query. This query is an at-rule, which checks the user's preferences regarding motion on the screen and allows us to apply conditional styles based on those preferences. The query has two values:

- `no-preference`
- `reduce`

We can choose to disable or reduce an animation when a user prefers reduced motion or enable it when they don't specify a preference. A user's preference for reduced motion doesn't mean that we can't use any animation, but we should be selective about which animations we keep. Aspects that may determine which animations to keep enabled include

- How fast it is
- How long it is
- How much of the viewport it uses
- What the flash rate is
- How essential it is to the functioning of the site or understanding of the content

TIP   It's worth mentioning that a user may prefer reduced or no animation but may not be aware of the system-preferences settings for opting out of animations. Providing an onsite opt-out button may be useful, depending on how much animation our website has.

Accessibility guidelines for animations

A user should be able to pause, stop, or hide animation that lasts more than 3 seconds and isn't considered to be essential (http://mng.bz/RldR). Loaders are a bit tricky in this respect, as they convey important information to the user (the application is doing something and isn't frozen) but can be large and have a lot of motion.

Our loader could be considered to be essential content, but we also provide a progress bar below it to give the user an indication of what the application is doing. Because the information is conveyed in a different medium, and because the animation is large, has a lot of movement, and could last more than 3 seconds, we're going to disable it for users who prefer reduced motion, using the code in the following listing.

Listing 3.13   Disabling the animation for users who prefer reduced motion

Conditionally applies styles within the at-rule
when the user enables prefer-reduced-motion

Disables the animation
previously applied to
the rectangles

```
@media (prefers-reduced-motion: reduce) {
  rect { animation: none; }
}
```

To check that we successfully disabled the animation, instead of editing our machine's settings, in most browsers we can do the following:

1. Go into our browser's developer tools.
2. In the console tab display, select the rendering tab.
   (In Google's Chrome browser, if this tab isn't already displayed, click the vertical ellipsis button and choose More Tools > Rendering from the drop-down menu.)
3. Enable the reduced-motion emulation.

Figure 3.13 shows the disabled animation and developer tools in the latest version of Chrome (http://mng.bz/51rZ) at this writing.

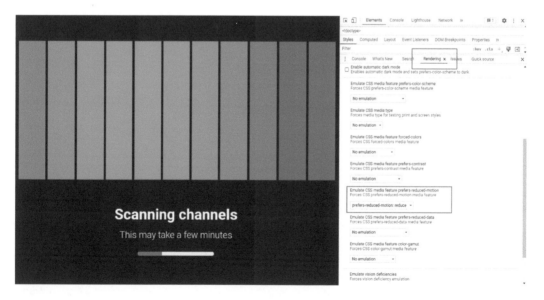

Figure 3.13   Emulating reduced-motion preference using Chrome DevTools

With our loader animation finished and accessibility needs handled, let's turn our attention to the progress bar at the bottom of the screen.

3.6 Styling an HTML progress bar

The `<progress>` HTML element can be used to show that something is loading or uploading, or that data has been transferred. It's often used to show the user how much of a task has been completed.

The default styles of the `<progress>` element vary among browsers and operating systems. Much of the functionality of the progress bar is handled at operating-system level; as a result, we have few properties available to restyle the control, especially when it comes to the colored progress indicator inside the bar itself. In this section, we'll look at some workarounds and their pitfalls. Let's start with an easy one.

Figure 3.14 shows our starting point generated by the HTML in listing 3.14. At this point, no styles have been applied to the control. The figure shows the defaults generated by Martine's machine.

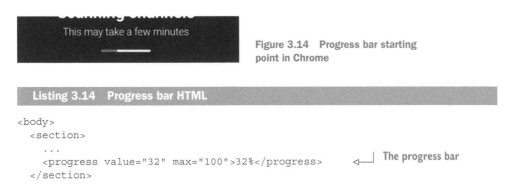

Figure 3.14 Progress bar starting point in Chrome

Listing 3.14 Progress bar HTML

```
<body>
  <section>
    . . .
    <progress value="32" max="100">32%</progress>          ⟵⎤ The progress bar
  </section>
```

3.6.1 Styling the progress bar

Let's start with changing the height and the width. To increase the width of the progress bar to match the width of the section, we'll give its `width` property a value of `100%`. We also want to increase the height to `24px`.

To change the color of the progress indicator (the colored portion of the control), we can use a fairly new property: `accent-color`. This property allows us to change the color of form controls such as check marks, radio inputs, and the `progress` element. We'll set it to `#128688`, matching the color of the last bar of our loader. The following listing shows our progress rule thus far.

Listing 3.15 Progress rule

```
progress {
  height: 24px;
  width: 100%;
  accent-color: #128688;
}
```

Figure 3.15 shows the styles in listing 3.15 applied to our control.

Figure 3.15   Width, height, and accent color applied to the progress element

If we try to add a background color to our element (background: pink), we'll notice that the addition doesn't work. As a matter of fact, it fails spectacularly (figure 3.16). It radically changes the appearance of the element and alters the accent-color we previously set. Furthermore, the background color changes to gray rather than pink.

Figure 3.16   background-color failure

How do we get around this problem? To restyle the control, we need to ignore the default and re-create the styles from scratch. To do that, though, we need to use vendor-prefixed properties.

VENDOR PREFIXES

Historically, when browsers introduced new properties, they were added with a vendor prefix before the property name. Each browser's prefix is based on the rendering engine that it uses. Table 3.1 displays major browsers and their prefixes.

Table 3.1   Vendor prefixes and their browsers

Prefix	Browsers
-webkit-	Chrome, Safari, Opera, most iOS browsers (including Firefox for iOS), Edge
-moz-	Firefox

Vendor prefixes are often incomplete or nonstandard implementations that browsers may choose to remove or refactor at any time. Although this fact has been clearly documented for years, developers who were eager to use the latest properties regularly used them in production nonetheless.

To prevent this continued behavior, most major browsers moved to shipping experimental features behind a feature flag. To enable the feature and play with it, the user must go into their browser settings and enable that specific flag.

By moving to a flag-based method, the browsers are able to let developers play with experimental, cutting-edge features without fear that a nonstandard implementation might be used in a piece of production code. But many vendor-prefixed properties are still available in the wild. For more information about vendor prefixing and feature flags, see the appendix.

The first thing we'll do to fix our `background-color` issue is to remove the default appearance of the control.

THE APPEARANCE PROPERTY

To reset the appearance of the `<progress>` element, we use the `appearance` property. By setting its value to `none`, we cancel the default styles provided by the user agent. Because we'll be creating all the styles from scratch, we can remove the `accent-color` property, as it will no longer have any effect.

We'll keep our height and width, and also add a `border-radius` because we're going to have a curved finish. The `appearance` property is supported by all new versions of major browsers, but we still need to include the vendor-prefixed versions, as some of the experimental properties we'll be using require them. The following listing shows our updated rule.

Listing 3.16 Updated progress rule

```
progress {
  height: 24px;
  width: 100%;
  border-radius: 20px;
  -webkit-appearance: none;
  -moz-appearance: none;
  appearance: none;
}
```

At this point, our progress bar looks the same as when we broke it by adding the background color. This result is to be expected. With `appearance:none` added, we can start altering the control in ways we previously couldn't. First, we'll focus on browsers with a `-webkit-` prefix.

3.6.2 Styling the progress bar for -webkit- browsers

We can use three vendor-prefixed pseudo-elements to edit the styles of our progress bar:

- `::-webkit-progress-inner-element`—The outermost part of the progress element
- `::-webkit-progress-bar`—The entire bar of the progress element, the portion below the progress indicator, and the child of the `::-webkit-progress-inner-element`
- `::-webkit-progress-value`—The progress indicator and the child of `::-webkit-progress-bar`

We'll use all three pseudo-elements to style our element. Let's start from the inside and work our way out. The first part we want to style is the progress indicator, for which we'll need to use ::-webkit-progress-value. We curve the edges and change the color of the bar to a light blue, as shown in the following listing.

> **Listing 3.17   Styling the progress indicator in Chrome**

```
::-webkit-progress-value {
  border-radius: 20px;
  background-color: #7be6e8;
}
```

Figure 3.17 shows our output in a WebKit browser.

Figure 3.17   Progress value styled in Chrome

Next, we'll edit the background behind the progress indicator by using ::-webkit-progress-bar. We'll also add rounded corners to the background and change the color to a linear gradient, going from a dark green to a light blue in keeping with the theme of the whole piece.

The linear-gradient() function takes a direction followed by a series of color and percentage pairs. The direction dictates the angle of the gradient; the color-percentage pairs dictate the points within the gradient at which we want to shift from one color to another. We'll use the keyword value to right as our direction. Then we'll set a starting color of #128688 and an ending color of #4db3ff. Our gradient, therefore, will go from left to right, fading from our start color to our end color.

> **CSS gradient generators and vendor prefixes**
>
> As gradients can be tedious to write by hand, many CSS gradient generators have been created and are freely available on the web. Many still include vendor prefixes in their generated code. These prefixes are no longer necessary, as gradients are now supported by all major browsers, and browsers that required them are almost completely nonexistent now.

Finally, we add a border radius to the outermost container. The CSS for our progress bar is shown in the following listing.

> **Listing 3.18   Styling the progress indicator container in Chrome**

```
::-webkit-progress-bar {
  border-radius: 20px;
```

```
    background: #4db3ff;
    background: linear-gradient(to right, #128688 0%,#4db3ff 100%);
}
::-webkit-progress-inner-element {
    border-radius: 20px;
}
```

Fallback color for
the gradient

Our progress indicator looks great in Chrome (figure 3.18). Next, let's take a look at what it looks like in Firefox.

Figure 3.18 Styled progress indicator in Chrome

In Firefox (figure 3.19), we see that our control remains fairly unstyled because instead of the -webkit- vendor prefix, it requires the -moz- prefix. Having written code for the -webkit- vendor prefix, we need to do the same for browsers that use the -moz- vendor prefix.

Figure 3.19 Unstyled progress bar in Firefox

3.6.3 *Styling the progress bar for -moz- browsers*

We'll approach the styles a bit differently for Firefox because we don't have as many properties to play with. The only -moz- prefixed property at our disposal is :::-moz-progress-bar. Also a pseudo-element, it targets the progress indicator itself. Therefore, we'll style it the same way that we styled ::-webkit-progress-value for Chrome because we want to achieve the same look in both browsers.

Because we're using the same styles, it's logical to add the -moz- selector to the existing rule: :::-moz-progress-bar, ::-webkit-progress-value { … }. It works well in Firefox (figure 3.20), but it will break Chrome (figure 3.21).

Having multiple selectors in the same rule shouldn't cause this side effect, but we're dealing with experimental properties, which sometimes have nonstandard

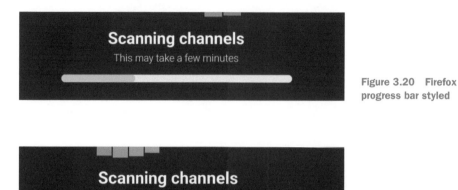

Figure 3.20   Firefox progress bar styled

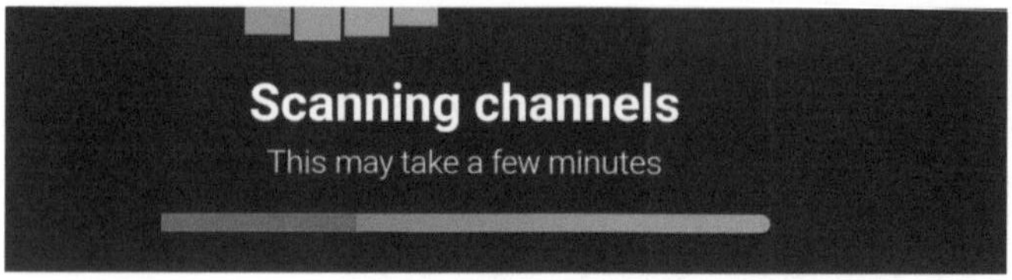

Figure 3.21   Adding both selectors in the same rule breaks Chrome.

behaviors. To prevent this unfortunate side effect, we'll write two identical rules, one for each selector, as shown in the following listing.

Listing 3.19   Styling the progress indicator container in Chrome

```
::-webkit-progress-value {          Rule for
  border-radius: 20px;              Chrome
  background-color: #7be6e8;
}
::-moz-progress-bar {               Rule for
  border-radius: 20px;             Firefox
  background-color: #7be6e8;
}
```

To change the background color for Firefox, we add a background property value to the progress element itself. We use the same gradient we used in the `::-webkit-progress-bar` rule. Figure 3.22 shows our progress in Firefox.

Figure 3.22   Firefox with background applied to the progress element

The last thing we need to do is remove the border, which we'll apply to the `progress` rule. To achieve this effect, we set the border property value to `none`. The following listing shows our final progress rule.

Listing 3.20   Final progress rule

```
progress {
  height: 24px;
  width: 100%;
  -webkit-appearance: none;
  -moz-appearance: none;
  appearance: none;                                          Gradient
  border-radius: 20px;                                       background
  background: linear-gradient(to right, #128688 0%,#4db3ff 100%);   ◁─┘
  border: none;      ◁─┐
}                      │  Removes the
                       │  border
```

As we can see in figure 3.23, we've achieved the same result in Chrome and Firefox.

Figure 3.23   Progress bar styles finished in Firefox

We must stress that the styles were achieved by using experimental features that are nonstandard and could change in the future. The value here is being able to experiment with new features before they become readily available. It's also an opportunity to get involved in the community; it's not uncommon for the working groups that develop browser features and specifications to request feedback before new standards are accepted and rolled out for general use.

Summary

- The `animation` property is a way to animate the values of the position, color, or some other visual element with CSS.
- The `@keyframes` at-rule is a way to define keyframes for your animations.
- We can delay the start of an animation by using the `animation-delay` property.
- The `animation-duration` sets how long a single iteration of the animation should take to complete.
- SVGs can be styled with CSS.
- The `prefers-reduced-motion` media query allows us to style animations conditionally per the user's settings.
- The HTML progress bar is a way to show how much of something has loaded.

- By default, the browser applies its own styling to the progress bar, but it can be reset by using the `appearance` property with a value of `none`.
- Our ability to style the `progress` element is fairly restricted unless we use experimental properties.
- Some nonstandard properties are available to style the `progress` element, but they require the use of vendor prefixes. Vendor-prefixed properties are experimental, which means that they sometimes have nonstandard implementations and could change at any time.

Creating a responsive
web newspaper layout

This chapter covers

- Using the CSS Multi-column Layout Module to create a newspaper layout
- Using the `counter-style` CSS at-rule to create custom list styles
- Styling images using the `filter` property
- Handling broken images
- Formatting captions
- Using the `quotes` property to add quotation marks to HTML elements
- Using media queries to change the layout based on screen size

In chapter 1, we looked at creating a single-column article, which taught us the basic principles of CSS. The design, however, was simple. Let's revisit the concept of formatting articles but make it much more visually interesting. In this chapter, we'll style our content to look like a page out of a newspaper, as shown in figure 4.1.

To create the content columns, we'll use the CSS Multi-column Layout Module. Along the way, we'll also look at how we can manage the space between the columns,

NEWSPAPER TITLE

TUESDAY, 5TH SEPTEMBER 2021

ARTICLE HEADING

John Doe

Maecenas faucibus mollis interdum. Cum sociis natoque penatibus et magnis dis parturient montes, nascetur ridiculus mus. Cras justo odio, dapibus ac facilisis in, egestas eget quam. Sed posuere consectetur est at lobortis. Morbi leo risus, porta ac consectetur ac, vestibulum at eros. Lorem ipsum dolor sit amet, consectetur adipiscing elit. Curabitur blandit tempus porttitor.

Integer posuere erat a ante venenatis dapibus posuere velit aliquet. Maecenas faucibus mollis interdum. Cum sociis natoque penatibus et magnis dis parturient montes, nascetur ridiculus mus. Vivamus sagittis lacus vel augue laoreet rutrum faucibus dolor auctor. Aenean eu leo quam. Pellentesque ornare sem lacinia quam venenatis vestibulum.

" Fusce dapibus, tellus ac cursus commodo, tortor mauris condimentum nibh, ut fermentum massa justo sit amet risus. "

Aenean lacinia bibendum nulla sed consectetur. Duis mollis, est non commodo luctus, nisi erat porttitor ligula, eget lacinia odio sem nec elit. Donec id elit non mi porta gravida at eget metus. Cras justo odio, dapibus ac facilisis in, egestas eget quam. Cras mattis consectetur purus sit amet fermentum. Nullam id dolor id nibh ultricies vehicula ut id elit. Cras mattis consectetur purus sit amet fermentum.

SUBHEADING

- List item 1
- List item 2
- List item 3

Cras justo odio, dapibus ac facilisis in, egestas eget quam. Lorem ipsum dolor sit amet, consectetur

adipiscing elit. Praesent commodo cursus magna, vel scelerisque nisl consectetur et. Cum sociis natoque penatibus et magnis dis parturient montes, nascetur ridiculus mus. Aenean lacinia bibendum nulla sed consectetur.

Donec ullamcorper nulla non metus auctor fringilla. Aenean eu leo quam. Pellentesque ornare sem lacinia quam venenatis vestibulum. Aenean lacinia bibendum nulla sed consectetur. Aenean lacinia bibendum nulla sed consectetur.

SUBHEADING

Praesent commodo cursus magna, vel scelerisque nisl consectetur et. Aenean eu leo quam. Pellentesque ornare sem lacinia quam venenatis vestibulum. Donec id elit non mi porta gravida at

Golden Gate Bridge

eget metus. Aenean lacinia bibendum nulla sed consectetur. Integer posuere erat a ante venenatis dapibus posuere velit aliquet. Aenean eu leo quam. Pellentesque ornare sem lacinia quam venenatis vestibulum. Integer posuere erat a ante venenatis dapibus posuere velit aliquet.

Morbi leo risus, porta ac consectetur ac, vestibulum at eros. Curabitur blandit tempus porttitor. Morbi leo risus, porta ac consectetur ac, vestibulum at eros. Duis mollis, est non commodo luctus, nisi erat porttitor ligula, eget lacinia odio sem nec elit.

Figure 4.1   The result we want to achieve

how to span elements across columns, and how to control where the content breaks to a new column.

Part of the newspaper page uses a list of items, which has some default styles provided to us by the user agent (UA) stylesheet. We'll look at how to use the CSS Lists and Counters Module, which allows us to customize how our `list-items` counters (the numbers and bullets) are styled.

Another concept we'll cover in this chapter is how to style images, including the use of the `filter` property in conjunction with functions to alter the image's appearance. We'll also look at solutions for broken images and ways to make them fail gracefully. When we say "fail gracefully" (sometimes known as *graceful degradation*), we're putting in place fallbacks to employ if the thing we're trying to load is having an problem or a feature we're trying to use isn't compatible with the user's browser.

You can find the code for our project in the `chapter-04` folder of the GitHub repository (http://mng.bz/OpOa) or on CodePen at https://codepen.io/michaelgearon/pen/yLxzbr. Our starting HTML consists of the elements in listing 4.1. Within the <body> element are the title of the newspaper and print date followed by an article. The article has a heading, author name, a quote, two subheadings, a list, some paragraphs, and an image.

Listing 4.1   Starting HTML

```
<body>
  <h1>Newspaper Title</h1>        ┌───  Newspaper title
  <time datetime="2021-09-07">    ←┘    (main heading)
    Tuesday, 5<sup>th</sup> September 2021        Print date
  </time>
  <article>
    <h2>Article heading</h2>                     Article author
    <div class="author">John Doe</div>       ←
    <p>Maecenas faucibus mollis interdum. Cum sociis nato...</p>
    <p>Integer posuere erat a ante venenatis dapibus posu...</p>
    <blockquote>
      Fusce dapibus, tellus ac cursus commodo, tortor ma...     Quote
    </blockquote>
    <p>Aenean lacinia bibendum nulla sed consectetur. Dui...</p>
    <h3>Subheading</h3>
    <ul>
      <li>List item 1</li>
      ...                           List
    </ul>
    <p>Cras justo odio, dapibus ac facilisis in, egestas ...</p>
    <p>Donec ullamcorper nulla non metus auctor fringilla...</p>
    <h3>Subheading</h3>
    <img src="./image.jpg" alt="">
    <p>Praesent commodo cursus magna, vel scelerisque nisl...</p>
    <p>Morbi leo risus, porta ac consectetur ac, vestibulu...</p>
  </article>       ←┐
</body>            │   End of the
</html>            │   article
```

Start of the article
Article heading
First subheading
Second subheading
Image

Figure 4.2 shows our starting point. The styles applied to the HTML are the defaults provided by the browser. No author styles have been applied to the page yet.

Before we worry about layout, let's define our theme.

4.1   Setting up our theme

The theme sets the tone for the page; it generally consists of colors, fonts, borders, and sometimes padding. Our theme will stay the same regardless of screen size or layout. Often, the theme of a website is tightly coupled to its logo and brand colors.

We'll set some defaults on the <body> element that can be inherited by its descendants. As a general rule, styles that revolve around typography (color, font-family, and so on) can be inherited by most elements. Exceptions are some form elements, which we cover in chapter 10. When we set inheritable properties on the parent, the styles trickle down to the descendents, relieving us of the need to apply them to every element.

Newspaper Title

Tuesday, 5th September 2021

Article heading

John Doe

Maecenas faucibus mollis interdum. Cum sociis natoque penatibus et magnis dis parturient montes, nascetur ridiculus mus. Cras justo odio, dapibus ac facilisis in, egestas eget quam. Sed posuere consectetur est at lobortis. Morbi leo risus, porta ac consectetur ac, vestibulum at eros. Lorem ipsum dolor sit amet, consectetur adipiscing elit. Curabitur blandit tempus porttitor.

Integer posuere erat a ante venenatis dapibus posuere velit aliquet. Maecenas faucibus mollis interdum. Cum sociis natoque penatibus et magnis dis parturient montes, nascetur ridiculus mus. Vivamus sagittis lacus vel augue laoreet rutrum faucibus dolor auctor. Aenean eu leo quam. Pellentesque ornare sem lacinia quam venenatis vestibulum.

> Fusce dapibus, tellus ac cursus commodo, tortor mauris condimentum nibh, ut fermentum massa justo sit amet risus.

Aenean lacinia bibendum nulla sed consectetur. Duis mollis, est non commodo luctus, nisi erat porttitor ligula, eget lacinia odio sem nec elit. Donec id elit non mi porta gravida at eget metus. Cras justo odio, dapibus ac facilisis in, egestas eget quam. Cras mattis consectetur purus sit amet fermentum. Nullam id dolor id nibh ultricies vehicula ut id elit. Cras mattis consectetur purus sit amet fermentum.

Subheading

- List item 1
- List item 2
- List item 3

Cras justo odio, dapibus ac facilisis in, egestas eget quam. Lorem ipsum dolor sit amet, consectetur adipiscing elit. Praesent commodo cursus magna, vel scelerisque nisl consectetur et. Cum sociis natoque penatibus et magnis dis parturient montes, nascetur ridiculus mus. Aenean lacinia bibendum nulla sed consectetur.

Donec ullamcorper nulla non metus auctor fringilla. Aenean eu leo quam. Pellentesque ornare sem lacinia quam venenatis vestibulum. Aenean lacinia bibendum nulla sed consectetur. Aenean lacinia bibendum nulla sed consectetur.

Subheading

Praesent commodo cursus magna, vel scelerisque nisl consectetur et. Aenean eu leo quam. Pellentesque ornare sem lacinia quam venenatis vestibulum. Donec id elit non mi porta gravida at eget metus. Aenean lacinia bibendum nulla sed consectetur. Integer posuere erat a ante venenatis dapibus posuere velit aliquet. Aenean eu leo quam. Pellentesque ornare sem lacinia quam venenatis vestibulum. Integer posuere erat a ante venenatis dapibus posuere velit aliquet.

Morbi leo risus, porta ac consectetur ac, vestibulum at eros. Curabitur blandit tempus porttitor. Morbi leo risus, porta ac consectetur ac, vestibulum at eros. Duis mollis, est non commodo luctus, nisi erat porttitor ligula, eget lacinia odio sem nec elit.

Figure 4.2   Starting point

4.1.1   Fonts

We apply a background color, font, and text color (listing 4.2). Notice that before the `body` rule, we import our chosen `font-family` from Google Fonts. Google Fonts (https://fonts.google.com) is a popular option with developers, as it's freely available, and users don't need to create an account or worry about licensing.

> **WARNING** When loading libraries or assets, including fonts, from a content delivery network (CDN), always check the privacy and data terms, and make sure that they're compliant with local laws such as General Data Protection

Regulation (GDPR) and European Union laws. When in doubt, ask your legal team. If CDNs aren't an option for you, check out chapter 9 for details on loading fonts locally.

PT Serif, for example, isn't a font we can expect a user to have already loaded on their computer; therefore, we have to import it for the browser to tell it what the *glyphs* (letters, numbers, and symbols) should look like. We also provide a default of serif as a fallback should the import fail.

Web-safe fonts

Only a few web-safe fonts (fonts we can assume that most devices will have access to) are available. According to W3Schools (http://mng.bz/Y6Ea), some safe options are Arial, Verdana, Helvetica, Tahoma, Trebuchet MS, Times New Roman, Georgia, Garamond, Courier New, and Brush Script MT. But no official standard specifies what constitutes a web-safe font or which ones would truly be available on all browsers and devices. Therefore, regardless of the font family we choose, it's good practice always to provide a fallback value (serif, sans-serif, monospace, cursive, or fantasy).

Although we'll do the bulk of the layout later in the chapter, we'll add some left and right padding on our body now to move our text away from the edge.

Listing 4.2 Defining some theme styles

```
@import url('https://fonts.googleapis.com/css2?family=PT+Serif&display=swap');    ◁──┐
                                                                          Imports PT
                                                                          Serif from
body {                                                                   Google Fonts
  background-color: #f9f7f1;
  font-family: 'PT Serif', serif;    ◁──┐ Applies PT Serif
  color: #404040;                        to our content and
  padding: 0 24px;                       provides a fallback
}
```

Figure 4.3 shows our updated page. Notice that all the elements in the <body> have inherited the color and font-family.

Next, we'll style the main heading and subheadings. Let's start with the newspaper title, which is the <h1> in the HTML. We want to change the font-family to use a typeface called Oswald, increase the text size, make it bold, transform the font to use all capital letters, set the line height, and center the text. Like PT Serif, Oswald isn't a font that we can expect most users' devices to know about, so we'll import it much as we did PT Serif.

Notice that for the text size, we use unit rem, which stands for "root em." An *em* is a relative unit based on the font size of the element's parent. If a container div has a font size of 12px, and we set a child element's size to .5em, the child element's size would equal to 12 x .5 or 6px. The rem unit works similarly, but instead of being relative

Newspaper Title

Tuesday, 5th September 2021

Article heading

John Doe

Maecenas faucibus mollis interdum. Cum sociis natoque penatibus et magnis dis parturient montes, nascetur ridiculus mus. Cras justo odio, dapibus ac facilisis in, egestas eget quam. Sed posuere consectetur est at lobortis. Morbi leo risus, porta ac consectetur ac, vestibulum at eros. Lorem ipsum dolor sit amet, consectetur adipiscing elit. Curabitur blandit tempus porttitor.

Integer posuere erat a ante venenatis dapibus posuere velit aliquet. Maecenas faucibus mollis interdum. Cum sociis natoque penatibus et magnis dis parturient montes, nascetur ridiculus mus. Vivamus sagittis lacus vel augue laoreet rutrum faucibus dolor auctor. Aenean eu leo quam. Pellentesque ornare sem lacinia quam venenatis vestibulum.

"Fusce dapibus, tellus ac cursus commodo, tortor mauris condimentum nibh, ut fermentum massa justo sit amet risus."

Aenean lacinia bibendum nulla sed consectetur. Duis mollis, est non commodo luctus, nisi erat porttitor ligula, eget lacinia odio sem nec elit. Donec id elit non mi porta gravida at eget metus. Cras justo odio, dapibus ac facilisis in, egestas eget quam. Cras mattis consectetur purus sit amet fermentum. Nullam id dolor id nibh ultricies vehicula ut id elit. Cras mattis consectetur purus sit amet fermentum.

Subheading

- List item 1
- List item 2
- List item 3

Cras justo odio, dapibus ac facilisis in, egestas eget quam. Lorem ipsum dolor sit amet, consectetur adipiscing elit. Praesent commodo cursus magna, vel scelerisque nisl consectetur et. Cum sociis natoque penatibus et magnis dis parturient montes, nascetur ridiculus mus. Aenean lacinia bibendum nulla sed consectetur.

Donec ullamcorper nulla non metus auctor fringilla. Aenean eu leo quam. Pellentesque ornare sem lacinia quam venenatis vestibulum. Aenean lacinia bibendum nulla sed consectetur. Aenean lacinia bibendum nulla sed consectetur.

Subheading

Praesent commodo cursus magna, vel scelerisque nisl consectetur et. Aenean eu leo quam. Pellentesque ornare sem lacinia quam venenatis vestibulum. Donec id elit non mi porta gravida at eget metus. Aenean lacinia bibendum nulla sed consectetur. Integer posuere erat a ante venenatis dapibus posuere velit aliquet. Aenean eu leo quam. Pellentesque ornare sem lacinia quam venenatis vestibulum. Integer posuere erat a ante venenatis dapibus posuere velit aliquet.

Morbi leo risus, porta ac consectetur ac, vestibulum at eros. Curabitur blandit tempus porttitor. Morbi leo risus, porta ac consectetur ac, vestibulum at eros. Duis mollis, est non commodo luctus, nisi erat porttitor ligula, eget lacinia odio sem nec elit.

Figure 4.3   Theme styles applied to the body being inherited by descendants

to the parent's font size, its base value is that of the root element—in our case, `<html>`. We didn't set a font size on the HTML element; therefore, our base will be the browser's default, which in most cases is `16px`. With that in mind, a font size of `4rem`—the size we set on our main heading—would be equivalent to 4 x 16 or `64px`.

To import Oswald from Google Fonts, we can add a second `@import` at the top of our file, or for better performance, we can combine the two imports into one `@import` statement. The ability to combine the two imports is specific to Google Fonts; not all CDNs have this ability.

Notice in listing 4.3 that in our `@import`, after the name of the font, we see `:wght@400;700`. This code indicates which Oswald font weights we want to import.

Listing 4.3   Styling the newspaper title

```
@import url('https://fonts.googleapis.com/css2?
    family=Oswald:wght@400;700&family=PT+Serif&display=swap');


h1 {
  font-weight: 700;
```

Updated import that includes both Oswald and PT Serif

Equivalent to using a value of bold

```
    font-size: 4rem;
    font-family:'Oswald', sans-serif;
    line-height: 1;
    text-transform: uppercase;
    text-align: center;
}
```

Figure 4.4 shows our updated title.

NEWSPAPER TITLE

Tuesday, 5th September 2021

Article heading

John Doe

Maecenas faucibus mollis interdum. Cum sociis natoque penatibus et magnis dis parturient montes, nascetur ridiculus mus. Cras iusto odio, dapibus ac facilisis in, egestas eget quam. Sed

Figure 4.4   Styled title

4.1.2   The font-weight property

The font-weight property can take either a number value between 100 and 900 or a keyword value (normal, bold, lighter, or bolder). normal is equivalent to 400, and bold to 700. lighter and bolder change the element's font weight based on the font weight of the parent element. Table 4.1 shows the relationships between numeric font-weight values and their common name equivalents.

Table 4.1   font-weight values and their common weight names

Value	Common weight name
100	Thin (Hairline)
200	Extra Light (Ultra Light)
300	Light
400	Normal (Regular)
500	Medium
600	Semi Bold (Demi Bold)
700	Bold
800	Extra Bold (Ultra Bold)
900	Black (Heavy)
950	Extra Black (Ultra Black)

If we don't import the weight that matches the one we set in the rule, the browser will apply the closest weight it has access to. Therefore, had we imported Oswald only with a weight of `400` and applied a `font-weight` value of `bold` to our element, the browser would have displayed our text with a weight of `400` because that value would be the only one it had to work with.

4.1.3   *The font shorthand property*

Using the `font` shorthand property, we can combine most of the styles in our rule. The `font` property requires us to provide a `font-family` and `size`, optionally followed by `style`, `variant`, `weight`, `stretch`, and `line-height`, using the following syntax: `font: font-style font-variant font-weight font-stretch font-size/line-height font-family`. The next listing shows our updated rule using `font`.

Listing 4.4   Title styles using the `font` shorthand property

```
h1 {
  font: 700 4rem/1 'Oswald', sans-serif;
  text-transform: uppercase;
  text-align: center;
}
```

Let's apply the concepts we've covered regarding importing fonts, `font-weight`, and the `font` shorthand property to style the article's main heading and subheadings.

4.1.4   *Visual hierarchy*

To create a visual hierarchy on the page, we'll set the article heading `<h2>` to be smaller than our newspaper's main heading `<h1>` but larger than the subheadings within the article `<h3>`. Generally speaking, the larger an element is, the more important it's perceived to be, so we use size to make our headers stand out. By using a different `font-family` from the one we use for the main body text and making all the heading letters uppercase, we further the distinction.

Creating a visual hierarchy is important, as it allows the user to glance at the screen and immediately recognize elements of interest. It also segments information into groups, making the information easier to process and understand.

Listing 4.5 shows our header rules. We'll keep the same font family, uppercase the lettering, and adjust the sizing. We'll also remove the browser-provided bottom margins of both article headers to keep them closer to the text they precede.

Listing 4.5   Article header rules

```
h2 {
  font: 3rem/.95 'Oswald', sans-serif;    ◁——┐ Article
  text-transform: uppercase;                   │ heading
  margin-bottom: 16px;
}
```

```
h3 {                                          ⊲──┐   Article
  font: 2rem/.95 'Oswald', sans-serif;           │   subheadings
  text-transform: uppercase;
  margin-bottom: 12px;
}
```

Now our article's headers look like figure 4.5.

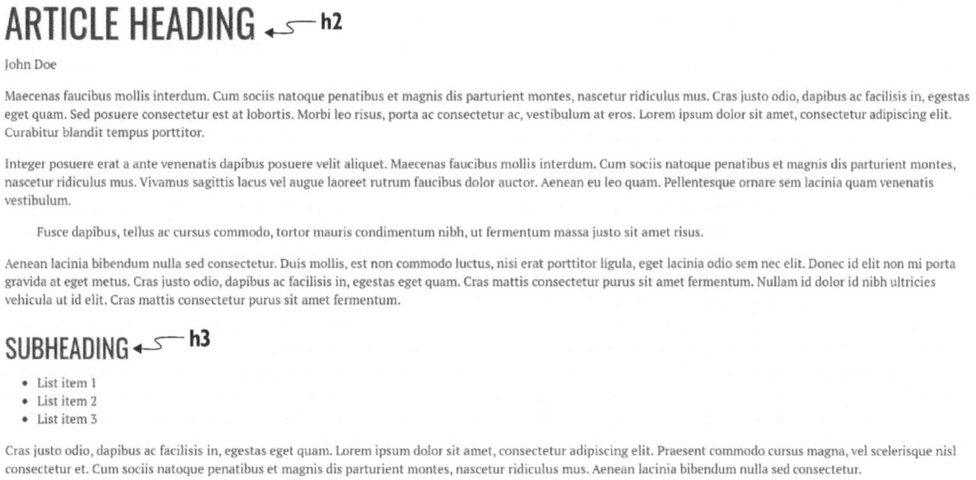

ARTICLE HEADING ←⌐ h2

John Doe

Maecenas faucibus mollis interdum. Cum sociis natoque penatibus et magnis dis parturient montes, nascetur ridiculus mus. Cras justo odio, dapibus ac facilisis in, egestas eget quam. Sed posuere consectetur est at lobortis. Morbi leo risus, porta ac consectetur ac, vestibulum at eros. Lorem ipsum dolor sit amet, consectetur adipiscing elit. Curabitur blandit tempus porttitor.

Integer posuere erat a ante venenatis dapibus posuere velit aliquet. Maecenas faucibus mollis interdum. Cum sociis natoque penatibus et magnis dis parturient montes, nascetur ridiculus mus. Vivamus sagittis lacus vel augue laoreet rutrum faucibus dolor auctor. Aenean eu leo quam. Pellentesque ornare sem lacinia quam venenatis vestibulum.

Fusce dapibus, tellus ac cursus commodo, tortor mauris condimentum nibh, ut fermentum massa justo sit amet risus.

Aenean lacinia bibendum nulla sed consectetur. Duis mollis, est non commodo luctus, nisi erat porttitor ligula, eget lacinia odio sem nec elit. Donec id elit non mi porta gravida at eget metus. Cras justo odio, dapibus ac facilisis in, egestas eget quam. Cras mattis consectetur purus sit amet fermentum. Nullam id dolor id nibh ultricies vehicula ut id elit. Cras mattis consectetur purus sit amet fermentum.

SUBHEADING ←⌐ h3

- List item 1
- List item 2
- List item 3

Cras justo odio, dapibus ac facilisis in, egestas eget quam. Lorem ipsum dolor sit amet, consectetur adipiscing elit. Praesent commodo cursus magna, vel scelerisque nisl consectetur et. Cum sociis natoque penatibus et magnis dis parturient montes, nascetur ridiculus mus. Aenean lacinia bibendum nulla sed consectetur.

Figure 4.5   Styled article headings

4.1.5   *Inline versus block elements*

Let's continue to make important elements stand out from the rest of the content, starting with the publication date, which is inside a `<time>` element in our HTML. The `<time>` element semantically denotes a specific period in time; it takes an optional `datetime` attribute that provides the date as a machine-readable format for search engines. Our `<time>` element looks like this: `<time datetime="2021-09-07">Tuesday, 5<sup>th</sup> September 2021</time>`. Figure 4.6 shows the look we want to achieve.

NEWSPAPER TITLE

TUESDAY, 5ᵀᴴ SEPTEMBER 2021

ARTICLE HEADING

Figure 4.6   Styled publication date

Starting with the typography, we center the text and use the Oswald font family, set the `font-size` to `1.5rem`, and make the text uppercase and bold. Then we change the text size of the *th* found in the superscript element (`<sup>`) to a slightly smaller font size and normal weight to decrease its prominence.

Next, we add the top and bottom borders to be 3-pixel-thick, solid, dark gray lines. After adding the borders, we add some top and bottom padding so that we have some breathing room between the text and the borders.

The `<time>` element is an inline-level element, meaning that it takes up only the exact amount of space it needs for its content, the same way that a `<span>` or `<a>` element does.

By contrast, block-level elements (such as `<div>`, `<p>`, and `<ul>`) place themselves on a new line and take the full width of their available space unless given a set width. To achieve the design in figure 4.6, we want our `<time>` element to behave as though it were a block-level element so that the text will place itself in the middle of the screen, and the borders will take the full width of the page.

To change the element's default behavior, we'll use the `display` property and give it a value of `block`. Figures 4.7 and 4.8 show the `<time>` element before and after we add the `display` property. In figure 4.7 (before adding the `display` property), the element is exhibiting its default behavior as an inline-level element. In figure 4.8 (after adding the `display` property), the element behaves like a block-level element, taking the full width of the screen.

NEWSPAPER TITLE

TUESDAY, 5TH SEPTEMBER 2021

ARTICLE HEADING

John Doe

Maecenas faucibus mollis interdum. Cum sociis natoque penatibus et magnis dis parturient montes, nascetur ridiculus mus. Cras justo odio, dapibus ac facilisis

Figure 4.7   The `<time>` element exhibiting inline behavior

NEWSPAPER TITLE

TUESDAY, 5TH SEPTEMBER 2021

ARTICLE HEADING

John Doe

Maecenas faucibus mollis interdum. Cum sociis natoque penatibus et magnis dis parturient montes, nascetur ridiculus mus. Cras justo odio, dapibus ac

Figure 4.8   The `<time>` element exhibiting block behavior

Styling the publication date in this manner serves two purposes: the styling makes it stand out, and it creates a visual divide between the newspaper information (the date and newspaper's main heading) and the article itself (everything below the date). The following listing contains the rules we wrote to achieve our design.

Listing 4.6   Styling the publication date

```
time {
    font: 700 1.5rem 'Oswald', sans-serif;
    text-align: center;                          Typography
    text-transform: uppercase;

    border-top: 3px solid #333333;
    border-bottom: 3px solid #333333;            Handles the borders
    padding: 12px 0;                             and padding

    display: block;            ←──────  Makes the element
}                                       behave like a block-
time sup {                              level element
    font-size: .875rem;
    font-weight: normal;
}
```

Styles the "th" ─────→ `time sup {`

4.1.6   Quotes

The last bit of text we want to feature is the `<blockquote>` after the second paragraph in the article. Sticking with our theme, as with all the other elements we want to make stand out, we'll make the font bigger and bolder. We'll also adjust the line height and add a margin to the element. Isolating an element from the content around it makes it easier to spot. By adding a top and bottom margin, we add space between the quote and the paragraphs above and below it, creating whitespace around the element. By adding left and right margins, we change its alignment, effectively indenting it. The added whitespace creates isolation.

Let's also add quotation marks to our `<blockquote>`. To add the quotation marks at the beginning and end of our quote, we could simply go into the HTML and add them manually, or we can do the job programmatically with CSS.

The `quotes` property allows us to define custom quotation marks. We can pass to this property the symbols we want to use as our double- and single-quote glyphs. Not all languages use the same symbols. American English, for example, uses "…" and '…', but French uses «…» and ‹…›. Using the `quotes` property, we can customize the symbols we want to use. If we don't provide a value for `quotes`, the browser's default behavior is to use what is customary for the language set on the document.

The `quotes` property, however, only defines the symbols; it doesn't add them. To add them, we use the `content` property values `open-quote` and `close-quote` in conjunction with the `::before` and `::after` pseudo-elements, as shown in listing 4.7. The pseudo-elements allow us to insert content via the `content` property before and after the element to which they're applied, respectively.

Listing 4.7   Styling the `blockquote`

```
blockquote {
  font: 1.8rem/1.25 'Oswald', sans-serif;
  margin: 1.5rem 2rem;
}
blockquote::before { content: open-quote; }
blockquote::after { content: close-quote; }
```

The `open-quote` and `close-quote` keywords represent opening and closing quotation marks as defined by the `quotes` property. Because we didn't add a `quotes` declaration to our `blockquote` rule, the browser will use what is conventional for the document's language, which we set to `en-US` in the language (`lang`) attribute of the `<html>` tag. The value of `en-US` specifies that our document is written in American English; therefore, the symbols that the browser renders are " and ", as we see in figure 4.9.

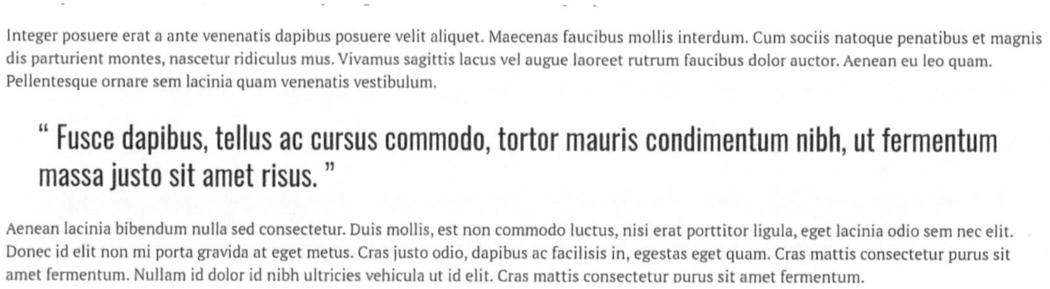

Integer posuere erat a ante venenatis dapibus posuere velit aliquet. Maecenas faucibus mollis interdum. Cum sociis natoque penatibus et magnis dis parturient montes, nascetur ridiculus mus. Vivamus sagittis lacus vel augue laoreet rutrum faucibus dolor auctor. Aenean eu leo quam. Pellentesque ornare sem lacinia quam venenatis vestibulum.

" Fusce dapibus, tellus ac cursus commodo, tortor mauris condimentum nibh, ut fermentum massa justo sit amet risus. "

Aenean lacinia bibendum nulla sed consectetur. Duis mollis, est non commodo luctus, nisi erat porttitor ligula, eget lacinia odio sem nec elit. Donec id elit non mi porta gravida at eget metus. Cras justo odio, dapibus ac facilisis in, egestas eget quam. Cras mattis consectetur purus sit amet fermentum. Nullam id dolor id nibh ultricies vehicula ut id elit. Cras mattis consectetur purus sit amet fermentum.

Figure 4.9   Styled title, heading, subheadings, and quote

With our quote styled, let's turn our attention to the bulleted list in the middle of the article.

4.2   *Using CSS counters*

Our article contains an unordered (bulleted) list. Currently, each list item has the default bullet before it. We can alter what our bullet looks like by using the `list-style-type` property. By default, we can choose disc (•), circle (○), square (▪), and numbers or letters in several languages, alphabets, and number formats. But let's say we want our bullet to be an emoji—specifically, the hot-beverage emoji (☕). We'll have to create a custom list style.

To create our custom list style, we'll use the `@counter-style` at-rule. We used at-rules in chapter 3 when we created keyframes. In this case, instead of defining how an animation will behave, we'll define how a list looks and behaves. The at-rule is called `counter-style` because it specifically addresses the built-in counting mechanism for list items in CSS. Under the covers, regardless of whether the list is ordered or unordered, the browser keeps track of the position of the item in the list—that is, it counts the items.

As with keyframes (which we named so we could reference them inside our `anima-tion` property), we'll name our `@counter-style` so we can reference it with the `list-style` property and apply it to our list. Let's name our list-style `emoji`. Our at-rule, therefore, will be `@counter-style emoji { }`.

Next, we'll define the behavior our `list-style` needs to have inside of our at-rule. We'll use three properties: `symbols`, `system`, and `suffix`.

4.2.1   The symbols descriptor

The `symbols` descriptor defines what will be used to create the bullet style. To define our emoji as the symbol to use, we can use the emoji directly or use its Unicode value.

Unicode is a character-encoding standard that specifies how a 16-bit binary value is represented as a string. In other words, it's the code representation of our emoji. The actual emoji image is determined by the operating system and browser, which is why we see variations in how emojis look between iOS and Android, for example. The Unicode value tells the machine what to render.

We use lookup tables such as the one at http://mng.bz/GRQJ to find this value for our emoji. ☕ is listed as having the following code: U+2615. To tell our CSS that we're using a Unicode value, we'll replace the U+ with a backslash (\\). Using the Unicode value, our declaration value will be `symbols: "\2615"`. If we use the emoji, our declaration value will be `symbols: ☕;`.

Next, we need to define our `system` descriptor.

4.2.2   The system descriptor

Regardless of type of list (ordered or unordered), under the covers the browser keeps track of the list item it's styling based on its position inside the list. The first item's integer value is 1, the second is 2, and so on. The `system` descriptor value defines the algorithm used to convert that integer value to the visual representation we see on the screen.

We're going to use the `cyclic` value. Earlier, we provided only one emoji in our `symbols` declaration, but we could have included multiple different emojis using a space-delimited list. A `cyclic` value tells the browser to loop through these values and, when it runs out, to start back at the beginning. Because we have only one value, the browser will apply the ☕ to the first list item and then run out of symbols. Having run out before the second list item, the browser starts back at the beginning of the list, applying the ☕ once again but to the second list item this time. Then the browser will run again, moving on to the third list item, and the cycle continues. Finally, we'll set a suffix.

4.2.3   The suffix descriptor

The `suffix` descriptor defines what comes between the bullet (our emoji) and the contents of the list item—by default, a period. We want to replace the period with plain whitespace between our emoji and list-item content. Therefore, we'll set our `suffix` descriptor value to `" "` (a blank space).

4.2.4   Putting everything together

With our `counter-style` defined, we can apply it to our list. Remember that we named the `counter-style` rule `emoji`. We'll apply the name as the `list-style` property value for our list, as shown in the following listing.

> **Listing 4.8   Styling the list**

```
@counter-style emoji {
    symbols: "\2615";              ◄──┐   The at-rule defining
    system: cyclic;                    │   the custom list-style's
    suffix: " ";                       │   behavior
}

article ul {                           Applies the custom
    list-style: emoji;          ◄──    list-style to the
}                                      article's lists
```

Figure 4.10 shows our newly styled list.

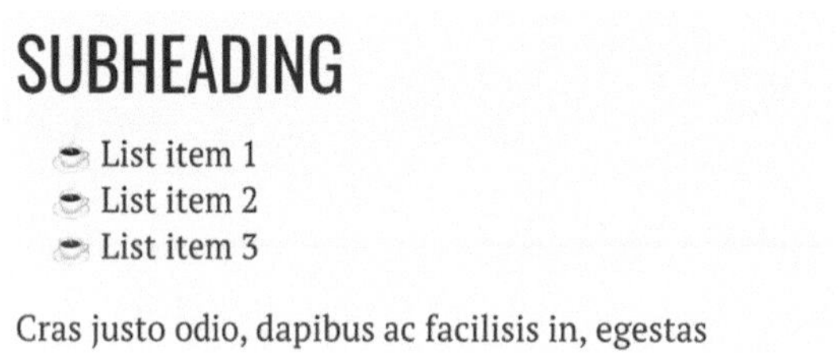

SUBHEADING

- List item 1
- List item 2
- List item 3

Cras justo odio, dapibus ac facilisis in, egestas

Figure 4.10   List styled using ☕ as counters

4.2.5   @counter versus list-style-image

Another way to change the list item marker being used is to use the `list-style-image` property and assign an image to it, similarly to the way we can set a background image by using the `background-image` property. We didn't use that approach in this project because we used an emoji, which is a Unicode character and not an image. The counter also provides us much more control, such as assigning a suffix or specifying how the counter cycles through the item markers being displayed.

   If we're looking only to change the marker to a specific image, `list-style-image` is perfect. But if we want to have more granular control or, as in our case, to use text, we need to use `@counter`. Let's continue going down the page, styling the image next.

4.3   Styling images

Historically, newspapers were printed in black and white. Colored ink in newsprint is a fairly new thing when we consider the history of print. To give our design a bit of a retro vibe, therefore, we'll make our image grayscale. First, we'll look at how to alter our image using filters. Unlike in print, on the web we need to worry about resources not loading or links being broken, so we'll also look at how to make the image fail gracefully should it fail to load. Finally, we'll add a caption to accompany the image.

4.3.1 *Using the filter property*

As in photo editors or on social-media websites like Instagram, we can apply filters to images with CSS. We can alter colors, blur, and add drop shadows, for example. Figure 4.11 shows examples of some of the things we can do to our images by using filters in CSS. Check out this code sample in CodePen to see it in action: https://codepen .io/michaelgearon/pen/porovxJ.

Figure 4.11 **Examples of images altered with the** `filter` **property**

If we think about pre-digital-era photography, when we used film and had to go to a shop to have it developed, we applied filters by adding a translucent disk over our lens, which altered the light coming into the camera box and onto the film. By altering the nature of the light, we altered the image being produced. If we used a red filter while taking a picture, for example, only the red-colored wavelength was allowed through; our picture was tinted red. Polarized sunglasses are another example of a filter that alters the light coming through a lens.

We can still use physical filters with digital cameras. In many cases, however, filters are applied digitally after the picture has been taken.

In CSS, we use the `filter` property to apply a filter to the image; then we use a function that defines the behavior we want the filter to have. You can find a list of the available functions at http://mng.bz/zmYA. We'll use the `grayscale()` function to make our picture appear to be a black-and-white photo.

The `grayscale()` function takes a percentage, which represents how much we want to reduce the amount of color in the image. We want to remove all the color, so we'll pass in a value of `100%`. Our rule, then, will be `img { filter: grayscale(100%) }`. Figure 4.12 shows the filter applied to our image.

SUBHEADING

Praesent commodo cursus magna, vel scelerisque   **Figure 4.12 Grayscale Image**

One consideration to make before using filters is their impact on website performance. Some of the filter functions, such as `grayscale()`, are relatively simple for the browser to process, but functions such as `drop-shadow()` and `blur()` can be resource-intensive. If we find that we're applying many filters to a large number of images, we should consider the impact of the filters on overall page performance and whether we should be preprocessing the image rather than applying the change with CSS.

4.3.2 *Handling broken images*

Even with the most thorough diligence and best testing practices, broken image links can happen. Let's add some fallbacks to ensure that if our image fails to load (regardless of the reason), we'll maintain a positive experience for our users.

First, let's deliberately break our link. In the HTML, we'll replace the path to the image with an image file that doesn't exist in our project, like so: `<img src="./my-broken-image.jpg" alt="my broken link" />`. The image will display as broken, as shown in figure 4.13.

SUBHEADING

my broken link

Praesent commodo cursus magna, vel scelerisque nisl consectetur et. Aenean eu leo quam. Pellentesque ornare sem laci
mi porta gravida at eget metus. Aenean lacinia bibendum nulla sed consectetur. Integer posuere erat a ante venenatis d
Pellentesque ornare sem lacinia quam venenatis vestibulum. Integer posuere erat a ante venenatis dapibus posuere veli

Figure 4.13 Broken link with `alt` text

Notice that the text provided in the `alt` attribute is displayed. The `alt` attribute allows assistive technologies to inform users about the image being displayed. A common use case is a blind user accessing content via a screen reader. In this particular case, because the image is broken, the text replaces the image. Although the situation isn't ideal, in the event of an image failure, users can still be informed of the content that the image was supposed to provide.

In our case, the image is purely decorative and doesn't provide any content value, so if the link is broken, we'll hide the image. Nothing will be there, but "nothing" is less unsightly than a broken-image icon. Because there's no way to detect that an image is broken in CSS, we need to use a little bit of JavaScript to know when to hide the image. We'll use the `onerror` JavaScript event handler to trigger a change in styles as follows: `<img src="..." alt="..." onerror="this.style.display='none'" >`. The bit of code that is of interest to us here is the `onerror` attribute. When an error occurs, the JavaScript inside the `onerror` attribute triggers and sets the image's `display` property to `none`, hiding the image. We can see that, in figure 4.14, our broken image is missing.

consectetur. Aenean lacinia bibendum nulla sed consectetur.

SUBHEADING — **Broken image is gone.**

Praesent commodo cursus magna, vel scelerisque nisl consectetur et. Aenean eu leo quam. Pellentesque ornare sem lacinia qua mi porta gravida at eget metus. Aenean lacinia bibendum nulla sed consectetur. Integer posuere erat a ante venenatis dapibus p Pellentesque ornare sem lacinia quam venenatis vestibulum. Integer posuere erat a ante venenatis dapibus posuere velit alique

Morbi leo risus, porta ac consectetur ac, vestibulum at eros. Curabitur blandit tempus porttitor. Morbi leo risus, porta ac consec

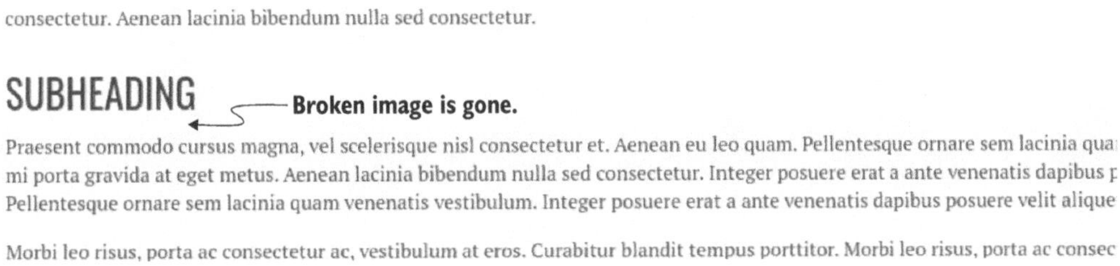

Figure 4.14 **The broken image is missing.**

The `onerror` code triggers only when the image fails to load, so let's fix our resource path to our image but keep the error handling: `<img src="./image.jpg" alt="" onerror="this.style.display='none'" >`. Now our image is restored (figure 4.15), but we have a safeguard in case it fails.

SUBHEADING

Praesent commodo cursus magna, vel scelerisque nisl consectetur et. Aenean eu leo quam. Pellentesque ornai non mi porta gravida at eget metus. Aenean lacinia bibendum nulla sed consectetur. Integer posuere erat a an

Figure 4.15 **Restored image with fallback**

Next, let's add a caption to the image.

4.3.3 Formatting captions

The image doesn't have a caption, so we're going to add one by using the `<figure>` and `<figcaption>` HTML elements. Then we'll style it.

These two elements go hand in hand. `<figure>` contains the image and then the optional `<figcaption>`. Often in books and other publishing material, a diagram, chart, or image has text below it that describes it or relates it to the text. Semantically, the benefit of grouping the image and the caption is that grouping programmatically links the image with its caption. From a styling perspective, having the elements together in a parent element allows us to position the element and its caption as a unit. The following listing shows how to change the HTML to add the figure and caption.

Listing 4.9   Adding a `<figure>` and `<figcaption>` to the HTML

```
<figure>            ⟵——| Start of the figure                              Our image
  <img src="./image.jpg" alt="" onerror="this.style.display='none'" />    ⟵——
  <figcaption>Golden Gate Bridge</figcaption>          ⟵——|
</figure>           ⟵——| End of the figure                   Our image
                                                              caption
```

Let's style the figure and the caption, starting by removing the browser-provided margins (figure 4.16) that are currently being applied to the figure.

SUBHEADING

Golden Gate Bridge

Praesent commodo cursus magna, vel scelerisque nisl consectetur et. Aenean eu leo quam. Pellentesque ornare sem lacinia quam venenatis vestibulum. Donec id elit non mi

Figure 4.16   `<figure>` with browser-provided styles

Next, we'll reinstate a bottom margin so that our caption is kept separate from the paragraph below it. Finally, we'll center the image and caption. We'll style the caption's text to use the Oswald font family (the one we used for all the headers) to differentiate it visually from the article text. The following listing shows the CSS used to style the figure and caption.

Listing 4.10   `figure` and `figcaption` styles

```
figure {
  margin: 0 0 12px 0;        ←——  Padding shorthand property:
  text-align: center;              top, left, and right padding set
}                                  to 0 and bottom set to 12px
figcaption {
  font-family: 'Oswald', sans-serif;
}
```

Figure 4.17 shows the progress we've made on our project thus far. At this point, the page looks good on narrow screens, but we still need to display our columns on wide screens. Next, we'll look at how to create a multicolumn layout using the CSS Multi-column Layout Module.

NEWSPAPER TITLE

TUESDAY, 5ᵀᴴ SEPTEMBER 2021

ARTICLE HEADING

John Doe

Maecenas faucibus mollis interdum. Cum sociis natoque penatibus et magnis dis parturient montes, nascetur ridiculus mus. Cras justo odio, dapibus ac facilisis in, egestas eget quam. Sed posuere consectetur est at lobortis. Morbi leo risus, porta ac consectetur ac, vestibulum at eros. Lorem ipsum dolor sit amet, consectetur adipiscing elit. Curabitur blandit tempus porttitor.

Integer posuere erat a ante venenatis dapibus posuere velit aliquet. Maecenas faucibus mollis interdum. Cum sociis natoque penatibus et magnis dis parturient montes, nascetur ridiculus mus. Vivamus sagittis lacus vel augue laoreet rutrum faucibus dolor auctor. Aenean eu leo quam. Pellentesque ornare sem lacinia quam venenatis vestibulum.

" Fusce dapibus, tellus ac cursus commodo, tortor mauris condimentum nibh, ut fermentum massa justo sit amet risus. "

Aenean lacinia bibendum nulla sed consectetur. Duis mollis, est non commodo luctus, nisi erat porttitor ligula, eget lacinia odio sem nec elit. Donec id elit non mi porta gravida at eget metus. Cras justo odio, dapibus ac facilisis in, egestas eget quam. Cras mattis consectetur purus sit amet fermentum. Nullam id dolor id nibh ultricies vehicula ut id elit. Cras mattis consectetur purus sit amet fermentum.

SUBHEADING

- List item 1
- List item 2
- List item 3

Cras justo odio, dapibus ac facilisis in, egestas eget quam. Lorem ipsum dolor sit amet, consectetur adipiscing elit. Praesent commodo cursus magna, vel scelerisque nisl consectetur et. Cum sociis natoque penatibus et magnis dis parturient montes, nascetur ridiculus mus. Aenean lacinia bibendum nulla sed consectetur.

Donec ullamcorper nulla non metus auctor fringilla. Aenean eu leo quam. Pellentesque ornare sem lacinia quam venenatis vestibulum. Aenean lacinia bibendum nulla sed consectetur. Aenean lacinia bibendum nulla sed consectetur.

SUBHEADING

Golden Gate Bridge

Praesent commodo cursus magna, vel scelerisque nisl consectetur et. Aenean eu leo quam. Pellentesque ornare sem lacinia quam venenatis vestibulum. Donec id elit non mi porta gravida at eget metus. Aenean lacinia bibendum nulla sed consectetur. Integer posuere erat a ante venenatis dapibus posuere velit aliquet. Aenean eu leo quam. Pellentesque ornare sem lacinia quam venenatis vestibulum. Integer posuere erat a ante venenatis dapibus posuere velit aliquet.

Morbi leo risus, porta ac consectetur ac, vestibulum at eros. Curabitur blandit tempus porttitor. Morbi leo risus, porta ac consectetur ac, vestibulum at eros. Duis mollis, est non commodo luctus, nisi erat porttitor ligula, eget lacinia odio sem nec elit.

Figure 4.17   Progress thus far, including styled figure and image caption

4.4 Using the CSS Multi-column Layout Module

The CSS Multi-column Layout Module is perhaps less known than Grid and Flexbox as a way to present content, but it's no less useful. The purpose of this module is to allow content to flow naturally between multiple columns. It works similarly to the way we create multiple column layouts in a Microsoft Word or Google Docs document. We assign columns to a section of content, and the content naturally flows from one column to another. Because we want our content to be placed in columns only on wider screens, we'll use a media query to apply our columns conditionally only after the window reaches a particular size.

4.4.1 Creating media queries

A *media query* is a type of at-rule; we looked at it briefly in chapter 2 when we changed our grid layout to depend on the width of the screen. Like `@counter-style`, which we used earlier in this chapter, it starts with an at (`@`) symbol followed by the identifier `media`. Then we set the instruction about what to do when the rules inside the media query apply. We want to place the content in columns when our window width is greater than or equal to 955 pixels. Therefore, our media query will be `@media(min-width: 955px) {}`. Figure 4.18 breaks down the individual pieces of the query. Inside the media query, we'll define our columns.

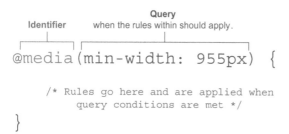

Figure 4.18 Media-query breakdown

4.4.2 Defining and styling columns

There are two ways we can define how the columns are created:

- *Dictate a column width.* The browser will create as many columns of that width as it can in the available space.
- *Dictate how many columns we want.* The browser will fit that number of equal-size columns in the available space.

We'll go with the second option because we already know that we want to create three columns. We specifically target the article, and using the `column-count` property, we set our quantity to 3, as shown in the following listing.

Listing 4.11 Conditionally breaking an article into three columns based on screen width

```
@media(min-width: 955px) {          ⟵──┐  Media query
  article {
    column-count: 3;       ⟵──┐  Sets how many
  }                            │  columns we want
}
```

Figure 4.19 shows our article laid out in three columns using the CSS from listing 4.11.

NEWSPAPER TITLE

TUESDAY, 5ᵀᴴ SEPTEMBER 2021

ARTICLE HEADING

John Doe

Maecenas faucibus mollis interdum. Cum sociis natoque penatibus et magnis dis parturient montes, nascetur ridiculus mus. Cras justo odio, dapibus ac facilisis in, egestas eget quam. Sed posuere consectetur est at lobortis. Morbi leo risus, porta ac consectetur ac, vestibulum at eros. Lorem ipsum dolor sit amet, consectetur adipiscing elit. Curabitur blandit tempus porttitor.

Integer posuere erat a ante venenatis dapibus posuere velit aliquet. Maecenas faucibus mollis interdum. Cum sociis natoque penatibus et magnis dis parturient montes, nascetur ridiculus mus. Vivamus sagittis lacus vel augue laoreet rutrum faucibus dolor auctor. Aenean eu leo quam. Pellentesque ornare sem lacinia quam venenatis vestibulum.

" Fusce dapibus, tellus ac cursus commodo, tortor mauris condimentum nibh, ut

fermentum massa justo sit amet risus. "

Aenean lacinia bibendum nulla sed consectetur. Duis mollis, est non commodo luctus, nisi erat porttitor ligula, eget lacinia odio sem nec elit. Donec id elit non mi porta gravida at eget metus. Cras justo odio, dapibus ac facilisis in, egestas eget quam. Cras mattis consectetur purus sit amet fermentum. Nullam id dolor id nibh ultricies vehicula ut id elit. Cras mattis consectetur purus sit amet fermentum.

SUBHEADING

- List item 1
- List item 2
- List item 3

Cras justo odio, dapibus ac facilisis in, egestas eget quam. Lorem ipsum dolor sit amet, consectetur adipiscing elit. Praesent commodo cursus magna, vel scelerisque nisl consectetur et. Cum sociis natoque penatibus et magnis dis parturient montes, nascetur ridiculus mus. Aenean lacinia bibendum nulla sed consectetur.

Donec ullamcorper nulla non metus auctor fringilla. Aenean eu leo quam. Pellentesque ornare sem lacinia quam venenatis vestibulum. Aenean lacinia bibendum

nulla sed consectetur. Aenean lacinia bibendum nulla sed consectetur.

SUBHEADING

Golden Gate Bridge

Praesent commodo cursus magna, vel scelerisque nisl consectetur et. Aenean eu leo quam. Pellentesque ornare sem lacinia quam venenatis vestibulum. Donec id elit non mi porta gravida at eget metus. Aenean lacinia bibendum nulla sed consectetur. Integer posuere erat a ante venenatis dapibus posuere velit aliquet. Aenean eu leo quam. Pellentesque ornare sem lacinia quam venenatis vestibulum. Integer posuere erat a ante venenatis dapibus posuere velit aliquet.

Morbi leo risus, porta ac consectetur ac, vestibulum at eros. Curabitur blandit tempus porttitor. Morbi leo risus, porta ac consectetur ac, vestibulum at eros. Duis mollis, est non commodo luctus, nisi erat porttitor ligula, eget lacinia odio sem nec elit.

Figure 4.19 Three-column layout

Next, we'll adjust the spacing between columns and add vertical lines between them. Let's start with the vertical lines.

4.4.3 *Using the column-rule property*

To create a clear separation between our columns, we'll add a vertical line between them, using the `column-rule` property. As with borders and outlines, we need to set a line type, width, and color. To keep our line work consistent, we'll use the same color and style of line that we set for the borders above and below the date at the top of the page. We'll make the lines slightly narrower, however.

The lines at the top of the screen separate content types (title, date, and article). Here, we're within the same content type. We add the lines to make visual separation of the columns easier; we don't want to break up the content. We want the lines to be less prominent, so we'll make them thinner.

To create the lines, we add `column-rule: 2px solid #333333;` to the existing article rule inside the media query. Now our article looks like figure 4.20.

NEWSPAPER TITLE

TUESDAY, 5ᵀᴴ SEPTEMBER 2021

ARTICLE HEADING

John Doe

Maecenas faucibus mollis interdum. Cum sociis natoque penatibus et magnis dis parturient montes, nascetur ridiculus mus. Cras justo odio, dapibus ac facilisis in, egestas eget quam. Sed posuere consectetur est at lobortis. Morbi leo risus, porta ac consectetur ac, vestibulum at eros. Lorem ipsum dolor sit amet, consectetur adipiscing elit. Curabitur blandit tempus porttitor.

Integer posuere erat a ante venenatis dapibus posuere velit aliquet. Maecenas faucibus mollis interdum. Cum sociis natoque penatibus et magnis dis parturient montes, nascetur ridiculus mus. Vivamus sagittis lacus vel augue laoreet rutrum faucibus dolor auctor. Aenean eu leo quam. Pellentesque ornare sem lacinia quam venenatis vestibulum.

" Fusce dapibus, tellus ac cursus commodo, tortor mauris condimentum nibh, ut fermentum massa justo sit amet risus. "

Aenean lacinia bibendum nulla sed consectetur. Duis mollis, est non commodo luctus, nisi erat porttitor ligula, eget lacinia odio sem nec elit. Donec id elit non mi porta gravida at eget metus. Cras justo odio, dapibus ac facilisis in, egestas eget quam. Cras mattis consectetur purus sit amet fermentum. Nullam id dolor id nibh ultricies vehicula ut id elit. Cras mattis consectetur purus sit amet fermentum.

SUBHEADING

- List item 1
- List item 2
- List item 3

Cras justo odio, dapibus ac facilisis in, egestas eget quam. Lorem ipsum dolor sit amet, consectetur adipiscing elit. Praesent commodo cursus magna, vel scelerisque nisl consectetur et. Cum sociis natoque penatibus et magnis dis parturient montes, nascetur ridiculus mus. Aenean lacinia bibendum nulla sed consectetur.

Donec ullamcorper nulla non metus auctor fringilla. Aenean eu leo quam. Pellentesque ornare sem lacinia quam venenatis vestibulum. Aenean lacinia bibendum nulla sed consectetur. Aenean lacinia bibendum nulla sed consectetur.

SUBHEADING

Golden Gate Bridge

Praesent commodo cursus magna, vel scelerisque nisl consectetur et. Aenean eu leo quam. Pellentesque ornare sem lacinia quam venenatis vestibulum. Donec id elit non mi porta gravida at eget metus. Aenean lacinia bibendum nulla sed consectetur. Integer posuere erat a ante venenatis dapibus posuere velit aliquet. Aenean eu leo quam. Pellentesque ornare sem lacinia quam venenatis vestibulum. Integer posuere erat a ante venenatis dapibus posuere velit aliquet.

Morbi leo risus, porta ac consectetur ac, vestibulum at eros. Curabitur blandit tempus porttitor. Morbi leo risus, porta ac consectetur ac, vestibulum at eros. Duis mollis, est non commodo luctus, nisi erat porttitor ligula, eget lacinia odio sem nec elit.

Figure 4.20 Columns with added vertical lines

With our lines in place, we see that we have some crowding between the article itself and the date and that we could use a bit more space between our lines and our text.

4.4.4 Adjusting spacing with the column-gap property

Now we need to do two things: increase the container spacing between the date of the article and the body of the article, and increase the gap between columns within the article. To adjust the spacing between the article and the date, we'll add `36px` of margin to the top of the article. Because working out a value to use isn't an absolute science, sometimes we need a bit of trial and error to determine what will look right on the page. We want to create enough room that each item has its own space and is clear, but not so much room that the items are too far apart and look separated.

> **Gestalt design principles**
>
> The *Gestalt principles* of design are a collection of principles of human perception that describe how humans group similar elements. One of the seven principles is proximity, which talks about how things that are close together appear to be more related than things that are spaced farther apart. For more information about the Gestalt principles, see http://mng.bz/OyNv.

With the space between the article and the date handled, let's turn our attention to the space between the columns. To add a gap between our vertical lines and our text, we'll use the `column-gap` property, which defines the amount of whitespace we want to have between our columns. We will set ours to `42px;`.

We continue to add these styles inside the media query as shown in listing 4.12 because we want them to apply only when our layout is columned. We don't want these style changes to apply to narrower screens.

Listing 4.12 Updated media query and article rule

```
@media (min-width: 955px) {
  article {
    column-count: 3;
    column-rule: 2px solid #333333;
    column-gap: 42px;
    margin-top: 36px;
  }
}
```

With these adjustments made (figure 4.21), let's turn our attention to the quote.

Earlier in this chapter, we styled the block quote so that it would stand out. But now that we have a multicolumn format, it gets a little lost in the other visual elements on the page. Let's make it span multiple columns to make it pop.

NEWSPAPER TITLE

TUESDAY, 5TH SEPTEMBER 2021

ARTICLE HEADING

John Doe

Maecenas faucibus mollis interdum. Cum sociis natoque penatibus et magnis dis parturient montes, nascetur ridiculus mus. Cras justo odio, dapibus ac facilisis in, egestas eget quam. Sed posuere consectetur est at lobortis. Morbi leo risus, porta ac consectetur ac, vestibulum at eros. Lorem ipsum dolor sit amet, consectetur adipiscing elit. Curabitur blandit tempus porttitor.

Integer posuere erat a ante venenatis dapibus posuere velit aliquet. Maecenas faucibus mollis interdum. Cum sociis natoque penatibus et magnis dis parturient montes, nascetur ridiculus mus. Vivamus sagittis lacus vel augue laoreet rutrum faucibus dolor auctor. Aenean eu leo quam. Pellentesque ornare sem lacinia quam venenatis vestibulum.

" Fusce dapibus, tellus ac cursus commodo, tortor mauris condimentum nibh, ut fermentum massa justo sit amet risus. "

Aenean lacinia bibendum nulla sed consectetur. Duis mollis, est non commodo luctus, nisi erat porttitor ligula, eget lacinia odio sem nec elit. Donec id elit non mi porta gravida at eget metus. Cras justo odio, dapibus ac facilisis in, egestas eget quam. Cras mattis consectetur purus sit amet fermentum. Nullam id dolor id nibh ultricies vehicula ut id elit. Cras mattis consectetur purus sit amet fermentum.

SUBHEADING

- List item 1
- List item 2
- List item 3

Cras justo odio, dapibus ac facilisis in, egestas eget quam. Lorem ipsum dolor sit amet, consectetur adipiscing elit. Praesent commodo cursus magna, vel scelerisque nisl consectetur et. Cum sociis natoque penatibus et magnis dis parturient montes, nascetur ridiculus mus. Aenean lacinia bibendum nulla sed consectetur.

Donec ullamcorper nulla non metus auctor fringilla. Aenean eu leo quam. Pellentesque ornare sem lacinia quam venenatis vestibulum. Aenean lacinia bibendum nulla sed consectetur. Aenean lacinia bibendum nulla sed consectetur.

SUBHEADING

Golden Gate Bridge

Praesent commodo cursus magna, vel scelerisque nisl consectetur et. Aenean eu leo quam. Pellentesque ornare sem lacinia quam venenatis vestibulum. Donec id elit non mi porta gravida at eget metus. Aenean lacinia bibendum nulla sed consectetur. Integer posuere erat a ante venenatis dapibus posuere velit aliquet. Aenean eu leo quam. Pellentesque ornare sem lacinia quam venenatis vestibulum. Integer posuere erat a ante venenatis dapibus posuere velit aliquet.

Morbi leo risus, porta ac consectetur ac, vestibulum at eros. Curabitur blandit tempus porttitor. Morbi leo risus, porta ac consectetur ac, vestibulum at eros. Duis mollis, est non commodo luctus, nisi erat porttitor ligula, eget lacinia odio sem nec elit.

Figure 4.21   Layout with adjusted spacing

4.4.5   *Making content span multiple columns*

We can make elements span multiple columns by using the `column-span` property. Our choices of values are `all` and `none`. Because we want the quote to go across the entire page, we'll choose `all`. Inside our media query, we'll add the following rule: `blockquote { column-span: all }`. This rule results in the layout shown in figure 4.22.

Notice that the flow of the content has changed. We added arrows to show the new flow introduced by making the quote span the screen. Instead of flowing the entire article from top left to bottom right, evenly distributed across the columns, we added `column-span: all` to the quote, so content that's before the quote now flows from top left to top right across the page above the quote. The content after the quote does the same. As a result of spanning content, we changed the flow of the text through our columns.

When we look at the content flow, we notice that the caption and the image have been split across two columns, which isn't ideal. Let's prevent that from happening.

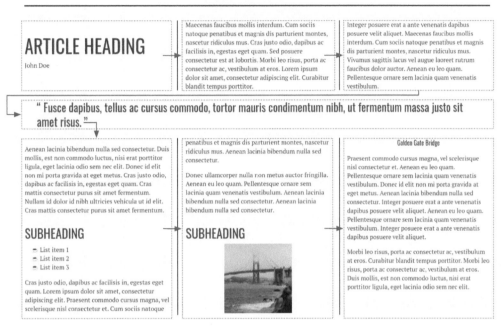

Figure 4.22 Content reflow due to spanning the `blockquote` across the columns

4.4.6 Controlling content breaks

To prevent the image and its caption from ending up in different columns, we can use the `break-inside` property with the keyword value `avoid`, which we set on the `<figure>` element. With this declaration, we inform the browser that when it's generating the columns, the contents of the element should stay together as a unit, not be split across multiple columns. In other words, the image and figure caption should remain together. The rule we add to the media query is `figure { break-inside: avoid }`. Figure 4.23 shows the resulting output.

4.5 Adding the finishing touches

With our content flowing the way we want it across the columns, let's polish some final details. One of the hallmarks of newspaper layouts is that the text is often justified.

mi porta gravida at eget metus. Cras justo odio, dapibus ac facilisis in, egestas eget quam. Cras mattis consectetur purus sit amet fermentum. Nullam id dolor id nibh ultricies vehicula ut id elit. Cras mattis consectetur purus sit amet fermentum.

SUBHEADING

- List item 1
- List item 2
- List item 3

Cras justo odio, dapibus ac facilisis in, egestas eget quam. Lorem ipsum dolor sit amet, consectetur adipiscing elit. Praesent commodo cursus magna, vel scelerisque nisl consectetur et. Cum sociis natoque penatibus et magnis dis parturient montes, nascetur

Aenean eu leo quam. Pellentesque ornare sem lacinia quam venenatis vestibulum. Aenean lacinia bibendum nulla sed consectetur. Aenean lacinia bibendum nulla sed consectetur.

SUBHEADING

Golden Gate Bridge

id elit non mi porta gravida at eget metus. Aenean lacinia bibendum nulla sed consectetur. Integer posuere erat a ante venenatis dapibus posuere velit aliquet. Aenean eu leo quam. Pellentesque ornare sem lacinia quam venenatis vestibulum. Integer posuere erat a ante venenatis dapibus posuere velit aliquet.

Morbi leo risus, porta ac consectetur ac, vestibulum at eros. Curabitur blandit tempus porttitor. Morbi leo risus, porta ac consectetur ac, vestibulum at eros. Duis mollis, est non commodo luctus, nisi erat porttitor ligula, eget lacinia odio sem nec elit.

Figure 4.23   Keeping the image and caption together

4.5.1   *Justifying and hyphenating text*

Justification refers to the alignment of the lines inside a body of text, as illustrated in figure 4.24. When text is *justified*, the lines of text start and end at the same spot, forming a box. By contrast, text that is left-aligned has ragged ends.

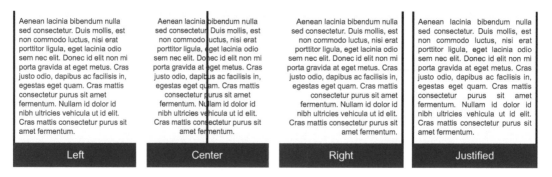

Figure 4.24   Text justification

Let's justify our paragraph text. To do this, we'll use the `text-align` property and give it a value of `justify`. To make the lines equal in length, we'll distribute extra space across the line. We can tune how the space is redistributed by using the `text-justify` property. If we don't set a `text-justify` value, the browser will choose what it thinks is best for the situation. We have a fluid design; it grows and shrinks with the window size. What is best may be different based on the window size, so we'll let the browser decide what will work best.

We'll add some hyphens, however. By default, browsers don't hyphenate a word at the end of a line; they simply continue to the next line. We can alter this behavior by setting the `hyphens` property to `auto`. Allowing the browser to hyphenate words at the end of lines will help diminish the amount of whitespace that's needed between our words to justify the text.

Listing 4.13 shows our paragraph rule. We continue to include our updates inside our media query, as these changes are relevant only when we switch to the columns layout.

Listing 4.13   Justifying paragraph text

```css
@media (min-width: 955px) {
  ...
  p {
    text-align: justify;
    hyphens: auto;
  }
}
```

Now our paragraphs look like those in figure 4.25.

ARTICLE HEADING

John Doe

Maecenas faucibus mollis interdum. Cum sociis natoque penatibus et magnis dis parturient montes, nascetur ridiculus mus. Cras justo odio, dapibus ac facilisis in, egestas eget quam. Sed posuere consectetur est at lobortis. Morbi leo risus, porta ac consectetur ac, vestibulum at eros. Lorem ipsum dolor sit amet, consectetur adipiscing elit. Curabitur blandit tempus porttitor.

Integer posuere erat a ante venenatis dapibus posuere velit aliquet. Maecenas faucibus mollis interdum. Cum sociis natoque penatibus et magnis dis parturient montes, nascetur ridiculus mus. Vivamus sagittis lacus vel augue laoreet rutrum faucibus dolor auctor. Aenean eu leo quam. Pellentesque ornare sem lacinia quam venenatis vestibulum.

" Fusce dapibus, tellus ac cursus commodo, tortor mauris condimentum nibh, ut fermentum massa justo sit amet risus. "

Aenean lacinia bibendum nulla sed consectetur. Duis mollis, est non commodo luctus, nisi erat porttitor ligula, eget lacinia odio sem nec elit. Donec id elit non mi porta gravida at eget metus. Cras justo odio, dapibus ac facilisis in, egestas eget quam. Cras mattis consectetur purus sit amet fermentum. Nullam id dolor id nibh ultricies vehicula ut id elit. Cras mattis consectetur purus sit amet fermentum.

SUBHEADING

- List item 1
- List item 2
- List item 3

Cras justo odio, dapibus ac facilisis in, egestas eget quam. Lorem ipsum dolor sit amet, consectetur adipiscing elit. Praesent commodo cursus magna, vel scelerisque nisl consectetur et.

Cum sociis natoque penatibus et magnis dis parturient montes, nascetur ridiculus mus. Aenean lacinia bibendum nulla sed consectetur.

Donec ullamcorper nulla non metus auctor fringilla. Aenean eu leo quam. Pellentesque ornare sem lacinia quam venenatis vestibulum. Aenean lacinia bibendum nulla sed consectetur. Aenean lacinia bibendum nulla sed consectetur.

SUBHEADING

Golden Gate Bridge

Praesent commodo cursus magna, vel scelerisque nisl consectetur et. Aenean eu leo quam. Pellentesque ornare sem lacinia quam venenatis vestibulum. Donec id elit non mi porta gravida at eget metus. Aenean lacinia bibendum nulla sed consectetur. Integer posuere erat a ante venenatis dapibus posuere velit aliquet. Aenean eu leo quam. Pellentesque ornare sem lacinia quam venenatis vestibulum. Integer posuere erat a ante venenatis dapibus posuere velit aliquet.

Morbi leo risus, porta ac consectetur ac, vestibulum at eros. Curabitur blandit tempus porttitor. Morbi leo risus, porta ac consectetur ac, vestibulum at eros. Duis mollis, est non commodo luctus, nisi erat porttitor ligula, eget lacinia odio sem nec elit.

Figure 4.25   Justified and hyphenated paragraph text

As we look at our layout, we notice that the image at the bottom of the second column looks a little odd and out of place. Let's fix that.

4.5.2   *Wrapping the text around the image*

To reconnect the image with the subsequent text, we'll push the image and its caption to the left and have the text wrap around the image. To create this effect, we'll use the `float` property. Applying the `float` property to an element pushes it to the left or the right, allowing text and inline elements to wrap around it.

In this situation, having the image and caption as a unit inside a `<figure>` element comes in handy for styling. Because both items are contained in the `<figure>`, we'll apply `float` to the figure, neatly wrapping the text around both the image and the caption.

Listing 4.14 shows how we float the figure. Notice that we added a right margin to the figure. Because we are floating the figure to the left, it places itself on the left side of the column, allowing the text to wrap around it in the leftover space to the right, as shown in figure 4.26. The right margin creates a space between the image and the text so that the text doesn't come right up against the edge of the image.

Listing 4.14   Floating the figure

```
@media (min-width: 955px) {
  ...
  figure {
    float: left;
    margin-right: 24px;
  }
}
```

NEWSPAPER TITLE

TUESDAY, 5ᵀᴴ SEPTEMBER 2021

ARTICLE HEADING
John Doe

" Fusce dapibus, tellus ac cursus commodo, tortor mauris condimentum nibh, ut fermentum massa justo sit amet risus. "

Maecenas faucibus mollis interdum. Cum sociis natoque penatibus et magnis dis parturient montes, nascetur ridiculus mus. Cras justo odio, dapibus ac facilisis in, egestas eget quam. Sed posuere consectetur est at lobortis. Morbi leo risus, porta ac consectetur ac, vestibulum at eros. Lorem ipsum dolor sit amet, consectetur adipiscing elit. Curabitur blandit tempus porttitor.

Integer posuere erat a ante venenatis dapibus posuere velit aliquet. Maecenas faucibus mollis interdum. Cum sociis natoque penatibus et magnis dis parturient montes, nascetur ridiculus mus. Vivamus sagittis lacus vel augue laoreet rutrum faucibus dolor auctor. Aenean eu leo quam. Pellentesque ornare sem lacinia quam venenatis vestibulum.

Aenean lacinia bibendum nulla sed consectetur. Duis mollis, est non commodo luctus, nisi erat porttitor ligula, eget lacinia odio sem nec elit. Donec id elit non mi porta gravida at eget metus. Cras justo odio, dapibus ac facilisis in, egestas eget quam. Cras mattis consectetur purus sit amet fermentum. Nullam id dolor id nibh ultricies vehicula ut id elit. Cras mattis consectetur purus sit amet fermentum.

SUBHEADING
▪ List item 1
▪ List item 2
▪ List item 3

Cras justo odio, dapibus ac facilisis in, egestas eget quam. Lorem ipsum dolor sit amet, consectetur adipiscing elit. Praesent commodo cursus magna, vel scelerisque nisl consectetur et. Cum sociis natoque penatibus et magnis dis parturient montes, nascetur ridiculus mus. Aenean lacinia bibendum nulla sed consectetur.

Donec ullamcorper nulla non metus auctor fringilla. Aenean eu leo quam. Pellentesque ornare sem lacinia quam venenatis vestibulum. Aenean lacinia bibendum nulla sed consectetur. Aenean lacinia bibendum nulla sed consectetur.

SUBHEADING
Praesent commodo cursus magna, vel scelerisque nisl consectetur et. Aenean eu leo quam. Pellentesque ornare sem lacinia quam venenatis vestibulum. Donec id elit non

Golden Gate Bridge

mi porta gravida at eget metus. Aenean lacinia bibendum nulla sed consectetur. Integer posuere erat a ante venenatis dapibus posuere velit aliquet. Aenean eu leo quam. Pellentesque ornare sem lacinia quam venenatis vestibulum. Integer posuere erat a ante venenatis dapibus posuere velit aliquet.

Morbi leo risus, porta ac consectetur ac, vestibulum at eros. Curabitur blandit tempus porttitor. Morbi leo risus, porta ac consectetur ac, vestibulum at eros. Duis mollis, est non commodo luctus, nisi erat porttitor ligula, eget lacinia odio sem nec elit.

Figure 4.26   Floated image

As you'll see in chapter 7, we can do a lot more cool things with floating images. For now, though, let's focus on our newspaper page. The last thing we'll address is handling how the page behaves in an extremely wide window.

4.5.3 *Using max-width and a margin value of auto*

Figure 4.26 shows that our layout starts to degrade as the window gets extremely wide. The wider the window, the worse the problem gets. More and more users have extra-wide screens, so we need to consider what would happen if they have the window maximized, taking up the entire screen. To handle this use case, we'll use the same trick that we used for the loader in chapter 2. We'll set a maximum width for our layout and then set its left and right margins to `auto`, which will center the container horizontally when the window is larger than our maximum width.

For our page, our container is the body, so we'll give our `body` a `max-width` of `1200px` and set our left and right margins to `auto`. We also need to move the `back-ground-color` from being set on the `body` to being set on the `html` element rule; otherwise, when our screen is wider than 1,200 pixels, we'll end up with a white band to the left and right sides of our page.

These changes won't go inside the media query. We'll edit the styles we set on the `body` at the beginning of this chapter and add an `html` rule to set the background color. The following listing shows our changes.

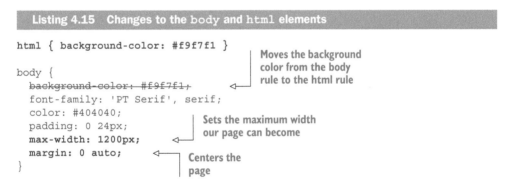

Listing 4.15 Changes to the `body` and `html` elements

```
html { background-color: #f9f7f1 }

body {
  background-color: #f9f7f1;          ← Moves the background
  font-family: 'PT Serif', serif;       color from the body
  color: #404040;                       rule to the html rule
  padding: 0 24px;                    ← Sets the maximum width
  max-width: 1200px;                    our page can become
  margin: 0 auto;     ← Centers the
}                        page
```

With these final changes, we have a page that works for both mobile and desktop users. Figure 4.27 shows our finished layout.

NEWSPAPER TITLE

TUESDAY, 5TH SEPTEMBER 2021

ARTICLE HEADING

John Doe

Maecenas faucibus mollis interdum. Cum sociis natoque penatibus et magnis dis parturient montes, nascetur ridiculus mus. Cras justo odio, dapibus ac facilisis in, egestas eget quam. Sed posuere consectetur est at lobortis. Morbi leo risus, porta ac consectetur ac, vestibulum at eros. Lorem ipsum dolor sit amet, consectetur adipiscing elit. Curabitur blandit tempus porttitor.

Integer posuere erat a ante venenatis dapibus posuere velit aliquet. Maecenas faucibus mollis interdum. Cum sociis natoque penatibus et magnis dis parturient montes, nascetur ridiculus mus. Vivamus sagittis lacus vel augue laoreet rutrum faucibus dolor auctor. Aenean eu leo quam. Pellentesque ornare sem lacinia quam venenatis vestibulum.

" Fusce dapibus, tellus ac cursus commodo, tortor mauris condimentum nibh, ut fermentum massa justo sit amet risus. "

Aenean lacinia bibendum nulla sed consectetur. Duis mollis, est non commodo luctus, nisi erat porttitor ligula, eget lacinia odio sem nec elit. Donec id elit non mi porta gravida at eget metus. Cras justo odio, dapibus ac facilisis in, egestas eget quam. Cras mattis consectetur purus sit amet fermentum. Nullam id dolor id nibh ultricies vehicula ut id elit. Cras mattis consectetur purus sit amet fermentum.

SUBHEADING

- List item 1
- List item 2
- List item 3

Cras justo odio, dapibus ac facilisis in, egestas eget quam. Lorem ipsum dolor sit amet, consectetur

adipiscing elit. Praesent commodo cursus magna, vel scelerisque nisl consectetur et. Cum sociis natoque penatibus et magnis dis parturient montes, nascetur ridiculus mus. Aenean lacinia bibendum nulla sed consectetur.

Donec ullamcorper nulla non metus auctor fringilla. Aenean eu leo quam. Pellentesque ornare sem lacinia quam venenatis vestibulum. Aenean lacinia bibendum nulla sed consectetur. Aenean lacinia bibendum nulla sed consectetur.

SUBHEADING

Praesent commodo cursus magna, vel scelerisque nisl consectetur et. Aenean eu leo quam. Pellentesque ornare sem lacinia quam venenatis vestibulum. Donec id elit non mi porta gravida at

Golden Gate Bridge

eget metus. Aenean lacinia bibendum nulla sed consectetur. Integer posuere erat a ante venenatis dapibus posuere velit aliquet. Aenean eu leo quam. Pellentesque ornare sem lacinia quam venenatis vestibulum. Integer posuere erat a ante venenatis dapibus posuere velit aliquet.

Morbi leo risus, porta ac consectetur ac, vestibulum at eros. Curabitur blandit tempus porttitor. Morbi leo risus, porta ac consectetur ac, vestibulum at eros. Duis mollis, est non commodo luctus, nisi erat porttitor ligula, eget lacinia odio sem nec elit.

Figure 4.27   Finished layout

Summary

- A theme is the general look and feel that we maintain throughout an application.
- We may need to import our fonts, as few fonts are universally available. Because no officially defined list of web-safe fonts exists, we should always use a keyword fallback.
- Creating a visual hierarchy will help our users orient themselves to the page and identify important information.
- We can control which symbols the browser uses when it's instructed to display quotation marks.
- We can customize the way our lists display their bullets by using the `counter-style` at-rule.
- Filters allow us to alter the appearance of an image.
- We can create multicolumn layouts by using the CSS Multi-column Layout Module.
- We can make content span all the columns when creating multicolumn layouts.
- We can make the browser use hyphens to break words at the end of lines.
- Floating allows us to wrap text around an element.

Summary cards
with hover interactions

This chapter covers

- Clipping static background images using the `background-clip` property
- Using transitions to reveal content on hover
- Using media queries to choose styles based on device capabilities and window size

Summary cards are used for a range of purposes, whether that be showing a preview for a film, buying a property, previewing a news article, or (in this chapter) showing a list of hotels. Usually, a summary card contains a title, description, and a call to action; sometimes, it also contains an image. Figure 5.1 shows the cards we'll create in this project.

The cards will be placed in a single line, using the CSS Grid Layout Module for layout. Each card will have its own background image, with the content placed on top. If the user is viewing the card on a device that supports hover and has a screen at least 700 pixels wide, they'll be able to see the title and then hover over the card, which will reveal the short description and an orange call-to-action button for contrast with the black background (figure 5.2).

121

Figure 5.1   Finished product

Figure 5.2   Hover effect on finished product

For users whose devices don't support hover or have a screen less than 700 pixels wide, we'll show all the information without hover so that the user experience isn't affected (figure 5.3).

Figure 5.3 Finished product on small or touch devices that can't handle the hover state

The other piece of this project is the header, which we want to make stand out and have some visual interest. To do this, we'll explore the `background-clip` property and see how we can clip an image around the text.

5.1 Getting started

Listing 5.1 and listing 5.2 include our starting CSS and HTML for the page that we'll build on in this chapter. To follow along as we style the page, you can download the starting HTML and CSS from the GitHub repository at http://mng.bz/KlaO or from CodePen at https://codepen.io/michaelgearon/pen/vYpaQPO.

The mobile and desktop experiences will use the same HTML and stylesheet. Similarly to what we did in chapter 4, we'll use media queries to alter the styles based on browser size and capabilities.

Listing 5.1 shows our starting HTML. Each card is wrapped in a `<section>` element and includes its title (`<h2>`), description (`<p>`), and call to action (`<a>`).

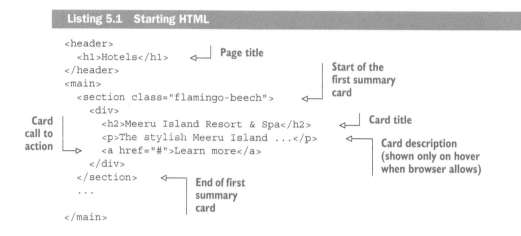

Our starting CSS (listing 5.2) includes some base styles to set up our page. For the body, we're increasing the margin by 40 pixels and adding padding of 20 pixels to all four sides. We're using Google Fonts—this time the font family Cardo, regular weight, italicized version—for the description of each card. For the headers, we'll use Rubik in both regular and bold weights. This font is a good choice because it combines good readability with rounded edges, providing a sense of informality that works well with the Cardo font. Notice that when we're loading multiple Google Fonts, we can combine the imports into one request.

Listing 5.2   Starting CSS

```
@import url("https://fonts.googleapis.com/css?
    family=Cardo:400i|Rubik:400,700&display=swap");

body {
  margin-top: 40px;
  padding: 20px;
}
```
> One request to load both the Cardo and Rubik fonts

As we begin styling our project, our page looks like figure 5.4.

5.2   *Laying out the page using grid*

A good starting point is reviewing the layout of our cards and the web page as a whole. We need to consider three aspects of our layout:

- The header and main content
- The container for the cards
- The content within the cards

We'll use the CSS Grid Layout Module for layout in all three use cases.

Hotels

Meeru Island Resort & Spa

The stylish Meeru Island Resort & Spa strikes the perfect note for a peaceful escape.

Learn more

Flamingo Beach

Plenty of pools and activities to keep children smiling, plus comfy apartments that are tailored for families.

Learn more

Protur Safari Park

The big, family-friendly complex dishes up plenty of pools and activities.

Learn more

Mountain View Resort

There are heaps of spots to soak in at the super-sized Holiday Village Costa del Sol.

Learn more

Figure 5.4 Starting point

> **NOTE** The CSS Grid Layout Module allows us to place and align elements across both the vertical and horizontal axes in a system of columns and rows. Check out chapter 2 to find out how this module works.

To lay out the elements on our page, we'll start by creating the styles for narrow screens and edit the layout as we build up to larger screen sizes by using media queries.

5.2.1 Layout using grid

Our layout consists of two landmarks: `<header>` and `<main>`, which are immediate children of `<body>` (listing 5.3). By giving the `<body>` a `display` property with a value of `grid`, we'll be affecting the position of the `<header>` and `<main>` elements.

Listing 5.3 Starting HTML

```
<body>
  <header>     <!-- title -->
  </header>
   <main>      <!-- cards -->
   </main>
</body>
```

Next, we use the `place-items` property to center the elements on the page. This property is a shorthand way to combine declaring values for the `align-items` and `justify-items` properties. We'll set its value to `center`, aligning all the items in the middle of their respective rows and columns. The following listing shows our updated body rule.

Listing 5.4   Positioning the `<header>` and `<main>` elements

```
body {
  display: grid;
  place-items: center;
  margin-top: 40px;
  padding: 20px;
}
```

Notice that we haven't defined any `grid-template-rows`, `grid-template-columns`, or `grid-template-areas`. By default, when none of these areas is declared, the browser creates a one-column grid with as many rows as there are elements to position. In our case, we have two elements: `<main>` and `<body>`. Therefore, our grid has one column and two rows (figure 5.5).

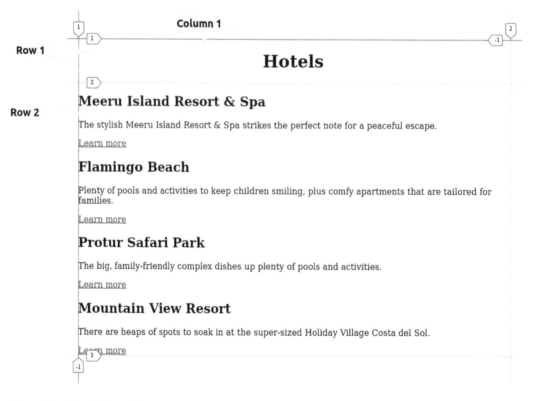

Figure 5.5   One-by-two grid

The widths of the <header> and <main> are altered by being within the grid to take only as much horizontal space as their content requires. Because the <header> has narrow content (the <h1> containing the word *hotel*), the page title centers itself on the page. The <main> element takes the full width available to it because the description of Flamingo Beach (in the second card) needs the full width and even wraps. If we extend the width of the screen further, we see that the <main> element also centers itself (figure 5.6).

Figure 5.6   Centered main **on a wide screen**

We'll also rely on the default functionality of the grid and omit defining rows and columns because we want to keep the cards stacked on narrow screens. To add space between cards, we include a gap of 1rem. We also restrict the width of the <main> element to a maximum 1024 pixels to prevent our cards being too spaced out on wide screens after we align them horizontally on wide screens (section 5.2.2). Our updated CSS, shown in the following listing, keeps the cards stacked but adds a 1-rem gap between cards (figure 5.7).

Listing 5.5   Positioning the cards on narrow screens

```
main {
  display: grid;
  max-width: 1024px;
  grid-gap: 1rem;
}
```

5.2.2   *Media queries*

At the moment, our cards are stacked vertically—the default behavior in most cases with HTML elements. This layout makes sense on mobile devices, which have rather

Figure 5.7   **Grid applied to** `<main>`

narrow screens. For desktop screens, however, because the browser window can be
much wider, we can take advantage of the horizontal space by using media queries. We
can define some media queries to adjust the layout:

- If the window width is greater than or equal to 700 pixels, we adjust the grid to
  have two equal-size columns and set the height of each section to exactly 350
  pixels.
- At 950 pixels, we adjust the layout again to have four equal-size columns over-
  riding the `grid-template-columns` value set in the preceding media query.
  The `height` property value remains 350 pixels because the condition for the
  preceding media query (`min-width: 700px`) is still being met.

If neither of the requirements for these media queries is met (when the browser window is less than 700 pixels wide), the cards will be stacked vertically in a single column. The following listing shows the two media queries being created.

Listing 5.6   Layout for the cards

```
@media (min-width: 700px) {
  main {
    grid-template-columns: repeat(2, 1fr);
  }
  main > section {
    height: 350px;
  }
}
@media (min-width: 950px) {
  main {
    grid-template-columns: repeat(4, 1fr);
  }
}
```

Media query to determine whether the browser window is at least 700 pixels wide. If so, the styles within the query are used.

Second media query to determine whether the browser window is at least 950 pixels wide. If so, this query overrides the preceding query and sets the grid to four columns wide.

Figure 5.8 and figure 5.9 show the output in browser windows that are 800 and 1000 pixels wide, respectively.

With our layout in hand, let's focus on styling our content, starting with the header. We're going to change the font for our <h1> element and look at how to use an image to color our text.

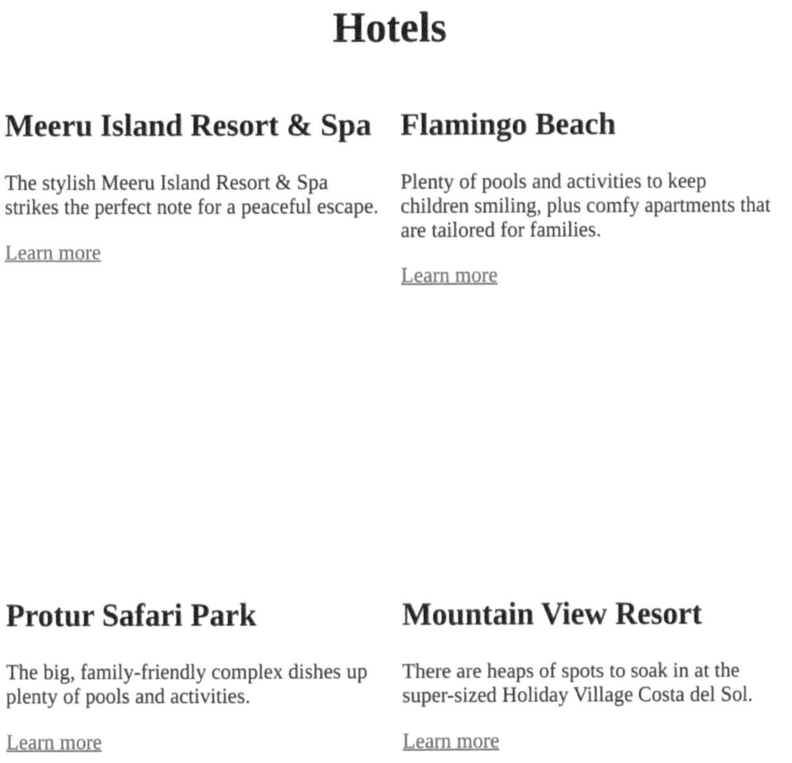

Hotels

Meeru Island Resort & Spa

The stylish Meeru Island Resort & Spa strikes the perfect note for a peaceful escape.

Learn more

Flamingo Beach

Plenty of pools and activities to keep children smiling, plus comfy apartments that are tailored for families.

Learn more

Protur Safari Park

The big, family-friendly complex dishes up plenty of pools and activities.

Learn more

Mountain View Resort

There are heaps of spots to soak in at the super-sized Holiday Village Costa del Sol.

Learn more

Figure 5.8   Layout on a screen 800 pixels wide

Hotels

Meeru Island Resort & Spa

The stylish Meeru Island Resort & Spa strikes the perfect note for a peaceful escape.

Learn more

Flamingo Beach

Plenty of pools and activities to keep children smiling, plus comfy apartments that are tailored for families.

Learn more

Protur Safari Park

The big, family-friendly complex dishes up plenty of pools and activities.

Learn more

Mountain View Resort

There are heaps of spots to soak in at the super-sized Holiday Village Costa del Sol.

Learn more

Figure 5.9   Layout on a screen 1000 pixels wide

5.3   Styling the header using the background-clip property

The title of this page—Hotels—could be more interesting visually. One way to liven it up could be to set a nice vibrant color and update the font family to something modern. Another way is to apply a background image to the text. These changes are possible through two experimental properties: `background-clip` and `text-fill-color`.

> **Experimental properties**
>
> Some properties' browser support may be value-specific. The `background-clip` property is one of those. This property is supported in all major browsers without a vendor prefix for all its possible values except `text`, which still required a vendor prefix in Microsoft Edge and Google Chrome when this book was written (https://caniuse.com/?search=background-clip).
>
> Experimental properties should be used with care because they often have nonstandard implementations. For more details about experimental properties, please refer to chapter 3.

We can reduce the risks from `background-clip: text` being an experimental property by setting a fallback color value so that if these two properties don't work, the user will see the text without the background image.

5.3.1   Setting the font

The first step is to update the `font-family`, `weight`, and `size`, as well as transform the text to uppercase. The following listing shows these changes.

Listing 5.7   Header typography

```
h1 {
  font: 900 120px "Rubik", sans-serif;      ◁──┐ Shorthand
  text-transform: uppercase;                   │ font property
}
```

We used the shorthand font property. The first value sets the weight, which in this case is heavy. The second value is the font size (120px), followed by the font-family we want to use. If this font can't be loaded, we fall back to a sans-serif font.

We transformed the text to uppercase through styling rather than by writing it all in uppercase letters within the HTML. Using all uppercase characters can affect accessibility, as some screen readers may interpret all caps as an acronym and read the letters individually. If we set the text to uppercase through CSS, we're styling the text only visually; the characters can be mixed-case.

Moreover, we're in a unique position with only one page to style. In a traditional project, our styles would most likely be applied to multiple pages. By adjusting our casing in our styles, we help ensure consistency throughout our website or application.

It's also worth noting that we should use all capitals sparingly, as that format can affect the readability of the content. Now our header looks like figure 5.10.

Meeru Island Resort & Spa

The stylish Meeru Island Resort & Spa strikes the perfect note for a peaceful escape.

Learn more

Flamingo Beach

Plenty of pools and activities to keep children smiling, plus comfy apartments that are tailored for families.

Learn more

Protur Safari Park

The big, family-friendly complex dishes up plenty of pools and activities.

Learn more

Mountain View Resort

There are heaps of spots to soak in at the super-sized Holiday Village Costa del Sol.

Learn more

Figure 5.10 Applied typography styles to headers

5.3.2 Using background-clip

Now we'll use an image to color the letters, essentially applying a background image to the letters themselves. The first thing we need to do is set a background image on the <h1> element. To ensure that the image covers the entirety of the <h1> element, we assign the background-size property a value of cover. This value automatically calculates the width and height the image needs to make sure that the image covers the entire element.

Next, we manipulate the image to apply only to the letters, rather than the entire <h1> element. This step is where the background-clip property comes into play. This property defines, based on the box model, which part of the element the background should cover. In our case, we'll give it a value of text because we want the image to show behind the letters. This property with the value of text still requires a browser prefix for WebKit-based browsers (Chrome, Edge, and Opera), so we also include the prefixed property for compatibility with those browsers.

Currently, our text is black, preventing the image from showing through. We must make the letters transparent so as not to obscure the image we set as our text background. The `text-fill-color` property allows us to set the color of the text. This property is similar to `color`, but if both properties are set, `text-fill-color` supersedes `color`. Because `text-fill-color` also requires a vendor prefix (for both WebKit- and Mozilla-based browsers), we can use the `color` property as a fallback in case the image doesn't load or any of the experimental properties fails.

We're using `text-fill-color` instead of using the `color` property with a value of `transparent` because we'll use the `color` to create a fallback in case `background-clip` doesn't work in a user's browser. We set its value to `white` because we'll add a black background to our page later in this chapter. That way, if `background-clip` fails or isn't supported, our text will still be visible to the user; it will be white instead of having the image coloring it. The following listing shows our updated header class.

Listing 5.8 `background-clip` text code

```
h1 {
  text-transform: uppercase;
  font: 900 120px "Rubik", sans-serif;
  background: url(background: url("bg-img.jpg"));        ◁── Adds the background image
  background-size: cover;
  -webkit-background-clip: text;                          │ Clips the background to be
  background-clip: text;                                  │ applied only behind the text
  -moz-text-fill-color: transparent;                      ┐ Makes the text transparent
  -webkit-text-fill-color: transparent;                   │ to allow the image to show
  color: white;        ◁── Fallback                       ┘ through
}                            color
```

When using prefixes, we add the `-moz-` and `-webkit-` properties before the non-prefixed version if an nonprefixed version is available. This allows the browser to make sure it's using the nonexperimental version when it becomes available.

With our header styled (figure 5.11), the next task is styling the cards. We'll focus on styling the cards without the hover effect first and then create our media query for handling cards on wide screens that support hover.

Meeru Island Resort & Spa

The stylish Meeru Island Resort & Spa strikes the perfect note for a peaceful escape.

Learn more

Flamingo Beach

Plenty of pools and activities to keep children smiling, plus comfy apartments that are tailored for families.

Learn more

Protur Safari Park

The big, family-friendly complex dishes up plenty of pools and activities.

Learn more

Mountain View Resort

There are heaps of spots to soak in at the super-sized Holiday Village Costa del Sol.

Learn more

Figure 5.11   Background image clipped to the heading

5.4 Styling the cards

Each card is created with an outer `<section>` element that has a background image and an inner `<div>`, which we'll give a background color to keep our text legible over the image. Within that `<div>` is the actual content. The following listing shows our card structure in isolation from the rest of the HTML.

Listing 5.9 Card HTML in isolation

```
<section class="meeru-island">          ⟵───  Outer card container. Each section has a
  <div>                                         class name based on the hotel it describes.
    <h2>Meeru Island Resort & Spa</h2>
    <p>The stylish Meeru Island Resort…</p>     Content
    <a href="#">Learn more</a>
  </div>
</section>
```

Content container

To style each part of the card, we'll work from the outside in, styling the container for each card, followed by the container for the content, and finally the content itself.

5.4.1 Outer card container

The outer container is the element that gets the background image. Each section gets an image for its hotel or resort. We'll select each section individually by its class name. Then we'll assign each of the sections a background image, as shown in the following listing.

Listing 5.10 Adding background images

```
.meeru-island {
  background-image: url("1.jpg");
}
.flamingo-beech {
  background-image: url("2.jpg");
}
.protur-safari {
  background-image: url("3.jpg");
}
.mountain-view {
  background-image: url("4.jpg");
}
```

With the background images added (figure 5.12), let's configure some general styles that apply to all the sections.

We can see that the images aren't properly centered and don't showcase the hotels and resorts well. We can adjust the size of the images by using the `background-size` property. We set this property to `cover` to maximize the amount of the picture being shown without leaving any whitespace visible if the aspect ratio of the image differs from that of our card. We also add a `background-color` of #3a8491 (turquoise) as a fallback. Finally, we add a `border-radius` to the card to curve our corners and soften our edges. Listing 5.11 shows our container styles.

Figure 5.12   Card background pictures

```
main > section {
  background-size: cover;
  background-color: #3a8491;
  border-radius: 4px;
}
```

With our outer container addressed (figure 5.13), let's move on to the content container.

Figure 5.13   Styled outer card container

5.4.2 *Inner container and content*

Currently, our text isn't readable; the dark text is hard to read against the image background and also close to the edge of the outer container. To improve readability, we'll give our inner container a background-color of rgba(0, 0, 0, .75), which is black with some transparency. We'll also change the text color to whitesmoke and center it. By not using pure black or pure white in our design, we achieve a softer feel for our overall composition.

With the added background color, we add 1rem of padding with our content container to keep the text away from the edge of our dark background and 1rem of margin to leave a gap between the edge of the picture and the beginning of the background. Finally, we adjust the font-size, font-weight, line-height, and font-family of our text inside our card. The following listing shows the CSS.

Listing 5.12 Card content styles

```
main > section > div {
  background-color: rgba(0, 0, 0, .75);
  margin: 1rem;                              Card
  padding: 1rem;                             content
  color: whitesmoke;                         container
  text-align: center;
  font: 14px "Rubik", sans-serif;
}

section h2 {
  font-size: 1.3rem;          Card
  font-weight: bold;          header
  line-height: 1.2;
}

section p {
  font: italic 1.125rem "Cardo", cursive;    Card
  line-height: 1.35;                         content
}
```

With our styles applied (figure 5.14), the last piece of content that needs styling is our link.

Because our link serves as a call to action, getting users to look at more information about the hotel or resort, we want to make it bold and flashy (listing 5.13). To achieve this end, because the majority of our elements inside our cards are rather dark, we'll give the link a bright yellowish-orange (#ffa600) background and change its text color to almost black. We'll also add padding. But because a link is an inline element by default, we'll want to change its display property's value to inline-block so that the padding will affect the height of the element.

Figure 5.14   Card inner container and typography

```
a {
  background-color: #ffa600;
  color: rgba(0, 0, 0, .75);
  padding: 0.75rem 1.5rem;
  display: inline-block;
  border-radius: 4px;
  text-decoration: none;
}

a:hover {
  background-color: #e69500;
}

a:focus {
  outline: 1px dashed #e69500;
  outline-offset: 3px;
}
```

To match our cards, we'll give the links a `border-radius` of 4px and finally handle hover and focus. Instead of underlining, which we'll remove, on `hover` we'll darken the background color slightly, and on `focus` we'll add a dashed outline offset from the link by 3 pixels. Figure 5.15 shows our styled links.

Not having all of the links aligned horizontally is a bit odd and doesn't seem to be organized. To have all the links aligned, we'll use `grid` once again. We'll give our inner container a `display` value of `grid` and set our `grid-template-rows` value to `min-content auto min-content`, at the same time setting the height of the inner container to `100%` minus the padding and margin we allotted to it (figure 5.16).

Earlier in this chapter, we gave the inner container a `margin` of `1rem` and `padding` of `1rem`, meaning that the height it needs to take up the full height of the space provided is equal to `100%` minus `4rem` (1 rem of padding and 1 rem of margin at the top and the same at the bottom, equaling 4 rems total). To achieve this effect in CSS, we

Figure 5.15 Styled links

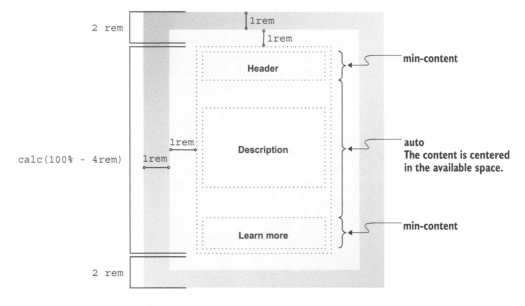

Figure 5.16 Aligning card elements horizontally

use the calc() function to do the math for us, assigning calc(100% - 4rem) to the height property. The combination of defined rows (grid-template-rows: min-content auto min-content) and set height creates a layout in which the header and link take only as much room as they need and the middle section (the paragraph element) gets what is left.

Finally, to center the paragraph content vertically in the middle of the card, we use the align-items property with a value of center and remove the bottom margin automatically added by the browser to the <h2>. If we left the margin at the bottom of the header, we'd have more room at the top of the paragraph than at the bottom because `min-content` takes the margin included on an element into account. Because the link at the bottom of the card has no margin, there would be a disproportionate amount of whitespace above the paragraph compared with below it. The following listing shows our layout adjustments.

Listing 5.14   Inner container layout adjustments

```
main > section > div {
  background-color: rgba(0, 0, 0, .75);
  margin: 1rem;
  padding: 1rem;
  color: whitesmoke;
  text-align: center;
  height: calc(100% - 4rem);
  display: grid;
  grid-template-rows: min-content auto min-content;
  align-items: center;
}

section h2 {
  font-size: 1.3rem;
  font-weight: bold;
  line-height: 1.2;
  margin-bottom: 0;
}
```

This last adjustment finishes our card layout (figure 5.17). Next, we'll focus on showing and hiding parts of the content for devices that are wide enough (width greater than or equal to 700 pixels) and have hover capabilities.

Figure 5.17   Styled cards

5.5 Using transitions to animate content on hover and focus-within

To start, we need to create a media query that checks whether the device supports the `hover` interaction, whether the browser window is at least 700 pixels wide, and whether our user has `prefers-reduced-motion` enabled on their machine.

Reduced-motion preference

Some users want to opt out of motion-heavy animations. They can do this by enabling a setting on their devices that is conveyed to the browser via the `prefers-reduced-motion` property. We want to make sure that we respect our users' settings. Therefore, we'll state that the setting isn't set (has a value of `no-preference`) as part of our query determining whether to animate our content. For more information about `prefers-reduced-motion`, refer to chapter 3.

Our media query is `@media (hover: hover) and (min-width: 700px) and (prefers-reduced-motion: no-preference) { }`. Notice that we can chain multiple parameters that need to be met for the CSS in the query to be applied.

To hide everything but the header, we'll shift the content down to the bottom of the card by using the `transform` property with a value of `translateY()`. The `translateY()` value allows us to move content vertically outside the flow of the page; the content around the element being moved is unaffected by the movement and won't reposition itself or get out of the way.

To calculate the distance that the element needs to move, we'll use the `calc()` function again. We'll move the header down by the height of the card (`350px`) minus `8rem` (the top margin of the container + top padding of the container + size of the header), as shown in the following listing.

Listing 5.15 Hiding the nonheader content

```
@media (hover: hover) and (min-width: 700px) and
➥ (prefers-reduced-motion: no-preference) {
  main > section > div {
    transform: translateY(calc(350px - 8rem));
  }
}
```

The inner portion of the card is moved down, as shown in figure 5.18.

Because we're going to animate showing the content when the user stops hovering over the section, we don't want the trailing content at the bottom to remain: if the user hovers on the content bleeding out of the picture, the content will move upward into the picture, lose the hover, and then move back down. This behavior will repeat, creating a flicker. Therefore, we'll set a height of `5rem` for our inner container and hide the overflow when the paragraph and link are hidden.

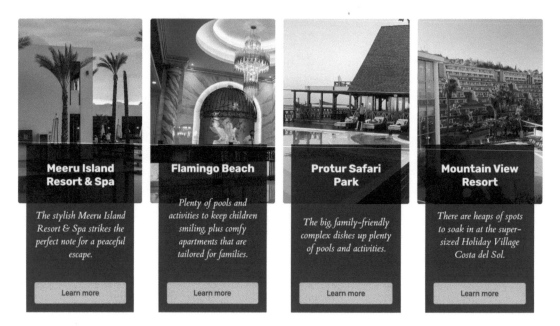

Figure 5.18   **Moving the content down**

Notice that in the second card, a little bit of the paragraph content will still be visible when the content should be hidden, so we'll also hide the nonheader content by using opacity when it shouldn't be seen. Additionally, we'll move that content down 1rem by using `translateY()`, which will give it a bit of motion when we animate it back in on `hover`.

All together, the CSS used to hide the content and shorten the inner container appears in the following listing. To select all the content that isn't the header, we can use the `:not()` pseudo-class.

Listing 5.16   Hiding the nonheader content

```
@media (hover: hover) and (min-width: 700px) and (prefers-reduced-motion:
 no-preference) {
  main > section > div {
    transform: translateY(calc(350px - 8rem));      Moves and
    height: 5rem;                                   shortens the inner
    overflow: hidden;                               content container
  }
  main > section > div > *:not(h2) {
    opacity: 0;                                     Hiding all the
    transform: translateY(1rem);                    non-<h2>
  }                                                 content
}
```

Media query ⟶

The `not()` pseudo-class allows us to filter selectors. In this case, we want to target anything that isn't an `<h2>`. Figure 5.19 diagrams the process.

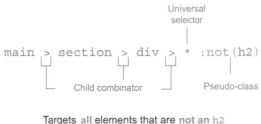

Targets **all** elements that are **not an** h2
that are **immediate children of a** div
that is an **immediate child of** section
that is an **immediate child of** main

Figure 5.19 Selecting anything
that isn't an <h2> inside the inner
container

Now that the content is hidden (figure 5.20), we can focus on showing it again.

Figure 5.20 Hiding content

To show the content again, we need to undo everything we did to hide it on both
hover and focus. Because we're not removing the links from the Document Object
Model (DOM), they're hidden only visually; programmatically, they still exist, and a
user can tab to a link via the keyboard. As a result, we need to show the content both
when the user hovers over the card and when a link gains focus. Because we want to
act on an ancestor (the content container) when a child (the link) is in focus, we can
use the :focus-within pseudo-class. This pseudo-class allows us to apply styles conditionally based on whether a descendant of the element is currently in focus.

So when either the link is in focus or the section is being hovered over, we move
the container back into place by setting the translateY() parameter to 0 (no vertical
displacement) and setting the height of the inner container to 350px (height of the
outer container) minus 4rem (total of the vertical padding and margin of the container). We also need to reinstate the paragraph and link, the opacity of which was set
to 0 and which had been moved down by 1rem.

We'll finish our hover and focus-within effect by adding a transition to elements
being shown and hidden. Because we have predefined states that we're changing
between and want the animation to run only once, when the change occurs, we don't

need to use keyframes. We can simply instruct the CSS to animate all the changes when they happen, using the `transition` property with a value of `all 700ms ease-in-out`. All the changes will be animated; the animation will take 700 milliseconds to complete; and the animation will start slow, accelerate, and then slow again before completing. The following listing shows our `hover` and `focus-within` CSS.

Listing 5.17 Showing content on `hover` and `focus-within`

```
@media (hover: hover) and (min-width: 700px) and
➥ (prefers-reduced-motion: no-preference) {
 main > section > div {
  transform: translateY(calc(350px - 8rem));
  height: 5rem;
  overflow: hidden;
  transition: all 700ms ease-in-out;      ◁──┐
 }                                            │   Animates
 div > *:not(h2) {                            │   the changes
  opacity: 0;
  transform: translateY(1rem);
  transition: all 700ms ease-in-out;      ◁──┘
 }
 section:hover div,                       ◁──────  On section hover, moves
 section:focus-within div {              ◁──────   container back into place
  transform: translateY(0);
  height: calc(350px - 4rem);               On section focus-within, moves
 }                                           container back into place

 section:hover div > *:not(h2),           ◁──────  On hover, moves all
 section:focus-within div > *:not(h2){   ◁──────   non-<h2> elements
  opacity: 1;                                       inside the container
  transform: translateY(0);                         back into place with
 }                                                   full opacity
}            On section focus-within, moves all non-
             <h2> elements inside the container
             back into place with full opacity
```

With these changes applied (figure 5.21), all that's left to do to complete the project is set the background on our page.

To make the pictures pop, we'll add a dark gray, almost black background to the entire page. To apply the background color, we'll add the `background` property with a value of `#010101` to our existing body rule, as shown in the following listing.

Listing 5.18 Adding the background

```
body {
  display: grid;
  place-items: center;
  margin-top: 40px;
  padding: 20px;
  background: #010101;
}
```

Figures 5.22, 5.23, and 5.24 show our finished project at various screen sizes.

Figure 5.21 The `hover` and `focus-within` effect

Figure 5.22 Project in window
600 pixels wide

Figure 5.23   Project in window 850 pixels wide

Figure 5.24   Project in window 1310 pixels wide with `prefers-reduced-motion` **enabled**

Summary

- Grid can be used for entire layouts or individual elements within the layout.
- The `text-transform` property can change text to uppercase without affecting the accessibility of the content.
- Use `text-transform: uppercase` sparingly, not on large areas of content.
- The `background-clip` property with a value of `text` can clip a background image around the text.
- The `background-clip` property with a value of `text` still needs to be prefixed, and this property can change while it's being implemented.
- We can use a media query to check whether a device supports `hover` and adjust our layout so that it prevents the user from seeing the content if their device doesn't support `hover`.
- We can chain multiple conditions in the same media query by using `and`.
- We can use `prefers-reduced-motion` in our media query to respect user preferences regarding animations and motion.
- The `:not()` pseudo-class represents elements that don't match a list of selectors.
- `translateY()` will move content vertically without affecting reflow.
- We can use the `transition` property to animate style changes between states.
- To apply styles conditionally based on an element's descendant being in focus, we use the `focus-within` pseudo-class.

Creating a profile card

6

This chapter covers

- Using CSS custom properties
- Creating a background using `radial-gradient`
- Setting image size
- Positioning elements using a flexbox

In this chapter, we'll create a profile card. In web design, a card is a visual element that contains information on a single topic. We're going to apply this concept to someone's profile information, essentially creating a digital business card. This type of layout is often used on social media and blog sites to give readers an overview of who wrote the content. It sometimes has links to a detailed profile page or opportunities to interact with the person to whom the profile belongs.

To create the layout, we'll do a lot of work revolving around positioning, specifically, using the CSS Flexbox Layout Module to align and center elements. We'll also look at how to make a rectangular image fit into a circle without distorting the image. By the end of the chapter, our profile card will look like figure 6.1.

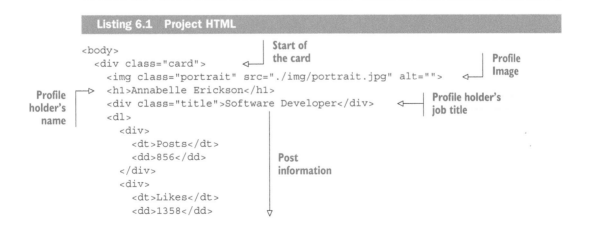

Figure 6.1   Final output

6.1   *Starting the project*

Let's dive right in and take a look at our starting HTML (listing 6.1), which you can find in the GitHub repository at http://mng.bz/5197 or on CodePen at https://codepen.io/michaelgearon/pen/NWyByWN. We have a `<div>` with a class of `card` that contains all the elements being presented in the profile card. To set our blog post information, we'll use a description list. Our technologies (CSS, HTML, and so on) are presented in a list.

> **Description list**
>
> A *description list* contains groups of terms, including a description term (`dt`) and any number of descriptions (`dd`). Description lists are often used to create glossaries or to display metadata. Because we're pairing terms (posts, likes, and followers) with their counts (the number), this project is a great use case for a description list.

Listing 6.1   Project HTML

```
<body>
  <div class="card">                          ⟵─ Start of the card
    <img class="portrait" src="./img/portrait.jpg" alt="">   ⟵─ Profile Image
    <h1>Annabelle Erickson</h1>               ⟵ Profile holder's name
    <div class="title">Software Developer</div>   ⟵─ Profile holder's job title
    <dl>
      <div>
        <dt>Posts</dt>
        <dd>856</dd>                           ⟵ Post information
      </div>
      <div>
        <dt>Likes</dt>
        <dd>1358</dd>
```

```
          </div>
          <div>
            <dt>Followers</dt>
            <dd>1257</dd>
          </div>
        </dl>
        <p class="summary">I specialize in UX / UI...</p>
        <ul class="technologies">
          <li>CSS</li>
          <li>HTML</li>
          <li>JavaScript</li>
          <li>Accessibility</li>
        </ul>
        <div class="actions">
          <button type="button" class="follow">Follow</button>
          <a href="#" class="message">Message</a>
        </div>
      </div>
  </body>
```

Post information

Personal summary/about

Technologies

Actions

End of the card

As we begin styling our card, our page looks like figure 6.2.

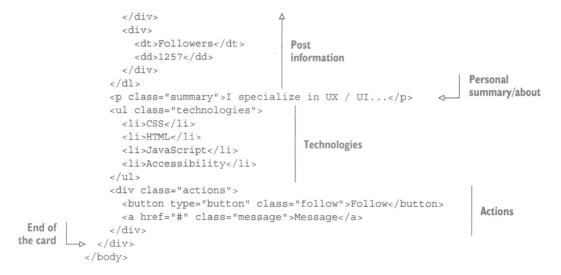

Figure 6.2   Starting point

6.2 Setting CSS custom properties

In our layout, specifically, when we style the profile image and colored portion at the top of the card below the image, we're going to need the image-size value for several calculations. In languages such as JavaScript, when we have a value that we're going to be referencing multiple times, we use *custom properties,* sometimes referred to as *CSS variables.*

To create a custom property, we prefix the variable name with two hyphens (--) immediately followed by the variable name. We assign the value to a custom property the same way that we do any other property: with a colon (:) followed by the value. A CSS variable declaration, therefore, looks like this: --myVariableName: myValue;.

As with any other declaration, we need to define our variables inside a rule. For our project, we're going to define our colors and image size and then declare them inside a body rule, as shown in listing 6.2. Because we define our variables on the body, the <body> element and any of its descendants will have access to the variables.

Listing 6.2 Defining CSS custom properties

```
body {
  --primary: #de3c4b;              ←┘  Red
  --primary-contrast: white;
  --secondary: #717777;           ←┘  Gray
  --font: Helvetica, Arial, sans-serif;
  --text-color: #2D3142;
  --card-background: #ffffff;      ←┐  Dark blue-gray
  --technologies-background: #ffdadd;
  --page-background: linear-gradient(#4F5D75, #2D3142);
  --imageSize: 200px;

  background: var(--page-background);
  font-family: var(--font);
  color: var(--text-color);
}
```

> **NOTE** Our linear gradient will go from top to bottom, fading from dark blue to darker blue. For an in-depth explanation of linear gradients, check out chapter 3.

Notice that we can assign different types of values to our variables. We assign colors, such as in our --primary variable (probably one of the most common uses for CSS custom properties), but we also define a size (--imageSize), a font family (--font), and a gradient (--page-background).

To reference the variable and use it as part of a declaration, we use the syntax var(--variableName). Therefore, to assign our text color, we declare color: var(--text-color);. With our background and the font color and family applied (figure 6.3), we notice that our background repeats at the bottom of the page.

Figure 6.3   Adding the background to the `<body>`

6.3   *Creating full-height backgrounds*

A *linear gradient* is a type of image. When we apply an image as a background to an element in CSS, if the image is smaller than the element, the image will repeat, or *tile*. In this particular case, we don't want the image to repeat. We have two ways to fix this situation:

- We can tell the background that we don't want it to repeat by using `background-repeat: no-repeat;`. Because our `<body>` element is only as tall as its contents, however, if the window is taller than the content, we'll be left with an unsightly white bar at the bottom of the page—which is not ideal.
- Our second option (the one we'll use) is to make the `<html>` and `<body>` elements take the full height of the screen rather than size to their contents.

We'll add the rule in listing 6.3 to our stylesheet. We reset the margin and padding to 0 because we want to ensure that we go edge to edge inside the window.

Listing 6.3   Making the background full height

```
html, body {
  margin: 0;
  padding: 0;
  min-height: 100vh;
}
```

To set the height, we use `min-height` because should the content length be greater than the height of the window, we want the user to have access to the content, and we want the background to be behind that content. By using `min-height`, we instruct the browser to make the `<body>` and `<html>` elements at least the height of the window. If the content forces the elements to be taller, the browser will use the height of the content.

The value we set for `min-height` is `100vh`. Viewport height (vh), a unit based on the height of the viewport itself, is percentage-based. So assigning a value of `100vh` to `min-height` means that we want the element to have, at minimum, a height equal to 100% of the viewport height. Now that we have our background set (figure 6.4), let's style the card.

Figure 6.4   Full-screen gradient background

6.4   *Styling and centering the card using Flexbox*

Let's start with styling the card itself. We'll give it a white background and shadow to give our layout some depth. Notice that instead of using the color value for the background, we use our `background` variable.

We're also going to set the width of the card to `75vw`. Viewport width (vw) is the horizontal counterpart to the viewport height (vh) unit we used earlier. It's also percentage based, so by setting our width to `75vw`, we're setting the width of the card to be 75% of the total width of the browser window.

Next, we'll further constrain the width of the card to a maximum 500 pixels wide. By using both the `width` and `max-width` properties, we allow the card to shrink when the screen size is narrow but constrain it from becoming too wide and unruly on larger screens. Last, we curve the corners of the card by using `border-radius` to soften the design. The following listing shows our card rule.

Listing 6.4   Styling the card

```
.card {
  background-color: var(--card-background);
  box-shadow: 0 0 55px rgba(38, 40, 45, .75);
  width: 75vw;
  max-width: 500px;
  border-radius: 4px;
}
```

Figure 6.5 shows the styles applied to our project. With some basic styles added to the card (we'll continue adding to them later in the chapter), let's place the card in the middle of the screen both vertically and horizontally.

Figure 6.5   Starting to style the card

To center the card in the exact middle of the screen, we're going to use a flex layout (sometimes referred to as *flexbox*), which allows us to place elements across a single axis either vertically or horizontally. Although we could position the card by using `grid` (and whether we should is a matter of personal preference), in this instance, we're concerned only with centering the item, not with its position in terms of columns and rows, so Flexbox seems to be a better choice.

The display property with a value of flex is used on the parent item of the child elements that should be placed on the screen with Flexbox. In our project, the element being positioned is the card, and its parent is the <body> element, so we'll add the display: flex declaration to our body rule.

Next, we define how we want the elements within the <body> to behave. In our case, we have one child (the card), and we want it to be centered. To center the card horizontally, we add a justify-content: center declaration to the body rule. This property allows us to dictate how elements are distributed across our axis. Figure 6.6 breaks down the options.

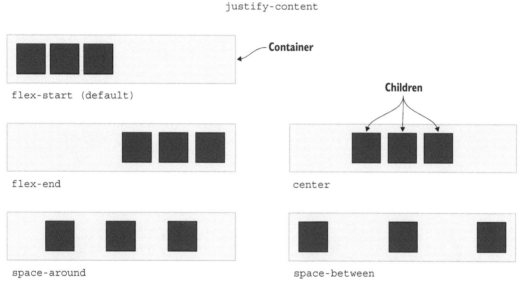

Figure 6.6 Values for the justify-content property

We also want to center the card vertically. For the vertical positioning, we'll use align-items: center. The align-items property enables us to dictate how elements should be positioned relative to one another and to the container, as shown in figure 6.7.

The following listing shows our updated body rule. Remember that the parent of the element being positioned is the one to which we apply flexbox-related declarations.

Listing 6.5 Centering the card

```
body {
  ...
  display: flex;              Centers the card
  justify-content: center;    horizontally
  align-items: center;
}                             Centers the
                              card vertically
```

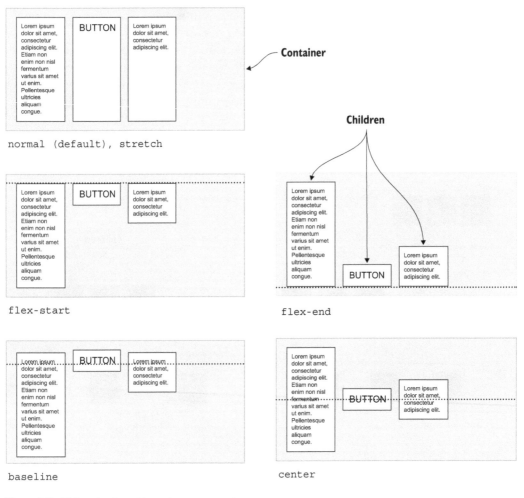

Figure 6.7   Values for the `align-items` **property**

Now that our card is centered (figure 6.8), let's focus on the content of the card, starting with the profile picture.

6.5   *Styling and positioning the profile picture*

We currently have a rectangular image. We want to make the image circular. We also want to center it on the card and have it stick out the top a little bit. Let's start by converting the image to a circle.

Figure 6.8   Centered card

6.5.1   *The object-fit property*

A circle's height is equal to its width, so as we can see in figure 6.9, if we set the height and width of the picture to equal our image-size variable, the picture will distort.

Figure 6.9   Distorted profile picture

To prevent the image from distorting, we must also dictate how the image behaves in relation to the size it's given. To do this, we'll use the `object-fit` property. By setting `object-fit`'s value to `cover`, we instruct the image to maintain its initial aspect ratio but fit itself to fill the space available. In this case, we'll lose a little of the top and bottom of the image due to the image being taller than it is wide.

When we use `object-fit`, the image is centered by default, and if parts of the image are clipped, those parts are the edges, which works well for our current use case and picture. But if we wanted to adjust the position of the image within its allotted size and clip only from the bottom, we would add an `object-position` declaration.

To make our image a circle 200 pixels wide, we use the CSS in listing 6.6. Remember that we set the image size as a CSS custom property in the `body`, so we set the width and height of the image equal to the `--imageSize` variable. We add the `object-fit` declaration to prevent the image from distorting. Finally, we give the image a 50% `border-radius` to make it a circle.

Listing 6.6   Centering the card

```
body {
  ...
  --imageSize: 200px;
}

img.portrait {
  width: var(--imageSize);
  height: var(--imageSize);       ⟵ Prevents distortion
  object-fit: cover;
  border-radius: 50%;             ⟵ Makes the image a circle
}
```

Now our image looks like figure 6.10.

Annabelle Erickson

Figure 6.10   Circle profile picture

Next, we need to position our picture.

6.5.2   *Negative margins*

To position our image to stick out above the card, we're going to use a negative margin. To move an element down and away from the content above it, we can add a positive `margin-top` value to the element. But if we add a negative margin, instead of being pushed down, the element will be pulled up. We're going to use margin in conjunction with text centering to position the image. Looking at the final design in figure 6.11, we notice that all the text is also centered.

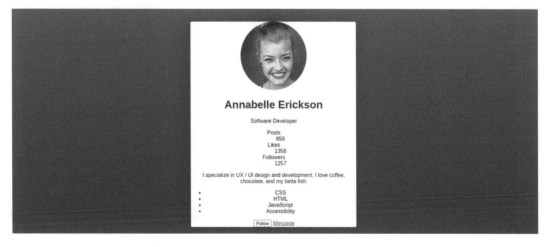

Figure 6.11   Final design

Because all the text is centered, let's add a `text-align: center` declaration to the card rule. Images are inline elements by default, so we notice that by centering the text, the image also gets centered (figure 6.12).

Figure 6.12   Centered text

Now all that's left to do is add the negative top margin to move the image upward. We want one third of the image to stick out from the top, and we'll use the `calc()` function to do the math for us. Our function is `calc(-1 * var(--imageSize) / 3);`. We divide the image size by 3 to get a third of the height of the image and then multiply by –1 to make it negative. Our margin will make a third of the image stick out from the top of the card, as shown in figure 6.13.

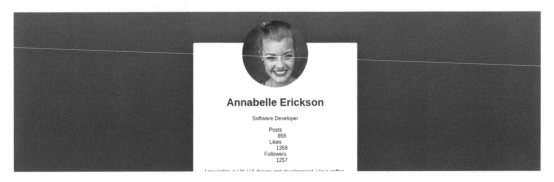

Figure 6.13   **Positioned image**

Next, we need to give our card some margin. Due to the negative margin we added to the image, if we have a short screen (figure 6.14), the top of the image disappears offscreen.

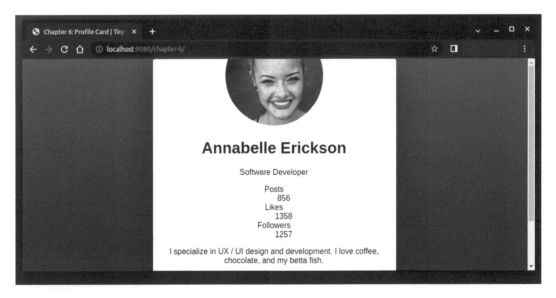

Figure 6.14   **Clipping the top of the image when the window height is small**

To prevent cutting off part of the picture when the window isn't especially tall, we want to add some vertical margin to the card itself—a margin that's greater than or equal to the amount of the picture that's sticking out of the card. To calculate the amount sticking out, we used `calc(-1 * var(--imageSize) / 3);`. For our card margin, we're going to use a similar concept, taking one third of the image height and then adding 24 pixels to move the card and image away from the edge. Our final function will be `calc(var(--imageSize) / 3 + 24px)`. The following listing shows the CSS we added to position the image.

Listing 6.7   Positioning the image

```
.card {
  ...
  text-align: center;
  margin: calc(var(--imageSize) / 3 + 24px) 24px;    ⊲─┐ Vertical margin of one
}                                                        third the image size
                                                         + 24px and horizontal
                                                         of 24px

img {
  width: var(--imageSize);
  height: var(--imageSize);
  object-fit: cover;                                      Negative top margin to
  border-radius: 50%;                                     make the image stick
  margin-top: calc(-1 * var(--imageSize) / 3);   ⊲─┐ out of the card
}
```

With our image positioned and margins added so that the top of the image doesn't get cut off on small screens (figure 6.15), let's turn our attention to the curved red background below the picture.

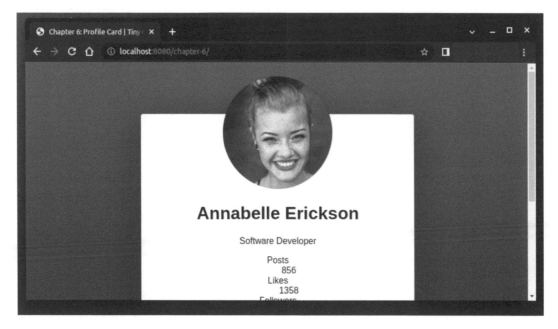

Figure 6.15   Added card margin

6.6   *Setting the background size and position*

To add the red curved background behind the picture, we're going to add the declaration in the following listing to our card rule.

Listing 6.8   Positioning the image

```
.card {
  background-color: var(--card-background);
  ...
  background-image: radial-gradient(
    circle at top,
    var(--primary) 50%,
    transparent 50%,
    transparent
  );
  background-size: 1500px 500px;
  background-position: center -300px;
  background-repeat: no-repeat;
}
```

Let's break down what this code does. First, we add a background-image consisting of a radial-gradient, as shown in figure 6.16.

Combining background color and image
We can add both a background color and a background image to the same element. We assign the color to the background-color property and the image to the background-image property. Or we can apply both in the background shorthand property as follows: background: white url(path-to-image);.

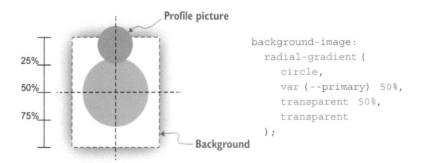

Figure 6.16   Adding background with radial-gradient

The radial-gradient takes an ending shape (circle or ellipse) and then defines where we want each color to start and stop to form the gradient. We define ours as radial-gradient(circle, var(--primary) 50%, transparent 50%, transparent);.

Our primary color is red, so our gradient will create a circle that's red until it reaches 50% of its container. At 50% of the container size, the color immediately shifts to transparent. Because the shift in color is immediate, no fade occurs, so we get a nice clean circle.

By default, radial gradients emanate from the center of their container, so next we add `circle at top` to the beginning of our `radial-gradient` function to shift the origin of the circle from the center of the background to the top. Our updated `radial-gradient` function is `radial-gradient(circle at top, var(--primary) 50%, transparent 50%, transparent);` (figure 6.17).

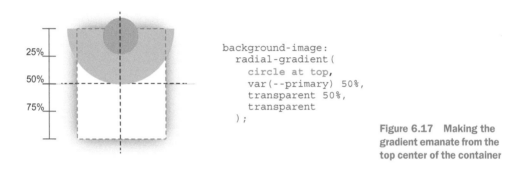

```
background-image:
   radial-gradient(
      circle at top,
      var(--primary) 50%,
      transparent 50%,
      transparent
   );
```

Figure 6.17   Making the gradient emanate from the top center of the container

Now we want to move the circle up so that the bottom of the circle is directly below the image. Figure 6.18 shows that if we move the background up -150 pixels and our card is rather short (our profile doesn't have a lot of content), we'll end up with gaps in the top corners between our circle and the edge of the card, which we don't want.

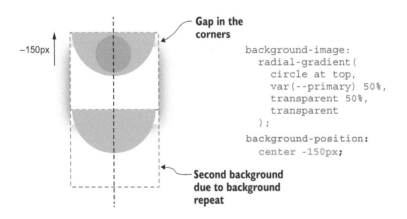

```
background-image:
   radial-gradient(
      circle at top,
      var(--primary) 50%,
      transparent 50%,
      transparent
   );
background-position:
   center -150px;
```

Figure 6.18   Altering the background position

To prevent this from happening, we're going to make the background image three times wider than the maximum card size: (3×500 =1500). When we create a `background-image` using gradients, the background image produced will grow and shrink with the container, so we're also going to give the background a set height. That way, no matter how much content is in the card, the shape of our background will be predictable (figure 6.19).

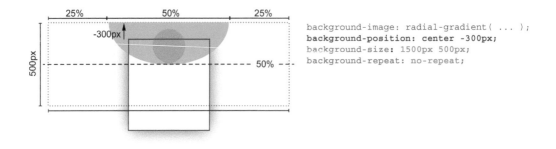

Figure 6.19   **Editing the** `background-size` **and handling the** `background-repeat`

After changing the dimensions of the background, we also increase the amount by which we move the background up so that it ends directly below the profile image. Finally, as mentioned earlier in the chapter, background images repeat by default. By moving the image up, we leave room for the background to tile. We want to have only one semicircle, so we add a `background-repeat` declaration with a value of `no-repeat`. Now our card background is defined as shown in the following listing.

Listing 6.9   **Positioning the image**

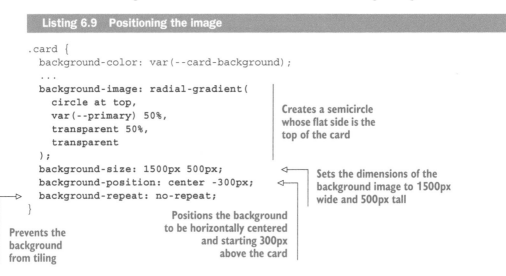

```
.card {
  background-color: var(--card-background);
  ...
  background-image: radial-gradient(
    circle at top,
    var(--primary) 50%,
    transparent 50%,
    transparent
  );
  background-size: 1500px 500px;
  background-position: center -300px;
  background-repeat: no-repeat;
}
```

Creates a semicircle whose flat side is the top of the card

Sets the dimensions of the background image to 1500px wide and 500px tall

Positions the background to be horizontally centered and starting 300px above the card

Prevents the background from tiling

Figure 6.20 shows the background added to the card. With the top of our card starting to look good, let's focus on the rest of the content.

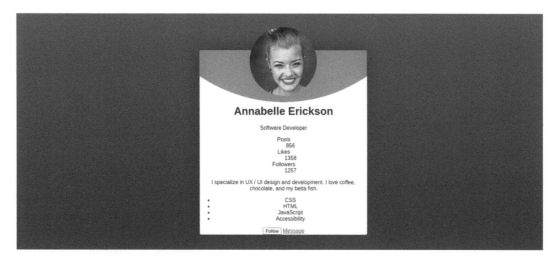

Figure 6.20   Finished background image

6.7   *Styling the content*

Our card currently doesn't have any padding, which means that if the name were longer, it could potentially go edge to edge on our card. In most cases, we would create a card as a component or template to reuse for multiple clients, so let's add some left and right padding to ensure that our text doesn't run to the edge of the card. We'll also add some bottom padding to move the links and bottom away from the bottom edge of the card.

Listing 6.10 shows our updated card rule, and figure 6.21 shows the new output. We use the padding shorthand property, which defines three values: it states that the top padding is 0, that the left and right are 24px, and that the bottom padding is 24px. We specifically don't add padding to the top because it would push the image down, forcing us to readjust our image positioning.

Listing 6.10   Adding padding to the card

```
.card {
  ...
  padding: 0 24px 24px;
}
```

6.7.1   *Name and job title*

Going down the card, we see that the first piece of content is the name. As an <h1>, it has some default styles provided by the browser, including some margin. We're going to edit the margin to increase the amount of room between the header and the image, and remove the bottom margin so that the job title appears directly below the name. We'll also change the color to red and set the font size to 2rem.

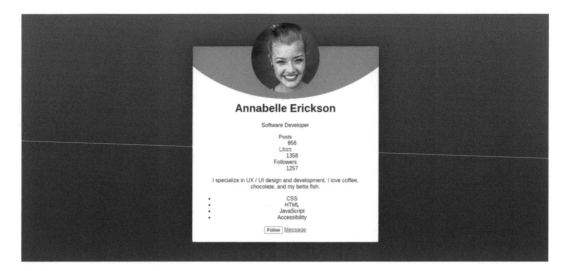

Figure 6.21   Added card padding

The rem unit

A *rem* is a relative unit based on the font size of the root element—in our case, HTML. For most browsers, the default is `16px`. We didn't set a font size on the `html` element in our project; therefore, when we set the `<h1>` `font-size` to `2rem`, the output size is `32px`, assuming a `16px` default.

The benefit of using relative font sizes such as `rem` and `em` is accessibility. These sizes help ensure that the text scales gracefully regardless of the user's settings or device.

For the job title, we'll increase the size and weight of the font, and we'll change the font color to our secondary color, which is gray. The following listing shows our new rules, and figure 6.22 shows the output.

Listing 6.11   Styling the name

```
h1 {
  font-size: 2rem;              Styles for
  margin: 36px 0 0;             the name
  color: var(--primary);
}

.title {
  font-size: 1.25rem;           Styles for
  font-weight: bold;            the job title
  color: var(--secondary);
}
```

Next, we're going to style the post, like, and follower information.

Figure 6.22   Styled name and job title

6.7.2   *The space-around and gap properties*

In our HTML, the description list (dl) contains the post, like, and follower counts (listing 6.12). Each grouping is contained within a <div>, so we'll apply a display value of flex to the definition list to align all three groups horizontally. Then we'll set the justify-content property to space-around to spread them out across the card.

Listing 6.12   Description-list HTML

```
<dl>
  <div>
    <dt>Posts</dt>
    <dd>856</dd>
  </div>
  <div>
    <dt>Likes</dt>
    <dd>1358</dd>
  </div>
  <div>
    <dt>Followers</dt>
    <dd>1257</dd>
  </div>
</dl>
```

The space-around value distributes the elements evenly across our axis by providing an equal amount of space between each element and half as much on each edge. Figure 6.23 shows how the spacing is applied.

Listing 6.13 shows our styles for the description list. Notice that we included a gap: 12px declaration, which ensures that the minimum amount of space between our elements will be 12 pixels. We could have given our <div>s inside the description list a margin, but a margin would have affected the outer edges. The gap property affects only the space between elements.

> **NOTE**   The gap property is supported in iOS version 14.5 and later. At this writing, many people still use earlier versions. To check global use of this property, see https://caniuse.com/flexbox-gap.

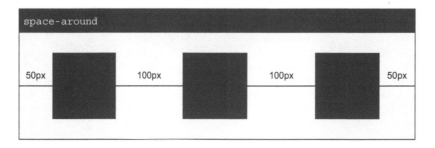

Figure 6.23   The `space-around` **property**

Listing 6.13   Styling the name

```css
dl {
  display: flex;
  justify-content: space-around;
  gap: 12px;
}
```

As shown in figure 6.24, now our profile stats are in a row and evenly spaced across the card.

Figure 6.24   Aligned profile stats

The numbers are offset, however. This offset comes from the description, which has some margins that come from the browser defaults. Let's get rid of those settings and style the text to be bold, bigger, and red, using the CSS in the following listing.

Listing 6.14   Description details rule

```css
dd {
  margin: 0;
  font-size: 1.25rem;
  font-weight: bold;
  color: var(--primary);
}
```

With the margin removed (figure 6.25), we notice that the likes still aren't centered on our card.

Figure 6.25 **Description list alignment**

The reason that the likes aren't centered is that three elements don't have exactly the same width. When the elements are distributed, the browser calculates the total amount of space each element needs and redistributes the leftovers equally. Therefore, because the <div> containing followers is larger than the <div> containing posts, the likes <div> doesn't land in the middle.

6.7.3 The flex-basis and flex-shrink properties

To center the likes, we'll assign the same width to all three <div>s. Instead of using the width property, however, we'll use flex-basis and set its value to 33%. flex-basis sets the initial size the browser should use when calculating the amount of space the element needs. We'll also set flex-shrink to 1.

flex-shrink dictates whether an element is allowed to shrink smaller than the size assigned by the flex-basis value if there's not enough room for the element in the container. If the flex-shrink value is 0, the size isn't adjusted. Any positive value allows for resizing.

We set our flex-basis to 33%. But remember that we also set a gap of 12 pixels between each of our elements. Therefore, the flex-basis size we set is too wide for the container when the gap setting is taken into consideration. By allowing the elements to shrink, we tell the browser to start its positioning calculations with each <div> taking up 33% of the width of the container and to shrink the <div>s evenly to fit the available space. This situation prevents us from having to do math, figuring out exactly how wide the <div>s should be and still be of equal sizes.

To write our rule (listing 6.15), we target the <div>s that are immediate children of the description list (dl) by using a child combinator (>), and we apply the flex-basis and flex-shrink declarations.

Listing 6.15   Centering the likes

```
dl > div {
  flex-basis: 33%;
  flex-shrink: 1;
}
```

With our likes centered (figure 6.26), let's turn our attention to the definition terms (dt).

Figure 6.26   **Centered likes**

6.7.4   *The flex-direction property*

In our original design, we have the description details (the numbers) above the description terms. To flip them visually, we're going to use the flex-direction property. We asserted that Flexbox can place elements across a single axis. So far, we've done our work across the horizontal axis, or x-axis.

To move the details above the terms, we're going to use Flexbox on the vertical (y-axis), sometimes called the *block* or *cross* axis. To change which axis we want Flexbox to operate on, we use the flex-direction property. By default, that property has a value of row, which makes Flexbox operate on the x-axis. By changing the value to column, we make it operate on the y-axis.

Furthermore, the flex-direction property allows us to dictate how the elements should be ordered. Setting the value to column-reverse tells the browser that we want to operate on the y-axis and that we want the elements to be placed in reverse HTML order, making the description details (<dd>) appear first and the description term (<dt>) second.

As before, we want to set the behavior on the parent—in this case, the <div>. We'll add to our previous <div> rule to reorder the elements (listing 6.16). We also decrease the size of the description term (<dt>) to emphasize the number over its term.

Listing 6.16   **Reversing content order**

```
dl > div {
  flex-basis: 33%;
```

```
    flex-shrink: 1;
    display: flex;
    flex-direction: column-reverse;
}
dt { font-size: .75rem; }
```

Accessibility concerns and content display order

For accessibility reasons, we want to make sure that the order in which our HTML is written follows the order in which it's displayed onscreen. A user who has their computer read the contents of the page to them as they follow along visually would be easily disoriented or confused if the content that's being read to them doesn't match what they're seeing. Use caution when using properties such as `flex-direction` to reorder content.

Figure 6.27 shows our styled description list (`<dl>`).

Figure 6.27 Styled description list

Continuing down the card, let's turn our attention to the summary paragraph below the profile stats.

6.7.5 Paragraph

The paragraph already looks good. The only thing we're going to do to it is add some vertical margin for breathing room and increase the line height for better legibility, as shown in listing 6.17.

Notice that the line height doesn't take a unit. By not setting a unit, we allow the line height to scale with the font size. This unitless value is specific to the `line-height` property. If we'd set it to a `12px` value, for example, the line height would remain 12 pixels regardless of the font size. So if the font size were increased radically, our letters would overlap vertically. It's always safest *not* to declare a unit.

Listing 6.17   Paragraph rule

```
p.summary {
  margin: 24px 0;
  line-height: 1.5;
}
```

With our paragraph taken care of (figure 6.28), let's style the list of technologies.

Figure 6.28   Styled summary paragraph

6.7.6   *The flex-wrap property*

First, we're going to style the list elements themselves. We'll use a design pattern sometimes referred to as a *pill*, *chip*, or *tags*, in which the element has a background color and rounded edges. Our CSS will look like listing 6.18. We also include some padding so that the text doesn't come right up against the edge of the tag.

Listing 6.18   Styling the list elements

```
ul.technologies li {
  padding: 12px 24px;
  border-radius: 24px;
  background: var(--technologies-background);
}
```

With the individual elements styled (figure 6.29), we can focus on the list's layout.

Figure 6.29   Styled list items

First, we'll remove the bullets by using `list-style: none`. Then we'll remove all padding, and set the margins to `24px` vertically and `0` horizontally.

To position the items, we'll use Flexbox, adding a `gap` of `12px` and setting the `justify-content` property value to `space-between`. `space-between` works similarly to `space-around` except that it doesn't add space to the beginning and end of the container, as shown in figure 6.30.

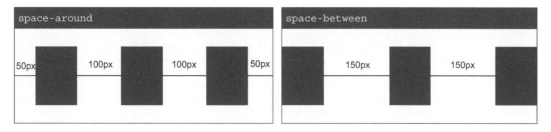

Figure 6.30   Comparing `space-around` **and** `space-between`

Our rule to lay out our chips will look like the next listing.

Listing 6.19   Styling the list of technologies

```
ul.technologies {
  list-style: none;
  padding: 0;
  margin: 24px 0;
  display: flex;
  justify-content: space-between;
  gap: 12px;
}
```

We notice that when we reduce the screen width (figure 6.31), however, our last tag extends beyond our card.

I specialize in UX / UI design and development. I love
coffee, chocolate, and my betta fish.

CSS   HTML   JavaScript   Accessibility

Follow Message

Figure 6.31   Tag extending beyond card width

On narrow screens, our list is wider than our card. To prevent the content from overflowing the card, we can use the `flex-wrap` property.

By default, flex items display in a straight line even if the container is too small, as we're experiencing with our list of technologies. To force the last element onto a new line when we run out of room, we can set the `flex-wrap` property to `wrap`. This setting tells the browser to start a new line of items below when it runs out of room.

Like `flex-direction`, `flex-wrap` can change the order in which the elements are displayed, but we won't need to change it here. The following listing contains our updated rule.

Listing 6.20   Adding `flex-wrap`

```
ul.technologies {
  list-style: none;
  padding: 0;
  margin: 24px 0;
  display: flex;
  justify-content: space-between;
  gap: 12px;
  flex-wrap: wrap;
}
```

Notice the gap between the CSS and Accessibility tags in figure 6.32, even though our list element doesn't have any margin. Our list has a `gap` property value of `12px`, which means not only that we'll have a minimum 12 pixels horizontally between our items, but also that when we wrap, we'll add a 12-pixel gap between the items vertically.

Figure 6.32   Wrapping the chips on narrow screens

6.8   *Styling the actions*

The last things we need to style in our profile card are the two actions the user can take at the bottom of the card: message or follow the profile owner. Even though these actions are semantically different—one is a link, and the other is a button—we're going to style both of them to look like buttons. Let's start with some basics that will apply to both elements. We create one rule with selectors for both elements to ensure that both element types are visually consistent. Then we create individual rules for use where they diverge.

We also create a `focus-visible` rule that will be applied to all elements by means of the universal selector (`*`) and the pseudo-class `:focus-visible` so that when a user navigates to our links and buttons via the keyboard, a dotted outline appears around the element, and they can clearly see what they're about to select. The following listing shows our styles.

Listing 6.21   Adding `flex-wrap`

```
.actions a, .actions button {          ←────  Applies to both the
  padding: 12px 24px;                          link and the button
  border-radius: 4px;
  text-decoration: none;               ←────  Removes the
  border: solid 1px var(--primary);            underline
  font-size: 1rem;
  cursor: pointer;
}

.follow {
  background: var(--primary);
  color: var(--primary-contrast);
}

.message {
  background: var(--primary-contrast);
  color: var(--primary);
}

*:focus-visible {
  outline: dotted 1px var(--primary);
  outline-offset: 3px;
}
```

Notice that in our base styles, we changed the cursor to pointer for both links and buttons. In most browsers, links will use the pointer by default but not the button. Because we want both elements to have a similar experience, we'll define the cursor to ensure consistency. Figure 6.33 shows our styled link and button.

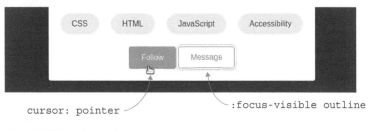

Figure 6.33   Styled actions

As these two buttons are quite close together, however, we're going to want to add some space between them. Let's use flex and gap one last time to position our action elements.

We're going to give the list a `display` property value of `flex` and add a `gap` of `16px`. To keep the two elements centered, we'll use the `justify-content` property with a value of `center`. Finally, we'll add some space between the list of technologies and our actions by giving the list a `margin-top` value of `36px`, as shown in the following listing.

Listing 6.22   Positioning the link and button

```
.actions {
  display: flex;
  gap: 16px;
  justify-content: center;
  margin-top: 36px;
}
```

With this last rule, we've finished styling our profile card. The final product is shown in figure 6.34.

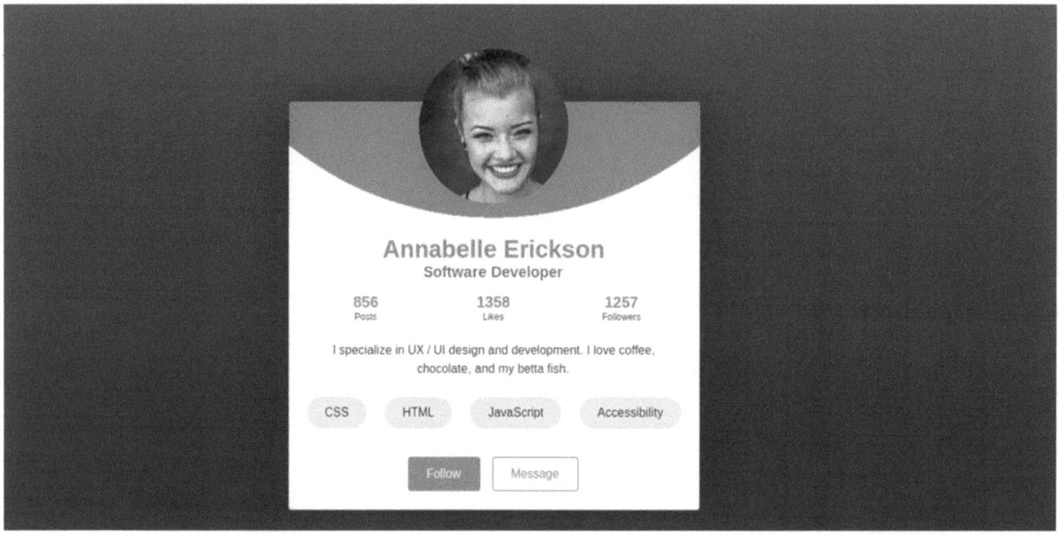

Figure 6.34   Finished profile card

Summary

- CSS custom properties allow us to set variables that can be reused throughout our CSS.
- The CSS Flexbox Layout Module allows us to position elements on a single axis either horizontally or vertically.
- `flex-direction` sets which axis Flexbox will operate on.
- Both `flex-direction` and `flex-wrap` can alter the order in which the elements are displayed.

- The `align-items` property sets how the elements are aligned on the axis relative to one another.
- The `justify-content` property dictates how the elements are positioned; leftover space will be distributed within the element to which it's applied.
- `flex-basis` sets a starting element size for the browser to use when laying out flexed content.
- `flex-shrink` dictates whether and how content can shrink when an element is being flexed.
- We can prevent images from distorting when we use fixed heights and widths that don't match the image's aspect ratio by using the `object-fit` property.

Harnessing the full
power of float

Grid and Flexbox have given us the ability to create layouts that once were incredibly difficult to realize, if not impossible. One of the most common examples is a three-column layout with all three columns the same height regardless of the contents. Another layout technique, which unlike its grid and flexbox counterparts has been around for quite some time, is float. Part of the CSS Logical Properties and Values Module, *float* is purpose-built to allow other content to wrap around the element being floated; as a result, it shines at manipulating images inside text and creating drop caps.

Drop caps are a way to style and add emphasis to text. They consist of creating a larger (sometimes more ornate) capital letter, usually at the beginning of a page or paragraph. Drop caps were often used in the illuminated manuscripts of the Middle Ages. The *F* at the beginning of the paragraph in figure 7.1 is an example of a drop cap in the Carmina Burana manuscript. Later, with the advent of the printing press, the concept carried over into print; printers created specialized glyphs and plates or simply used a larger font size. Drop caps are much rarer on the web, but they're by no means impossible to create, and they're a great way to make our online typography more interesting.

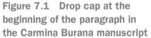

Figure 7.1 Drop cap at the beginning of the paragraph in the Carmina Burana manuscript

Another way to make content more visually striking is to style our images to fit nicely in the text. When we add images to content, we often add our image element and maybe some margin, and don't think about the process much more. Using CSS shapes in conjunction with float, however, we can make our text wrap in the actual shape of the image to create a much more striking effect. We can flow text around virtually any shapes we create, even curves.

In this chapter, we'll take a close look at our typography and images to make our content more visually interesting while making sure to keep it accessible. We'll start with an unstyled excerpt from *The Call of the Wild*, by Jack London (http://mng .bz/61WR). We'll use float to add a drop cap to our first paragraph. Then we'll wrap our text around our images (both raster and vector), following the content of those images. Figure 7.2 shows the starting point and the finished product.

Chapter I: Into the Primitive

"Old longings nomadic leap,
Chafing at custom's chain;
Again from its brumal sleep
Wakens the ferine strain."

Buck did not read the newspapers, or he would have known that trouble was brewing, not alone for himself, but for every tide-water dog, strong of muscle and with warm, long hair, from Puget Sound to San Diego. Because men, groping in the Arctic darkness, had found a yellow metal, and because steamship and transportation companies were booming the find, thousands of men were rushing into the Northland. These men wanted dogs, and the dogs they wanted were heavy dogs, with strong muscles by which to toil, and furry coats to protect them from the frost.

Buck lived at a big house in the sun-kissed Santa Clara Valley. Judge Miller's place, it was called. It stood back from the road, half hidden among the trees, through which glimpses could be caught of the wide cool veranda that ran around its four sides. The house was approached by gravelled driveways which wound about through wide-spreading lawns and under the interlacing boughs of tall poplars. At the rear things were on even a more spacious scale than at the front. There were great stables, where a dozen grooms and boys held forth, rows of vine-clad servants' cottages, an endless and orderly array of outhouses, long grape arbors, green pastures, orchards, and berry patches. Then there was the pumping plant for the artesian well, and the big cement tank where Judge Miller's boys took their morning plunge and kept cool in the hot afternoon.

And over this great demesne Buck ruled. Here he was born, and here he had lived the four years of his life. It was true, there were other dogs, There could not but be other dogs on so vast a place, but they did not count. They came and went, resided in the populous kennels, or lived obscurely in the recesses of the house after the fashion of Toots, the Japanese pug, or Ysabel, the Mexican hairless,—strange creatures that rarely put nose out of doors or set foot to ground. On the other hand, there were the fox terriers, a score of them at least, who yelped fearful promises at Toots and Ysabel looking out of the windows at them and protected by a legion of housemaids armed with brooms and mops.

London, Jack. "The Project Gutenberg EBook of The Call of the Wild, by Jack London." Project Gutenberg, https://www.gutenberg.org/files/215/215-h/215-h.htm. Accessed 25 3 2021.

Chapter I: Into the Primitive

*"Old longings nomadic leap,
Chafing at custom's chain;
Again from its brumal sleep
Wakens the ferine strain."*

B uck did not read the newspapers, or he would have known that trouble was brewing, not alone for himself, but for every tide-water dog, strong of muscle and with warm, long hair, from Puget Sound to San Diego. Because men, groping in the Arctic darkness, had found a yellow metal, and because steamship and transportation companies were booming the find, thousands of men were rushing into the Northland. These men wanted dogs, and the dogs they wanted were heavy dogs, with strong muscles by which to toil, and furry coats to protect them from the frost.

Buck lived at a big house in the sun-kissed Santa Clara Valley. Judge Miller's place, it was called. It stood back from the road, half hidden among the trees, through which glimpses could be caught of the wide cool veranda that ran around its four sides. The house was approached by gravelled driveways which wound about through wide-spreading lawns and under the interlacing boughs of tall poplars. At the rear things were on even a more spacious scale than at the front. There were great stables, where a dozen grooms and boys held forth, rows of vine-clad servants' cottages, an endless and orderly array of outhouses, long grape arbors, green pastures, orchards, and berry patches. Then there was the pumping plant for the artesian well, and the big cement tank where Judge Miller's boys took their morning plunge and kept cool in the hot afternoon.

 And over this great demesne Buck ruled. Here he was born, and here he had lived the four years of his life. It was true, there were other dogs, There could not but be other dogs on so vast a place, but they did not count. They came and went, resided in the populous kennels, or lived obscurely in the recesses of the house after the fashion of Toots, the Japanese pug, or Ysabel, the Mexican hairless,—strange creatures that rarely put nose out of doors or set foot to ground. On the other hand, there were the fox terriers, a score of them at least, who yelped fearful promises at Toots and Ysabel looking out of the windows at them and protected by a legion of housemaids armed with brooms and mops.

London, Jack. "The Project Gutenberg EBook of The Call of the Wild, by Jack London." Project Gutenberg, https://www.gutenberg.org/files/215/215-h/215-h.htm. Accessed 25 3 2021.

Figure 7.2   The starting point (left) and finished product (right)

NOTE   A *raster image* is created by using a grid of pixels, whereas a *vector image* is drawn with the help of mathematical formulas. For in-depth information about the difference between rasters and vectors, check out chapter 3.

Listing 7.1 and listing 7.2 contain the starting HTML and CSS, respectively, for the page we'll build on in this chapter. To follow along as we style the page, you can download the starting code from the GitHub repository at http://mng.bz/oJXD or from Code-Pen at https://codepen.io/michaelgearon/pen/MWodXxM. Our HTML consists of a `<main>` element inside which we have a header (`<h1>`), block quote (`<blockquote>`), three paragraphs (`<p>`), two images (`<img>`), and the source citation (`<cite>`).

Listing 7.1 Starting HTML

```
<main>
  <h1>Chapter I: Into the Primitive</h1>
  <blockquote>"Old longings nomadic…</blockquote>
  <p>Buck did not read the newspapers, or he…</p>
  <img class="compass" src="./img/compass.png"          Compass
      width="175" height="175" alt="a black and gray compass">  │ image
  <p>Buck lived at a big house in the…</p>
  <img class="dog" src="./img/dog.svg"            Dog
      width="126" alt="line drawing of a dog">    │ image
  <p>And over this great demesne Buck ruled…</p>
  <cite>London, Jack…</cite>
</main>
```

Our CSS includes some base styles to set up our page, including `margin`, `padding`, and `background-color`. The body's width is restricted to `78ch`, and margins center the content when the screen width exceeds our maximum value. We also set up the default font for the page, which is Times New Roman. Last, to ensure that the images don't overflow on small screens, we give them a maximum width, which is set to `100%`. In other words, the images can't be wider than their container.

> **NOTE** Notice that we use `ch` for our `max-width`. `ch` is a relative unit based on the font family being used. `1ch` is equal to the width of—or, more precisely, the horizontal amount of space occupied by—the glyph `0` (zero).

Listing 7.2 Starting CSS

```
html {
  padding: 0;
  margin: 0;
}

body {
  background-color: rgba(206, 194, 174, 0.24);
  padding: 4rem;
  font-size: 16px;           ┐ Prevents our content from
  max-width: 78ch;        ◄──┘ becoming excessively wide
  margin: 0 auto;      ◄── Centers the content
  font-family: 'Times New Roman', Times, serif;
  border-left: double 5px rgba(0,0,0,.16);
  min-height: 100vh;    ◄──┐ Regardless of window size, the
  box-sizing: border-box;  └ background covers the whole window.
}
```

```
img {
  max-width: 100%;
}
```

7.1   *Adding a drop cap*

We have some base CSS to style the page, so now we're going to turn our attention to the text. By virtue of the fact that the width of our body is capped at a width that works well for our text, we don't need to worry about line length. But we do need to address the leading.

7.1.1   *Leading*

Leading (pronounced 'le-diŋ) is the amount of space between lines. The term comes from the days of the printing press when compositors used lead bars of various widths to adjust the spacing between lines of text. The CSS property we're going to use to accomplish the same outcome is `line-height`. This property can take a number value (`line-height: 2`) or a number with a unit (`line-height: 5px`). The unit can be relative, such as ems, or fixed, such as pixels. Unless the unit is relative to the font size when we provide a unit (such as em), if the font is scaled or a child element has a different font size, the line height may not look correct and can negatively affect legibility. When we use a unitless number, the line height is automatically calculated relative to the font size of the element, eliminating this concern. Therefore, we'll use a unitless `line-height`. We'll set a `line-height` of `1.5` on all paragraphs by creating a rule specifically for the paragraph element and then applying the height as follows: `p { line-height: 1.5; }`.

> **TIP**   Research shows that text with a `line-height` between `1.5` and `2` makes line tracking easier for people with cognitive disabilities (https://www.w3.org/TR/WCAG20-TECHS/C21.html).

7.1.2   *Justification*

For optimum effect when we have the text follow the image, we're going to justify our text. *Justifying* the text means we're going to make all our lines the same width—a technique often used in newspapers to make the right edge of a column on text straight rather than ragged.

> **WARNING**   The Web Content Accessibility Guideline (WCAG) includes three levels of conformance that build on one another: A, AA, and AAA. A is the least restrictive, and AAA is the most stringent. Most often, websites aim for an AA level of conformance. But if we're required to conform to AAA, it's worth mentioning that justifying text goes against accessibility guideline 1.4.5, which is a requirement for AAA (http://mng.bz/v1ja).

To justify our text, we're going to use the `text-align` property, which can take a value of `left`, `right`, `center`, or `justify`. We'll add `text-align: justify;` to our paragraph rule. Now that rule has two properties, `text-align` and `line-height`, that take care of styling the paragraph. The following listing shows the completed paragraph rule, and figure 7.3 shows the result.

Listing 7.3   Completed paragraph rule

```
p {
  line-height: 1.5;
  text-align: justify;
}
```

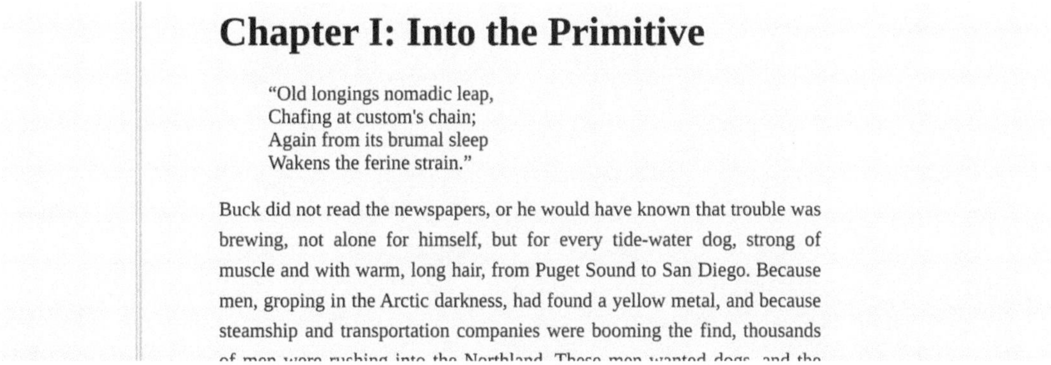

Chapter I: Into the Primitive

"Old longings nomadic leap,
Chafing at custom's chain;
Again from its brumal sleep
Wakens the ferine strain."

Buck did not read the newspapers, or he would have known that trouble was brewing, not alone for himself, but for every tide-water dog, strong of muscle and with warm, long hair, from Puget Sound to San Diego. Because men, groping in the Arctic darkness, had found a yellow metal, and because steamship and transportation companies were booming the find, thousands of men were rushing into the Northland. These men wanted dogs, and the

Figure 7.3   Styled paragraphs

With the paragraph taken care of, we can hone in on the first letter of the first paragraph to create our drop cap.

7.1.3   *First letter*

We don't need to add any elements to the HTML to select the first letter of our first paragraph. We can use the pseudo-class `:first-of-type` to select the first paragraph and then the pseudo-element `::first-letter` to get to the letter, in this case a *B*, both of which can be chained. In code, these selections translate to `p:first-of-type::first-letter {}`.

> **NOTE**   A pseudo-class is added to a selector to target a specific state; a pseudo-element allows us to select part of the element.

With the letter selected, we can start styling it to make it look like a drop cap. To make it stand out from the rest of the text, we're going to pick a more ornate typeface. In this case, we'll import Passions Conflict (http://mng.bz/X5vE; figure 7.4) from Google Fonts.

Because this typeface has particularly ornate capital letters, it's well suited for use as our drop cap. We'll also use it later in this chapter to style the quote at the beginning of the text. Using a beautiful typeface such as this one is a wonderful way to embellish a page—but only for short bits of content. Handwriting and display fonts

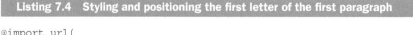

Figure 7.4 Passions Conflict glyphs

can be quite difficult to read, so they're not well suited for large blocks of text. For a drop cap, large header, or short quote, however, these fonts differentiate the element from the rest of the content and give the page some personality.

This particular font has glyphs that are quite a bit smaller than those of Times New Roman (the font we're using for the rest of our content). Because we're creating a drop cap, which by definition is larger than the rest of the text, we're going to have to adjust the font size. We're also going to adjust the line height of the letter to make it fit nicely with the text. Finally, we're going to float our first letter to the left so that the text flows around the letter, accomplishing our desired effect.

The `float` property places an element to the right or left of its container based on the value passed to it. According to the Mozilla Developer Network, "The element is removed from the normal flow of the page, though still remaining a part of the flow" (http://mng.bz/ydle). Inline elements around it (our text) use the leftover space to wrap around the floated element.

The `float` property can take one of three values: `left`, `right`, and `none` (element isn't floated). Because our text is in English, which flows from left to right, we want to keep the letter *B* to the left, so we're going to float the first letter of the first paragraph (*B*) to the left by adding `float: left;` to our rule. The following listing shows the completed CSS rule we create to style our drop cap, as well as the import of the Passions Conflict typeface.

Listing 7.4 Styling and positioning the first letter of the first paragraph

```
@import url(
  'https://fonts.googleapis.com/css2?          ← Import of the
➥ family=Passions+Conflict&display=swap'         Passions Conflict
);                                                typeface

p:first-of-type::first-letter {        Rule that styles the letter B
  font-size: 6em;                      at the beginning of our
  float: left;                         first paragraph
```

```
   line-height: .5;
   font-family: 'Passions Conflict', cursive;
}
```

△ **Rule that styles the letter B at the beginning of our first paragraph**

Notice that we altered the line height of the first letter to adjust the space below the *B*. By default, line height is proportional to font size. Because our letter is large, the line height it requires is tall, so we decrease it to make the text flow more naturally below the drop cap. Figure 7.5 shows the output generated.

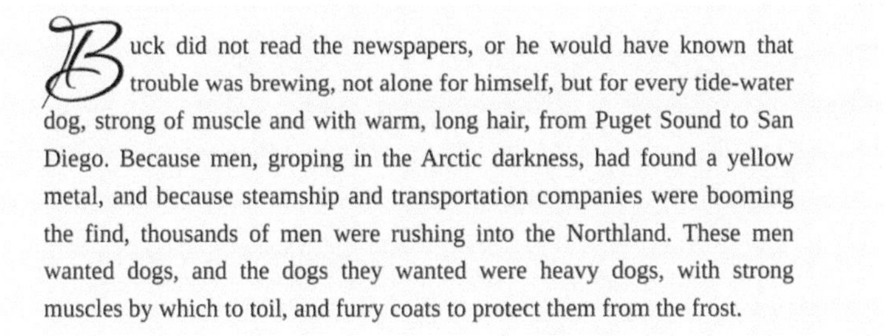

Figure 7.5 Drop cap

We use ems and a unitless line-height so that if we ever change the font size of the paragraph, the drop cap will scale accordingly. The value of 6em is set based on the font-size of the parent element, which in this case is our paragraph tag.

To reposition our *B* to fit well with the text, we edited the line-height of the letter. But we could have used another technique. We could have set the position of the *B* to relative and then used top, bottom, left, and right to alter its position relative to the rest of the text. With our drop cap created, we're going to turn our attention to the quote at the start of the page.

7.2   Styling the quote

The quote at the top of the page is rather drab at the moment and gets a little lost in the rest of the text. To make it stand out, we're going to use the same font we used for our drop cap. Because of the previously mentioned differences in size and line height, we're going to adjust those parameters so that the paragraphs and the quote are uniformly sized and spaced. Listing 7.5 shows the CSS we'll add to accomplish this task, and figure 7.6 shows the output.

Listing 7.5   `<blockquote>` formatting

```
blockquote {
  font-family: 'Passions Conflict', cursive;
  font-size: 2em;
  line-height: 1;
}
```

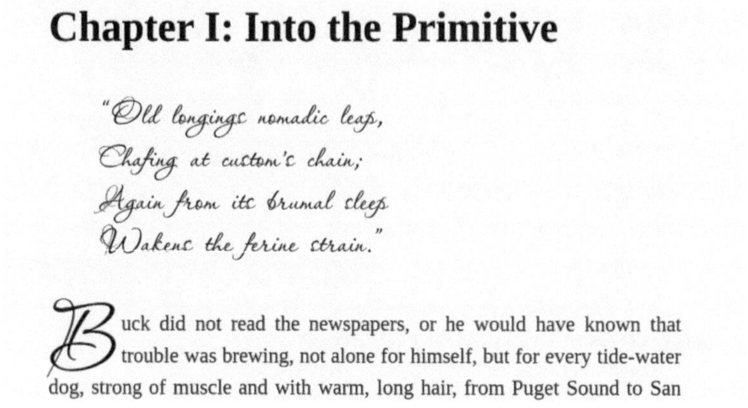

Chapter I: Into the Primitive

"Old longings nomadic leap,
Chafing at custom's chain;
Again from its brumal sleep
Wakens the ferine strain."

Buck did not read the newspapers, or he would have known that trouble was brewing, not alone for himself, but for every tide-water dog, strong of muscle and with warm, long hair, from Puget Sound to San

Figure 7.6   Styled `<blockquote>`

Again, we use relative units so that if the rest of the content's font size changes, so will the quote. You may have noticed that we used a `line-height` of 1 even though we stated earlier (section 7.1.1) that for optimal legibility, a line height of 1.5 to 2 is ideal. We make an exception here because by default the font already has a large line height; we don't need to increase the size. Occasionally, we'll encounter fonts that have naturally tall line heights by default, especially when we're dealing with cursive or display fonts. When this happens, sometimes we have to make an exception to the line-height-legibility guidance due to the design of the font.

Now, with our text taken care of, we can focus on the images.

7.3   *Curving text around the compass*

The first thing we need to do to make the text wrap around our compass image is float the compass to the right. Our compass is a PNG image, and because it's a rectangular image, the text follows a rectangular path in wrapping around the image. Figure 7.7 shows the floated compass. A border has been applied to the image to expose its bounding box.

Buck lived at a big house in the sun-kissed Santa Clara Valley. Judge Miller's place, it was called. It stood back from the road, half hidden among the trees, through which glimpses could be caught of the wide cool veranda that ran around its four sides. The house was approached by gravelled driveways which wound about through wide-spreading lawns and under the interlacing boughs of tall poplars. At the rear things were on even a more spacious scale

Figure 7.7
Square compass

7.3.1   Adding shape-outside: circle

To make the text follow the curve of the compass, we need to add a curve to the image for the text to wrap around. The property we'll use is `shape-outside`. This property allows us to define a shape around which the adjacent text will flow. The shape doesn't have to be rectangular; instead, it can be any of the following:

- Circle or ellipse
- Polygon
- Derived from an image (uses the alpha channel [transparency] of the image to determine what the shape should be)
- Path (in the specification but not implemented in any browser at this writing; see http://mng.bz/aMWX)
- Box model values (`margin-box`, `content-box`, `border-box`, and `padding-box`)
- Linear gradient

Because we have a circular graphic, the shape we're going to aim for is a circle. This decision gives us a couple of options:

- Use CSS shapes (http://mng.bz/aMWX).
- Use `border-radius`.

Let's first take a look at using shapes. To define our circle, we're going to use the `circle()` function, which takes an optional `radius` property and an optional `position` property to define where the center of the circle starts. If no `radius` is provided, the value defaults to `closest-side`. If the `position` property is omitted, the origin of the circle defaults to the center of the image:

```
circle(<shape-radius>, at <position> )
```

In our case, we want the center of the circle to be the middle of the image, so we won't pass a `position` property. We have to define a `radius`, however, and we're going to set it to `50%`.

How the math works

We want the radius to equal half the width of our image, which under the covers will resolve to the square root of our width squared plus our height squared divided by the square root of 2:

$$radius = \% \times \frac{\sqrt{height^2 + width^2}}{\sqrt{2}} = .5 \times \frac{\sqrt{175^2 + 175^2}}{\sqrt{2}} = 87.5$$

Because our image is square and has a width of 175, when we pass a `radius` of `50%`, it's logical that our radius would be 87.5. But if the image were rectangular, understanding how a percentage-based radius is calculated is important for understanding what the resulting output will look like.

(continued)

If we had a landscape image of height 100px and width 300px, the radius needed to inscribe the circle when choosing a percentage-based value is much less obvious. We can use the following formula to calculate what the radius would be:

$$radius = \% \times \frac{\sqrt{height^2 + width^2}}{\sqrt{2}} = .5 \times \frac{\sqrt{100^2 + 300^2}}{\sqrt{2}} \approx 111.8$$

Figure 7.8 shows how the radius would be applied to our square image versus a rectangular image when we use a value of 50% in the circle() function.

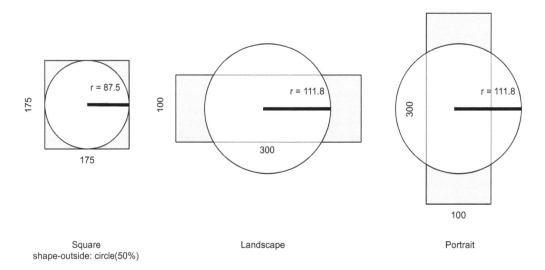

Figure 7.8   Radius applied to a square versus a rectangular image

Our image is square, so we use a shape-outside property with a value of circle(50%) for our image. Listing 7.6 shows the CSS rule. Our image is square, so it has an aspect ratio of 1 (width / height = 175 ÷ 175 = 1).

DEFINITION   The *aspect ratio* of an image is the proportional relationship of the image's height and width calculated by dividing the width by the height.

Adding the aspect ratio isn't strictly necessary to create our shape but helps reduce layout shifts on load.

DEFINITION   When an element is added to the page or its size is changed, everything after the element moves to make room for the element or fill the void left behind. The movement of elements on the page is referred to as a *layout shift.*

When the image has a set height and width or has a defined aspect ratio, the browser can save room for the image while it's being loaded, therefore reducing the layout shift. Accordingly, it's good practice to define aspect ratios and/or height and width for our images.

Listing 7.6 `shape-outside`

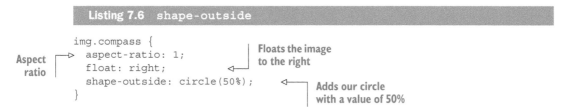

```
img.compass {
    aspect-ratio: 1;
    float: right;
    shape-outside: circle(50%);
}
```

Aspect ratio

Floats the image to the right

Adds our circle with a value of 50%

Figure 7.9 displays our output. The text wraps around the image and follows the curve, but the image isn't clipped in any way. This effect works because our image has a transparent background.

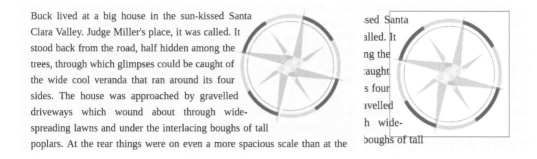

Figure 7.9 Floated compass with curved text

7.3.2 Adding a clip-path

We've curved the text, but the image is still square. If we add a background to the image, this fact becomes obvious. To make the image appear to be truly circular, we need to add a `clip-path`. The `clip-path` property also takes a shape, so we're going to pass it the same value we passed to `shape-outside`. We're also going to add some margin to our image to add a little breathing room between it and the text. Listing 7.7 shows the complete CSS for our image.

Listing 7.7 `clip-path`

```
img.compass {
  aspect-ratio: 1;
  float: right;
  shape-outside: circle(50%);
  clip-path: circle(50%);
  margin-left: 1rem;
}
```

We added a `clip-path` that matches our `shape-outside` and some margin to the left of the image to prevent the text from getting too close to the image, especially because the compass has arrows protruding from the circular outline that our `circle()` doesn't create. Figure 7.10 shows the finished output.

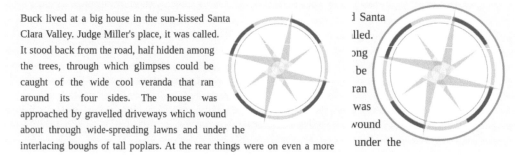

Buck lived at a big house in the sun-kissed Santa Clara Valley. Judge Miller's place, it was called. It stood back from the road, half hidden among the trees, through which glimpses could be caught of the wide cool veranda that ran around its four sides. The house was approached by gravelled driveways which wound about through wide-spreading lawns and under the interlacing boughs of tall poplars. At the rear things were on even a more

Figure 7.10   Round floated compass

When we add the `clip-path`, we observe that now the image itself, including the background, appears to be round. The corners have been clipped, and the previously square background is circular. Also, the added margin moves the text around our compass arrow, making it look less crowded.

We've demonstrated that we can create a circle by using CSS shapes. Now let's look at how to make the circle by using `border-radius`.

7.3.3   Creating a shape using border-radius

We can create a CSS shape from an element's contours when we use `border-radius` to shape the element. We still use `shape-outside`, but instead of passing in a shape, we specify the level of the box model at which we want the shape to form. Our options are

- `margin-box`—Shape follows the margins.
- `border-box`—Shape follows the borders.
- `padding-box`—Shape follows the padding.
- `content-box`—Shape follows the content.

Let's start with a clean slate, with our image floated to the right and some margin added to keep the text from crowding the image. Listing 7.8 contains our starting CSS, and figure 7.11 shows the current display.

Listing 7.8   Starting point

```
img.compass {
  aspect-ratio: 1;
  float: right;
  margin-left: 1rem;
}
```

Buck lived at a big house in the sun-kissed
Santa Clara Valley. Judge Miller's place, it was
called. It stood back from the road, half
hidden among the trees, through which
glimpses could be caught of the wide cool
veranda that ran around its four sides. The
house was approached by gravelled driveways
which wound about through wide-spreading
lawns and under the interlacing boughs of tall poplars. At the rear things

**Figure 7.11   Resetting
to float and adding a
margin**

Now let's add a `border-radius` of 50%, which will make our image a circle. At this
point, though, the text doesn't follow the curve. We still need to add the `shape-out-
side` property.

   Our image has a margin that (ideally) we want the shape to respect, so we're going
to use the `margin-box` value. The next listing shows this concept applied in code.

Listing 7.9   Adding `border-radius` and `shape-outside`

```
img.compass {
  aspect-ratio: 1;
  float: right;
  margin-left: 1rem;
  border-radius: 50%;
  shape-outside: margin-box;
}
```

Figure 7.12 shows the output with a white background and border added to emphasize the shape of the image.

Buck lived at a big house in the sun-kissed Santa
Clara Valley. Judge Miller's place, it was called.
It stood back from the road, half hidden
among the trees, through which glimpses
could be caught of the wide cool veranda that
ran around its four sides. The house was
approached by gravelled driveways which wound
about through wide-spreading lawns and under the
interlacing boughs of tall poplars. At the rear things were on even a more

Figure 7.12   Compass shape with `border-radius` **of** 50% **and a** `shape-
outside` **value of** `margin-box`

Unlike when we used `shape-outside` with the `circle()` function, our image is already
cropped into a circular shape, eliminating the need to use `clip-path`. This outcome
is a direct result of using `border-radius`, which is doing the clipping for us.

We've seen two different ways to accomplish the same result. CSS offers more than one way to approach many problems, including this one. Neither option is particularly superior to the other. border-radius requires slightly less code, which gives it a slight edge, but in this case the choice is a matter of preference.

Now that we've handled the compass image, we're going to move on to wrap the text around the dog.

7.4   Wrapping text around the dog

Unlike the compass, which is a standard shape, the dog has an irregular outline. This image is line art composed of a single path, so we might be tempted to grab the path from the SVG file and use the path() function to create our shape. As we're about to see, however, although it's defined in the CSS specification (https://www.w3.org/TR/css-shapes), this technique won't work.

7.4.1   Using path() . . . or not yet

Let's open the image file in an editor to inspect the code. The following listing shows the image code redacted for brevity to highlight the important information.

Listing 7.10   dog.svg

```
<svg xmlns="http://www.w3.org/2000/svg" viewBox="0 0 152 193">
  <defs>
    <style>
      .cls-1{
        fill:none;
        stroke:#000;
        stroke-miterlimit:10;
        stroke-width:2px;
      }
    </style>
  </defs>
  <path class="cls-1" d="M21.9135,115.62c-17.2115,4.7607-37.3354,..."/>
</svg>
```

We have the <defs> element, which includes the styles for the image. This part defines what the individual elements in the SVG will look like. Then we have a <path>, which is the element displaying the dog. This element is 1,988 characters long and quite complex, and when shape-outside: path('M21.913…'); is pasted into the path() function, it doesn't seem to do anything. The reason is that when this book was written, no browser fully implemented path().

When this feature is implemented, creating our paths with a graphics editor and copying them to create our shapes will be a valuable technique. But this method will have a drawback: the paths can get quite long, making maintainability dubious. In the meantime, we have a couple of alternatives:

- Creating a polygon shape that roughly matches our image, similar to the technique we used for the circle

- Using the `url()` function, which pulls in the image and bases the shape on the alpha channel

We're going to go with the second option: the `url()` function.

7.4.2 *Floating the image*

As we did when we handled the compass image (section 7.3), we're going to start by floating the image, but this time we'll float it to the left to break up the visual monotony of our page. Then, to create the shape, we'll use the `url()` function and pass the path to the image to it. Listing 7.11 shows the CSS applied to the dog image.

> **Serving the image file**
>
> When using URLs with `shape-outside`, we need to make sure we're running our code through a server so that the image is getting fetched by the browser, not read directly from the file system. This approach is related to Cross-Origin Resource Sharing (CORS) and security policies set by the browser. You can find a detailed explanation in the CSS specification at http://mng.bz/pdMw.
>
> To mitigate this problem, the sample code in the GitHub repository uses `http-server`, serving the files on `localhost:8080` to accomplish this task. Another option would be to reference the hosted file in GitHub by using `shape-outside: url("https://raw.githubusercontent.com/michaelgearon/Tiny-CSS-Projects/main/chapter-07/before/img/dog.svg")`.

Listing 7.11 Dog floated left

```
img.dog {
  aspect-ratio: 126 / 161;
  float: left;
  shape-outside: url("https://raw.githubusercontent.com/michaelgearon/Tiny-
    CSS-Projects/main/chapter-07/before/img/dog.svg");
}
```

We float the image left and then add our `shape-outside`, passing in a reference to the image itself. The browser will look at the transparency of the image and determine where to create the shape based on where the transparency ends. Figure 7.13 shows our output.

Because our image has an opaque line with a transparent background, the cutoff is straightforward. If our image had a gradient that went from opaque to transparent, we could tailor the cutoff by using the `shape-image-threshold` property. This property takes a value between `0` (fully transparent) and `1` (fully opaque).

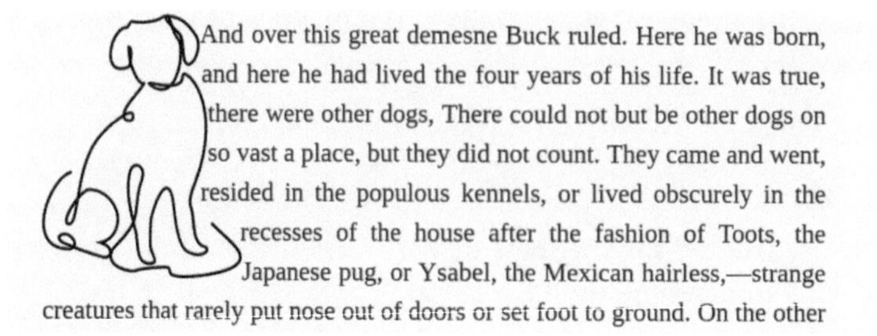

And over this great demesne Buck ruled. Here he was born, and here he had lived the four years of his life. It was true, there were other dogs, There could not but be other dogs on so vast a place, but they did not count. They came and went, resided in the populous kennels, or lived obscurely in the recesses of the house after the fashion of Toots, the Japanese pug, or Ysabel, the Mexican hairless,—strange creatures that rarely put nose out of doors or set foot to ground. On the other

Figure 7.13   Floated dog

7.4.3   *Adding shape-margin*

The next step is adding some margin to move the text away from the image because it looks rather crowded. We can't simply add a margin to the image, as we did when we floated to the right; if we try, we'll notice that the margin is ignored. Instead, we need to use shape-margin. The shape-margin property allows us to adjust the amount of space between our shape and the rest of the content. We're going to add 1em worth of space, as shown in the following listing and figure 7.14.

Listing 7.12   Adding `shape-margin` to our rule

```
img.dog {
  aspect-ratio: 126 / 161;
  float: left;
  shape-outside: url("https://raw.githubusercontent.com/michaelgearon/Tiny-
    CSS-Projects/main/chapter-07/before/img/dog.svg");
  shape-margin: 1em;
}
```

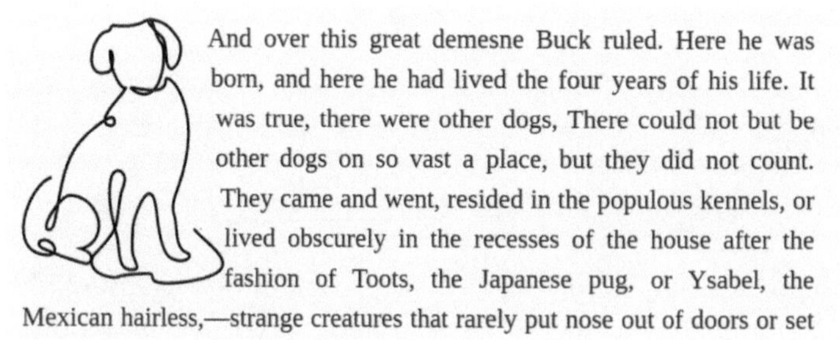

And over this great demesne Buck ruled. Here he was born, and here he had lived the four years of his life. It was true, there were other dogs, There could not but be other dogs on so vast a place, but they did not count. They came and went, resided in the populous kennels, or lived obscurely in the recesses of the house after the fashion of Toots, the Japanese pug, or Ysabel, the Mexican hairless,—strange creatures that rarely put nose out of doors or set

Figure 7.14   `shape-margin` applied to the image

The text at the bottom of the image is still quite close. At this point, we can add some margin to increase the space as long as the margin added is less than or equal to the shape-margin amount. If the value is greater than the shape-margin amount, the margin will still take effect, but only as much as the shape-margin amount. Keeping this caveat in mind, we'll add 1em of margin to the right of the image. The next listing shows the completed CSS for the dog image.

Listing 7.13   Completed dog image

```
img.dog {
  aspect-ratio: 126 / 161;
  float: left;
  shape-outside: url('img/dog.svg');
  shape-margin: 1em;
  margin-right: 1em;
}
```

The combination of shape-margin and margin-right pushes the text away from our image, creating the polished result we see in figure 7.15.

And over this great demesne Buck ruled. Here he was born, and here he had lived the four years of his life. It was true, there were other dogs, There could not but be other dogs on so vast a place, but they did not count. They came and went, resided in the populous kennels, or lived obscurely in the recesses of the house after the fashion of Toots, the Japanese pug, or Ysabel, the Mexican hairless,—strange creatures that rarely put nose out of doors or set

Figure 7.15   Finished floated dog

With this last piece completed, we've finished styling our page (figure 7.16). We have a layout that's visually appealing and much more interesting than the one we started with.

We've created a layout made possible by the use of float. We couldn't have achieved the same result by using Flex or Grid easily. Whether we use it on its own, as in our drop-cap example, or in conjunction with shapes (which, granted, are rather new as well), float continues to be a valuable asset for us to keep in our toolbox.

Chapter I: Into the Primitive

"Old longings nomadic leap,
Chafing at custom's chain;
Again from its brumal sleep
Wakens the ferine strain."

Buck did not read the newspapers, or he would have known that trouble was brewing, not alone for himself, but for every tide-water dog, strong of muscle and with warm, long hair, from Puget Sound to San Diego. Because men, groping in the Arctic darkness, had found a yellow metal, and because steamship and transportation companies were booming the find, thousands of men were rushing into the Northland. These men wanted dogs, and the dogs they wanted were heavy dogs, with strong muscles by which to toil, and furry coats to protect them from the frost.

Buck lived at a big house in the sun-kissed Santa Clara Valley. Judge Miller's place, it was called. It stood back from the road, half hidden among the trees, through which glimpses could be caught of the wide cool veranda that ran around its four sides. The house was approached by gravelled driveways which wound about through wide-spreading lawns and under the interlacing boughs of tall poplars. At the rear things were on even a more spacious scale than at the front. There were great stables, where a dozen grooms and boys held forth, rows of vine-clad servants' cottages, an endless and orderly array of outhouses, long grape arbors, green pastures, orchards, and berry patches. Then there was the pumping plant for the artesian well, and the big cement tank where Judge Miller's boys took their morning plunge and kept cool in the hot afternoon.

And over this great demesne Buck ruled. Here he was born, and here he had lived the four years of his life. It was true, there were other dogs, There could not but be other dogs on so vast a place, but they did not count. They came and went, resided in the populous kennels, or lived obscurely in the recesses of the house after the fashion of Toots, the Japanese pug, or Ysabel, the Mexican hairless,—strange creatures that rarely put nose out of doors or set foot to ground. On the other hand, there were the fox terriers, a score of them at least, who yelped fearful promises at Toots and Ysabel looking out of the windows at them and protected by a legion of housemaids armed with brooms and mops.

London, Jack. "The Project Gutenberg EBook of The Call of the Wild, by Jack London." Project Gutenberg, https://www.gutenberg.org/files/215/215-h/215-h.htm. Accessed 25 3 2021.

Figure 7.16
Finished layout

Summary

- Leading, the amount of space between lines, is important for legibility.
- Float can be used in conjunction with `::first-letter` to create drop caps.
- Not all typefaces have the same size and line heights when given the same size value.
- The `shape-outside` property uses CSS shapes to alter the shape of an element.
- Circular shapes can be created with `border-radius`.
- Inline content adjacent to a floated CSS shape will follow the shape.
- When we use `url()` with `shape-outside`, the image file must be fetched by the browser (hosted or via `http-server` or the equivalent).
- The `shape-margin` property sets the margin of a shape.
- Some layouts can't be created without the use of float.

Designing a checkout cart

This chapter covers

- Using responsive tables
- Autopositioning using Grid
- Formatting numbers
- Conditionally setting CSS based on viewport size via media queries
- Using the `nth-of-type()` pseudo-class

Many of us regularly go online to buy items ranging from food to books to entertainment and everything in between. Common to this experience is the checkout cart. We make our selections by adding them to a virtual cart or basket in which we can review our chosen items before making our final purchase. In this chapter, we'll look at how to style a checkout cart so that it works on both narrow and wide screens. We'll also look at how to handle tables for narrow and wide screens. Tables are incredibly useful for displaying data, but they can be a bit difficult to style for mobile devices, so we'll look at a CSS solution for narrow screens.

First, though, we'll handle some theming. Regardless of the width of our screen, elements such as our input fields, links, and buttons will look the same, so we'll style them first. Defining a theme early in the process of putting together a user interface can significantly reduce redundant code. It also increases our ability to keep our styles consistent, so that whether we're creating a checkout cart or any other page or application, we can apply this process to any number of designs.

Next, we'll focus on the layout, moving from narrow to wide. On devices with narrow screens, such as phones, we tend to stack things. As screens grow larger, we add rules to make use of the full width available to us. Often, it's easier to start with the mobile layout and add to our styles as the screen gets wider than to start with wide-screen layout and have to override previously set layout elements as screens become smaller.

8.1   Getting started

We'll create styles to accommodate three sizes of screens:

- *Narrow* (most phones)—Maximum width of 549 pixels
- *Medium* (tablets and small screens)—Between 500 and 955 pixels
- *Wide* (desktop computers and high-resolution tablets)—Wider than 955 pixels

Figure 8.1 shows our starting point and the final output for each screen size.

Figure 8.1   Start and end outputs for small, medium, and large screens

Regardless of the screen size, we're going to use the same HTML. We'll have one stylesheet and use media queries to adjust how our elements look depending on screen size. Our starting HTML is on GitHub at http://mng.bz/GRpJ and on Code-Pen at https://codepen.io/michaelgearon/pen/ExmLNxL. The code consists of two sections, one for the cart and one for the summary, which are wrapped in a container that we'll use on wide screens to place the sections side by side. The cart section includes a heading and a table that contains each of the items in the cart. The summary section contains a heading, a description list, and two links. Figure 8.2 diagrams the HTML elements.

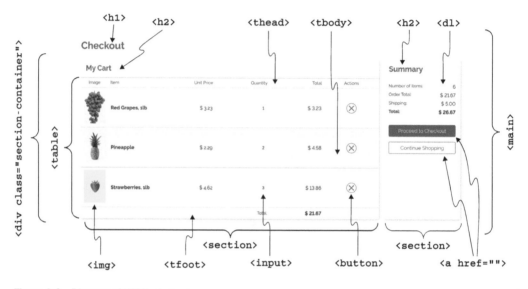

Figure 8.2   Diagram of HTML elements

The following listing is an abridged version of the HTML we're starting with.

Listing 8.1   Starting HTML

```html
<body>
  <main>
    <h1>Checkout</h1>
    <div class="section-container">
      <section class="my-cart">
        <h2>My Cart</h2>
        <table>
          <thead>
            <tr>
              <th>Image</th>
              <th>Item</th>
              <th>Unit Price</th>
              <th>Quantity</th>
              <th>Total</th>
              <th>Actions</th>
            </tr>
```

```
    </thead>
    <tbody>
      <tr>
        <td>
          <img src="./img/grapes.jpg" width="75" height="105"
            loading="lazy" alt="Red grapes">
        </td>
        <td data-name="Item">Red Grapes, 1lb</td>
        <td data-name="Unit Price">$ 3.23</td>
        <td data-name="Quantity">
          <input name="grapes" type="number"
            aria-label="Pounds of grape baskets"
            min="0" max="99"
            value="1">

        </td>
        <td data-name="Total">
          <!-- value calculated & inserted by JS -->
        </td>
        <td>
          <button type="button" class="destructive">
            <img width="24" height="24"
src="./img/icons/remove.svg" alt="remove grapes">
          </button>
        </td>
      </tr>
      ...
    <tfoot>
      <tr>
        <th colspan="4" scope="row">Total:</th>
        <td id="total">
          <!-- value calculated & inserted by JS -->
        </td>
      </tr>
    </tfoot>
  </table>
</section>

<section class="summary">
  <h2>Summary</h2>
  <dl>
    <dt>Number of Items</dt>
    <dd id="itemQty">
      <!-- value calculated & inserted by JS -->
    </dd>
  ...

  </dl>
  <div class="actions">
    <a href="#" class="button primary">
      Proceed to Checkout
    </a>
    <a href="#" class="button secondary">
      Continue Shopping
    </a>
```

```
        </div>
      </section>
    </div>
  </main>
  <script src="./script.js"></script>
</body>
```

In addition to the starting HTML, we'll use a JavaScript file (`script.js`). We won't be editing or interacting with the file; it's there simply to update the totals for the summary sections.

8.2 Theming

Although our layout has two clearly defined sections (the cart and the summary) and needs to work across screen sizes, some styles aren't going to change regardless of where they are or what size the screen is. These styles include

- Fonts
- Buttons and link styles
- Input and error-message styles
- Header size and color

These styles can be referred to as our *theme*, and to keep them consistent across our page, we generally want to write them once and apply them everywhere. Let's start with our fonts.

8.2.1 Typography

Currently, our `font-family` is our browser's default. For this project, we're going to import Raleway from Google Fonts and apply it to the body. We'll import both regular and bold, as we'll need both throughout this project. We'll also set a default text color of `#171717`, which looks almost black, for our text. We aren't using black with this design because it's a soft design, and pure black can be quite harsh.

Next, we're going to handle our numbers. A font family by default has either old-style or modern numbers. The difference is how the numbers are aligned compared with the meanline and baseline, as shown in figure 8.3.

Figure 8.3 Old-style versus modern figures

Numbers in old style have portions that peek above and below the baseline; modern ones don't. Because we're creating a shopping cart, and we want to stack numbers to show them being added to create a total, we want to use modern figures so that they line up nicely. However, Raleway (the font family we've chosen for the page) uses old-style figures by default. To make our typeface use modern figures, we can use the font-variant-numeric property, which lets us set how we want our numbers to display. This lesser-known property is handy for handling numbers because it allows us to control multiple facets of their display, including

- Whether zeros are displayed with a slash in them
- How the numbers are aligned
- How fractions are displayed

We're going to use a font-variant-numeric: lining-nums property that will change our numbers from old-style to modern. Figure 8.4 shows the summary section before and after we apply font-variant-numeric to our body rule. In the before version, the numerals are different sizes; in the after version, they're aligned and uniformly sized.

Before (old-style figures)   After (modern figures)

Figure 8.4 Before and after applying the font-variant-numeric **property**

Last, we'll change the color of our headers to teal. After that change, we'll have set the base typography for our page. We applied it directly in the <body> element so that other child elements within our page will inherit the values. Listing 8.2 shows the rules we've constructed up to this point.

Listing 8.2   Typography-related styles applied to the <body> element

```
@import url('https://fonts.googleapis.com/css2?
  family=Raleway:wght@400;700&display=swap');

body {
  font-family: 'Raleway', sans-serif;
  color: #171717;
  font-variant-numeric: lining-nums;
}

h1, h2 {
  color: #2c6c69;
}
```

Figure 8.5 shows our updated output.

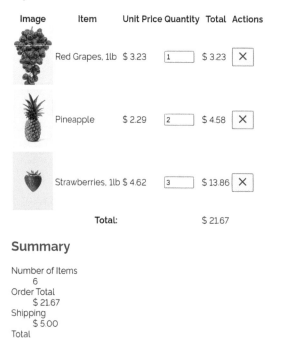

Figure 8.5   Applied typography

Let's turn our attention to links and buttons.

8.2.2   *Links and buttons*

Our page has several links and buttons, but stylistically, all these elements look like buttons. They can be categorized by purpose:

- *Primary call to action*—Proceed to Checkout link
- *Secondary call to action*—Continue Shopping link
- *Destructive*—Button with an *X* to remove items from the cart

We're going to use these categories to name our classes so that our rules will be easy to reuse.

In this chapter, we're dealing with a single page, but this situation is an anomaly. In a full application, we have multiple pages or components that will reuse the same styles, so instead of naming a class something like `proceed-to-checkout`, we're going to use `primary` so that the class can easily be reused in a different context.

Links versus buttons

We have both links and buttons in our project. The decision to use one or the other isn't a matter of preference; it's based on the intended functionality or purpose. For navigating, we should use a link. For performing an action, such as removing an item from our cart, we should use a button. We can style these elements however we please, but the underlying element should match the intended use case.

The reason for the distinction is that links and buttons have information and behaviors tied to them automatically by the browser. These behaviors include their capability to focus and, more important, their roles. The role of the element is used by assistive technologies to help users interact with the page.

A specific example of a difference in the behavior of a link and a button is the user's ability to right-click it to open the link in a new tab or window. If the link is created with a button and JavaScript, this functionality isn't available to the user.

Before we address the differences among button types, let's consider the similarities and write a baseline for all of our links that look like buttons (which were given a class of `button`) and for buttons. After we've written a baseline, we'll make rules for each of the button types.

To create our baseline, we'll start by removing the default gray background set by the browser, which we'll do by using `background: none`. We'll also update the padding, `border`, and `border-radius` values.

Finally, because we're applying this rule to the links and buttons and because links are underlined by default, we're going to remove the underline from the links by setting the `text-decoration` property to none. The following listing shows our base rule for our buttons and links with a class of `button`.

Listing 8.3 Base styles for buttons

```
button, .button {              ◁──┐   This rule will be applied
  background: none;                  to all button elements
  border-radius: 4px;                and to all elements
  padding: 10px;                     with a class of button.
  border: solid 1px #ddd;
  text-decoration: none;
}
```

With the default state of the buttons taken care of, we'll add style changes to apply when a user hovers over a button with their mouse or focuses on it via their keyboard. To achieve this goal, we'll use the `:hover` and `:focus` pseudo-classes.

NOTE A pseudo-class is added to a selector to target a specific state. Adding style changes on `hover` and `focus` is important for accessibility, as it provides visual feedback, letting the user know that they can interact with the item. For keyboard navigation, style changes on `focus` let the user know which element they're about to interact with. Without these visual cues, it's difficult to know what we can click and where we're focused (http://mng.bz/zmdA).

On hover, we're going to add a dotted teal outline around our buttons, and to give the outline some breathing room, we're going to offset it by 2 pixels. We'll use two properties: outline and outline-offset. outline works similarly to border, taking the same three properties, which are style, width, and color. outline-offset takes a length value (which can be negative) that dictates the amount of space we want between the outline and the edge of the element.

For focus, we have the same styles as those for hover, but instead of having a dotted-line outline, we'll make the line solid. The following listing shows our final CSS for the hover and focus states.

Listing 8.4   Button hover and focus states

```
button:hover,
.button:hover {
  outline: dotted 1px #2c6c69;
  outline-offset: 2px;
}

button:focus,
.button:focus {
  outline: solid 1px #2c6c69;
  outline-offset: 2px;
}
```

Figure 8.6 shows the styled links and buttons for the hover and focus states.

Now that we have a baseline, we can start focusing on each individual use case. We'll start with our calls to action (the Proceed to Checkout and Continue Shopping links). Because we already have a baseline set, all we need to do is edit the colors for these use cases, as shown in listing 8.5. We differentiate between the two actions based on which we prefer (or expect) the user to select to highlight the primary choice. Being consistent about styling action types throughout the application helps us guide our users through the choices they'll have to make.

Listing 8.5   Call-to-action styles

```
button.primary,
.button.primary {
  border-color: #2c6c69;          Applies to
  background: #2c6c69;            the Proceed to
  color: #ffffff;                Checkout link
}

button.secondary,
.button.secondary {
  border-color: #2c6c69;          Applies to
  color: #2c6c69;                the Continue
}                                Shopping link
```

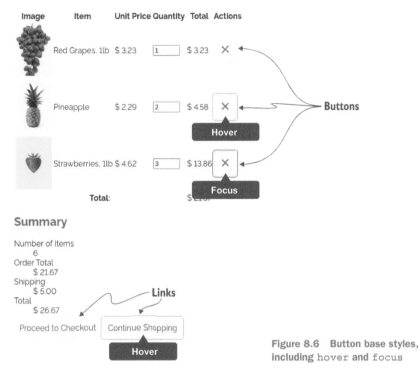

Figure 8.6 **Button base styles,** including `hover` and `focus`

Left to style is the Remove button in the table for the items in the cart. This button has been given a class of `destructive`. As for the previous two button types, we'll want to change the border, text, and outline colors, this time to red instead of teal to emphasize that this action is destructive. We make the button look circular by giving it a `border-radius` of `50%`. We also decrease the `padding` value; otherwise, the Remove button becomes the most prominent element in our table, which is undesirable. Finally, we center the image in the middle of the button via the `vertical-align` property. This property, which can be applied to both inline- and inline-block-level elements, dictates how the element is aligned vertically based on the inline and inline-block elements around it. We want to center the image vertically inside the button, so we'll use a property value of `middle`.

Listing 8.6 shows the CSS for the Remove button. Figure 8.7 shows the output for each state.

Listing 8.6 Remove button

```
button.destructive {
  border-color: #9d1616;
```

```
  color: #9d1616;
  border-radius: 50%;
  padding: 5px;
}

button.destructive img {          | Centers the
  vertical-align: middle;         | image inside
}                                 | the button

button.destructive:hover,
button.destructive:focus {
  outline-color: #9d1616;
}
```

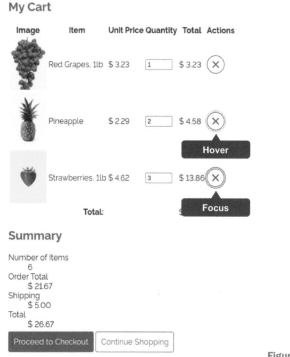

Figure 8.7   Link and button styles

8.2.3   *Input fields*

We're going to do some minimal styling of the input fields. We won't handle styles for invalid inputs or error messages here because the focus of this chapter is creating a responsive layout that contains a table. For a detailed look at styling forms, see chapter 10.

For this layout, we're going to give our input fields the same base styles we gave the buttons and links. Instead of writing a new rule, however, we'll add the `input` selector to the existing ruleset, as shown in the following listing.

Listing 8.7 Adding `input` to base button styles

```
button,
.button,
input {
  background: none;
  border-radius: 4px;
  padding: 10px;
  border: solid 1px #ddd;
  text-decoration: none;
}
```

Figure 8.8 shows the styled input fields.

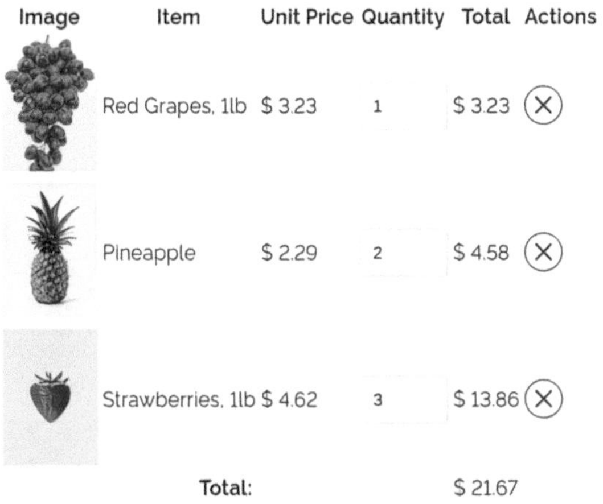

Image	Item	Unit Price	Quantity	Total	Actions
	Red Grapes, 1lb	$ 3.23	1	$ 3.23	⊗
	Pineapple	$ 2.29	2	$ 4.58	⊗
	Strawberries, 1lb	$ 4.62	3	$ 13.86	⊗
	Total:			$ 21.67	

Figure 8.8 Formatted fields

8.2.4 Table

Next, we're going to style the table. We're going to concern ourselves only with styles that relate to the theme, such as colors and borders. We'll handle layout and responsiveness in sections 8.3 through 8.5.

Our table is divided into three sections, which we'll address in order:

- *Header*—`<thead>`
- *Body*—`<tbody>`
- *Footer*—`<tfoot>`

STYLING THE TABLE HEADERS

We're going to start by styling our table headers. Because the headers aren't as important as the content of the table itself, we'll give them a slightly smaller font size and lighter color than the rest of the text. We'll also decrease their default font-weight of bold to normal. By subduing the headers a bit, we're creating a visual hierarchy in the table and emphasizing what the user cares most about (the items in their shopping cart). The rule is shown in the following listing.

Listing 8.8   Styling the cells' contents

```
th {
  color: #3a3a3a;
  font-weight: normal;
  font-size: .875em;
}
```

At this point, our table headers look like figure 8.9.

Figure 8.9   Styled header cells

BOLDFACING ITEMS IN THE SECOND CELL

In the table body (`<tbody>`), we're going to emphasize the item name (in the second column) by making the text bold. To add the `font-weight` property with a value of bold to the item, we're going to use the pseudo class `:nth-of-type()`, which allows us to select an element based on its position among its siblings of the same tag. To target the second cell—the second `<td>` element—of each row in the table's body, we use `tbody td:nth-of-type(2)`. Listing 8.9 shows our rule.

Listing 8.9   Boldfacing the second cell of each row in the table's body

```
tbody td:nth-of-type(2) {
  font-weight: bold;
}
```

Figure 8.10 shows our updated table with the item names in bold.

STRIPING THE ROWS

Next, we'll stripe the table rows. We'll use `:nth-of-type()` again, but instead of passing in a number, we'll use the keyword even. The rule in the following listing selects the even-numbered rows in the table body (`<tbody>`), to which we give a light-teal background color.

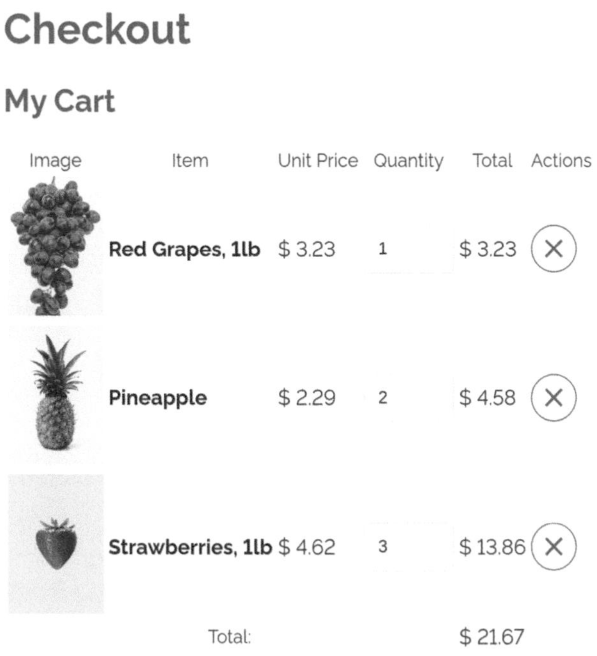

Checkout

My Cart

Image	Item	Unit Price	Quantity	Total	Actions
	Red Grapes, 1lb	$ 3.23	1	$ 3.23	⊗
	Pineapple	$ 2.29	2	$ 4.58	⊗
	Strawberries, 1lb	$ 4.62	3	$ 13.86	⊗
	Total:			$ 21.67	

Figure 8.10   Item name in bold

Listing 8.10   Striping the table body's rows

```
tbody tr:nth-of-type(even) {
  background: #f2fcfc;
}
```

Figure 8.11 shows our updated rows.

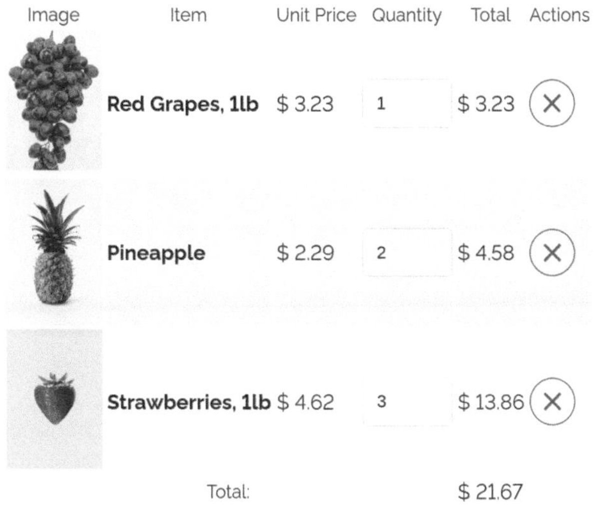

Image	Item	Unit Price	Quantity	Total	Actions
	Red Grapes, 1lb	$ 3.23	1	$ 3.23	⊗
	Pineapple	$ 2.29	2	$ 4.58	⊗
	Strawberries, 1lb	$ 4.62	3	$ 13.86	⊗
	Total:			$ 21.67	

Figure 8.11   Striped rows

We want to bold the grand total, which appears in the table's footer cell. Because we already have a rule that boldfaces text—the one we created to boldface item names—we can add the `tfoot td` selector to that existing rule, as shown in the following listing.

Listing 8.11   Boldfacing the footer

```
tbody td:nth-of-type(2),
tfoot td {
  font-weight: bold;
}
```

Our updated footer looks like figure 8.12.

Figure 8.12   Grand total in bold

HANDLING BORDERS

We'll add a top border to all the rows, regardless of where they are in the table. We also want to remove the protruding white lines that appear between cells. If we darken the background color of the row, it becomes particularly visible (figure 8.13).

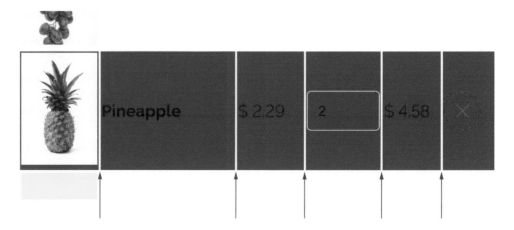

Figure 8.13   White lines between cells

Let's start by removing the gaps between our cells. But first, why are these white lines present? If we decided to give each cell in our table a border, our table would look like figure 8.14.

Image	Item	Unit Price	Quantity	Total	Actions
	Red Grapes, 1lb	$ 3.23	1	$ 3.23	⊗
	Pineapple	$ 2.29	2	$ 4.58	⊗
	Strawberries, 1lb	$ 4.62	3	$ 13.86	⊗
Total:				$ 21.67	

Figure 8.14   Borders on individual cells

Notice that each cell has a square around it. The gap we see in our row is the gap between the individual cells. If we collapse the borders so that only one line appears between the cells, the gap disappears (figure 8.15).

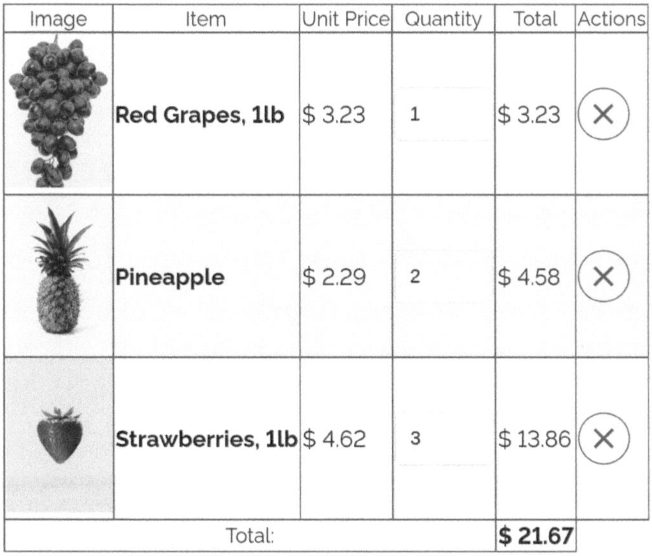

Image	Item	Unit Price	Quantity	Total	Actions
	Red Grapes, 1lb	$ 3.23	1	$ 3.23	⊗
	Pineapple	$ 2.29	2	$ 4.58	⊗
	Strawberries, 1lb	$ 4.62	3	$ 13.86	⊗
Total:				$ 21.67	

Figure 8.15   Table with collapsed borders

The CSS property we use to remove the gap and combine the borders is `border-collapse` with a value of `collapse`. With this property added, we can also give our rows a border. Before we collapsed the borders, only the individual cells could take a border. In our project, therefore, we collapse the borders on the table and apply a border to the top of each row, as shown in the following listing.

Listing 8.12   Handling the table's borders

```
table { border-collapse: collapse; }
tr { border-top: solid 1px #aeb7b7; }
```

Figure 8.16 shows our updated table.

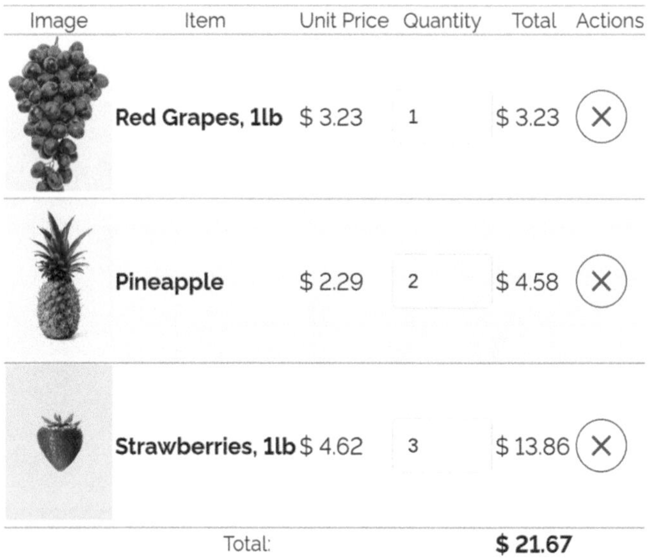

Image	Item	Unit Price	Quantity	Total	Actions
	Red Grapes, 1lb	$ 3.23	1	$ 3.23	✕
	Pineapple	$ 2.29	2	$ 4.58	✕
	Strawberries, 1lb	$ 4.62	3	$ 13.86	✕
	Total:			**$ 21.67**	

Figure 8.16   Styled table borders

Next, let's move on to the description list inside the summary section of the project.

8.2.5   Description list

Still to be themed is the description list (<dl>) in the summary section. Commonly used for creating glossaries or displaying metadata, a description list is perfect for our summary, which contains items and their values. We're going to style the description term (<dt>) the same way we did our table headers. We want to deemphasize them from the descriptions themselves (<dd>), which contains the dollar value of each element. Because we want to style them the same way as the table headers, we'll add dt as a selector to the existing rule, similar to what we did to add input to the button rule in section 8.2.3.

   After that, we'll add two colons after each <dt> by using the pseudo-element ::after with a property of content to insert the character. The CSS and output are shown in listing 8.13 and figure 8.17.

Listing 8.13   Styling the description list

```
th, dt {
  color: #3a3a3a;
  font-weight: normal;
  font-size: .875em;
}
```

◁—┐ Adds a description
│ term to our existing
│ header styles

```
dt::after {
  content: ": ";
}
```

Adds a colon after
each description
term

Summary

Number of Items:
      6
Order Total:
      $ 21.67
Shipping:
      $ 5.00
Total:
      $ 26.67

[Proceed to Checkout]   [Continue Shopping]

Figure 8.17   Description list theme

8.2.6   Cards

To give the layout some depth and achieve separation between sections, we're going to style our sections' containers as cards. *Cards* are a design pattern commonly used to separate content by encapsulating it in a box or container reminiscent of a playing card. This concept is the same as the one we used to create a profile card in chapter 6.

To pull off our card design, we'll add a pale teal background to the <body> and outline the sections with a shadow that looks like it's hovering slightly above the <body>. To create the shadow, we'll use the box-shadow property, which allows us to control the amount of shadow to add on the x- and y-axes, as well as the amount of blur (fuzziness), the distance it should spread, and the color the shadow should be. Figure 8.18 details how the property values are applied.

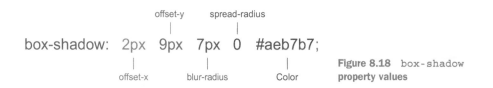

```
                 offset-y   spread-radius
                    |            |
box-shadow:  2px  9px  7px  0  #aeb7b7;
                |         |         |
             offset-x  blur-radius  Color
```

Figure 8.18 box-shadow
property values

Optionally, we can also set a value of inset to indicate that the shadow should be turned inward within the element rather than around the outside. To finish the appearance of our card, we'll curve the corners with a border-radius value of

4px—the same value we used for our links, buttons, and inputs. The following listing shows our section rule.

Listing 8.14   Styling the sections

```
body {
  font-family: 'Raleway', sans-serif;
  color: #171717;
  font-variant-numeric: lining-nums;
  background: #fbffff;                        ◁——┤ Adds a background
}                                                  color to the page

section {
  background: #ffffff;                            ┐ Makes our
  border-radius: 4px;                             ├ sections look
  box-shadow: 2px 2px 7px #aeb7b7;                ┘ like cards
}
```

Figure 8.19 shows our styled sections. Notice, however, that at the bottom of the summary card, the links extend out beyond the card. This effect happens because links have a `display` value of `inline` by default.

Figure 8.19   Themed sections with overflowing links

When vertical padding is added to an inline element—the links, in this case—the height of the element doesn't increase inside the flow of the page. Thus, it takes up only as much room as its content (the text), which is why it isn't increasing the height of the card. To fix this problem, we'll change their `display` value from `inline` to `inline-block`. The following listing shows the updated rule.

Listing 8.15   Section styles

```
button, .button, input {
  background: none;
  border-radius: 4px;
  padding: 10px;
```

```
    border: solid 1px #ddd;
    text-decoration: none;
    display: inline-block;
}
```

With the fix in place, our layout looks like figure 8.20.

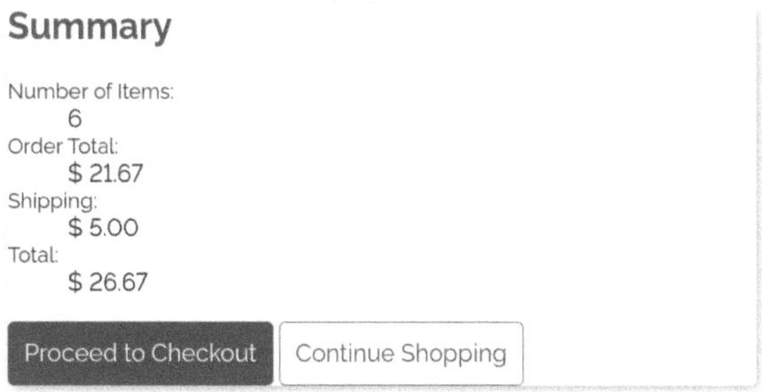

Summary

Number of Items:
6
Order Total:
$ 21.67
Shipping:
$ 5.00
Total:
$ 26.67

Proceed to Checkout   Continue Shopping

Figure 8.20   Styled cards

With our theme taken care of, we can start focusing on the layout.

8.3   *Mobile layout*

We'll start with the mobile layout. The first thing we're going to do is make our table responsive.

8.3.1   *Table mobile view*

A traditional table layout doesn't work well on mobile devices because tables need a lot of width, which phone screens don't offer. To accommodate mobile phones, we'll make the table rows and cells act more like cards on narrow screens.

USING A MEDIA QUERY

We'll start by using a media query to apply a set of rules to the table when the viewport is less than or equal to `549px`. The query will be `@media(max-width: 549px) { }`. Notice that we use `max-width` here. In previous chapters, we used `min-width` because we wanted the styles to be applied only when the screen reached a certain size. In this case, we're doing the opposite: we want the styles to be applied *until* the screen reaches a certain width.

Inside this media query, we'll define what we want the table to look like on narrow screens. Figure 8.21 shows what our table currently looks like and what we're trying to achieve.

To view the narrow-screen or mobile version, most browsers' developer tools allow us to make the browser simulate the screen of a particular device. In Google Chrome, to select a particular device, we toggle the device toolbar by clicking the icon with the phone on it at the top of the DevTools bar and then choosing the device we want to use, as shown in figure 8.22. It's worth noting, however, that this simulation is limited and shouldn't replace testing on the physical device itself.

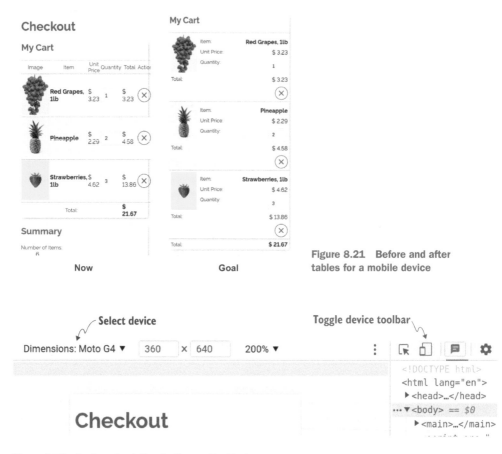

Figure 8.21 Before and after tables for a mobile device

Figure 8.22 Device simulation in Chrome DevTools

CHANGING THE TABLE'S DISPLAY STRUCTURE

First, we'll stack everything vertically rather than have the elements of each row represented horizontally. We accomplish this task by giving our rows and cells a display value of block. By default, table cells have a display value of table-cell, whereas rows have a display value of table-row.

Next, we float the image to the left (chapter 7) so that the rest of the contents of the row wrap around it. We also include some margin around the image to create some whitespace between the image and the rest of the row content. The following listing shows the start of our media query and our updated cell styles.

Listing 8.16 Mobile cell and row layout

```
@media(max-width: 549px) {
  td, tr { display: block; }
  table td > img {
    float: left;
```
Specifically targets images that are immediate children of the cell to avoid floating the image in the button (the red X)

```
        margin-right: 10px;
    }
}
```

We're getting closer to our goal, but our header information isn't where we need it to be. As we see in figure 8.23, header information is at the top of the table rather than before each piece of information in the table-body rows.

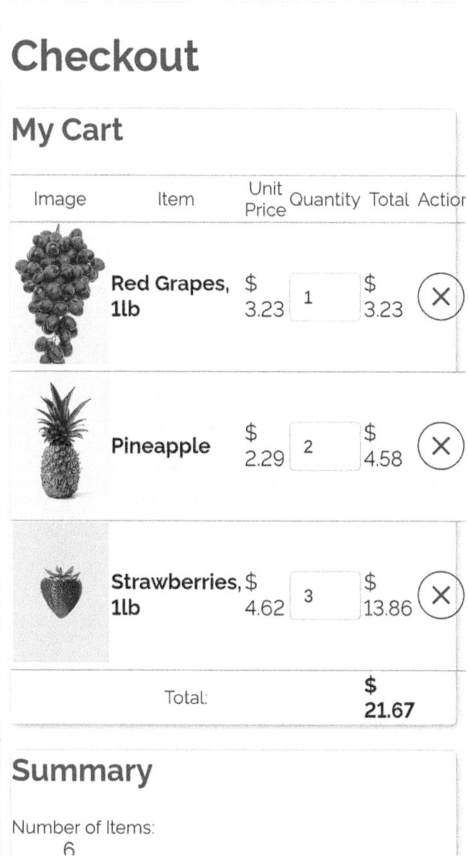

Checkout

My Cart

Image	Item	Unit Price	Quantity	Total	Action
	Red Grapes, 1lb	$ 3.23	1	$ 3.23	⊗
	Pineapple	$ 2.29	2	$ 4.58	⊗
	Strawberries, 1lb	$ 4.62	3	$ 13.86	⊗
	Total:			$ 21.67	

Summary

Number of Items:
6

Figure 8.23   The table header is at the top of the mobile table.

DISPLAYING CONTENT FROM A DATA ATTRIBUTE

To place the header information before each piece of content, we aren't going to use the header. Instead, we'll add some data attributes to the cells in our HTML: `<td data-name="Item">Red Grapes, 1lb</td>`. This data will drive labeling each row rather than the header contents in the table head.

We move the table header offscreen by using absolute positioning, as shown in listing 8.17. We don't want to use `display:none`, as the information available in the header is still needed by assistive technologies. By absolutely positioning it offscreen (using a large negative value), we hide it visually but not programmatically.

Listing 8.17   Hiding the table headers

```
@media(max-width: 549px) {
  ...
  thead {
    position: absolute;
    left: -9999rem;
  }
}
```

With our table head out of the way (figure 8.24), we can focus on extracting the data from the data-name attribute and displaying it to the user. We notice that our content shifted a bit after we removed the header because our table currently isn't taking up the full width of the screen. We'll remedy that problem later in this section. For now, let's finish handling our header information.

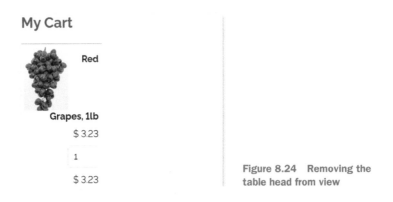

Figure 8.24   Removing the table head from view

To display the attribute value, we use the attr() function, which takes an attribute name and returns a value. For our use case, our content property will be td[data-name]: before { content: attr(data-name) ":"; }. Figure 8.25 breaks it down in detail.

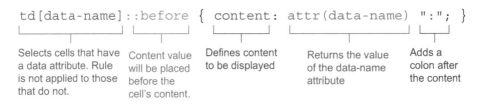

Figure 8.25   Adding the header information before the cell

To align our labels and content, we use a combination of text-align and float. We use text-align: right in the cell to right-justify the cell contents—the item name, unit price, input field, total, and button—and then float the label (the content we get from the `data-name` attribute) to the left to create a gap between the two elements, as shown in figure 8.26. We also give the cell some padding for added whitespace between the lines of content. Listing 8.18 shows the CSS used to align the contents of the table cells.

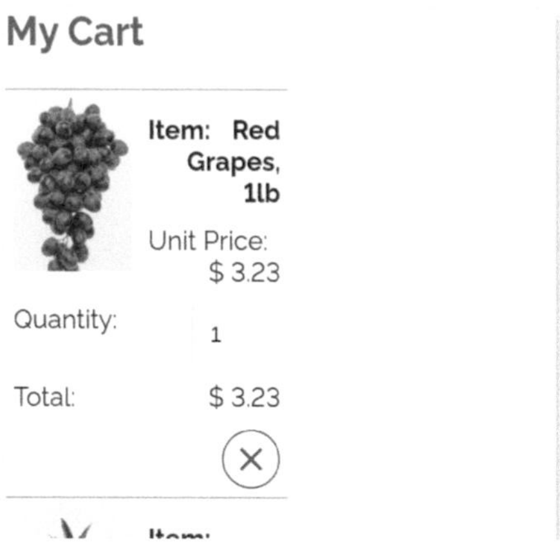

Figure 8.26   Aligning the labels and the content

Listing 8.18   Displaying the contents of the `data-name` attribute

```
@media(max-width: 549px) {
  ...
  td {
    text-align: right;
    padding: 5px;
  }
  td[data-name]::before {
    content: attr(data-name) ":";
    float: left;
  }
}
```

Now that the data in the `data-name` attribute is being displayed, let's style it to match the definition titles. Rather than copy the styles, we can append the selector to the existing rule as shown in the following listing.

Listing 8.19   Finishing touches

```
@media(max-width: 549px) {
  ...
  th, dt, td[data-name]::before {
    color: #3a3a3a;
    font-weight: normal;
    font-size: .875em;
  }
}
```

FULL WIDTH

With the labels styled, let's turn our attention back to the fact that our table isn't taking up the full width that's available to it. We can fix this problem by giving it a width of 100% by using the rule `table { width: 100%; }`. Because we'll want the table to take up the full width available to it regardless of screen size, we add this rule *outside* the media query.

We're almost done with the mobile styles of the table (figure 8.27). The only thing left to do is handle the table foot.

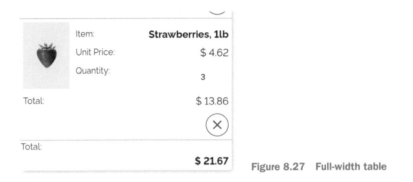

Figure 8.27   Full-width table

TABLE FOOTER

In the table footer (`<tfoot>`), we want to align the text on a single line. For this task, we'll use Flexbox with a `justify-content` property value of `space-between` and an `align-items` value of `baseline` to align the label and total at opposite ends of the row on the same line. (To see how the CSS Flexbox Layout Module works, check out chapter 6.)

Looking at our table-footer HTML (listing 8.20), we notice that our first cell is a table header (`<th>`), not a table data cell (`<td>`), which makes sense because it describes the contents of that row.

Listing 8.20   Table-footer HTML

```
@media(max-width: 549px) {
  <tfoot>
    <tr>
      <th colspan="4" scope="row">Total:</th>
      <td id="total">
        <!-- value calculated & inserted by JS -->
      </td>
    </tr>
  </tfoot>
}
```

If we look closely at figure 8.27, we notice that the footer content doesn't have any padding; it goes right up against the edge of the card and row border. Earlier, we added padding to all the table data cells, not the headers, so now we'll add padding to the footer. The following listing shows a recap of the styles we edited and created to create our mobile table layout along with our changes for the table footer.

Listing 8.21 Mobile table CSS

```
th, td, td[data-name]::before {
  color: #3a3a3a;
  font-weight: normal;
  font-size: .875em;
}
@media(max-width: 549px) {
  td, tr { display: block }
  table td > img {
    float: left;
    margin-right: 10px;
  }
  thead {
    position: absolute;
    left: -9999rem;
  }
  td {
    text-align: right;
    padding: 5px;
    vertical-align: baseline;
  }
  td[data-name]::before {
    content: attr(data-name) ":";
    float: left;
  }

  tfoot tr {
    display: flex;
    justify-content: space-between;
    align-items: baseline;
  }
  tfoot th { padding: 5px }
}
  table { width: 100% }
```

Figure 8.28 shows the finished table.

Now that the table looks good on mobile devices, we'll turn our attention to the description list and the overall layout. Unlike the rules that created styles specific to small screens, this next set of rules will apply regardless of the width of the screen, so they won't be inside a media query. We'll start by addressing the description list (`<dl>`).

8.3.2 *Description list*

Unlike the table, which looks completely different on mobile and desktop screens, the description list will look the same regardless of screen width. Its position will change on wider screens, but the list itself will not. Because the description list is the same regardless of screen size, we won't put the layout styles inside a media query.

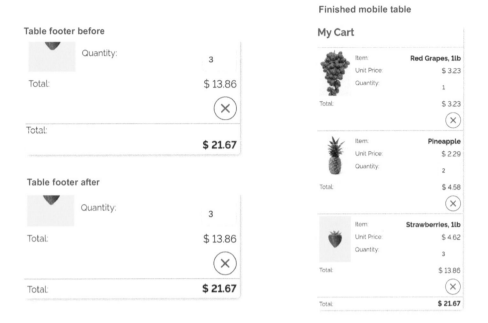

Figure 8.28   Table displayed as cards for narrow screens

To display the description list, we'll use `grid` (chapter 2). We'll define two columns and let items autoposition themselves within the two columns. When not given specific placement instructions, child elements of a grid container place themselves in the first available space, which is exactly the behavior we're going to exploit. We'll also define a gap and add some padding to the container to space the elements within the grid and card. Finally, we'll left-justify numbers. Listing 8.22 shows the CSS, and figure 8.29 shows the before and after versions of the description list.

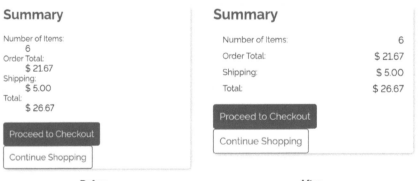

Figure 8.29   Before and after layouts for the description list

Listing 8.22 Description list styles

```
dl {
  display: grid;
  gap: .5rem;
  grid-template-columns: auto max-content;   ⊲──┐
  padding: 0 1rem;
}
dd { text-align: right; }
```

> We use max-content for our second column because we don't want the numbers to wrap, which would make them difficult to read.

8.3.3 Call-to-action links

Our description list looks a lot better, but the call-to-action links still need some help. As we did for the description list in section 8.3.2, we want our call-to-action links to be laid out the same regardless of screen size, so styles will go outside our media query.

First, we'll give the links' containers some padding and use the text-align property to center them. When there isn't enough room for links to be side by side and they end up stacked, we'll give them some margin to prevent them from running right up against one another. Listing 8.23 displays the code. Figure 8.30 shows before and after versions of the output.

Listing 8.23 Action links

```
.actions {
  padding: 1rem;
  text-align: center;
}
.actions a {
  margin: 0 .25rem .5rem;
}
```

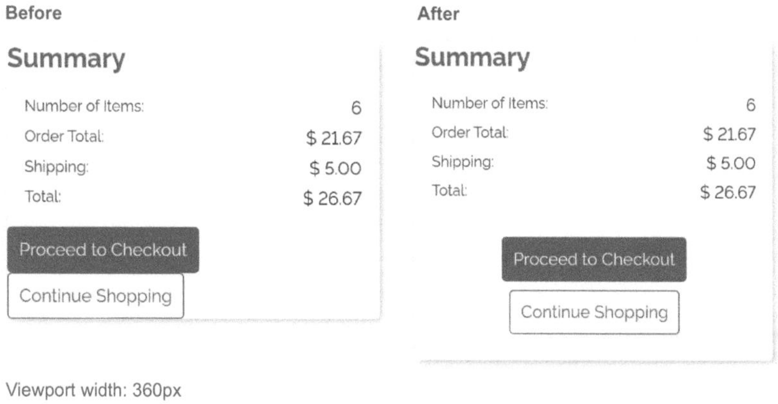

Before

Summary

Number of Items:	6
Order Total:	$ 21.67
Shipping:	$ 5.00
Total:	$ 26.67

Proceed to Checkout

Continue Shopping

After

Summary

Number of Items:	6
Order Total:	$ 21.67
Shipping:	$ 5.00
Total:	$ 26.67

Proceed to Checkout

Continue Shopping

Viewport width: 360px

Figure 8.30 Before and after layout of call-to-action links

8.3.4 *Padding, margin, and margin collapse*

All the content within our sections except the headers is laid out for mobile devices. The browser gives headers a margin by default, but that setting isn't accomplishing what we want it to; instead of creating vertical space between the edge of the card and the header, it's pushing the card down. A margin pushes content but doesn't affect how much room an element or its content occupies, which is why the top margin (header) is bleeding out of the card.

If we remove the header's margin and give it padding instead, the card will expand, but the gap between the two cards will disappear. Therefore, we need to give the section itself some margin to add space between the two cards. If we give the sections a margin with a value of 1rem 0 (1-rem top and bottom, but not left and right), we'll still have a 1-rem gap between the two cards—a direct result of margin collapse. Unless the positioning of the elements has been altered via float or flex, two margins that run up against each other will collapse to equal the greater of the two margins. Figure 8.31 diagrams this effect.

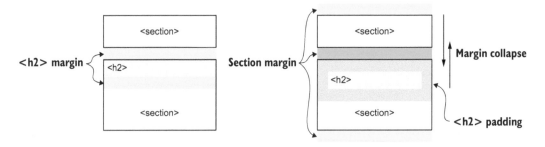

Figure 8.31 **Effects of margins and margin collapse**

To add space between the edges of the card and the header, we'll replace the card header's margin with padding. Then we'll add section margins to the card to regain the lost vertical space. Finally, we'll add padding to the body so that the cards aren't stuck against the left and right edges of the screen. The following listing shows how.

Listing 8.24 **Section margin and header padding**

```
body {
  font-family: 'Raleway', sans-serif;
  color: #171717;
  font-variant-numeric: lining-nums;
  background: #fbffff;
  padding: 1rem;
}

section { margin: 1rem 0 }
```

```
section h2 {
  padding: 1rem;
  margin: 0;
}
```

With the mobile layout finished (figure 8.32), let's increase the width of the screen for tablets and laptops.

Section header changes

Before

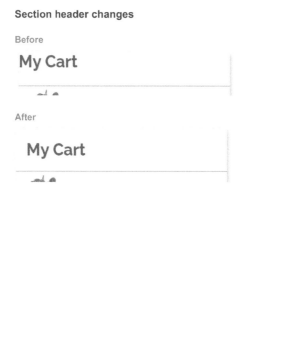

After

Figure 8.32   Before and after card headers

Mobile layout

8.4   *Medium screen layout*

Most of what we did for mobile devices will look great on medium-size screens. Because we used a media query to restrict table-layout changes to screens less than or equal to 549 pixels wide, the styles we wrote to edit the table won't apply to any screen that's 550 pixels wide or wider. Figure 8.33 shows the table when the viewport is 549 pixels wide and when it's 550 pixels wide. At 550 pixels of width, we're back to a standard table layout.

8.4.1   *Right-justified numbers*

Next, we're going to update the alignments of the values in the table. Because it makes computation at a glance easier, it's customary to right-justify numbers, especially if

Checkout

My Cart

	Item	Red Grapes, 1lb
	Unit Price:	$ 3.23
	Quantity:	1
Total:		$ 3.23
		⊗

	Item	Pineapple
	Unit Price:	$ 2.29
	Quantity:	2
Total:		$ 4.58
		⊗

	Item	Strawberries, 1lb
	Unit Price:	$ 4.62
	Quantity:	3
Total:		$ 13.86
		⊗

| Total: | | **$ 21.67** |

Summary

Number of Items:	6
Order Total:	$ 21.67
Shipping:	$ 5.00
Total:	$ 26.67

Proceed to Checkout   Continue Shopping

Checkout

My Cart

Image	Item	Unit Price	Quantity	Total	Actions
	Red Grapes, 1lb	$ 3.23	1	$ 3.23	⊗
	Pineapple	$ 2.29	2	$ 4.58	⊗
	Strawberries, 1lb	$ 4.62	3	$ 13.86	⊗
	Total			**$ 21.67**	

Summary

Number of Items:	6
Order Total:	$ 21.67
Shipping:	$ 5.00
Total:	$ 26.67

Proceed to Checkout   Continue Shopping

| Viewport width: | **549px** | **550px** |

Figure 8.33   Break point for table

they're being totaled in a column. We'll update both the header and the cells of the unit price, quantity, and total to be right-justified.

To select the headers and cells, we could use the :nth-of-type(n) selector. To select the header and cells of the Unit Price column (third column), we'd use th:nth-of-type(3), td:nth-of-type(3) { … } and repeat the same process for all the other columns (Quantity, Total, and Actions).

We could also think about the process a little differently. We want to right-align all columns after the first two. Inside :nth-of-type(), we can pass not only numbers, but also patterns. In section 8.2.4, we used this trick when we set our background colors on our rows by passing a parameter of even. In this case, we're going to pass a custom pattern, using the parameter n+3. This pattern indicates that we want to select all matching elements starting with the third instance where n is the iterator and 3 is the starting point. Figure 8.34 illustrates the pattern.

:nth-of-type(n+3)

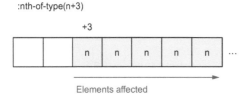

Figure 8.34   nth-of-type(n+3) explained

Using this technique, we can select the third, fourth, fifth, and sixth cells for each row and right-align their contents, as shown in listing 8.25. Notice that we put our rule inside a media query with a `min-width` of `550px`. We don't want to apply these changes to smaller screens (defined by our previous media query as any screen smaller than or equal to 549 pixels), so we use a second media query to apply these styles only to screens that are 550 pixels wide or wider.

Listing 8.25 Right-aligning contents

```
@media (min-width: 550px) {
  th:nth-of-type(n+3),
  td:nth-of-type(n+3) {
    text-align: right;
  }
}
```

After our styles are applied (figure 8.35), we notice a few things:

- Our first two columns need their titles to be left-justified to match their content.
- The numbers inside the fields didn't right-justify themselves.
- The Remove button is up against the edge of the card.

Let's address these problems in order.

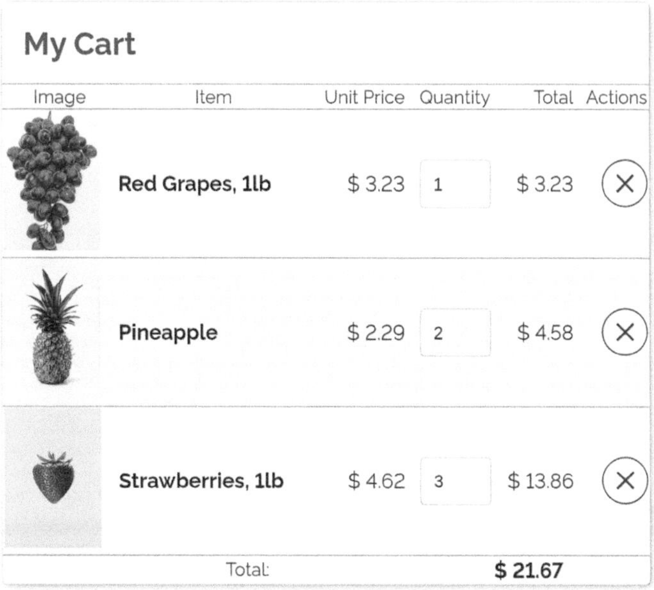

Image	Item	Unit Price	Quantity	Total	Actions
	Red Grapes, 1lb	$ 3.23	1	$ 3.23	⊗
	Pineapple	$ 2.29	2	$ 4.58	⊗
	Strawberries, 1lb	$ 4.62	3	$ 13.86	⊗
	Total:			$ 21.67	

Figure 8.35 Right-aligned number and action columns

8.4.2   *Left-justifying the first two columns*

We'll use specificity to our advantage to handle the headers. Because, as a selector, `th` is less specific than `th:nth-of-type(n+3)`, we can make a `th` rule that aligns the text to the left and keeps our previous rule for the other columns. The `th` rule will left-justify the header content for all columns. Then we'll override the `text-align` property value for our number and button columns in our `th:nth-of-type(n+3)` rule. The following listing shows the changes.

Listing 8.26   Updating the table header rules

```
@media (min-width: 550px) {

  th { text-align: left }

  th:nth-of-type(n+3),
  td:nth-of-type(n+3) {
    text-align: right;
  }
}
```

Now our first two table headers are left-justified instead of centered (the browser's default setting), and our other columns kept their right justification (figure 8.36).

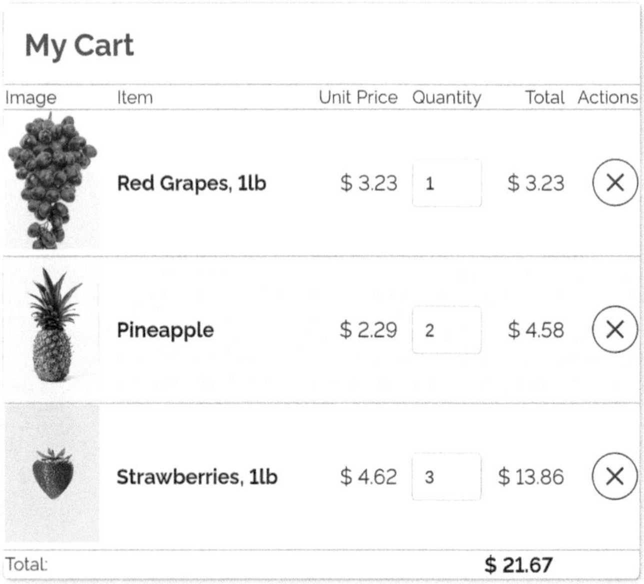

Figure 8.36   Styled headers

8.4.3   Right-justifying numbers in the input fields

We can choose to right-justify the text inside the input field only in this table view or all the time regardless of screen size, and we do that outside the media queries. Because we right-aligned our numbers and totals in the mobile view as well, it seems logical to update the input-field style for all display sizes and include the update in our theme.

  To select inputs of a type number, we can use an attribute selector: `input[type= "number"] { … }`. We'll add `input[type="number"] { text-align: right }` to our stylesheet *outside* our media queries, as we want to apply it regardless of screen size.

  With the text inside the input fields aligned (figure 8.37), the last piece we need to address is padding in all our table data cells and table headers.

Figure 8.37   Right-aligned text in input field

8.4.4   Cell padding and margin

To complete our table (medium-size screen) view, we'll add padding and margin to our cells in the table header, body, and footer. To achieve this effect, we add `td`, `th` `{ padding: 10px }` to our medium-size screen (`min-width: 550px`) media query. The following listing shows the full set of changes we make to achieve the table layout.

Listing 8.27   Medium-size screens

```
input[type="number"] { text-align: right }

@media (min-width: 550px) {

  th { text-align: left }

  th:nth-of-type(n+3),
  td:nth-of-type(n+3) {
    text-align: right;
  }

  td, th { padding: 10px }
}
```

Now that we have both small and medium-size screens styled (figure 8.38), let's go a bit further and handle wide screens.

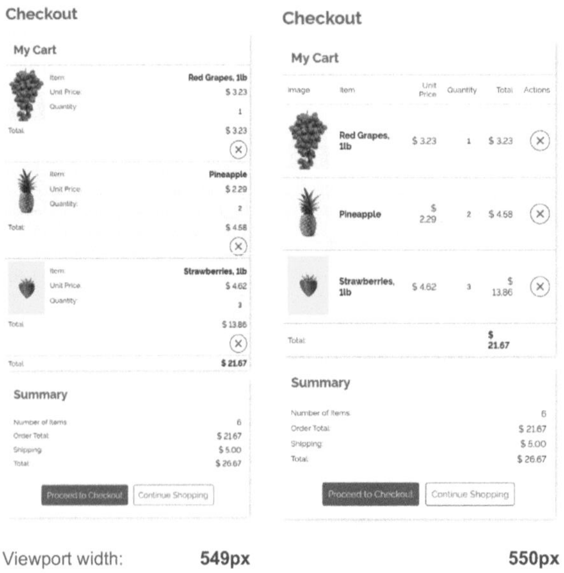

Viewport width: **549px**   **550px**

Figure 8.38   Finished mobile and tablet layouts

8.5   Wide screens

As we continue to increase the width of the screen, the summary section becomes harder to read because of the increasing distance between the definition titles and descriptions (figure 8.39).

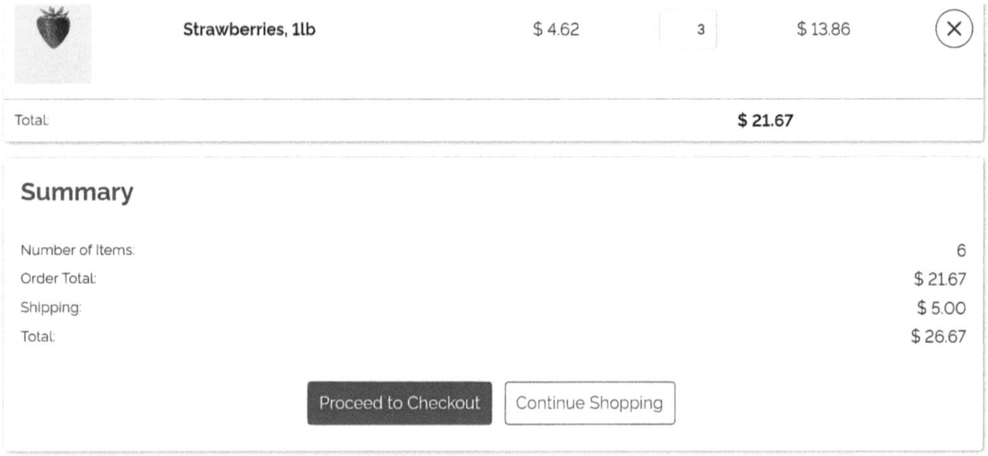

Figure 8.39   Desktop view of summary (viewport width 955 pixels)

Because we have more horizontal real estate to play with as the screen gets wider, we'll bring the summary section up beside the cart section when the viewport reaches 995 pixels wide or larger, as shown in the wireframe in figure 8.40.

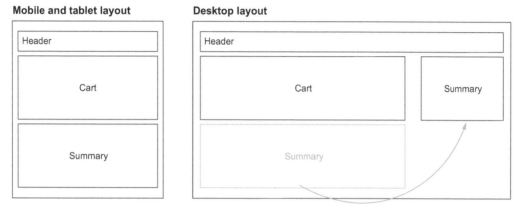

Figure 8.40 Layout wireframes

To change our layout conditionally based on the screen being 955 pixels wide or larger, we'll create the media query `@media (min-width: 995px) { }`. In the HTML shown in the following listing, we have a container `<div>` around our two sections with a class of `section-container`.

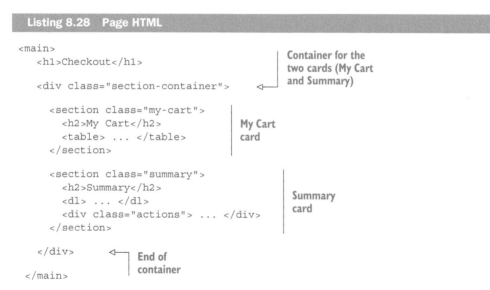

Listing 8.28 Page HTML

```
<main>
    <h1>Checkout</h1>

    <div class="section-container">        Container for the
                                            two cards (My Cart
                                            and Summary)

        <section class="my-cart">
          <h2>My Cart</h2>              My Cart
          <table> ... </table>         card
        </section>

        <section class="summary">
          <h2>Summary</h2>
          <dl> ... </dl>               Summary
          <div class="actions"> ... </div>   card
        </section>

    </div>        End of
                  container
    </main>
```

Inside our new media query, we'll give the container a `display` property value of `flex`. This value allows the two items to come side by side and align themselves on the x-axis. Then we'll add a gap of `20px` between the two sections.

Flexbox will autocalculate the amount of space to give each section. We can influence how the browser assigns dimensions via the properties `flex-grow`, `flex-shrink`, and `flex-basis`. We're going to give the summary section a `flex-basis` value of `250px` and the cart section a `flex-grow` value of 1.

Applied to the summary card, `flex-basis` will set the initial size of the section when the browser starts calculating how much room to assign each section. If the content to which flex is being applied can accommodate the section's being 250 pixels wide, the browser won't alter the section's dimensions; otherwise, the browser will adjust the section as necessary. The `flex-grow` property tells the browser that if space is left over after `flex` has been applied to the content, this element should be made wider to use the extra space. Figure 8.41 shows our sections with and without these two properties influencing how the elements are sized.

Figure 8.41   Influencing the size of elements to which `flex` has been applied

With `flex-grow` and `flex-basis`, we can control the width of the table relative to the summary card. Therefore, we use the media query in the following listing for our project.

Listing 8.29   **Placing the two cards side by side on wide screens**

```
@media (min-width: 955px) {
  .section-container {
    display: flex;
    gap: 20px;
  }
  section.my-cart { flex-grow: 1; }
  section.summary { flex-basis: 250px }
}
```

Figure 8.41 shows our layout when the screen is 955 pixels wide. But if we make the screen even wider, such as for the extra-wide curved displays, we eventually get to a point where the content once again becomes unreadable (figure 8.42). Because we set a `flex-basis` value on the summary card, it stays readable, but because the table is made to keep growing (via the `flex-grow` property), it becomes unwieldy.

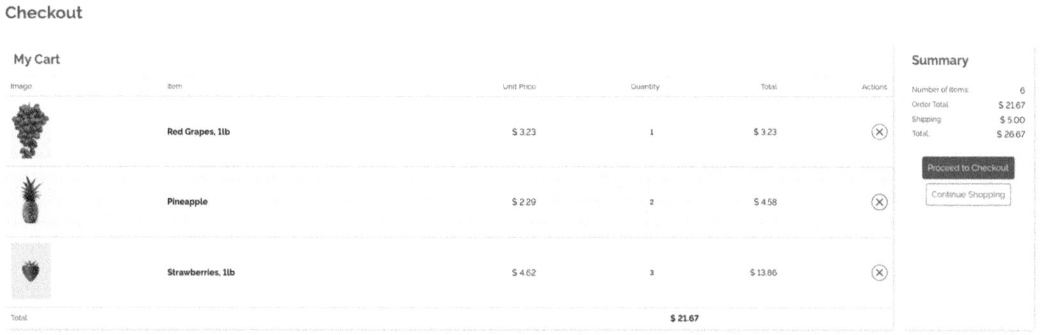

Figure 8.42   Layout on a screen 2,000 pixels wide

To prevent this growth, we can limit the width of the `<main>` element (inside which our main header and cards are contained). This change ensures that no matter how wide the user's display is or how the user chooses to extend the window, the content remains usable. We can center the body by giving the left and right margins a value of `auto`, as shown in the following listing.

Listing 8.30   Maximum width of the `main` element

```
main {
  max-width: 1280px;
  margin: 0 auto;
}
```

If we look at our layout again on an extremely wide screen with these last styles applied (figure 8.43), we see that we've constrained and centered our content.

With these final edits, our project is complete. From one HTML file, we created three distinct layouts based on the width of the screen (figure 8.44).

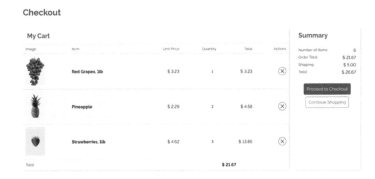

Figure 8.43   Constrained-width layout

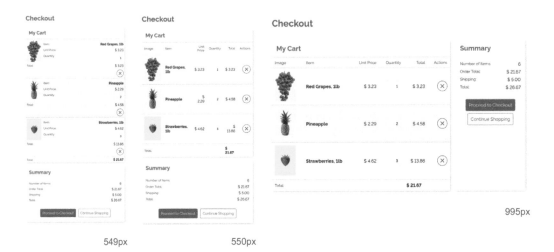

Figure 8.44   Final output for three screen sizes

Summary

- Numeral styles can be controlled via the `font-variant-numeric` property.
- Media queries allow us to apply styles conditionally based on screen size.
- Naming CSS classes based on the content they're styling or the content they represent can be helpful for creating names that are easy to understand and maintain.
- HTML attribute values can be used to select elements.
- HTML attributes can be displayed via CSS using pseudo-elements, the `content` property, and the `attr()` function.
- Margins can collapse.

- Elements set to `display:flex` can be controlled via `flex-grow`, `flex-shrink`, and `flex-basis`.
- `:nth-of-type` can take numbers, keywords, or custom patterns to target elements based on their position relative to others of the same type of elements inside a container.

Creating
a virtual credit card

This chapter covers

- Using Flexbox and `position` in layout
- Working with background images and sizing
- Loading and applying local fonts
- Using transitions and the `backface-visibility` property to create a 3D effect
- Working with additional styles such as the `text-shadow` and `border-radius` properties

As we saw in chapter 3, animation in CSS opens lots of opportunities to create interactive web experiences. In chapter 3, we used animations to give users the sense that something was happening in the background as they waited for a task to complete. Now we'll use animation to respond to users' interactions and create a flip effect for a credit card image. On one side, the animation will show the front of a credit card; on hover or on click for mobile devices, it will flip to show the back of the credit card.

This effect is useful to users, as we're re-creating what their credit cards may look like, showing which information from the cards they need to enter when buying something online, such as the expiration date or the security code. Animation is a way to represent something in real life by re-creating it for the web. This project goes hand in hand with the one in chapter 8, in which we designed a checkout cart.

We'll also explore styling images to set the background of the credit card and icons on the card. We'll use the CSS Flexbox Layout Module for the layout, as well as styling properties such as shadows, colors, and border radius. By the end of the chapter, our layout will look like figure 9.1.

Figure 9.1 Final output of the front and back of the credit card

As we go through the project, feel free to try customizing it to match your style. Try a different background image or typeface, for example. This project is a great opportunity to tweak the styling to suit your style. Let's get started.

9.1 Getting started

Our HTML is made up of two main parts. Within the overall section representing the virtual card are a front side and a back side. You can find the starting HTML in the chapter-09 folder of the GitHub repository (http://mng.bz/Bm5g), on CodePen (https://codepen.io/michaelgearon/pen/YzZKMKN), and in the following listing.

Listing 9.1 Project HTML

```
<section class="card-item">
  <section class="card-item__side front">
    <div class="card-item__wrapper">
      <div class="card-item__top">
        <img src="chip.svg" class="card-item__chip" alt="card chip">
        <div class="card-item__type">
          <img src="logo.svg" alt="Card Type" class="card-item__typeImg"
            height="37" width="152">
        </div>
      </div>
      <div class="card-item__number">
        <div>1111</div>
        <div>2222</div>
        <div>3333</div>
```

The container for the whole credit card

The container for the front of the card

The section for the top front of the card

The section for the middle front of the card, showing the card number

The section for the bottom front of the card, showing the expiration date and cardholder name

```
          <div>4444</div>
        </div>
      <div class="card-item__content">
        <div class="card-item__info">
          <div class="card-item__holder">Card Holder</div>
          <div class="card-item__name">John Smith</div>
        </div>
        <div class="card-item__date">
          <div class="card-item__dateTitle">Expires</div>
          <div class="card-item__dateItem">02/22</div>
        </div>
      </div>
    </div>
  </section>
  <section class="card-item__side back">
    <div class="card-item__band"></div>
    <div class="card-item__cvv">
      <div class="card-item__cvvTitle">CVV</div>
      <div class="card-item__cvvBand">999</div>
      <div class="card-item__type">
        <img src="card-type.svg" class="card-item__typeImg"
 height="30" width="50">
      </div>
    </div>
  </section>
</section>
```

We also have some starting CSS to change the background color to a light blue and increase the margin at the top of the page, as shown in the following listing.

Listing 9.2   Starting CSS

```css
* {
  box-sizing: border-box;
}
body {
  background: rgb(221 238 252);
  margin-top: 80px;
}
```

We're using the universal selector that we looked at in chapter 1 to set the `box-sizing` value for all HTML elements to `border-box`. This selector has two values:

- `content-box`—This setting is the default value for calculating the width and height of an element. If the `content-box` height and width are `250px`, any borders or padding will be added to the final rendered width. Given a border of `2px` all around, for example, the final rendered width would be `254px`.
- `border-box`—The difference between this value and `border-box` is that if we set the element height to `250px`, any borders and padding will be included in this specified value. The `content-box` will reduce as the padding and border increase.

Figure 9.2 shows an example. Our starting point looks like figure 9.3.

content-box | **border-box**

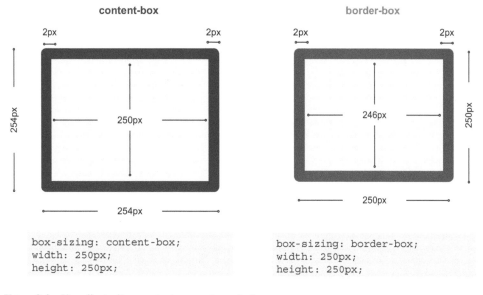

```
box-sizing: content-box;
width: 250px;
height: 250px;
```

```
box-sizing: border-box;
width: 250px;
height: 250px;
```

Figure 9.2 The effect of `box-sizing` on element size

Credit card

1111
2222
3333
4444
Card Holder
John Smith
Expires
02/22
CVV
999

Figure 9.3 Starting point

9.2 Creating the layout

Both the front and the back have a class name of `card-item__side`. The front also has a second class assignment of `front`, and the back has a second class of `back`. Having two class names—one that's identical on both sides and a second, different one—allows us to assign styles that are common to both sides using the `.card-item__side` selector (the class they have in common) and styles that are unique to a side in their individual rules of `.front {}` or `.back {}`.

Let's start by centering the card on the screen. The first step is setting the height and width of the card to a maximum width of `430px` and a fixed height of `270px`.

We're also setting its position to relative, which will be useful when we place the back of the card on top of the front to create the flip effect later in this chapter (section 9.5).

The final piece is setting the left and right margins of the card to auto to center the card horizontally in the browser window. To do this, we use the .card-item selector to create the rule shown in the following listing.

Listing 9.3 Container styling

```
.card-item {
  max-width: 430px;
  height: 270px;
  margin: auto;
  position: relative;
}
```

Figure 9.4 shows the updated positioning.

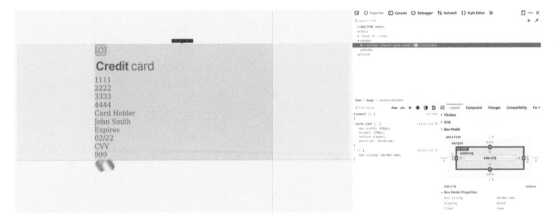

Figure 9.4 Centered credit card

9.2.1 Sizing the card

Now that we've set a maximum width and height for the card, we want to ensure that the front and back faces fill the entire space available to them within their parent container (the card). Therefore, we'll assign a height and width of 100% to both sides of the cards by using the class selector .card-item__side, as shown in the following listing.

Listing 9.4 Container shared between the front and back

```
.card-item__side {
  height: 100%;
  width: 100%;
}
```

With this piece of code added, our card faces (front and back) expand to match the size of its parent container, as figure 9.5 shows.

Figure 9.5 The card faces (front and back) match the parent's container size.

9.2.2 Styling the front of the card

For the front of the card, we have three main sections (figure 9.6):

- The top of the card has two images, one showing the chip and the other showing the type of credit card (such as Visa or MasterCard).
- In the middle is the card number, which is spread evenly across the width of the card.
- At the bottom are the cardholder's name and the card's expiration date. These elements are on opposite ends.

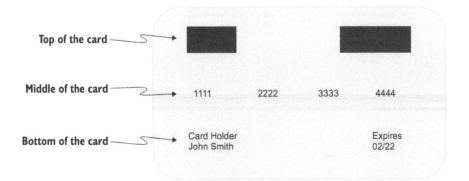

Figure 9.6 A wireframe of the front of the card

Before we start styling the individual parts of the front of the card, let's give the card face some padding so that the contents aren't positioned right up against the edge. We'll give them some breathing room. The following listing shows the code.

Listing 9.5   Container styling for the front of the card

```
.front {
  padding: 25px 15px;
}
```

Remember that in the styles originally provided with the project, we set the `box-sizing` of all elements to `border-box`. With the added padding, we see that changing the `box-sizing` didn't increase the dimensions of the card face `<section>`; rather, it decreased the space available to the content (figure 9.7).

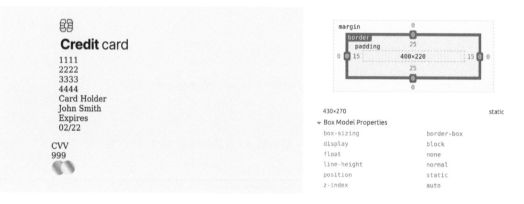

Figure 9.7   Card with added padding and box model diagram

TOP OF THE CARD

We're using Flexbox for the layout of the card. As we've learned, Flexbox is likely to be the best choice for placing items in a single-axis layout. Also, we need to take advantage of the extra functionality Flexbox gives us with spacing and alignment—functionality that float doesn't give us.

> NOTE   For details on the CSS Flexbox Layout Module and its associated properties, check out chapter 6. Chapter 7 covers float.

With these facts in mind, we'll set the top of the card to have a `display` property value of `flex` and set the alignment so that the tops of the elements align. The default property of `align-items` is `stretch`, which increases the heights of the `flex` items so that their heights match that of the tallest element in the set.

We don't want this distortion, though; we want the elements to be aligned vertically to the tops of the items. So we'll set the `align-items` property to `flex-start`. Then we'll set the `justify-content` property to `space-between`, which distributes the elements evenly along the axis, creating a gap between the two elements and placing them at the extreme edges of the card.

We'll give the top some margin and padding to position them further relative to the edge of the card. Then we'll increase the width of the chip to 60px. As this image is an SVG, we can increase its size without affecting its quality. Because we're manipulating only the width and haven't altered the default height, the image's height will scale proportionally by default. The following listing shows the rules used to style the top portion of the card.

Listing 9.6   Layout for the top front of the card

```
.card-item__top {
  display: flex;
  align-items: flex-start;
  justify-content: space-between;
  margin-bottom: 40px;
  padding: 0 10px;
}
.card-item__chip {
  width: 60px;
}
```

Our updated card looks like figure 9.8.

Before   After

Figure 9.8   Styled top portion of the card

MIDDLE OF THE CARD

In the middle front of the card, we find the card number. Again, we use a `display` property value of `flex`, with `justify-content: space-between` distributing the number groups evenly across the card's width. We also add padding and margin to add space between the numbers and the elements around them, as shown in the following listing.

Listing 9.7   Layout for the middle of the front of the card

```
.card-item__number {
  display: flex;
  justify-content: space-between;
  padding: 10px 15px;
  margin-bottom: 35px;
}
```

Figure 9.9 shows our number groups distributed evenly across the width of the card.

Before   After

Figure 9.9   Evenly distributed numbers

BOTTOM OF THE CARD

In the bottom front of the card, we have two elements: cardholder name and card expiration date. As we did in the top and middle of the card, we want to separate the bits of information and place them at opposite edges of the card.

We'll follow the same pattern of using Flexbox, justify-content, and padding to place the elements. We don't need any margin this time, however. The following listing shows the rule we'll use.

Listing 9.8   Layout for the bottom front of the card

```
.card-item__content {
  display: flex;
  justify-content: space-between;
  padding: 0 15px;
}
```

Figure 9.10 shows the updated layout. Next, we'll position the elements on the back of the card.

Before   After

Figure 9.10 Layout for the front of the card

9.2.3 *Laying out the back of the card*

The layout for the back includes the security code number and a semitransparent band (the magnetic strip), as shown in figure 9.11. Let's start with the semitransparent back strip.

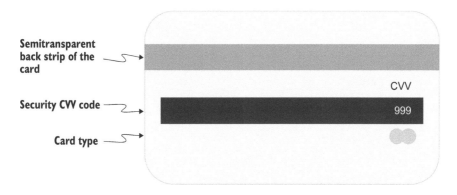

Figure 9.11 A wireframe of the back of the card

SEMITRANSPARENT STRIP

The strip has a class of `card-item__band`. We want to make it 50px in height and position it 30px from the top of the card. We'll use the `height` property to indicate how tall it should be. Even though the `<div>` is empty, it automatically takes the full width available to it because `<div>`s are block-level elements.

To move the strip down rather than keep it at the top of the back of the card, we'll add some padding to the back of the card itself. We can't give it margin, because it would push against the previously existing content (in the top card) rather than the top edge of the back.

Although we'll manage most of the theming later in this chapter, let's add the background color now so that we can see what we're doing (listing 9.9). The background is dark blue at 80% opacity, which will allow some of the background image we place on the card to show through.

Listing 9.9   Positioning the strip

```
.back { padding-top: 30px }
.card-item__band {
  height: 50px;
  background: rgb(0 0 19 / 0.8);
}
```

Now our strip looks like figure 9.12.

Before   After

Figure 9.12   Styled strip on back of card

SECURITY CODE

The security code has the letters *CVV* above it and a white band (usually intended for the user's signature) that includes the security code. Both the letters and the numbers are right-justified and nested inside a `<div>` with a class name of `card-item__cvv`.

For the letters *CVV*, because we don't need to distribute elements across the width of the card, we don't need to use Flexbox. Aligning the text to the right by using the `text-align` property is sufficient to accomplish the task. But we'll use Flexbox on the white band that contains the security numbers, not because it's needed to right-justify the text but because it makes vertically aligning the content inside the band much easier. Let's start by giving the `card-item__CVV` container some basic styles: `padding` to space elements and the `text-align` property so that our text will place itself on the right of the card, as shown in the following listing.

Listing 9.10   Positioning the text

```
.card-item__cvv {
  text-align: right;
  padding: 15px;
}
```

With the container taken care of (figure 9.13), we can style the letters and security code individually.

Before   After

Figure 9.13   Aligning the text

For the *CVV* letters, all we need to do is give this text some margin and padding to off-set it from the right edge and away from the number below. Because we want the number to be inside a white band of a specific height, we'll use the `height` property with a value of `45px`. To align the text vertically in the middle of the box, instead of trying to calculate the amount of vertical padding necessary based on the text size, we'll use Flexbox with an `align-items` property value of `center`. We'll still use padding to separate the text from the right edge of the box, however.

Because Flexbox's default property value for `justify-content` is `flex-start` (which would reposition our text to the right of the box), we need to assign it a value of `flex-end` explicitly so that the elements within (the text) stay to the right. The following listing shows the CSS we use to style *CVV* and the security code.

Listing 9.11   Layout for the back of the card

```
.card-item__cvvTitle {
  padding-right: 10px;
  margin-bottom: 5px;
}
.card-item__cvvBand {
  height: 45px;
  margin-bottom: 30px;
  padding-right: 10px;
```

```
    display: flex;
    align-items: center;
    justify-content: flex-end;
    Background: rgb(255, 255, 255);
}
```

At this point, our card looks like figure 9.14.

Before   After

Figure 9.14 Elements positioned on the card

The card is starting to take shape. Now we need to apply the background image to both the front and back, as well as the colors and typography. These steps will make a huge difference and get us one step closer to the final look.

9.3 *Working with background images*

Our credit card needs to have some sort of background image. To add one, we'll use the background-image property. The image could be in any format that's valid for the web.

9.3.1 *Background property shorthand*

When setting the background for an element, we can set each related property independently (background-image, background-size, and so on) or can use the shorthand background property. We're going to use the following properties and values:

- background-image: url("bg.jpeg")
- background-size: cover
- background-color: blue
- background-position: left top

If we use the shorthand background property, our declaration ends up being background: url("bg.jpeg") left top / cover blue; . The URL to the image is truncated here to make the code easier to read and discuss, but it'll be required in its entirety in our code to retrieve the image, as we'll do several times in this chapter. Figure 9.15 breaks down the property value.

Figure 9.15 **Shorthand** `background` **property**

Notice that we're using a `background-size` property value of `cover`. We're using this setting so that the browser will calculate the optimal size the image should be to cover the entire element while still showing as much of the image as possible without distortion. If the image and our element don't have the same aspect ratio, the excess image will be clipped. If we don't want any part of the image to be clipped, we can use `contain` instead. Figure 9.16 shows examples of using `cover` and `contain`.

background-position: center;
background-size: cover;
background-color: blue;

background-position: center;
background-size: contain;
background-color: blue;

background-position: center;
background-size: contain;
background-color: blue;
background-repeat: no-repeat;

Figure 9.16 **Examples of** `background-cover`

Although we use a `background-size` of `cover`, we still include a background color. When both an image and background color are provided, the image always appears on top of the color. We may want to do this for multiple reasons. If the image were smaller than the element or transparent, for example, including a background color would provide a uniformly colored background behind the image. It would also provide something for the browser to display while the image is loading or if the image fails to load. We don't have to provide this value in our project, but having a color that differs from the page's background helps distinguish the card from the page itself, making it a good fallback position if the image fails to load. Because we want the front and back of the card to have the background image, we'll update our .card-item__side rule, which affects both the front and back of the card, as shown in the following listing.

Listing 9.12   Background image for the front and back of the card

```
.card-item__side{
  height: 100%;
  width: 100%;
  background: url("bg.jpeg") left top / cover blue;
}
```

With the background image applied (figure 9.17), we can focus on styling the text.

Before   After

Figure 9.17   Background image added to both the front and back of the card

9.3.2   Text color

Now that we have the background image in place, we notice that the text is difficult to read, so we'll change it from black to white by updating our .card-item selector. Listing 9.13 shows our updated .card-item rule.

Color contrast and background images

Verifying that color contrast is accessible when text overlaps an image is notoriously difficult and requires manual testing. In many cases as the window is resized, the content reflows, and where the text overlaps, the image changes. One technique to ensure that contrast is always sufficient is to test the text color against both the lightest and darkest points of the image.

Also worth mentioning, and as clearly demonstrated in this project, the busier the image is, the more difficult achieving good readability becomes.

Listing 9.13   Setting the container color

```
.card-item {
  max-width: 430px;
  height: 270px;
  margin: auto;
  position: relative;
  color: white;
}
```

By updating this rule, we've made all text on the card white (figure 9.18). Our security code is on a white background, however, so we need to update its rule to change its text color to something darker.

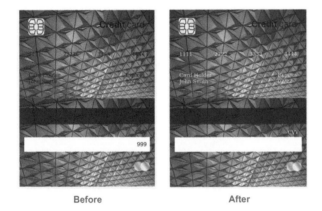

Before   After

Figure 9.18   Text color changed to white

To change the color of the text, we'll update the .card-item__cvvBand rule (listing 9.14), which currently gives us the white band and positions the security code within. We'll change the text color to a dark blue-gray.

Listing 9.14   Back-of-card white background

```
.card-item__cvvBand {
  background: white;
  height: 45px;
  margin-bottom: 30px;
  padding-right: 10px;
  display: flex;
  align-items: center;
  justify-content: flex-end;
  color: rgb(26, 59, 93);
}
```

With the visibility of our security code restored (figure 9.19), let's turn our attention to the two text elements on the front of the card: *Card Holder* and *Expires*.

In terms of information, these two pieces of text are there only to label the elements with which they're paired, so they're less important than the actual name and

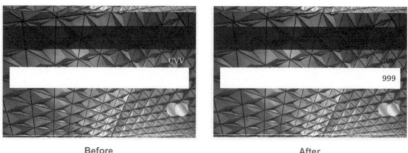

Before   After

Figure 9.19   Restored security code

date. To diminish their importance visually, we'll decrease their opacity (listing 9.15) to render them mildly translucent and decrease their brightness. In section 9.4, when we handle the typography, we'll diminish their size for the same reason.

Listing 9.15   Styling the labeling text

```
.card-item__holder, .card-item__dateTitle {
  opacity: 0.7;
}
```

At this point, the final appearance of the card is coming through (figure 9.20). We've styled the layout, format, images, and colors. But we still need to adjust the typography and create the main effect: the flip on hover. The next step is looking at the fonts.

Before   After

Figure 9.20   Diminished text opacity

9.4   *Typography*

For other projects, we used the free online resource Google Fonts to load the fonts we needed. We did this by linking to the Google Fonts application programming interface (API), requesting the fonts we needed, and then setting the property value to the font family we're using. But in some cases, we may want to load our font files ourselves rather than depend on an API or a content distribution network (CDN).

> **WARNING**   Like images and other forms of media, fonts are subject to licensing. Always make sure that you have the appropriate licenses, regardless of how a font is being imported (API, CDN, or locally hosted) before using it on a website or in an application. When in doubt, ask your legal team!

Both approaches have benefits and drawbacks. Neither is overwhelmingly better than the other, so the choice comes down to the needs of the project we're working on.

The benefits of using local or self-hosted fonts include

- We don't have to depend on a third party.
- We have more control in terms of cross-browser support and performance optimization, which can make the font load time faster than that of a third-party font.

Drawbacks include

- We have to do our own performance optimization.
- The user won't already have the font cached.

The advantages of using fonts hosted by a third party include

- The user may already have the font cached on their device.
- Importing is easier.

Drawbacks include

- We need to make an extra call to fetch the font file.
- There are privacy concerns about what the third party is tracking.
- The service can discontinue the font at any time.

To load our own fonts from our local project folder, we need to create `@font {}` at-rules to define and import the fonts we want to use. To understand this at-rule, let's start by looking at font formats.

9.4.1 *@font-face*

Fonts can come in a few file types. Some well-known ones are

- *TrueType (TTF)*—Supported by all modern browsers; not compressed
- *Open Type (OTF)*—Evolution of TTF; allows for more characters such as small caps and old-style figures
- *Embedded Open Type (EOT)*—Developed by Microsoft for the web; supported only by Internet Explorer (obsolete because Internet Explorer has been end-of-lifed)
- *Web Open Font Format (WOFF)*—Created for the web; is compressed; includes metadata within the font file for copyright information; and is recommended by the World Wide Web Consortium (https://www.w3.org/TR/WOFF2)
- *Web Open Font Format 2 (WOFF2)*—Continuation of WOFF; 30% more compressed than WOFF
- *Scalable Vector Graphic (SVG)*—Created to allow embedding glyph information in SVGs before web fonts became widespread

When you select a font type to use, we generally recommend using WOFF or WOFF2.

NOTE   Only recently have we been able to rely on WOFF2 files without having to upload multiple font formats. You can still find a lot of outdated information about fonts on the web. A trick that helps is looking at when the information was published—the more recently, the better.

When dealing with fonts, we know from previous chapters that we need to import each weight we want to use. The same is true for dealing with fonts locally: each variation (weight and style) needs to be included in the project individually unless we use a variable font.

Variable fonts are fairly new. Rather than having each style in a separate file, all the permutations are included inside a single file. So if we wanted regular, bold, and semi-bold, we could import only one file instead of three, and we'd have access not only to those three font weights, but also to everything from thin to extra-bold. Italics may not be in the same file; in some typefaces, the italic glyphs are different from those of the non-italic versions.

For our project, we want to load three fonts: Open Sans normal, Open Sans bold, and Open Sans Italic. These fonts are variations within the same family. Open Sans has both static and variable font versions. The variable version separates italic and regular styles into two separate files. For our non-italic needs, because we're loading multiple weights, we'll use the variable version.

For italic, however, we're going to use only one weight: regular. It doesn't make sense to load the variable font version for that weight. Because the variable font includes all the information necessary to cross the full gamut of weights, it's significantly larger (314.8 KB) than the file that holds only one weight (17.8 KB). For performance reasons, it makes sense to stick with the static version.

For each font, we need to create a separate `@font-face` rule. This at-rule defines the font and includes where the font is being loaded from, what its weight is, and how we want it to load.

First, we declare the `@font-face { }` rule. Inside the curly braces, we'll define its characteristics and behavior, including four descriptors:

- `font-family`—The name we use to refer to our font when we apply it to an element via the `font-family` property.
- `src`—Where the font is being loaded from. This descriptor takes a comma-delimited list of locations to fetch the font from and what format to expect from each source. The browser will go down the list, starting with the first one, until it fetches the font successfully.
- `font-weight`—What weight this particular font file represents. In the case of variable fonts, we'll include a range.
- `font-display`—Dictates how the font is loaded. We'll use the descriptor value `swap`. Fonts are load-blocking, in that the browser will wait until they're loaded before moving on to load other resources. `swap` limits the amount of time the font is allowed to be load-blocking. If the font isn't done loading when that

period is over, the browser will move on to load other resources and finish applying the font whenever the font is done loading. This setting allows content to be shown and the user to interact with the interface even if the font is not available yet.

Listing 9.16 shows both of our rules, which must be added *at the top of the stylesheet*. Also, with a few exceptions, a rule can't be declared inside an existing rule. `.myClass { @font-face { ... } }` wouldn't work, for example. One exception is the `@supports` at-rule, which we expand on in the next section.

Listing 9.16 Declaring our fonts

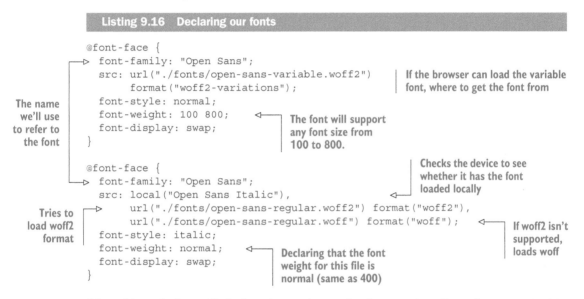

```
@font-face {
    font-family: "Open Sans";
    src: url("./fonts/open-sans-variable.woff2")
        format("woff2-variations");
    font-style: normal;
    font-weight: 100 800;
    font-display: swap;
}

@font-face {
    font-family: "Open Sans";
    src: local("Open Sans Italic"),
        url("./fonts/open-sans-regular.woff2") format("woff2"),
        url("./fonts/open-sans-regular.woff") format("woff");
    font-style: italic;
    font-weight: normal;
    font-display: swap;
}
```

The name we'll use to refer to the font

The font will support any font size from 100 to 800.

If the browser can load the variable font, where to get the font from

Tries to load woff2 format

Checks the device to see whether it has the font loaded locally

If woff2 isn't supported, loads woff

Declaring that the font weight for this file is normal (same as 400)

After this code is applied, there's no change in the user interface; the `font-family` being used is still the browser's default because we haven't applied the fonts to any of our elements yet. We also want to create a fallback in case the browser doesn't support variable fonts. Before we apply the font to our elements, let's look at browser support.

9.4.2 Creating fallbacks using @supports

Because variable fonts are fairly new, and because not everyone is good at running updates on their devices, we'll include a fallback in case variable fonts aren't supported by a user's browser. For this purpose, we'll use the `@supports` at-rule. This rule allows us to check whether the browser supports a particular property and value, and allows us to write CSS that gets applied only if the provided condition is met.

Our feature query will be `@supports not (font-variation-settings: normal) { ... }`. Because our query has the keyword `not` before the condition, the styles it contains will be applied when the condition is *not* being met. In other words, if the browser doesn't support variable font behaviors, we want to load the static version.

Inside the `@supports` at-rule, which we place at the top of our file, we include the `@font-face` rules for both weights of the normal style version we want to include

(listing 9.17). We also create an `@supports (font-variation-settings: normal) { }`
rule, this time without the not. In this second at-rule for browsers that do support variable fonts, we move the two rules we created in section 9.4.1. This way, we load the
variable fonts only if they're supported by the browser and prevent the file from being
loaded if the browser doesn't support variable fonts.

Listing 9.17   Fallback for browsers that don't support variable fonts

Applies styles when variable
fonts are supported

```
@supports (font-variation-settings: normal) {
  @font-face {
    font-family: "Open Sans";
    src: url("./fonts/open-sans-variable.woff2")
    format("woff2-variations");
    font-weight: 100 800;
    font-style: normal;
    font-display: swap;
  }
}
```

Our previously
created rule for
the variable font,
moved into the
at-rule

```
@supports not (font-variation-settings: normal) {
  @font-face {
    font-family: "Open Sans";
    src: local("Open Sans Regular"),
        local("OpenSans-Regular"),
        url("./fonts/open-sans-regular.woff2") format("woff2"),
        url("./fonts/open-sans-regular.woff") format("woff");
    font-weight: normal;
    font-display: swap;
  }

  @font-face {
    font-family: "Open Sans";
    src: local("Open SansBold"),
        local("OpenSans-Bold"),
        url("./fonts/open-sans-regular.woff2") format("woff2"),
        url("./fonts/open-sans-regular.woff") format("woff");
    font-weight: bold;
    font-display: swap;
  }
}
```

Applies styles when
variable fonts aren't
supported

Rule for
normal
style, font
weight
regular
(400)

Rule for normal style,
font weight bold (700)

With our fallback added, let's update our body rule to apply Open Sans to our project
(listing 9.18). Although we added fallbacks for loading the font, we'll still include
`sans-serif` in the `font-family` property value in the body rule in case our font files
fail to load.

Listing 9.18   Applying the fonts to our project

```
body {
  background: rgb(221, 238, 252);
```

```
    margin-top: 80px;
    font-family: "Open Sans", sans-serif;
}
```

When the font is applied, we see that our text has been updated to use Open Sans rather than the browser default (figure 9.21). Now we can edit our individual elements for font weight and style.

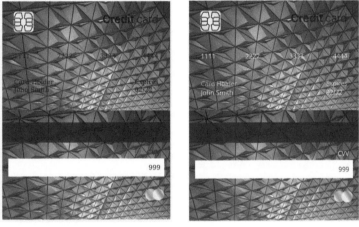

Before   After

Figure 9.21   Open Sans applied to the project

9.4.3   *Font sizing and typography improvements*

Starting with the front of the card, we'll increase the font size of the numbers and make them bold. We'll add to our existing rule, as shown in the following listing.

> **Listing 9.19   Boldfacing and increasing the size of the numbers**

```
.card-item__number {
  display: flex;
  justify-content: space-between;
  padding: 10px 15px;
  margin-bottom: 35px;
  font-size: 27px;
  font-weight: 700;
}
```

Figure 9.22 shows our styled numbers.

Moving on to the text below the numbers, we want to decrease the size of *Card Holder* and *Expires*. We'll set their font-size to 15px and increase the size and font-weight of the name and date, as shown in the following listing.

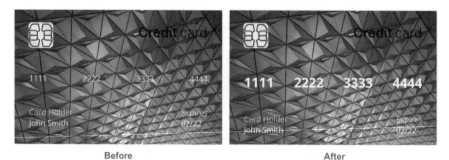

Before   **After**

Figure 9.22   Styled numbers

```
.card-item__holder, .card-item__dateTitle {
  opacity: 0.7;
  font-size: 15px;
}
```
Card Holder
and Expires

```
.card-item__name, .card-item__dateItem {
  font-size: 18px;
  font-weight: 600;
}
```
Name and
expiration
date

With the text elements on the front of the card taken care of (figure 9.23), let's turn our attention to the back.

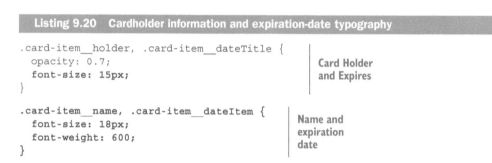

Before   **After**

Figure 9.23   Typography of the front of the card

On the back, we need to update the security code to be in italics. We'll update our existing rule with `font-style: italic`, as shown in the following listing.

```
.card-item__cvvBand {
  background: white;
  height: 45px;
  margin-bottom: 30px;
```

```
    padding-right: 10px;
    display: flex;
    align-items: center;
    justify-content: flex-end;
    color: #1a3b5d;
    font-style: italic;
}
```

Now that our card is styled (figure 9.24), we're ready to apply the flip effect.

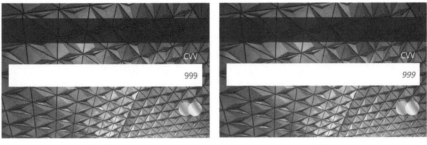

Before   After

Figure 9.24   Completed typography styles

9.5   *Creating the flipping-over effect*

Next, we'll create the flipping-over effect for devices that support the `hover` interaction. We'll start by adjusting the position to overlay the back of the card on top of the front. Then we'll use the `backface-visibility` and `transform` properties to place the card. To animate the change, we'll use a transition.

9.5.1   *Position*

To achieve the flip effect, we stack the card faces on top of one another via the `backface-visibility` property. Then we'll toggle which side is shown. When we use the `backface-visibility` property and expose the back side, we perform a rotation on the horizontal axis; therefore, we need to invert the back so that its contents are mirrored. Imagine taking a piece of tracing paper and drawing an image on the back. When we look at the front, the image that appears through it from the back is mirrored. That effect is what we're building here. The CSS we use to stack front and back and then flip the back is in listing 9.22. We place our code inside a media query that checks whether the browser has `hover` functionality. We want to have the flip effect only on devices that support `hover`. For devices that don't (such as mobile phones), we'll show the front and the back at the same time.

Listing 9.22   Positioning the back over the front

```
@media (hover: hover) {
  .back {
    position: absolute;
```

```
    top: 0;
    left: 0;
    transform: rotateY(-180deg);    ◁───| Flips the
  }                                       card
}
```

Earlier in this chapter, we set the `position` property value to `relative` in our `.card-item` rule. Using relative positioning on a parent or ancestor element goes hand in hand with the fact that we're setting the `position` property value of the back of our card to `absolute`. The top and left positions of `0` will be the top-left section with the `card-item` class (the container that holds the two card faces).

Whenever we use `position: absolute`, we take the element out of the regular flow of the page and can set a specific position on the page on which to place the element. The position is calculated based on the closest ancestor with a `position` value of `relative`. If none is found, the top left will be the top-left corner of the page.

What gets a bit confusing here is that if no values are set to position the element (`top`, `left`, `right`, `bottom`, or `inset`), the element is placed wherever it normally would lie but takes up no space in the flow. The height and width of the element are also affected. If a value is provided in the CSS, the element maintains that value; otherwise, it takes up only as much room as it needs. Even if it's a block-level element, it no longer takes up the full width available to it. Furthermore, if the width is set using a relative unit such as percentage, it will be calculated against the element to which it's relative. Figure 9.25 shows some scenarios for using `position: absolute`.

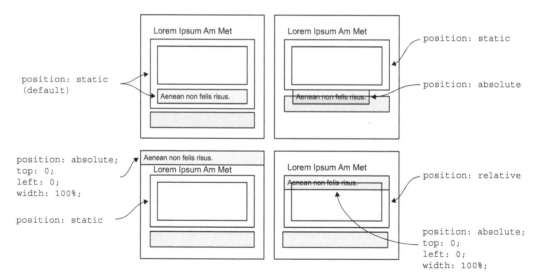

Figure 9.25   Absolute positioning

With our CSS applied (figure 9.26) and the back of the card flipped and on top of the front, we can apply the `backface-visibility` property.

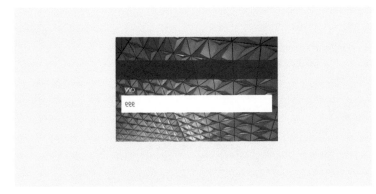

Figure 9.26   Back of the card positioned on top of front and flipped

9.5.2   Transitions and backface-visibility

Up to now, we've looked at objects in 2D space—in other words, a flat perspective. We've looked at width and height but not depth. Now we'll consider that third dimension.

With the back flipped, we need it to be hidden unless the user is hovering over the card. We have two sides, the second of which has a `transform: rotateY(-180deg)` declaration (the back). In a 3D space, therefore, that side is facing away from us. If we set the `backface-visibility` property value to be `hidden` on both sides, whichever side is facing away from us is hidden.

Our back, which currently faces away from us, is hidden. If we rotate the entire card, the back faces us, and the front is hidden. Figure 9.27 diagrams how our CSS and HTML interact to create the flip effect.

In our CSS, we add the following rules and properties to our media query (listing 9.23). They instruct the card to hide the side if it's facing away from us and to rotate the entire card 180-degrees on the y-axis on hover. Notice a property that we haven't talked about yet: `transform-style`, to which we've given a value of `preserve-3d`. Without this property, the flip won't work. It tells the browser that we're operating in 3D space rather than 2D space, establishing the concept of a front and a back.

Listing 9.23   Hiding the back and exposing it on `hover`

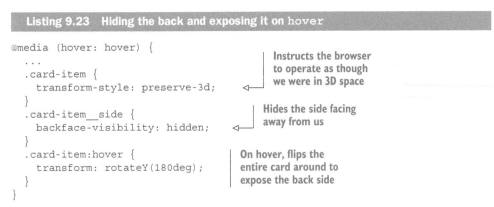

```
@media (hover: hover) {
  ...
  .card-item {
    transform-style: preserve-3d;     ◁── Instructs the browser to operate as though we were in 3D space
  }
  .card-item__side {
    backface-visibility: hidden;      ◁── Hides the side facing away from us
  }
  .card-item:hover {
    transform: rotateY(180deg);       ◁── On hover, flips the entire card around to expose the back side
  }
}
```

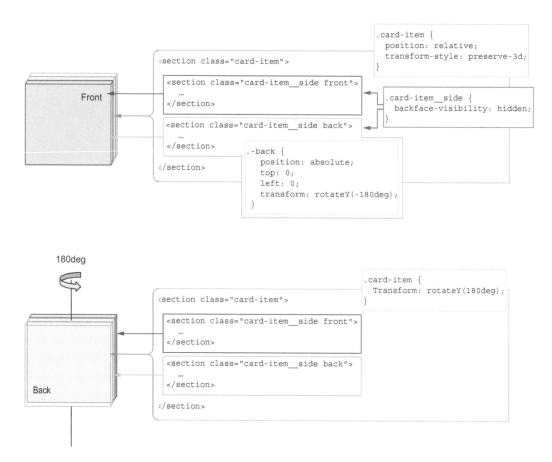

Figure 9.27   The `backface-visibility` property applied to our use case

With our hover functionality exposing the back of our card (figure 9.28), we need to add the animation to make it look more like a card flip. Notice that the back is no longer mirrored.

Figure 9.28   Card default state and on `hover`

Currently, when we hover over the card, the back is shown instantaneously. We want to make it look as though the card is actually being flipped.

9.5.3   *The transition property*

To animate the card flip, we'll use a transition. You may recall from chapter 5 that transitions are used to animate the change of CSS. In this case, we'll animate the change in the rotation of the card by adding a transition declaration to the `card-item` (container that holds the two faces). We'll also add a condition to our media query.

Because this animation is motion-heavy, we want to make sure to respect our users' settings. Therefore, we'll add a `prefers-reduced-motion: no-preference` condition to our media query, as shown in the following listing.

Listing 9.24   Transitions and `transform`

```
@media (hover: hover) and (prefers-reduced-motion: no-preference) {
  ...
  .card-item {
    transform-style: preserve-3d;
    transition: transform 350ms cubic-bezier(0.71, 0.03, 0.56, 0.85);
  }
  ...
}
```

Our animation, which takes 350 milliseconds, affects the `transform` property (the rotation) and is present only for users who don't have `prefers-reduced-motion` set to `reduce` on their devices. Figure 9.29 shows the progression of the animation, and figure 9.30 shows the user interface when the user has `prefers-reduced-motion` enabled.

Time

Figure 9.29   Animation over time

For our timing function, we used a `cubic-bezier()` function. Next, let's take a closer look at what this function represents.

9.5.4   *The cubic-bezier() function*

The Bézier curve is named after French engineer Pierre Bézier, who used these curves on the bodywork of Renault cars (http://mng.bz/d1NX). A Bézier curve is composed of four points: P_0, P_1, P_2, and P_3. P_0 and P_3 represent the starting and ending points,

Figure 9.30 `prefers-reduced-motion: reduce` **emulation in Chrome DevTools**

and P_1 and P_2 are the handles on the points. Point and handle values are set with x and y coordinates (figure 9.31).

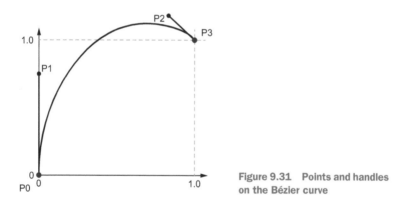

Figure 9.31   Points and handles on the Bézier curve

In CSS, we need to worry about only the handles because the P_0 and P_3 values are set for us to `(0, 0)` and `(1, 1)`, respectively. By manipulating the curve, we change the acceleration of the animation. In CSS, our function takes four parameters that represent the x and y values of P_1 and P_2: `cubic-bezier(x1, y1, x2, y2)`, where the x values must remain between `0` and `1`, inclusive.

The premade timing functions we used in previous chapters for both our transitions and our animations have `cubic-bezier()` values by which they can be represented (figure 9.32).[1]

---

[1] *Architecting CSS: The Programmer's Guide to Effective Style Sheets,* by Martine Dowden and Michael Dowden (2020, Apress).

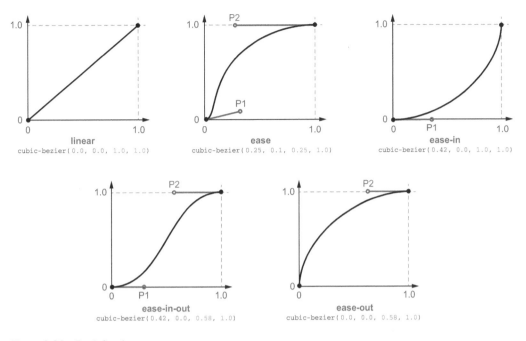

Figure 9.32   Predefined curves

Writing our own `cubic-bezier()` functions to animate our designs can be tedious. Luckily, online tools such as https://cubic-bezier.com allow us to see the curve and determine the values (figure 9.33).

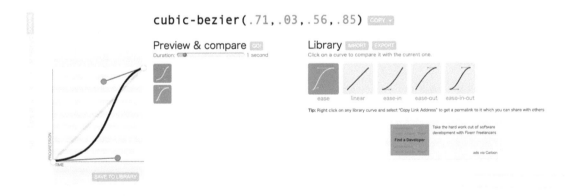

Figure 9.33   An example `cubic-bezier()` function from cubic-bezier.com

We can also see the `cubic-bezier()` in some browser developer tools, such as those of Mozilla Firefox (figure 9.34).

Figure 9.34 Firefox DevTools curve details

With our animation completed, let's add some finishing touches to our project.

9.6 *Border radius*

Most credit cards have rounded corners, so we're going to round ours as well. We'll also round the corners of the white CVV box on the back of the card.

Adding rounded corners to a user interface can be a balancing act. We'll add rounded corners to the card to make it look more natural and realistic. Sharp corners can come across as aggressive, but overuse of rounded corners can make an interface look too soft and playful, which may not work in all cases. The "correct" amount of curve is design-specific. To make our card look more realistic, we'll add the following CSS.

Listing 9.25 Adding `border-radius`

```
.card-item__side {          ⬅—— The card
  height: 100%;
  width: 100%;
  background: url("bg.jpeg") left top / cover blue;
  border-radius: 15px;
}
.card-item__cvvBand {       ⬅—— White
  background: white;              CVV band
  height: 45px;
  margin-bottom: 30px;
  padding-right: 10px;
  display: flex;
  align-items: center;
  justify-content: flex-end;
  color: #1a3b5d;
  font-style: italic;
  border-radius: 4px;
}
```

With the rounded corners, our card looks like figure 9.35.

Default   Hover

Figure 9.35   Rounded corners on the card and CVV band

9.7   Box and text shadows

In chapter 4, we looked briefly at the `drop-shadow` value, which can be applied to the `filter` property for image filters. Another way to apply a shadow to an element is via the `box-shadow` property, which applies a shadow to the element box.

9.7.1   The drop-shadow function versus the box-shadow property

We may be wondering about the difference between the `drop-shadow` filter property and the `box-shadow` property. Both have the same base set of values, but the `box-shadow` property has an additional two nonmandatory values: `spread-radius` and `inset`.

The benefit of using a filter with the `drop-shadow` property on images is that when we're using a filter, the shadow is applied to the alpha mask rather than the bounding box. So if we have a PNG or SVG image, and that image has transparent areas, the shadow is applied around that transparency. If we add a `box-shadow` to the same image rather than the filter, the shadow is applied only to the outer image container (figure 9.36).

Figure 9.36   Comparing
`box-shadow` **(left) and**
`drop-shadow` **(right)**

To reinforce the 3D effect on the card and make the card appear to be floating, we're going to give our card a shadow. Because we're concerned only about giving the bounding area of the card a shadow, we can use the `box-shadow` property, which will give the project a sense of depth and further emphasize that something is on the back. The shadow will be large, soft, and fairly transparent. To achieve that effect, we'll add `box-shadow: 0 20px 60px 0 rgb(14 42 90 / 0.55);` to our `.card-item__side` rule. Our updated rule looks like the following listing.

Listing 9.26   Using `box-shadow` on our card

```
.card-item__side {
  height: 100%;
  width: 100%;
  background: url("bg.jpeg") left top / cover blue;
  border-radius: 15px;
  box-shadow: 0 20px 60px 0 rgb(14 42 90 / 0.55);
}
```

Figure 9.37 shows our updated card.

Figure 9.37   Added shadow to make the card appear to be floating

9.7.2   Text shadows

We can also add shadows to text. If we applied a `box-shadow` to text, the shadow would be applied to the box containing the text, not to the individual letters. To add a shadow to the letters, we use the `text-shadow` property, which has the same syntax as the `box-shadow` property. We'll use this property on the front of the card to lift the text from the background. We need to add this property to our `.front` rule, as shown in the following listing.

Listing 9.27   Text shadow for all the text elements on the front of the card

```
.front{
  padding: 25px 15px;
  text-shadow: 7px 6px 10px rgb(14 42 90 / 0.8);
}
```

Figure 9.38 shows the card before and after.

Although the effect is subtle, the added shadow makes the numbers pop out a bit. It's worth noting that this effect is best used with finesse and sparingly, as it can easily impede readability rather than help it.

Before   After

Figure 9.38   Before and after adding the `text-shadow`

9.8   *Wrapping up*

The last detail we need to handle deals with users who aren't interacting with the flip effect but are viewing both sides of the card at the same time (devices that don't have hover capabilities, such as phones and tablets, and users with a `prefers-reduced-motion` setting). Currently when both sides are displayed, there's no space between the card faces. So let's add some margin to the bottom of the faces to separate them, as shown in the following listing.

Listing 9.28   Separating the card faces

```
.card-item__side {
  height: 100%;
  width: 100%;
  background: url("bg.jpeg") left top / cover blue;        URL truncated
  border-radius: 15px;                                      for legibility
  box-shadow: 0 20px 60px 0 rgb(14 42 90 / 0.55);
  margin-bottom: 2rem;
}
```

On a Moto G4 device, our card looks like figure 9.39.

With this last addition, our project is complete. Using a combination of media queries, shadows, positioning, and transitions, we created a realistic-looking card (figure 9.40).

Figure 9.39   Our project
on a mobile device

Figure 9.40 Finished project

Summary

- We can alter the box model's behavior through the `box-sizing` property.
- The `background` property value `cover` allows us to show as much of a background image as possible while still covering the full element.
- Although fonts come in a range of formats, for the web we need only the WOFF and WOFF2 formats.
- Fonts can be static or variable.
- We use the `@font-face` at-rule to define where and how fonts are imported and how they should behave.
- The `@font-face` at-rule needs to be at the top of the stylesheet.
- The `@supports` at-rule allows us to create styles specific to a browser's functionality.
- The `backface-visibility` property used in conjunction with `transform-style: preserve-3d` creates a flip effect.
- The `cubic-bezier()` function defines how our elements will animate over time.
- The `box-shadow` property allows us to add a shadow to an element's box.
- `text-shadow` rather than `box-shadow` is the property we use to add a shadow to individual letters of text.

Styling forms

Forms are everywhere in our applications. Whether they're contact forms or login screens, whether or not they're core to an application's functionality, they're truly omnipresent. The design of a form, however, can easily make or break the user's experience. In this chapter, we'll style a form and look at some of the accessibility considerations we need to make sure to address. We'll look at some of the challenges that come with styling some radio and check-box inputs and drop-down menus, and we'll cover some options for styling error messaging.

A *form* in this context is a section of code in an HTML `<form>` element containing controls (form fields) that the user interacts with to submit data to a website or application. Because contact forms are so prevalent across applications and websites, we'll use a contact form as the basis for our project.

10.1 Setting up

Our form contains two input fields, a drop-down menu, radio buttons, a check box, and a text area. We also have a header at the top and a Send button at the end of the form. Figure 10.1 shows our starting point—the raw HTML without any styles applied—and what we aim to accomplish.

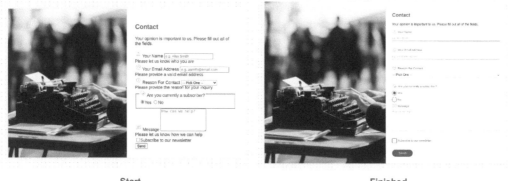

Start   Finished

Figure 10.1   Starting point and finished product

Our starting HTML is fairly simple; it contains our form, inside which our labels, fields, error messages, and buttons are placed. The starting and final code are on GitHub (http://mng.bz/rWYZ), on CodePen (https://codepen.io/michaelgearon/pen/poeoNbj), and in the following listing.

Listing 10.1   Starting HTML

```html
<body>
  <main>
    <section class="image"></section>          Left
    <section class="contact-form">            image
      <h1>Contact</h1>
      <form>
        <p>Your opinion is important to us…</p>
        <label for="name">
          <img src="./img/name.svg" alt="" width="24" height="24">
          Your Name                           Name
        </label>                              input with
        <input type="text"                    associated
               id="name"                      label and
               name="name"                    error
               maxlength="250"                message
               required
```

```
                        aria-describedby="nameError"
                        placeholder="e.g. Alex Smith"
          >
          <div class="error" id="nameError">
            <span role="alert">Please let us know who you are</span>
          </div>

          <label for="email">
            <img src="./img/email.svg" alt="" width="24" height="24">
            Your Email Address
          </label>
          <input type="email"
                 id="email"
                 name="email"
                 maxlength="250"
                 required
                 aria-describedby="emailError"
                 placeholder="e.g. asmith@email.com"
          >
          <div class="error" id="emailError">
            <span role="alert">Please provide a...</span>
          </div>

          <label for="reasonForContact">
            <img src="./img/reason.svg" alt="" width="24" height="24">
            Reason For Contact
          </label>
          <select id="reasonForContact"
                  required
                  aria-describedby="reasonError"
          >
            <option value="">-- Pick One --</option>
            <option value="sales"> Sales inquiry</option>
              ...
          </select>
          <div class="error" id="reasonError">
            <span role="alert">Please provide the...</span>
          </div>

          <fieldset>
            <legend>
              <img src="./img/subscriber.svg" alt=""
    width="24" height="24">
              Are you currently a subscriber?
            </legend>
            <label>
<input type="radio" value="1" name="subscriber"
        checked required>
    Yes
            </label>
            <label>
              <input type="radio" value="0" name="subscriber" required>
              No
            </label>
          </fieldset>
```

Name input with associated label and error message

Email input with associated label and error message

Reason for Contact drop-down menu and associated label

Fieldset containing subscription radio buttons

```
            <label for="message">
              <img src="./img/message.svg" alt="" width="24" height="24">
              Message
            </label>
            <textarea id="message"
                      name="message"
                      rows="5"
Message              required
textarea             maxlength="500"
                     aria-describedby="messageError"
                     placeholder="How can we help?"
            ></textarea>
            <div class="error" id="messageError">
              <span role="alert">Please let us know how we can help</span>
            </div>

            <label>
              <input type="checkbox" name="subscribe">          Subscription
              Subscribe to our newsletter                        check mark
            </label>

            <div class="actions">
              <button type="submit" onclick="send(event)">Send</button>
            </div>
          </form>
        </section>

      </main>

      <script src="./script.js"></script>   ←—  JavaScript that
    </body>                                      handles errors
```

You may have noticed that a JavaScript file is included. We'll use this file to show and hide errors later in the chapter (section 10.8).

So that we can focus specifically on styling form elements, the CSS to lay out the page is provided in the starting project. We use `grid` to place the image and form side by side. We also use a gradient to create the dots in the background. Our theme colors have been set up with CSS custom properties and some basic typography settings, including using a sans-serif font and changing the default text size for our project to 12pt. The following listing shows our starting CSS.

Listing 10.2   Starting CSS

```
html {
  --color: #333333;
  --label-color: #6d6d6d;
  --placeholder-color: #ababab;          Sets up our
  --font-family: sans-serif;             theme colors
  --background: #fafafa;                 using custom
  --background-card: #ffffff;            properties
  --primary: #e48b17;
  --accent: #086788;
```

```
  --accent-contrast: #ffffff;
  --error: #dd1c1aff;
  --border: #ddd;
  --hover: #bee0eb;

  color: var(--color);
  font-family: var(--font-family);
  font-size: 12pt;
  margin: 0;
  padding: 0;
}
```
→ Sets up our theme colors using custom properties

```
body {
  background-color: var(--background);
  background-image: radial-gradient(var(--accent) .75px,
                    transparent .75px);
  background-size: 15px 15px;
  margin: 0;
  padding: 2rem;
}
```
Adds the polka-dotted background

```
main {
  display: grid;
  grid-template-columns: 1fr 1fr;
  margin: 1rem auto;
  max-width: 1200px;
  box-shadow: -2px 2px 15px 0 var(--border);
}
```
Grid to place the two sections side by side

Prevents our design from getting too wide and centers it horizontally on the page

```
.image {
  background-image: url("/img/illustration.jpeg");
  background-size: cover;
  background-position: bottom center;
  object-fit: contain;
}
```
Adds the image to the left side

```
.contact-form {
  background-color: var(--background-card);
  padding: 2rem;
}
```

```
h1 { color: var(--accent); }
```

10.2 Resetting fieldset styles

Fieldsets are purpose-built to group controls and labels. Radio groups are a perfect use case for fieldsets, as they allow us to identify the controls effectively and explicitly as belonging together. They also give us a ready-built way of labeling the group of controls via the <legend>. Stylistically, however, we can agree that they're rather unsightly.

Let's reset the styles on the group to make it disappear visually. Programmatically, we want to keep the group, as it's helpful for users of assistive technology, but we're going to make it blend in a little more. To make the <fieldset> styles disappear, we need to reset three properties: `border`, `margin`, and `padding`. The following listing shows our rule.

Listing 10.3   Resetting fieldset styles

```
fieldset {
  border: 0;
  padding: 0;
  margin: 0;
}
```

With browser default styles on the `<fieldset>` removed (figure 10.2), let's turn our attention to our input fields.

Figure 10.2   Reset fieldset

10.3   Styling input fields

We have four types of input fields in our form, broken down as follows:

- *Your Name*—`text`
- *Your Email Address*—`email`
- *Yes/No*—`radio`
- *Subscribe to our newsletter*—`checkbox`

HTML has many more types of fields, including `date`, `time`, `number`, and `color`, each with its own semantic meaning and styling considerations. We chose the preceding four types because they're commonly used on the web today.

The unstyled appearance of these fields dictates what we'll do to style them. We'll treat the radio buttons and check box differently from the text input, for example, but we can reuse code across multiple types. We'll group them by how the unstyled controls look, so we'll handle the text and email together and then handle the radio buttons and check box together. Let's start with the text and email inputs.

10.3.1   Styling text and email inputs

The first thing we want to figure out is how to select only the text and email input fields—rather, all input fields that aren't a radio button or check box. One solution would be to add a class to each input we want to handle. This approach is hard to maintain and will get quite noisy, however, especially in a form-heavy application or complex form. Therefore, we'll use the pseudo-class `:not()` in conjunction with the type selector `selector[type="value"]`.

The `:not()` pseudo-class allows us to select elements that don't meet a particular criterion. In our case, we want to select all input fields that don't have a type of `radio` or `checkbox`. Our selector, therefore, will be `input:not([type="radio"], [type="checkbox"])`. Now we can start styling the input fields, which currently look like figure 10.3.

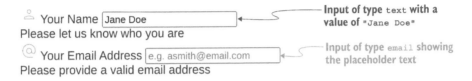

Figure 10.3   Input type `text` **and type** `email`

We see in figure 10.3 that the font is smaller than the `12pt` size we set on the body. Small font sizes are difficult to read on mobile devices; they're also hard to read for many users, especially young children and the elderly. If we want our form to be easily usable across a wide population and across devices, we'll need to increase it, so we'll set it to `1rem` to match the rest of our application. Inputs don't inherit font styles by default, so we'll also explicitly set `color` and `font-family` to `inherit`.

> **NOTE**   `inherit` is a handy property value. It allows an element to inherit a property value from the parent forcibly when inheritance doesn't happen by default.

Next, we're going to give the inputs some padding and custom borders, as well as curve their corners. In this case, we'll make these changes for stylistic purposes. Most applications have a general style (look and feel). The styles we choose to apply to our fields should be in the same vein as the rest of our application's general theme to help the form blend with the page and look as though it belongs. From a marketing perspective, sticking with our theme also helps reinforce brand recognition.

To create the bottom border gradient effect, we'll use a linear gradient that goes from our primary color to our accent color. Because a gradient is an image we can't assign to the `border-bottom` property, we need to use `border-image`, which allows us to style our borders with images. We'll still provide a color in the `border-bottom` property as a fallback. Our code looks like the following listing.

Listing 10.4   Styling input fields that aren't of type `radio` **or** `checkbox`

```
input:not([type="radio"], [type="checkbox"]) {

  font-size: 1rem;
  font-family: inherit;
```

```
    color: inherit;
    border: none;                              ←——| Removes all borders
    border-bottom: solid 1px var(--primary);        from the field
    border-image: linear-gradient(to right, var(--primary), var(--accent)) 1;   ←——
    padding: 0 0 .25rem;
    width: 100%;                                                    Adds the gradient
}                                                                    for our border
```

**Adds the border back in, but only
on the bottom, with our primary
color as a fallback color**

Pixels and rems

Notice that our border uses pixels whereas the rest of our declarations use rems. In
some instances, we want some elements of our design to be relative to the text size.
In other words, if the text size increased or decreased, we'd want those elements to
scale accordingly. Our padding and margin in this case use rems because if the text
size increases, we don't want the design to start looking cramped; on the flip side, if
the text size decreases, we want to shrink that space accordingly. For these cases,
we want to use a relative unit such as rems.

We want to keep the border at 1 pixel, however, regardless of the text size. Therefore,
we use a fixed unit.

We have some basic styles set for our text and email inputs, as shown in figure 10.4.
We've started to develop a theme for our form controls.

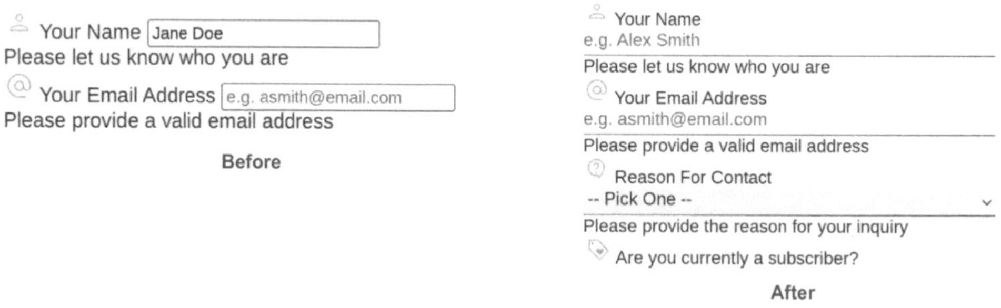

Figure 10.4   Text and email input styles

10.3.2 *Making selects and textareas match the input styles*

To make sure that the look and feel are consistent across our controls, let's apply the
same styles we applied to the input field to the <textarea> and <select> elements.
We're not going to create new rules or copy and paste the code. To keep our styles
consistent and maintainable, we'll add select and textarea as selectors to our existing rules, as shown in the following listing.

Listing 10.5 Adding `textarea` and `select` to existing rule

```
input:not([type="radio"], [type="checkbox"]),
textarea,
select {
  font-size: 1rem;
  font-family: inherit;
  color: inherit;
  border: none;
  border-bottom: solid 1px var(--primary);
  border-image: linear-gradient(to right, var(--primary), var(--accent)) 1;
  padding: 0 0 .25rem;
  width: 100%;
}
```

Adds textarea and select to our rule

Adds the border back in, but only on the bottom, with our primary color as a fallback color

Adds the gradient for our border

When the rule is applied, we notice that both fields still need a little bit of extra styling. Let's focus on the `<textarea>` first. Figure 10.5 shows our updated `<textarea>`.

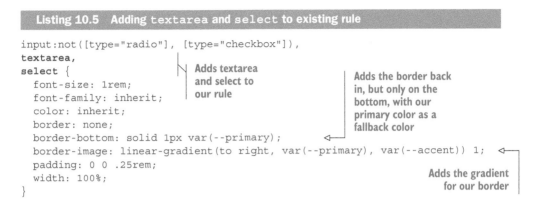

Before

After

Figure 10.5 Updated `<textarea>` styles

By default on the web, users can resize the width and height of `<textarea>`s by clicking and dragging the bottom-right corner. In our layout, increasing or decreasing the height doesn't cause any layout issues. Changing the width, however, hides our image and eventually makes our form uncentered, as we can observe in figure 10.6.

The `<textarea>` extends outside the container in an unsightly fashion. When we resize vertically, the container resizes appropriately, but this isn't the case horizontally. By changing the value of the `<textarea>`'s `resize` property from its default setting (`both`) to `vertical`, we limit users' ability to resize the element. Users will continue to be able to change its height but not the width, as shown in the following listing.

Listing 10.6 Updated styles for `textarea`

```
textarea { resize: vertical }
```

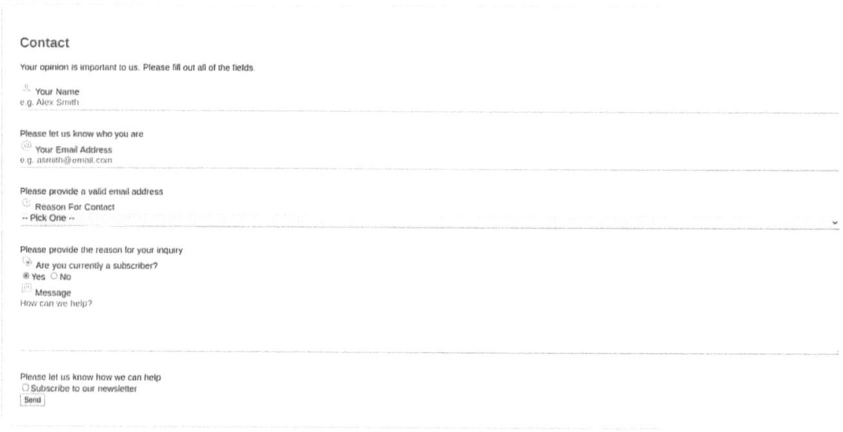

Figure 10.6 `<textarea>` **resize issue**

Visually, the text box looks the same and still has the resize control in the bottom-right corner (figure 10.7). When the user interacts with the resize control, however, they'll be constrained to resizing vertically.

Figure 10.7 `<textarea>` **vertical resize only**

We still need to address the `<select>`, but this process will be a bit more complicated than editing the `<textarea>`. So let's finish styling the input fields first and then circle back to finish styling the `<select>` control.

10.3.3 *Styling radio inputs and check boxes*

Some form controls are notoriously difficult to style because the number of styles that can be applied to them are incredibly limited. Radio buttons and check boxes fall squarely into that category. Until recently, no properties whatsoever affected the radio-button circle or the check-box square. Our only option was to replace the native control styles with our own.

> **Why are some form fields so hard to style?**
> Some form fields, radio buttons and check boxes included, have a reputation for being hard to style. This reputation stems from the limited number of CSS properties we have to alter how they look. The reason we have only limited properties is that the bulk of their appearance is driven by the operating system, not the browser.

Now we have the ability to change the native control's color. The `accent-color` property allows us to replace the user agent's chosen color with the color we specify. Applying `accent-color: var(--accent);` to our check box and radio buttons (listing 10.7) yields the results shown in figure 10.8.

Listing 10.7   Updated styles for `textarea`

```
input[type="radio"],
input[type="checkbox"] {              Styles are being applied
  accent-color: var(--accent);        only to inputs that have a
}                                     type of radio or checkbox.
```

Are you currently a subscriber?
◉ Yes ○ No
Message
How can we help?

Are you currently a subscriber?
◉ Yes ○ No
Message
How can we help?

Please let us know how we can help
☑ Subscribe to our newsletter
Send

Please let us know how we can help
☐ Subscribe to our newsletter
Send

Before   **After**

Figure 10.8   Accent color applied to radio buttons and check boxes

The elements have taken our set accent color instead of the light blue default color they used before. If we increase the `font-size` in the application, however, the controls don't increase in size (figure 10.9).

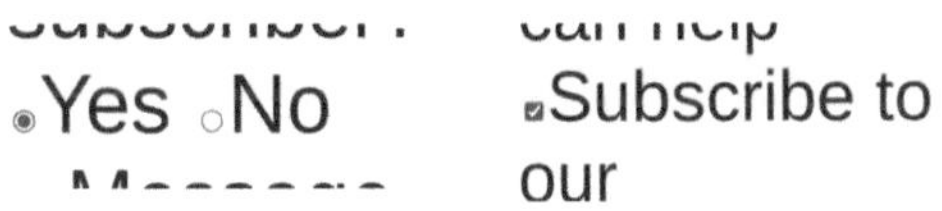

● Yes ○ No

☑ Subscribe to our

Figure 10.9   Increasing font size on radio buttons and check boxes

Although we can change the color of the element (which is an effective way to style the control quickly and efficiently to fit our styles better), if we want to allow a control to scale with our font size or make any further customizations, we'll need to replace the control's styles with our own. Because we want to keep the functionality of the control and replace only its visual aspect, our HTML stays the same. We're going to hide the native control provided by the browser and replace the visual portion with our own custom styles. To hide the native control, we'll use the `appearance` property and give it a value of `none`. This property allows us to control the native appearance of the control. By setting its property to `none`, we're saying that we don't want it to display the styles provided by the operating system. We'll also set the `background-color` to our own background color (because some operating systems include a background for the controls) and then reset our margins.

We can remove the `accent-color` declaration we created earlier; we're re-creating the visual aspect of the control from scratch, so the declaration will have no effect. The following listing shows the completed reset.

Listing 10.8   Reset of `radio` and `checkbox` inputs

```
input[type="radio"],
input[type="checkbox"] {
  accent-color: var(--accent);
  appearance: none;
  background-color: var(--background);
  margin: 0;
}
```

Figure 10.10 shows that the radio buttons have disappeared. We can start creating our own styles for those controls.

| Before | After |

Figure 10.10   Reset radio and check box styles

To start, we want to create a box. For radio-button inputs, we'll give that box a `border-radius` to make it round. At the core, whether an input element is a check box or group of radio buttons, an input needs a box. We'll create one by giving the input a `height` and a `width` of `1.75em`. We use em units because they're a percentage of the parent's font size. By setting our height and width to `1.75em`, we're setting them to equal 1 3/4 times the value of the parent's font size. If our label—the container and therefore the parent of our input—has a font-size of 16px, our box will be 28 pixels wide by 28 pixels tall (16 x 1.75 = 28).

Next, we'll add a border that inherits our label's font color. This step may sound a little weird: how are we going to make border-color inherit from font-color? We're going to use the keyword value currentcolor, which allows properties to inherit font color when they otherwise could not. We're going to set the border color to current-color to make the border color match the font color. To set our border width, we'll use em to allow the width of our border to scale with the size of our radio buttons.

Because inputs are inline elements by default, to apply our height and width, we'll also need to change the display property. We'll set it to inline-grid because when we handle the checked state for our inputs, we need to center the inner disk or check mark. Grid allows us to do so easily by means of the place-content property.

inline-grid is to grid as inline-block is to block. inline-block has all the same characteristics as block but places itself inline in the page flow. inline-grid works the same way. We have access to all the features of grid, but the element places itself inline in the page flow rather than below the previous content. For our purposes, this fact means that the input will place itself with the text label without our having to create special rules for labels containing radio-button inputs or check boxes.

Finally, we need to handle border-radius. This step is where the check box and the radio buttons diverge, because the check box is square and the radio buttons are circular. Because our fields have rounded edges, we're going to add a small border-radius (4px) to the check box. To make the radio buttons circular, we'll add a border-radius of 50%. Our updated rule is shown in the following listing.

Listing 10.9   Styled radio and checkbox inputs

```
input[type="radio"],
input[type="checkbox"] {
  appearance: none;
  background-color: var(--background);
  margin: 0;
  width: 1.75em;
  height: 1.75em;
  border: 1px solid currentcolor;       ◁── Sets the border to the
  display: inline-grid;                     same color as the parent
  place-content: center;                    element's text color
}
```
Sets up to center the inner disk or check mark when the element is checked

```
input[type="radio"] { border-radius: 50% }

input[type="checkbox"] { border-radius: 4px }
```

Our unchecked inputs are styled. Now we need to address the styles to use when those inputs are selected. In figure 10.11, selected (checked) and unselected elements look identical.

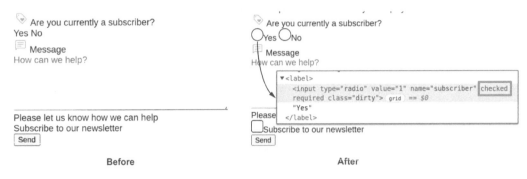

Figure 10.11   Unselected radio **and** checkbox **styles**

10.3.4   *Using the :where() and :is() pseudo-classes*

At this junction, we're going to look at two pseudo-classes that will help us keep our code clean and concise: :is() and :where(). Both pseudo-classes work similarly in that they take a list of selectors and apply the rule if any of the selectors within the list matches. Both are incredibly helpful for writing long lists of selectors. Instead of writing

```
input:focus, textarea:focus, select:focus, button:focus { ... }
```

we can use :where or :is and write an equivalent like so:

```
:where(input, textarea, select, button):focus { ... }
```

The :is() pseudo-class would be applied in the same manner. The difference between :is() and :where() is in their level of specificity. :where() is less specific and therefore easy to override. :is(), on the other hand, takes the specificity value of the most specific selector in the list.

> **NOTE**   To see how specificity is calculated, check out chapter 1. We'll go into a bit more depth on calculating specificity with :where() and :is() in section 10.3.9.

> **WARNING**   Use caution in using :is(), because if we have an id selector in our list of selectors (id selectors are most specific), we can create rules that are difficult to override.

We'll use :where() and :is() in conjunction with pseudo-classes such as :checked, :hover, and :focus, and with the ::before pseudo-element to finish styling our checkbox and radio inputs.

10.3.5   *Styling selected radio and checkbox inputs*

To add the inner disk of the selected radio button and the check mark for the check box, we'll apply a method similar to the one we used for unselected inputs. We created some base styles that applied to both types of inputs and then added the finishing touches to each element individually when the styles diverged. As before, we'll start by creating a box. Next, we'll place that box in the center of the existing styles, and then we'll shape it to be a disk or check mark.

To create this second box to be placed inside our current element, we'll use the ::before pseudo-element. At this point, the :where() pseudo class (introduced in section 10.3.4) comes into play; we'll use it to select both of our input types and then add the ::before pseudo-elements. Our selector will look like this: :where(input[type= "radio"], input[type="checkbox"])::before { }.

Our content will be empty, so we'll use a content property value of "" (empty quotes), and we'll give it a display value of block so that we can assign a width and a height.

When we created the outer box earlier, we gave it a height and width of 1.75em. We used an em unit so that control would scale relative to the text size. We'll do the same thing here. We want the inner disks and check mark to be smaller than their containers, so we'll set the height and width to 1em. Assuming that the font-size applied to the input is 16px, our box will be 16px by 16px (16 x 1 = 16).

We don't need to do anything to position our inner box. Remember that earlier, we set the input display to inline-grid and then added the place-content property with a value of center in listing 10.8. The grid layout automatically places the inner box in the center of the input. The CSS for our inner disk and check mark looks like the following listing.

Listing 10.10   Centering the inner box

```
:where(input[type="radio"], input[type="checkbox"])::before {
  display: block;
  content: '';
  width: 1em;
  height: 1em;
}
```

When we apply this code, we see no changes, as demonstrated in figure 10.12. Our inner box does exist but isn't visible yet.

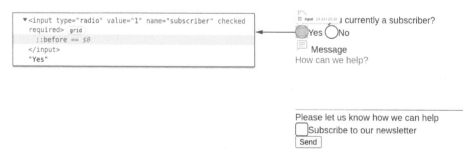

Figure 10.12   Invisible inner box

The box isn't visible because it doesn't have any content or background color. We'll add a background color next.

10.3.6 Using the :checked pseudo-class

We're not going to apply the same background color to our element all the time. We're going to use our accent color when the element is selected and our hover color when the element is being hovered over.

The `:checked` pseudo-class selector can be used on an input of type `radio` or `checkbox`, or on the option element (`<option>`) in a drop-down menu (`<select>`) to apply styles when the element is selected. The ability to use it on `<option>` is browser-dependent.

When we apply the `background-color` for the `checked` and `hover` states, if the selectors have the same level of specificity (as our example will), the order in which we write these rules matters. If we write the checked state rule first and the hover state rule second, the hover color will be applied to a selected input on hover; the hover state rule will override the checked state rule because it appears later in the CSS file. Therefore, we want to make sure that the hover state rule is placed before the checked state rule in the CSS file. Figure 10.13 illustrates these two scenarios.

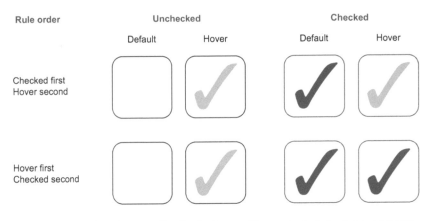

Figure 10.13 Rule order regarding the background for a selected check box on hover

Let's see how we'd go about applying our background colors in our CSS file. The following listing shows our `hover` and `checked` code so far.

Listing 10.11 Inner element background color

```
:where(input[type="radio"], input[type="checkbox"]):hover::before {
  background: var(--hover);
}
```

Adds a background color
to the inner box on hover

```
:where(input[type="radio"], input[type="checkbox"]):checked::before {
  background: var(--accent);
}
```

**Adds a background color to the
inner box when input is selected**

Figure 10.14 shows that we have a box we can shape inside our elements. The box is displayed in our accent color when the element is selected, and when a user hovers over unselected radio-button or check-box inputs, we see a gray box.

Before   **After**

Figure 10.14   Setting up for the selected state

Next, we need to shape the inner box, where our code will diverge to create disks and a check mark for the radio buttons and check box, respectively.

10.3.7   Shaping the selected radio buttons' inner disk

Starting with the radio-button inputs, we turn our inner box into a circle by adding a border-radius of 50%, as shown in listing 10.12. We don't differentiate between the hover and checked states because we want the shape to be a disk regardless of the state of the element.

Listing 10.12   Radio-button inner disk

```
input[type="radio"]::before {
  border-radius: 50%;
}
```

Now we have traditional-looking radio buttons that scale nicely regardless of text size (figure 10.15). With our radio buttons styled, we'll turn our attention to shaping the check mark inside our check box.

⬛Yes ◯No

▤ Message
How can we help?

⬜ Are you currently a subscriber?
⦿Yes ◯No

▤ Message
How can we help?

Please let us know how we can help
⬛Subscribe to our newsletter
[Send]

Please let us know how we can help
⬛Subscribe to our newsletter
[Send]

Before   **After**

Figure 10.15   Styled radio **inputs**

10.3.8 *Using CSS shapes to create the check mark*

Shaping our radio inputs was simple: we used border-radius to achieve a disk shape. Creating a check mark isn't quite as simple. To do that, we'll use clip-path.

> **NOTE**   clip-path allows us to create shapes by creating a clipping region that defines which parts of the element should be displayed and which parts should be hidden. We used clip-path in chapter 7.

The shape we'll apply to the clip-path to create our check mark is a polygon. Polygons are created by setting a series of X and Y percentage-based coordinates between which a line is created. The (0,0) coordinate is the top-left corner of the shape. If the shape isn't explicitly closed, it automatically joins the first and last points. Our polygon() function will be polygon(14% 44%, 0% 65%, 50% 100%, 100% 16%, 80% 0%, 43% 62%). Figure 10.16 explains the point-by-point construction of the shape.

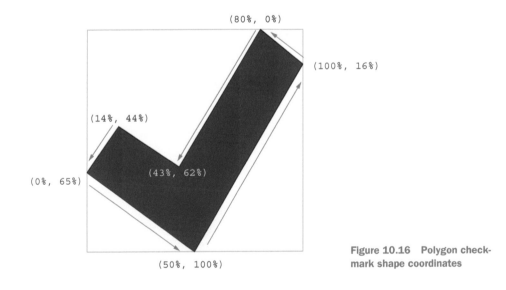

Figure 10.16   Polygon check-mark shape coordinates

NOTE The coordinates for simple shapes are easy enough to figure out. But as shapes get more complex, determining the coordinates manually can be cumbersome. In those situations, we can turn to vector-graphic drawing programs such as Inkscape and Illustrator, or to one of the many CSS shape-generator websites, including https://bennettfeely.com/clippy.

With our shape created, we can create our `clip-path` and apply it to the inner portion of our check box, as shown in the following listing.

Listing 10.13   Check mark in our check box

```
input[type="checkbox"]::before {
  clip-path: polygon(14% 44%, 0% 65%, 50% 100%, 100% 16%, 80% 0%, 43% 62%);
}
```

With the `clip-path` added, we have a fully functional check box. Next, let's add some finishing touches. Notice in figure 10.17 that the outlines of the selected radio buttons and check box are still in our font color rather than the accent color.

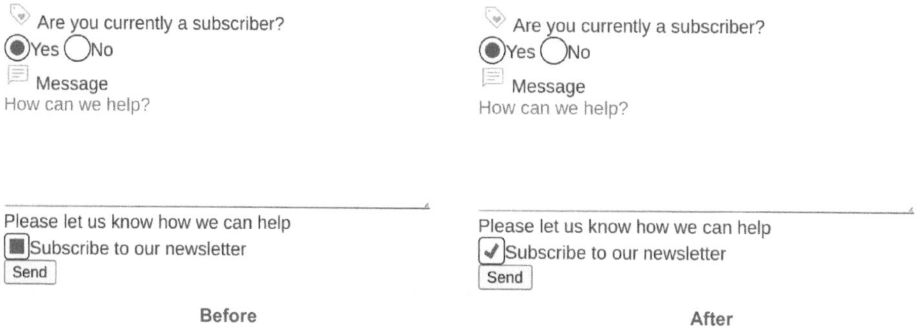

Figure 10.17   Styled check mark in the check box

To add the outline color to both the radio buttons and the check box when they're selected, we're going to use the `:checked` pseudo-class again to change the border color to our accent color only when the control is selected. This procedure translates to the code shown in listing 10.14. We use `:is()` instead of `:where()` for reasons of specificity.

Listing 10.14   Accent-color outline for selected inputs

```
:is(input[type="radio"], input[type="checkbox"]):checked {
  border-color: var(--accent);
}
```

10.3.9 *Calculating specificity with :is() and :where()*

We mentioned earlier that `:where()` has a specificity of 0, meaning that it's the least specific selector available to us. We set our default border color in the selector `input[type="radio"], input[type="checkbox"] { … }`, which has a specificity of 11, calculated according to table 10.1. In each column, we count the number of each type of selector, with columns A, B, and C forming the specificity value.[1]

Table 10.1   Calculating specificity

Selector	A ID selectors (×100)	B Class selectors, attribute selectors, & pseudo-classes (×10)	C Type selectors, pseudo- elements (×1)	Specificity
`:where(input[type="radio"], input[type="checkbox"])`	Ignores specificity rules and always equals 0			0 0 0
`:where(input[type="radio"], input[type="checkbox"]):checked`	Ignores specificity rules and always equals 0			0 0 0
`input[type="radio"]`	0	1	1	0 1 1
`input[type="radio"]:checked`	0	2	1	0 2 1
`:is(input[type="radio"], input[type="checkbox"]):checked`	0	2	1	0 2 1

Because `:is()` bases its specificity value on the value of the most specific selector within it, in this case the specificity will be 11 plus another 10 for the `:checked` state, giving us a specificity of 21. Because 21 is greater than 0, we override the styles, and our border becomes our accent color.

Now our radio buttons and check box are styled both when they're selected and unselected, and on hover for both states. Figure 10.18 shows our progress so far.

Let's turn our attention to the drop-down menu next.

10.4   *Styling drop-down menus*

Although we applied the same default styles to `<select>` elements as we did for the text-based `<input>`s and `<textarea>`s (listing 10.5), we see in figure 10.19 that the drop-down menu (`<select>`) is still rough. We also see in the expanded view that our options list doesn't match our theme.

Let's start by fixing the background color. Although it's not obvious because the background behind our form is white, the input fields have a white background by default. We're going to add a rule to the existing declaration that affects the `<input>`s,

---

[1] *Architecting CSS: The Programmer's Guide to Effective Style Sheets,* by Martine Dowden and Michael Dowden (2020, Apress).

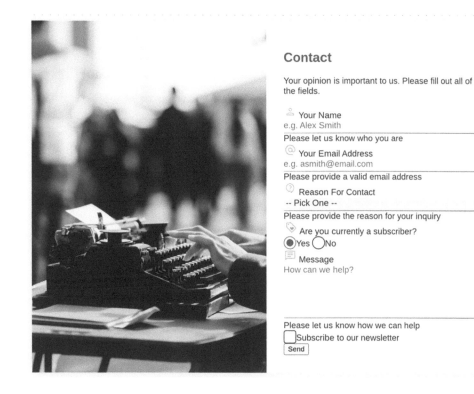

Figure 10.18   Styled check box and radio-button inputs

Closed

Expanded

Figure 10.19   Drop-down menu closed and expanded

<textarea>, and <select> elements to set the background color to the card background (listing 10.15). That way, should the card background change, our form controls will have the appropriate background color.

Listing 10.15   Default styles applied to `select`

```
input:not([type="radio"], [type="checkbox"]),
textarea,
select {
  font-size: 1rem;
```

```
font-family: inherit;
color: inherit;
border: none;
border-bottom: solid 1px var(--primary);
border-image: linear-gradient(to right, var(--primary), var(--accent)) 1;
padding: 0 0 .25rem;
margin-bottom: 2rem;
width: 100%;
background-color: var(--background-card);                      Adds background-
}                                                              color declaration
```

With the background color added, we see that the input and options have a white background (figure 10.20).

Before   **After**

Figure 10.20 `select` **element styled**

Although it would be nice to update the drop-down menu options to match our theme better, these menus, like the radio inputs and check boxes, get a lot of their styles and functionality from the operating system itself. Therefore, we're limited in what we can style with CSS alone, and for this design, these changes are about as far as we can go. We can use JavaScript and ARIA to replace the entire control, but because this book is about CSS, we're going to style as much as we can with CSS alone.

What is ARIA?

ARIA (which stands for Accessible Rich Internet Applications) is a set of roles and attributes that can be added to HTML elements to supplement missing information about the use, state, and functionality of an element that otherwise isn't available to the user. For more information, check out https://www.w3.org/WAI/standards -guidelines/aria.

NOTE When creating a custom control, it's important to be mindful of the underlying accessibility information and functionality that the browser provides automatically and to make sure we're re-creating that functionality along with the visual aspects of the control. Libraries or frameworks can be helpful when a custom control is needed, assuming that the library or framework was built with accessibility in mind. Usually, the best place to find out is the documentation.

10.5 Styling labels and legends

To style our labels and the legend, we're going to start by giving them a vertical margin for breathing room between the label and the control. We'll also use Flexbox to align the text and the icons, radio inputs, and check box. Finally, we'll decrease their font size and change their color. Most important here are the values entered by the user, not the labels. By decreasing their size, we diminish their importance in the visual hierarchy. We end up with the code displayed in the following listing.

Listing 10.16 Added margin and updated font size

```css
label, legend {
    display: flex;
    align-items: center;       Aligns the label
    gap: .25rem;               text and the icon
    margin: 0 0 .5rem 0;
    font-size: .875rem;
    color: var(--label-color);
}
```

With our labels and legend styled (figure 10.21), let's turn our attention to the placeholders.

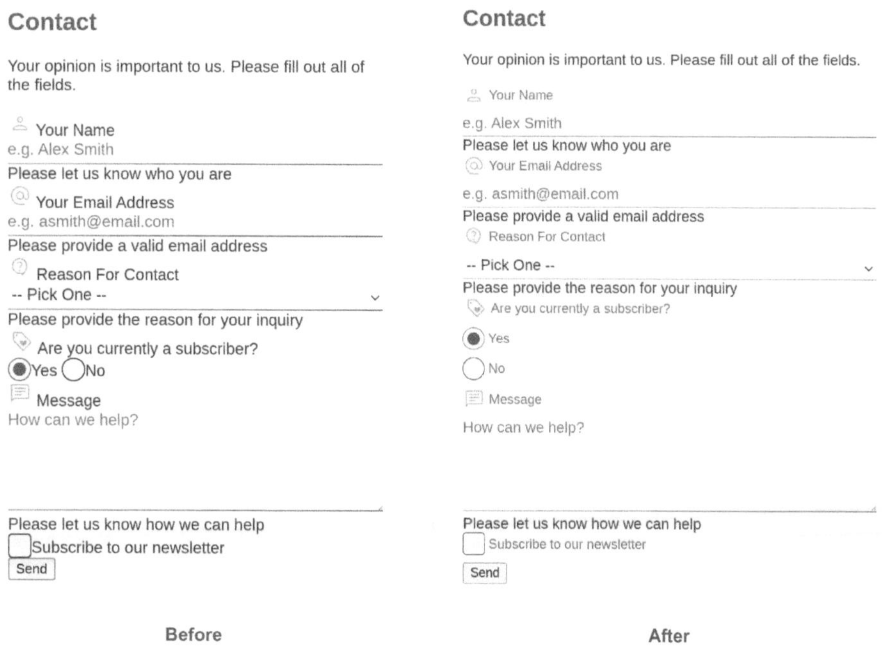

Contact

Your opinion is important to us. Please fill out all of the fields.

Your Name
e.g. Alex Smith
Please let us know who you are

Your Email Address
e.g. asmith@email.com
Please provide a valid email address

Reason For Contact
-- Pick One --
Please provide the reason for your inquiry

Are you currently a subscriber?
Yes No

Message
How can we help?

Please let us know how we can help
Subscribe to our newsletter
Send

Before

Contact

Your opinion is important to us. Please fill out all of the fields.

Your Name
e.g. Alex Smith
Please let us know who you are

Your Email Address
e.g. asmith@email.com
Please provide a valid email address

Reason For Contact
-- Pick One --
Please provide the reason for your inquiry

Are you currently a subscriber?
Yes
No

Message
How can we help?

Please let us know how we can help
Subscribe to our newsletter
Send

After

Figure 10.21 Styled labels and legend

10.6   *Styling the placeholder text*

In our form, it's difficult to distinguish what fields are user filled from what is placeholder text. As we did for our labels, we're going to deemphasize the placeholder text to make it easier to distinguish from user responses.

Labels and placeholder text

Our project has both labels and placeholder text. Although placeholder text can be helpful to guide the user, it doesn't replace labels. In fact, the Web Content Accessibility Guidelines (WCAG) accessibility standards specifically require form fields to have a label (http://mng.bz/mVzW).

Placeholder text disappears after the user enters a value in the field. This arrangement is problematic because the user doesn't have a way to reference the instructions after they enter a value.

Furthermore, labels are required for assistive technologies such as screen readers, which rely on this information to indicate to the user what is expected in the field.

To style our placeholder text, we're going to use the ::placeholder pseudo-element. Because we want the placeholder to be styled the same way regardless of the type, we'll write one rule that targets all placeholder text regardless of element type. In this new rule, we'll decrease the size of the placeholder text and lighten its color, as shown in the following listing.

Listing 10.17   Styling the placeholder text

```
::placeholder {                          ◁──┐  Targets any placeholder
  color: var(--placeholder-color);          │  text regardless of
  font-size: .75em;                         │  element type
}
```

Figure 10.22 shows our updated fields.

Next, let's style the button at the bottom of the form.

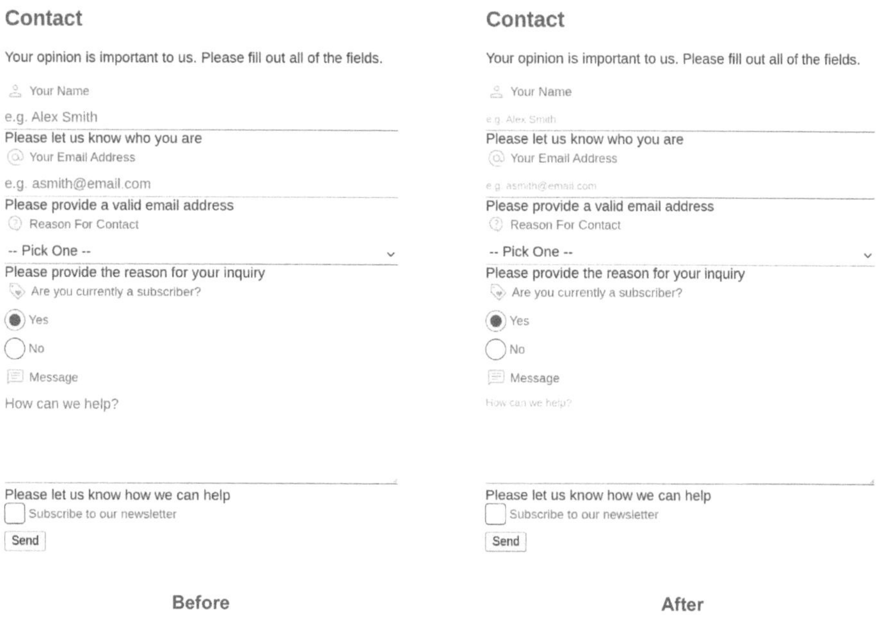

Before   **After**

Figure 10.22   Styled placeholder text

10.7   *Styling the Send button*

We have a Send button at the bottom of our form. Let's make it a bit more prominent and make it match the rest of our form. We'll create a rule that targets this button.

Next, we'll remove the border, curve the corners, and edit the text and background colors. In the "before" part of figure 10.23, the button text is smaller than our default font size, so we also change `font-size` to `1rem`. Finally, we set our button padding.

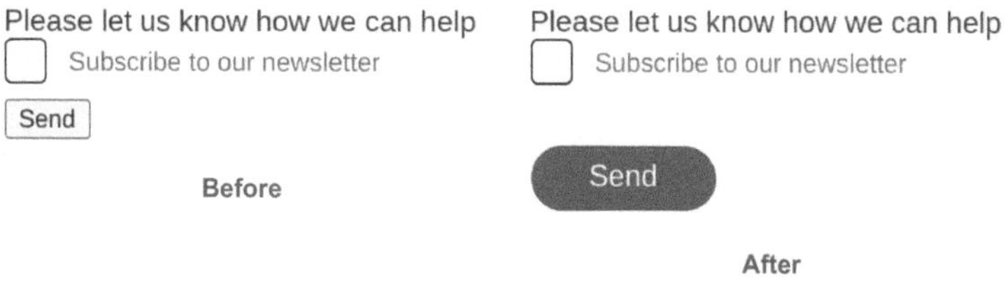

Before

After

Figure 10.23   Styled Send button

To make our button stand out even more, we'll separate it a little bit from the rest of our fields. The button is located inside a `<div>` with a class of `actions`. We'll give this

<div> a top margin of 2rem, which will move the button down a little farther from the Subscribe check box. The following listing shows our new rules, and figure 10.23 shows our progress.

Listing 10.18   Resetting button styles

```
button[type="submit"] {
  border: none;
  border-radius: 36px;
  background: var(--accent);
  color: var(--accent-contrast);
  font-size: 1rem;
  cursor: pointer;
  padding: .5rem 2rem;
}

.actions { margin-top: 2rem }
```

Next, let's style the error messages.

10.8   *Error handling*

Below the Name, Email, and Message controls are error messages. Currently, they're un-styled, so they aren't easy to identify as error messages or to match them with the fields that the errors describe. Furthermore, we don't want to show this error message until the user has interacted with the control. Nobody wants an error message yelling at them before they've even started.

We're going to style the error messages to look like error messages; then we'll hide them by default and show them only when appropriate. This task is where our Java-Script file comes into play.

We're going to make our text red, like most error messages on the web, by setting that color in our --error custom property. We'll also make the text bold and preface our error with an error icon to present it clearly as such; we don't want to use color alone to convey meaning or intent.

> **NOTE** Color is a great way to differentiate content types. But we should always use something else with it—such as an icon; text; or a change in size, weight, or shape—because people who are color-blind may not be able to differentiate between colors. Furthermore, some colors don't have the same meaning across cultures. For reasons of accessibility and clarity, it's best practice to use more than color alone to convey a message.

So that we can keep our error icon consistent instead of adding it before each error, we'll add it programmatically via CSS, using the ::before pseudo-element. To size and position the icon, we'll use two relative units: the character unit (ch), which we used in chapter 7 and which is based on the font's width; and ex, which is relative to the font's X-height, which is the distance between the baseline and meanline of a font (figure 10.24). We use these particular units because they're relative to not only the font size, but also the characteristics of the typeface being used. Using ch and ex units helps make the size and spacing between the icon and the text seem like an extension of the font that's being used.

Figure 10.24   A visual representation of typography terms

We'll also add some margin to our error <div> to give our input fields some breathing room. Our rules to style errors look like the following listing.

Listing 10.19   Error styles

```
.error {
  color: var(--error);          ⟵┤ Makes the
  margin: .25rem 0 2rem;           │ text red
}
.error span::before {
  content: url('./img/error.svg');
  display: inline-block;
  width: 1.25ex;                │ Makes the icon
  height: 1.25ex;               │ 1.25ex by 1.25ex
  vertical-align: baseline;     ⟵┐
  margin-right: .5ch;            │ Aligns the icon to
}                                │ the text's baseline
```

Notice that when we added the icon before the text, we added it to the span, not the error <div> itself, because we're going to be showing and hiding the span inside the error and the entire error <div>. Let's take a closer look at the HTML to understand why.

Listing 10.20 shows the complete control for the Name field, including its label and error message. Notice that the error <div> has an id of nameError, which is referenced by the aria-describedby attribute on the input field. The aria-describedby attribute tells screen readers and assistive technologies that the element whose id it references contains extra information pertaining to the input field.

If we hide the error <div> in its entirety by using display:none, the element to which the aria-describedby is pointing won't exist. Therefore, we hide only the contents (the span) so as not to break the programmatic connection between the element and its error. Because we'll be hiding only the span, we need to apply the icon to the span so that it can be hidden when we hide the error message.

Listing 10.20   Name-field HTML

```
<label for="name">Your Name</label>
<input type="text" id="name" name="name" maxlength="250" required
    aria-describedby="nameError">
<div class="error" id="nameError">
  <span role="alert">
    Please let us know who you are
  </span>
</div>
```

Indicates which <div>
provides extra information
about the input (referenced
by id)

The ID referenced by the
aria-describedby attribute

Figure 10.25 shows our styled error messages.

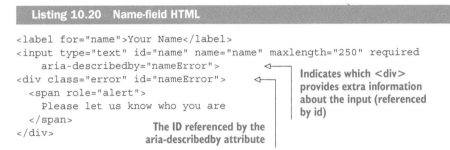

Before   After

Figure 10.25   Styled error messages

With our error messages styled, we can handle showing them only when appropriate. In figure 10.25, we see that the inputs have valid values, yet the error messages still appear. To show the error message only when the field is invalid, we'll start by hiding the error message by default. We apply a `display` property value of `none` to the `span` contained in the error `<div>`; then we use the `:invalid` pseudo-class to show it conditionally (only when the field is invalid).

The validity of the field in this case is determined by the properties we set on the field itself. Let's look at the Name input HTML again: `<input type="text" id="name" name="name" maxlength="250" required aria-describedby="nameError">`. We included `required` and `maxlength` attributes; therefore, if there's no value in the field or if the value's length is greater than 250 characters, the field value will be invalid, and styles in the `:invalid` pseudo-class will be applied.

The Email element (`<input type="email" id="email" name="email" max-length="250" required aria-describedby="emailError">`) also has a `maxlength` and a `required` attribute, so it would be invalid under the same conditions as the Name field. It also has a type of `email`. In HTML, some field types have validation built in, and `email` is one of them. If we were to enter an email address value of `"myEmail"`, it would be invalid.

Using the `:invalid` pseudo-class helps us prevent errors from being displayed when the field is valid, but it doesn't prevent errors from showing up if the user hasn't interacted with the field yet. We could use the `:user-invalid` pseudo-class instead of `:invalid`, which would trigger one time and only after the user interacted with the field, but at this writing, Mozilla Firefox is the only browser that supports this property. So we turn to JavaScript due to the current lack of cross-browser support. In the future, when the `:user-invalid` property is better supported, we'll no longer need to use JavaScript to show/hide our error messages based on user interaction. The script included in the project listens for blur events, which happen when an element loses focus. When we click or tab away from a field, a blur event occurs. Our script listens for these events and adds a class of `dirty` to the field that we've navigated away from, letting us know which fields have been interacted with and which haven't. Those with a class of `dirty` have; without a class of `dirty` have not.

Because we have this `dirty` class, in conjunction with the `:invalid` pseudo-class, we'll show the error message only below controls that are invalid and that the user has touched, preventing us from showing error messages before the user has had a chance to fill out the form. We use the selector `.dirty:invalid + .error span`. We select the `span` contained in an element that has a class of `error` located immediately after an element that is both invalid and has a class of `dirty`.

Last, we'll change the border color of the field to our error color when it's both invalid and `dirty`. Because we used a border image to create the gradient effect, we need to remove it. The following listing shows the full rules for showing and hiding the error messages.

Listing 10.21   Error-handling CSS

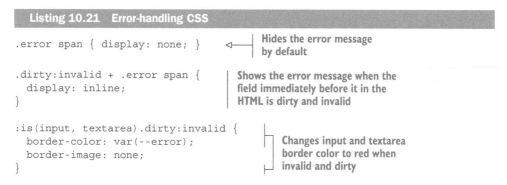

```
.error span { display: none; }          ⟵———  Hides the error message
                                                by default

.dirty:invalid + .error span {                 Shows the error message when the
  display: inline;                              field immediately before it in the
}                                               HTML is dirty and invalid

:is(input, textarea) .dirty:invalid {
  border-color: var(--error);                   Changes input and textarea
  border-image: none;                           border color to red when
}                                               invalid and dirty
```

Figure 10.26 shows fields in their three possible states: invalid and dirty, valid, and invalid but not yet touched.

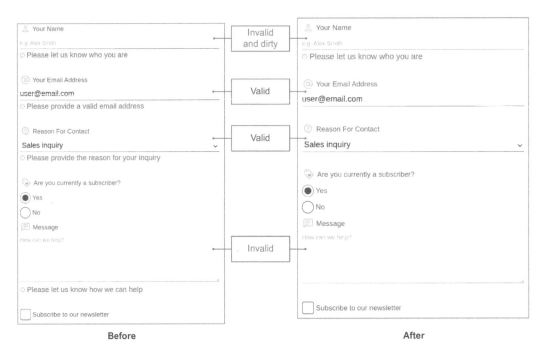

Figure 10.26   Error-handling and field states

On the surface, our form seems to be finished, but we still have some finishing touches to add.

10.9   *Adding hover and focus styles to form elements*

Because we want our form to be accessible, we need to make sure to include hover styles and to update the default focus styles to match our theme for our controls and buttons. We've already handled the hover styles for radio buttons and check boxes but not the focus. For the other elements, we haven't considered the hover and focus states.

Let's start with focus because we still need to apply it to everything on our form. Focus is important for users who navigate the web via the keyboard rather than clicking elements with a mouse. It gives the user a visual indicator of which element currently has focus. Therefore, if we don't like the default focus styles, it's fine to restyle them but not remove them.

10.9.1   Using :focus versus :focus-visible

Because showing the focus styles all the time regardless of how the user is navigating the web can be overwhelming depending on the design, a new property was recently added to the CSS specification to apply focus styles based on the user's modality: keyboard or mouse. The pseudo-class :focus-visible allows us to add styles when the user is interacting with the keyboard but won't apply it when the user is using a mouse. By contrast, :focus always applies regardless of the user's method of interacting with the element.

For our text and email input fields, drop-down menu, and text area, we'll remove the default outline and change the border's color from the gradient to a solid color. Because (as we mentioned earlier in this chapter) we don't want to rely on color alone for differentiation, we'll also change the border style from solid to dashed, as shown in listing 10.22. We also need to consider what to do with our fields when they're dirty and invalid (show the error message and have a red border). We want to keep the color differentiation between the fields in an error state, so we write a second rule to maintain the red border color.

Listing 10.22   Styling text fields and drop-down menu when focused

```
:is(
  input:not([type="radio"], [type="checkbox"]),
  textarea,
  select
):focus-visible {                        Removes the
  outline: none;              ◄─────     default outline
  border-bottom: dashed 1px var(--primary);
  border-image: none;         ◄────┐ Removes the
}                                   │ gradient image

:is(
  input:not([type="radio"], [type="checkbox"]).dirty:invalid,    Maintains the
  textarea.dirty:invalid,                                        border color when
  select.dirty:invalid                                           the field has been
):focus-visible {                                                interacted with and
  border-color: var(--error);                                    its value is invalid
}
```

Figure 10.27 shows our updated fields when in focus.

Next, we need to handle the focus state for our radio buttons and check boxes. For those elements, we'll keep the outline but edit its appearance. As we did for our other fields, we'll use a dashed line and the primary color. We also offset the outline to create separation between the border and the outline, as shown in listing 10.23.

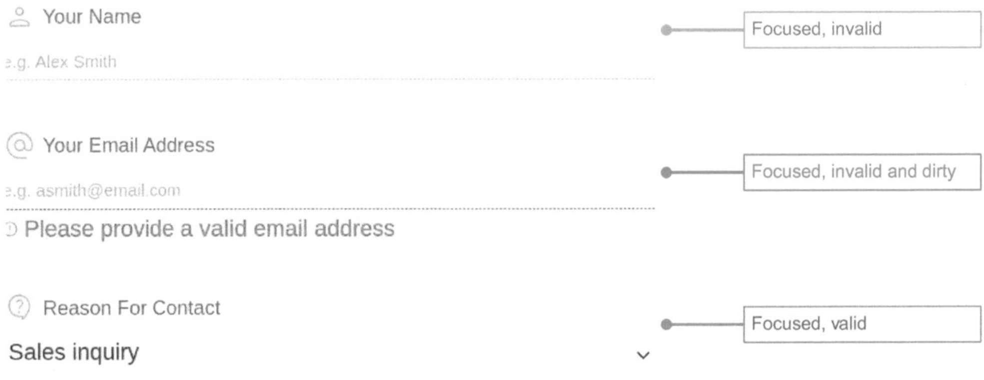

Your Name

e.g. Alex Smith

Focused, invalid

Your Email Address

e.g. asmith@email.com

Please provide a valid email address

Focused, invalid and dirty

Reason For Contact

Sales inquiry

Focused, valid

Figure 10.27   Text fields and drop-down menu when focused

Listing 10.23   Styling radio buttons and check boxes when focused

```
:where(input[type="radio"], [type="checkbox"]):focus-visible {
  outline: dashed 1px var(--primary);
  outline-offset: 2px;                    ⟵———  Moves the outline out 2 pixels so that
}                                                it isn't right up against the border
```

Figure 10.28 shows our radio buttons and check box when focused.

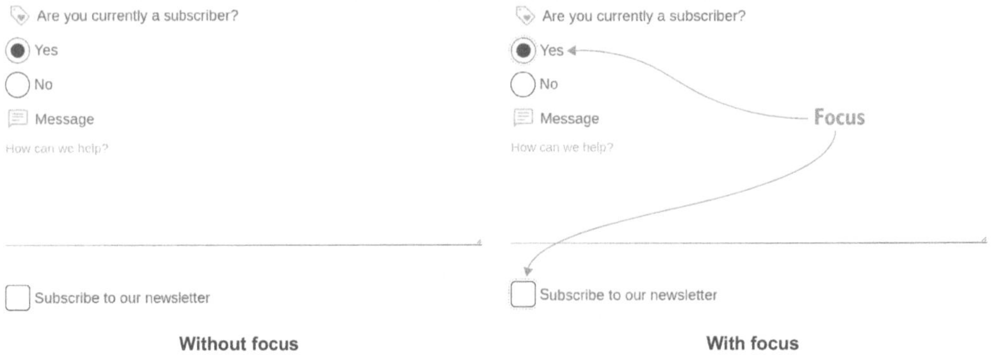

Are you currently a subscriber?
◉ Yes
◯ No
Message
How can we help?

Subscribe to our newsletter

Are you currently a subscriber?
◉ Yes ◄
◯ No
Message ———— Focus
How can we help?

Subscribe to our newsletter

Without focus   **With focus**

Figure 10.28   Focus styles for radio buttons and check box

With focus handled, let's turn our attention to hover.

10.9.2 Adding hover styles

Fields in which the user inputs text, such as inputs with a type of `text` and `email` or `<textarea>`s, already change the cursor type from the default to text on hover. Figure 10.29 shows what each cursor type looks like. Note that cursors may look slightly different depending on the operating system, browser, and user settings.

Although our text and email inputs and text area already have some differentiation on hover, our drop-down menu doesn't. Let's change its cursor to a pointer to emphasize that the field is clickable, as shown in the following listing.

Figure 10.29   Cursors in Chrome

Listing 10.24   Selecting hover styles

```
select:hover { cursor: pointer }
```

With focus and hover handled, the last thing we need to worry about is making sure that our styles work for users who have `forced-colors: active` enabled.

10.10 Handling forced-colors mode

The `forced-colors` mode is a high-contrast setting that allows a user to limit the color palette to a series of colors that they set on their device. Windows' High Contrast mode is an example of this use case. When this mode is enabled, it affects many CSS properties, including some that we've used in this project, most notably `background-color`. We used `background-color` to determine whether the inner portion of the `radio` and `checkbox` inputs were visible for selected versus unselected elements. We also used it to restyle the arrow for the `select` control.

In Chrome, we can use DevTools to emulate enabling `forced-colors` mode on our machine without having to edit our computer settings. In the console of our DevTools, choose the rendering tab. If it isn't already displayed, we can click the ellipsis button to display the possible tabs and choose it from the drop-down menu. On the tab, we look for the `forced-colors` emulation drop-down menu and set it to `forced-colors: active`. This setting updates the page's styles to act as though we had `forced-colors` set to `active` on our machine. Figure 10.30 shows the Chrome DevTools settings that enable the emulation. (Note: Browsers other than Chrome may not have this functionality, or the technique for enabling it may be different.)

When the emulation is applied, our page styles change (figure 10.31). We can't tell which radio button is selected or whether the check box is checked. This example demonstrates the importance of using more than color to differentiate meaning, because our error message is no longer red.

We won't try to reinstate our colors in this mode, because we want to respect the user's settings. But we need to make sure that selected inputs are distinguishable from those that aren't selected.

Console   Search | Rendering ✕ | Issues   Quick source   Network conditions   Animations   ✕

No emulation   ▾

Emulate CSS media type
Forces media type for testing print and screen styles

No emulation ▾

Emulate CSS media feature forced-colors
Forces CSS forced-colors media feature

forced-colors: active ▾

Emulate CSS media feature prefers-contrast
Forces CSS prefers-contrast media feature

No emulation   ▾

Emulate CSS media feature prefers-reduced-motion
Forces CSS prefers-reduced-motion media feature

No emulation   ▾

Emulate CSS media feature prefers-reduced-data
Forces CSS prefers-reduced-data media feature

No emulation   ▾

Emulate CSS media feature color-gamut
Forces CSS color-gamut media feature

Figure 10.30   A `forced-colors:active` emulation setup in Chrome DevTools

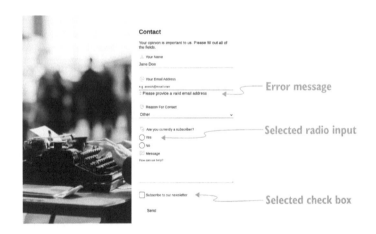

Figure 10.31   Emulated `forced-colors: active`

To create rules that apply only when users have `forced-colors` set to `active`, we'll use the media query `@media (forced-colors: active) { }`. Rules created inside the media query will take effect only when users have `forced-colors` enabled.

The reason why our check box and radio buttons are no longer visible is that the system-defined background color (in this case, white) is being applied to them. So we'll change our background to use a system color rather than our accent color. The CSS Color Module Level 4 specification (http://mng.bz/o1Vy) lists the colors available to us. We're going to use `CanvasText`, meaning that the color we'll apply will be the same as the color being used for the text. The following listing shows our full media query.

Listing 10.25 `forced-colors: active` media query

```
@media (forced-colors: active) {
  :where(input[type="radio"], input[type="checkbox"]):checked::before {
    background-color: CanvasText;
  }
}
```

Figure 10.32 shows our page in `forced-colors` mode with our media query applied, fixing the styles that were creating problems for our users.

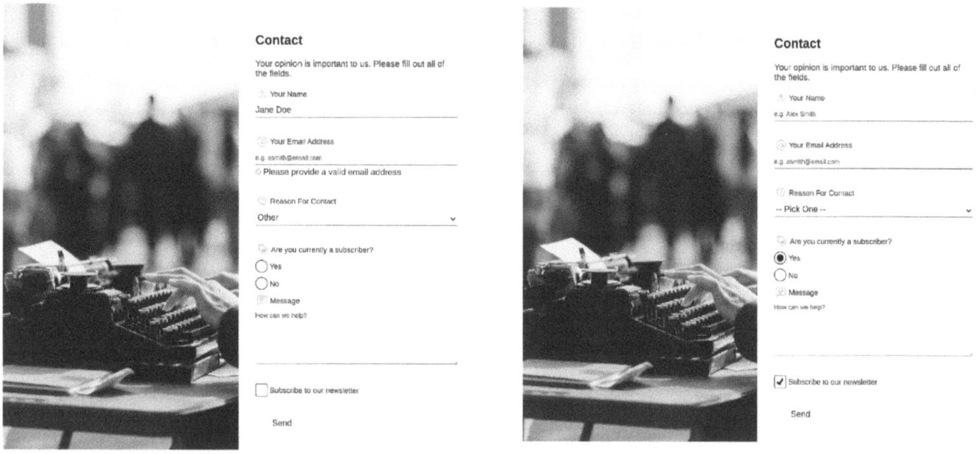

Before   After

Figure 10.32 `forced-colors: active` **styles fixed**

When we turn the emulation off, our previously set styles remain as they were; they're not affected by those set inside the media query (figure 10.33).

With this last task complete, we've finished styling our form.

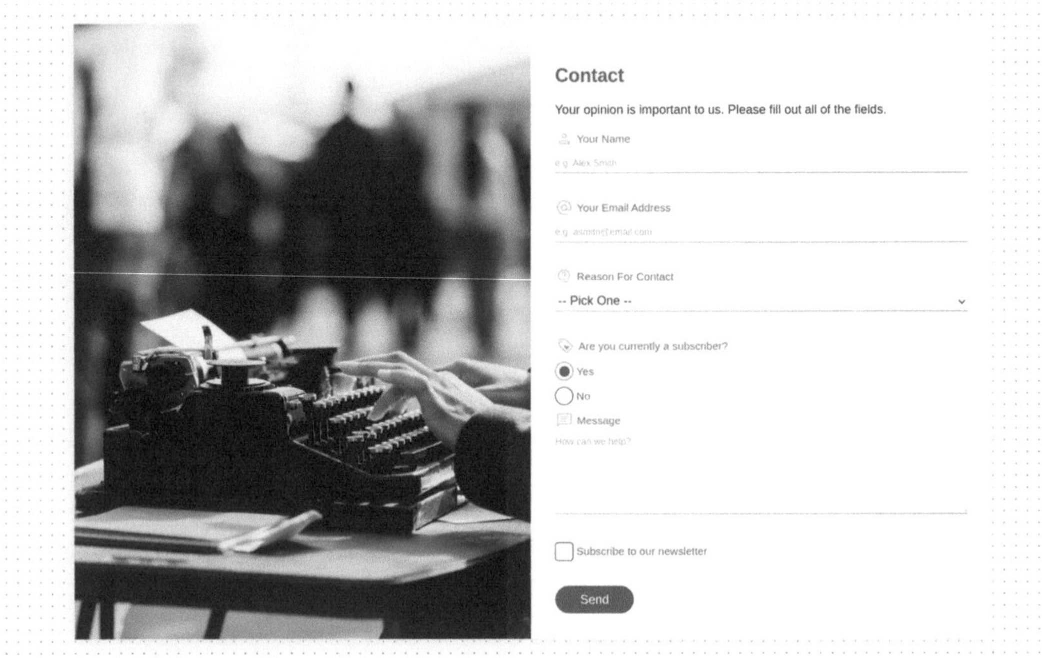

Figure 10.33   Finished product

Summary

- Form controls whose functionality is tightly coupled with the operating system, such as drop-down menus, are harder to style than those that lack this coupling.
- We can create shapes by using gradients.
- By using em, we can size elements to scale with text size.
- To inherit font-color when doing so isn't possible otherwise, we can use the keyword value currentcolor.
- The :where() and :is() pseudo-classes work similarly but have different levels of specificity.
- The :checked pseudo-class allows us to target form elements when they're selected.
- The :invalid pseudo-class can be used to format fields conditionally when they're invalid.
- The validity of a field's value is determined by the attributes set on the field in the HTML.
- :focus styles are necessary to make our designs accessible.
- We can use :focus-visible to make focus style show only for keyboard users.
- In some browsers, we can forcibly make the browser apply hover and focus styles.

- It's important to use more than color alone to convey meaning, as demonstrated by the error messages in this project.
- `forced-colors` mode changes how some properties behave and the colors we can apply to the user interface.
- Media queries can be used to apply styles conditionally when `forced-colors` is set to `active`.
- In some browsers, we can emulate `forced-colors` mode to check our designs.

Animated social media share links

11

This chapter covers

- Using the OOCSS, SMACSS, and BEM architecture patterns
- Scoping CSS when working with components
- Working with social media icons
- Creating CSS transitions
- Using JavaScript to overcome CSS limitations

One of the core reasons why the internet was created was to share and distribute information. One way we do this today is through social media. In this chapter, we'll style and animate some links that can be used to share a web page via email or social media.

As in the previous chapters, we'll be using HTML and CSS for this project without any frameworks. We chose this approach to focus on the CSS itself without the complexity and intricacies of using external packages. But many applications in the wild do use frameworks, some of which include the concept of the component.

A common reason to turn a piece of functionality into a component is to reuse the piece of code or element in multiple places in applications. With reusability comes the possibility of naming collisions. Some systems automatically restrict the scope of the CSS of the component to itself, preventing any possible collision between component styles. But many systems don't restrict the scope, leaving it up to the developer to organize the code to prevent changing the styles in another component when styling a new one.

Regardless of the framework and how it does (or doesn't) handle CSS scoping, we have a variety of architecture options to help us organize and standardize our styles. Before we dive into this chapter's project, let's take a quick look at some CSS architecture options.

11.1 *Working with CSS architecture*

Some of the most popular CSS architecture methodologies are OOCSS, SMACSS, and BEM. We'll be using BEM in this chapter, but we'll take a look at all three options so that we'll understand the high-level differences among them.

11.1.1 *OOCSS*

Introduced at Web Directions North in Denver by Nicolle Sullivan, OOCSS (Object-Oriented CSS; https://github.com/stubbornella/oocss/wiki) aims to help developers create CSS that's fast, maintainable, and standards-based. Sullivan describes the *Object* part of OOCSS as "a repeating visual pattern, that can be abstracted into an independent snippet of HTML, CSS, and possibly JavaScript. That object can then be reused throughout a site"—in other words, what we might think of today as a component or widget. To achieve this reusability, OOCSS follows two main principles:

- *Separate structure and skin*—Keeps visual features (background, borders, and so on, sometimes referred to as the theme) in their own classes, which can be mixed and matched with objects to create a variety of elements.
- *Separate container and content*—By refraining from using location-dependent styles, we can ensure that the objects look the same no matter where they're placed in the application or on the website.

11.1.2 *SMACSS*

Developed by Jonathan Snook, SMACSS (Scalable and Modular Architecture for CSS; http://smacss.com), organizes CSS rules into five categories:

- *Base*—The defaults applied by using element, descendent, or child selectors and pseudo-classes
- *Layout*—Used to lay elements out on the page, such as headers, articles, and footers
- *Module*—More discrete parts of the layout, such as carousels, cards, and navigation bars
- *State*—Something that augments or overrides other styles, such as an error state or the state of a menu (open or closed)
- *Theme*—Defines the look and feel; doesn't have to be separated in its own classes if it's the only theme for the page or project

11.1.3 BEM

Developed by a company named Yandex, BEM (Block Element Modifier; https://en
.bem.info/methodology) is a component-based architecture that aims to break the
user interface into independent, reusable blocks:

- *Block*
  - Describes the block's purpose.
  - An example would be a class name for an element, such as `header`.
- *Element*
  - Describes the element's purpose.
  - The class name is the block name followed by two underscores and the element, such as `header__text`.
- *Modifier*
  - Describes the appearance, state, and behavior.
  - The class pattern is `block-name_modifier-name` (example: `header_mobile`) or `block-name__element-name_modifier-name` (example: `header__menu_open`).

Choosing an architectural approach for CSS is a team-dependent task. The needs of
the project, the size and experience of the team, and the libraries and frameworks
being used are factors to consider. No one-size-fits-all approach exists, so the decision
needs to be made by the team. Because of BEM's component-based nature, we'll use it
in this chapter to scope and style our social media share links.

11.2 Setting up

Now that we've chosen our methodology, which dictates the naming convention we'll
use for the project, let's take a look at what we'll be building. We'll style a Share button that, when clicked, opens a set of links that let the user share the page via email or
to Facebook, LinkedIn, or Twitter. Then we'll use transitions to animate opening and
closing the share options and the hover/focus effects of the individual links. Figure 11.1
shows our goal.

Closed   Open

Figure 11.1   Goal

Our starting HTML (listing 11.1) consists of a container for our component, a Share
button, and a menu that lets users choose how to share the page. The code includes a
linked JavaScript file, which makes our component usable via keyboard navigation
and triggers showing/hiding the links inside the component when the Share button is

clicked. As we'll see in section 11.6, a few limitations apply to animating elements with CSS alone, so we'll rely on a couple of lines of JavaScript to support our CSS. We'll look at JavaScript in more detail later in the chapter (also in section 11.6); first, we'll focus on our HTML and CSS.

Listing 11.1 Starting HTML

```html
<main>
  <div class="share" id="share">          ⟵—  Component
                                                container

    <button id="shareButton"
      class="share__button"
      type="button"
      aria-controls="mediaList"
      aria-expanded="false"
      aria-haspopup="listbox">
        <img src="./icons/share.svg" alt="" width="24" height="24">
        Share
    </button>

    <menu aria-labelledby="share"
          role="menu"                           Media
          id="mediaList"                        menu
          class="share__menu">

                                                      Menu
      <li role="menuitem" class="share__menu-item">   ⟵—  item
        <a href="mailto:?subject=Tiny%20..."
          target="_blank"
          rel="nofollow noopener"
          tabindex="-1"
          class="share__link"
        >
          <img src="./icons/email.svg"              Media
              alt="Email" width="24" height="24">   icon
        </a>
      </li>
      <li role="menuitem" class="share__menu-item">
        <a href="https://www.facebook.com/sh..."
          target="_blank"
          rel="nofollow noopener"
          tabindex="-1"
          class="share__link"                       Link to share
        >                                           via social
          <img src="./icons/facebook.svg"           media
              alt="Facebook" width="24" height="24">
        </a>
      </li>
      ...
    </menu>
  </div>
</main>
                                          Script used for
                                          keyboard interactions
                                          and supplementing CSS
<script src="./scripts.js"></script>  ⟵—┘
```

Share button to open and close the list of social media links

First link is a mailto to share via email rather than social media.

We also have some basic starter CSS applied to the `main` element to move the component away from the edge of the screen: `main { margin: 48px; }`.

You can find all the starter code (HTML, CSS, and JavaScript) on GitHub at http://mng.bz/KeR4 or CodePen at https://codepen.io/michaelgearon/pen/YzZzpWj. Our starting point looks like figure 11.2.

As you can see, the icons have been provided, but let's discuss where and how we got them.

**Figure 11.2
Starting point**

11.3 Sourcing icons

Any time we use iconography from someone else's brand, we need to answer the following questions:

- Are we authorized to use the icon?
- Are there any restrictions on how the icon can be used?

When we use social media icons, those brands are being represented in our work, so we must follow their guidelines on when, how, and in what context we can use the brand. When we use icons that don't represent a brand (such as the icons we used for the `mailto` link and Share button), unless we created the icon ourselves, we're subject to copyright laws, just as we would be for any other piece of media (image, sound, video, and so on) that we use in our projects.

> **NOTE** We're not lawyers, and we don't intend to offer legal advice in this chapter. When in doubt, contact a legal professional.

11.3.1 Media icons

An effective way to find how a branded icon can be used is to look for that brand's guide by doing a web search for terms such as *style guide* and *brand guide*. Many social media outlets have specific instructions on how the brand can be represented, including icon and logo downloads. Table 11.1 lists the social media platforms we included in our component and the links to their brand information. For this project, we sourced our social media icons directly from the respective brand guides.

Table 11.1   Social media brand resources

Brand	Icon	Link to assets
Facebook		http://mng.bz/9Dza
LinkedIn		https://brand.linkedin.com/downloads
Twitter		http://mng.bz/jPry

11.3.2 Icon libraries

Looking for icons can be a bit tedious, especially in large projects, so it's common practice to use icon fonts and libraries, which also are subject to terms of use. Each library and icon font has its own rules about where and how icons can be used. Some also require attribution. Therefore, we must be aware of any rules we need to follow while sourcing our icons.

For this project, we sourced our non-brand-related icons from Material Symbols (https://fonts.google.com/icons). Because we needed only two—share ⟨ and email @—we downloaded the individual SVGs and included them in our icon folder rather than importing the entire library into the project. The icons have been provided in the starter code, so we're ready to start styling.

11.4 Styling the block

Because we're using BEM for our naming convention, our block name will be `"share"`. Therefore, the container `<div>` that wraps the entire component will have a class of `share`. This block name will be included in all future classes that use the BEM naming convention (section 11.1.3), which scopes our CSS to that component and helps prevent any styling collisions between our component and any other parts of the application it may be used in.

As shown in listing 11.2, we define the `font-family`, `background`, and `border-radius` for the block. We also give the component a `display` value of `inline-flex`. `inline-flex` works the same way as `flex` but makes the element an inline-level element rather than a block-level element. By making our component behave like an inline element (the same as links, spans, buttons, and so on), we give it the greatest versatility in terms of placement in an application. Furthermore, buttons are inline elements by default, and when closed, what's presented is essentially a button, so we'll give our component the same flow behavior as a button.

NOTE To find out how Flexbox works and discover its associated properties, check out chapter 6.

Listing 11.2 Styling the container

```
.share {
  font-family: Verdana, Geneva, Tahoma, sans-serif;
  background: #ffe46a;              ◄─────┐  Yellow
  border-radius: 36px;                    │
  display: inline-flex;
}
```

With the block styled (figure 11.3), let's address the individual elements inside the block.

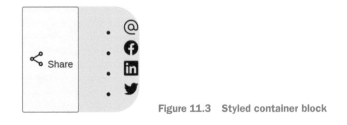

Figure 11.3   Styled container block

11.5   Styling the elements

Our block has three descendent elements, all of which we want to style:

- The Share button
- The menu containing the list of links
- The individual links inside the menu

Let's start with the Share button and work our way down the list.

11.5.1   Share button

The class name given to the button will include the block name followed by two underscores and then the element. In our case, we'll call this element button, so our class name will be share__button. By prefixing our class name with share__, we ensure that the only button we'll be styling is the one within our block.

We want to override the defaults provided by the browser and align the icon and text within the button (listing 11.3). We remove the background and border, adjust the font size and padding, and curve our corners.

To align the icon and text, we give the button a display value of flex and then use align-items to align the icon and text vertically. To add whitespace between the icon and text, we use the gap property.

Listing 11.3   Styling the Share button

```
.share__button {
  background: none;
  border: none;
  font-size: 1rem;
  padding: 0 2rem 0 1.5rem;
  border-radius: 36px;
  display: flex;
  align-items: center;
  gap: 1ch;
}
```

Figure 11.4 shows our output.

Next, let's handle the hover and focus styles. We use the :hover and :focus-visible pseudo-classes to change the cursor style conditionally and add a black outline to the

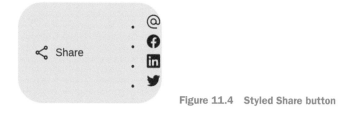

Figure 11.4 Styled Share button

button. Then we offset the outline by -5px so that the outline places itself 5-pixels inside the button rather than on the outer edge.

The outline-offset property allows us to control where the outline is placed. Positive numbers move the outline farther out or away from the element; negative numbers inset the outline. The following listing shows our hover and focus CSS.

Listing 11.4   Share button hover and focus CSS

```
.share__button:hover,
.share__button:focus-visible {
  cursor: pointer;
  outline: solid 1px black;
  outline-offset: -5px;
}
```

Figure 11.5 shows our button being hovered over with a mouse.

Figure 11.5   Share-button hover

11.5.2 Share menu

To style the menu and its items, we want to remove the bullets and then place the elements in a row beside the Share button. To remove the bullets, we give the list items a list-style value of none. Then we give the menu a display property value of flex. Finally, we remove the default margin and padding that the browser applies to the menu item automatically. The following listing shows our CSS.

Listing 11.5   Share menu and menu items

```
.share__menu-item { list-style: none; }

.share__menu {
  display: flex;
```

```
  margin: 0;
  padding: 0;
}
```

When we look at our output (figure 11.6), we notice that we need some space between the edge of our container and our elements. We'll handle this task while styling the individual links.

 Figure 11.6   Styled menu

11.5.3   Share links

To make sure that the links have a circle border on hover (rather than an ellipse), we set both their `height` and `width` to 48 pixels. Next, we curve their corners. This step also resolves our spacing problem because, as we see in listing 11.6, we've set the icon `height` and `width` to 24. Because we're making the links 48 pixels in both height and width, when the links are centered, we'll have 12 pixels of whitespace between each icon and the edge of its link.

Listing 11.6   List Item HTML

```
<li role="menuitem" class="share__menu-item">
  <a href="https://www.facebook.com/sha..."
    target="_blank"
    rel="nofollow noopener"
    tabindex="-1"
    class="share__link"
  >
    <img src="./icons/facebook.svg" alt="Facebook" width="24" height="24">
  </a>
</li>
```

We also give the links a transparent border. Borders take up space, so to prevent the content from shifting on hover or focus when we expose the border, we add a transparent border by default and then color it when we want to show it. This approach ensures that the space needed for the border is allotted and prevents the content succeeding the element from shifting when the border is exposed.

    To center the icon in the middle of the circle, we use `flex`, justifying the content and aligning the items to the center. Our CSS looks like the following listing.

Listing 11.7   Styling the links

```
.share__link:link,
.share__link:visited {
  height: 48px;
  width: 48px;
  border-radius: 50%;
  display: flex;
```

```
   align-items: center;
   justify-content: center;
   border: solid 1px transparent;
}
```

With our links styled (figure 11.7), we can style the links for the hover and focus states.

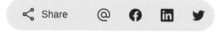

Figure 11.7   Styled share links

11.5.4 scale()

On hover and focus, we're going to expose the border by changing its color from transparent to black. When we set the border on the links, we used the `border` shorthand property, which allows us to define the style, border width, and border color in one declaration. Because we're changing only the color, we'll use `border-color` rather than the `border` shorthand. By using `border-color`, we can edit the border's color without worrying about the rest of the already defined properties.

Next, we'll use the `scale()` function to increase the size of the icon to make it look as though it's magnified. In chapter 2, while expanding the loader bars, we used `scaleY()` to grow and shrink the bar vertically. In this project, we want our links to grow proportionally, so we'll use `scale()`. When passed a single parameter, this function grows the element (both horizontally and vertically) proportionally by the same amount.

The `scale()` function is the shorthand for combining `scaleX()` and `scaleY()`. If only one value is passed, the `scale()` amount is applied both vertically and horizontally. If two parameters are passed, the first parameter defines horizontal scale, and the second defines vertical scale.

On hover or focus, we want the links to be 25% larger than when they're not being interacted with, so we'll give our function a single parameter of `1.25` and apply it to the `transform` property. Our CSS looks like the following listing.

Listing 11.8   Styling the links on hover and focus

```
.share__link:hover,
.share__link:focus-visible {
  border-color: black;
  outline: none;
  transform: scale(1.25);
}
```

With the styles applied, our links grow on hover (figure 11.8), but because now the link is taller than the container, gaps at the top and bottom of the link don't have the yellow background.

Figure 11.8   Link on hover

To create our magnification effect, we want the entire link to remain yellow. We could add a yellow background to the link, which would accomplish that task, but the background needs to be yellow because the block's background color is yellow. If we changed the background color of the container, we'd want the link's background color to change as well. To make sure that the colors stay in sync, we could use a custom property (CSS variable) or make the element inherit the color from its parent.

11.5.5 *The inherit property value*

The `background-color` property isn't inherited by default. We want to explicitly instruct the link to inherit the background color. To this inheritance from its parent, we can set the `background-color` property value for the link to `inherit`. Inheritance, however, goes up only to the parent. In our case, the element that controls the background color is the link's great-grandparent, as shown in figure 11.9.

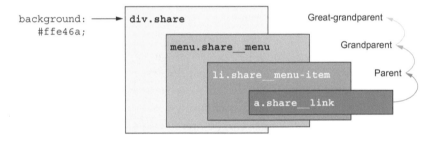

Figure 11.9   Ancestors of the media links

We need to make the `link`, `menu`, and `menu-item` rules inherit the `background-color` to make it trickle down to the link. After we give all three elements a `background-color` value of `inherit` (figure 11.10), we notice that although we've fixed the gaps in the link being hovered over, we've lost the curve on the right side of the component.

**Figure 11.10   Inherited
`background-color`**

We lost our curve because, like `background-color`, `border-radius` isn't inherited. To fix the problem, we apply the same logic that we used for `background-color`. Listing 11.9 shows our edited CSS. Notice that the `border-radius` of the link wasn't edited. We want to keep the link's shape as a circle, so we keep the `border-radius: 50%` declaration on the link.

Listing 11.9   Inheriting property values

```
.share__menu-item {
  list-style: none;
```

```
    background: inherit;
    border-radius: inherit;
}

.share__menu {
    display: flex;          ⟵──  Makes the
    margin: 0;                    link a circle
    padding: 0;
    background: inherit;
    border-radius: inherit;
}

.share__link:hover,
.share__link:focus-visible {
    border-color: black;
    outline: none;
    transform: scale(1.25);
    background: inherit;
}
```

Although inheriting values in this manner can be a bit cumbersome, it allows us to make sure that the color is controlled from one place. This approach benefits maintainability in case we decide to change the background's color, and it sets us up to expand our component to support multiple themes. Another option would be to use a custom property for our color.

With the `border-radius` and `background-color` inherited, our hover and focus styles are complete (figure 11.11), but the change when we hover over the link is abrupt. Let's animate the size change.

Figure 11.11   Share-link hover effect

11.6 Animating the component

In chapter 2, we used keyframes to create animation, which allowed us to define steps for our animation. For our hover state, we already have our start and end states defined. We're transitioning from one state (not hovered or focused) to another (hovered or focused), whose styles are already defined in rules. So instead of using an animation, we're going to use a transition.

11.6.1 Creating a transition

A transition doesn't require a keyframe but still allows us to animate the change of styles from one state to another. The `transition` property allows us to define which property changes should be animated, as well as the duration and timing function. By adding `transition: transform ease-in-out 250ms;` to our `.share__link` rules, we tell the browser to animate the size change of our link (listing 11.10).

To choose the amount of time the transition needs to take, we choose something relatively fast: 250 milliseconds. We want to keep the animation slow enough to be visible but fast enough to be snappy. If we make the transition too slow, our project will look laggy and distract users from performing the task they're trying to accomplish (sharing the content).

Listing 11.10 Transitioning the link size change

```
.share__link:link,
.share__link:visited {
  text-decoration: none;
  display: flex;
  flex-direction: column;
  align-items: center;
  justify-content: center;
  height: 48px;
  width: 48px;
  border-radius: 50%;
  border: solid 1px transparent;
  transition: transform ease-in-out 250ms;
}
```

> **NOTE** You may notice that after adding the transition, the outline gets chopped off on hover. The reason is that JavaScript drives the opening and closing of the component and toggles overflow and visibility. We go into detail on what the JavaScript is doing in section 11.6.2. Clicking the Share button toggles this behavior.

In our transition, we specifically tell the browser to animate the changes that occur on the `transform` property, but we don't have a `transform` property in our `.share__link:link, .share__link:visited` rule. When we run the code, however, we notice that our size change is animated and that the code works. This behavior occurs because, when not defined, `scale()` equals `scale(1)` by default. Therefore, we're animating going from `scale(1)` to `scale(1.25)` when we hover or focus the link and then animating the scale back to `scale(1)` when we move away from the link.

Next, we're going to animate hiding and exposing the links when the button is clicked.

11.6.2 Opening and closing the component

Remember that our goal is for the component to hide our menu of links by default and expose it only when the Share button is clicked (figure 11.12).

The first thing we need to do is hide the menu items by default. To achieve this task, we'll give the `menu` a `width` of `0` and hide the `overflow`, as shown in listing 11.11.

Closed   Open

Figure 11.12 Closed and expanded states

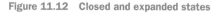

Listing 11.11 Hiding the menu

```
.share__menu {
  display: flex;
  margin: 0;
  padding: 0;
  background: inherit;
  border-radius: inherit;
  width: 0;
  overflow: hidden;
}
```

Makes the width of the menu equal to 0

Hides the overflow so that the links within are also hidden

With our menu hidden (figure 11.13), we need to toggle exposing and hiding the menu when the Share button is clicked.

Figure 11.13 Hidden menu

Our JavaScript handles part of the behavior for us. At the beginning of this chapter, we mentioned that we'll need some JavaScript for this project. When we open the JavaScript file, we notice that it contains a lot of code (listing 11.12).

Listing 11.12 JavaScript file

```
(() => {
  'use strict';

  let expanded = false;
  const container = document.getElementById('share');
  const shareButton = document.getElementById('shareButton');
  const menuItems = Array.from(container.querySelectorAll('li'));
  const menu = container.querySelector('menu');

  addButtonListeners();
  addListListeners();
  addTransitionListeners();

  function addButtonListeners() {
    shareButton.addEventListener('click', toggleMenu);
    shareButton.addEventListener('keyup', handleToggleButtonKeypress);
  }
```

Adds event listeners to the Share button for clicks and keypresses to open and close the menu via both keyboard and mouse

```
function addListListeners() {
  menuItems.forEach(li => {
    const link = li.querySelector('a');
    link.addEventListener('keyup', handleMenuItemKeypress);
    link.addEventListener('keydown', handleTab);
    link.addEventListener('click', toggleMenu);
  })
}
```

Adds event listens to the links for clicks and keypresses to handle keyboard navigation within the menu

Adds event listeners to the menu to know when transitions start and end

```
function addTransitionListeners() {
  menu.addEventListener('transitionstart', handleAnimationStart);
  menu.addEventListener('transitionend', handleAnimationEnd);
}
```

```
function handleToggleButtonKeypress(event) {
  switch(event.key) {
    case 'ArrowDown':
    case 'ArrowRight':
      if (!expanded) { toggleMenu(); }
      moveToNext();
      break;
    case 'ArrowUp':
    case 'ArrowLeft':
      if (expanded) { toggleMenu(); }
      break;
  }
}
```

Handles keyboard up- and down-arrow functionality or the Share button

```
function handleMenuItemKeypress(event) {
  switch(event.key) {
    case 'ArrowDown':
    case 'ArrowRight':
      moveToNext();
      break;
    case 'ArrowUp':
    case 'ArrowLeft':
      if (event.altKey === true) {
        navigate(event);
        toggleMenu();
      } else {
        moveToPrevious();
      }
      break;
    case 'Enter':
      toggleMenu();
      break;
    case ' ':
      navigate(event);
      toggleMenu();
      break;
    case 'Tab':
      event.preventDefault();
      toggleMenu();
      break;
    case 'Escape':
```

Handles keypress on links for keyboard navigation within the menu, including exiting the menu

```
        toggleMenu();
        break;
      case 'Home':
        moveToNext(0);
        break;
      case 'End':
        moveToNext(menuItems.length - 1);
        break;
    }
  }
```

> Handles keypress on links for keyboard navigation within the menu, including exiting the menu

```
function handleTab(event) {
  if (event.key !== 'Tab') { return; }
  event.preventDefault();
}
```

> Prevents tab from navigating between the links because on tab, we want to return focus to the Share button rather than go to the next link

```
function toggleMenu(event) {
  expanded = !expanded;
  shareButton.ariaExpanded = expanded;
  container.classList.toggle('share_expanded');
  if (expanded) {
    menuItems.forEach(li => li.removeAttribute('tabindex'));
  }
  if (!expanded) {
    menuItems.forEach(li => {
      li.removeAttribute('data-current');
      li.tabIndex = -1;
    })
    shareButton.focus();
  }
}
```

> Opens and closes the menu

When next is defined, moves the focus to the specific item by index; otherwise, cycles through the links, returning to the top when the user reaches the last item in the menu

```
function moveToNext(next = undefined) {
  const selectedIndex = menuItems.findIndex(
    li => li.dataset.current  === 'true'
  );
  let newIndex
  if (next) {
    newIndex = next;
  } else if (
    selectedIndex === -1 || selectedIndex ===  menuItems.length - 1) {
    newIndex = 0;
  } else {
    newIndex = selectedIndex + 1;
  }

  if (selectedIndex !== -1) {
    menuItems[selectedIndex].removeAttribute('data-current');
  }
  menuItems[newIndex].setAttribute('data-current', 'true');
  menuItems[newIndex].querySelector('a').focus();
}
```

Moves
focus to the
previous link
and returns
the user to
the bottom
of the list
when they
reach the
first item in
the menu

```
function moveToPrevious() {
  const selectedIndex = menuItems.findIndex(li => li.dataset.current);
  const newIndex = selectedIndex < 1
    ? menuItems.length - 1
    : selectedIndex - 1;
  if (selectedIndex !== -1) {
    menuItems[selectedIndex].removeAttribute('data-current');
  }
  menuItems[newIndex].setAttribute('data-current', 'true');
  menuItems[newIndex].querySelector('a').focus();
}
```

```
function navigate(event) {
  const url = event.target.href;
  window.open(url);
}
```
Navigates the user when the action is
keyboard-triggered and not the default
click or keypress; used when the user
presses the spacebar on a menu item

```
function handleAnimationStart() {
  if (!expanded) { menu.style.overflow = 'hidden' };
}
```
Hides overflow when
the menu is closing

```
function handleAnimationEnd() {
  if (expanded) { menu.style.overflow = 'visible' }
}
})()
```
If open, shows overflow to
allow the magnified icon to
expand outside the container

Most of the code handles keyboard accessibility for the component, and listing 11.13
shows the parts that are relevant to the button click. When the page loads, we default
the component to being closed and find the element's container, which we assign to
the `container` variable. Then we add event listeners to the button so that when the
button is clicked, the `toggleMenu()` function is triggered. When the button is clicked,
we change the `expanded` variable to its inverse. If the setting was `true`, it becomes
`false`, and vice versa. Finally, we add or remove the `share_expanded` class.
`classList.toggle()` adds the class if it's not present and removes it if it is.

Listing 11.13   Opening and closing the menu (JavaScript)

```
(() => {
  ...
  let expanded = false;
  const container = document.getElementById('share');
  ...
  function addButtonListeners() {
    shareButton.addEventListener('click', toggleMenu);
    ...
  }

  function toggleMenu(event) {
    expanded = !expanded;
    ...
    container.classList.toggle('share_expanded');
    ...
```
Defines a variable
to hold our
current state

Defines a variable
for our HTML
container element

Defines what
happens when the
button is clicked

Toggles the expanded
variable value

Handles adding and
removing share_expanded

```
  ...
}
```

NOTE Because this book is about CSS, the JavaScript is included in the starter code. If you're following along, you don't need to make any edits to the Java-Script to make it work.

All put together, this code adds the share_expanded class to the container when the Share button is clicked. If share_expanded is already open, the code removes it. We had hidden our menu items, but now we'll show them when the share_expanded class is present.

NOTE Remember that we decided to use BEM for our class-name convention. Our class name has only one underscore because expanded is our modifier. We use a modifier because we're changing (modifying) the style based on the state (open/closed). We have the block (share) and the modifier (expanded); therefore, our class name is block_modifier or share_expanded.

To show the links when the component is marked as expanded, we must increase the width of the menu, as shown in listing 11.14. We also add a little horizontal padding to create some room around the menu.

To calculate the width of the menu, we multiply the number of links by their width. The link's width is 48 pixels (which we hard-set) plus the border (1 pixel on each side). Therefore, the menu's width is $width = 4 \times (48 + 2) = 200px$.

Listing 11.14   Showing the menu

```
.share_expanded .share__menu {
  width: 200px;
  padding: 0 2rem 0 1rem;
}
```

After clicking the button and hovering over the first link, we see that our link no longer expands outside the menu (figure 11.14). We also see that after we hover over the links and close the menu, our menu items continue to display until we hover over them again.

1 Click Share.

2 Hover over first link.
   Will cut off before
   expanding correctly.

3 Click Share.
   Won't hide the menu items
   until we hover over the links.

Figure 11.14 · **Expanded component on click**

Remember that our JavaScript triggers when transitions start and end and is responsible for controlling our overflow. Although we've already animated the style changes for hovering over the individual menu items, we haven't added the transition for opening and closing the menu yet. When we add that transition, overflow will be set correctly when the transition activates and finishes, making these problems go away.

The next task we need to accomplish is to maintain the button outline that's usually present on hover when the component is open. Because we already have a rule to add the border on hover and focus, we're going to edit the rule to trigger when the component is open. By reusing the rule, we ensure that the styles will be consistent in the hover and focus states and when the list is visible. To add the condition, we add the `.share_expanded .share__button` selector to the rule, as shown in the following listing.

> **Listing 11.15 Adding button border to Share button when list is displayed**

```
.share__button:hover,
.share__button:focus-visible,
.share_expanded .share__button {
  cursor: pointer;
  outline: solid 1px black;
  outline-offset: -5px;
}
```

With the selector added, our button keeps its border after the component is expanded (figure 11.15); and when the component is closed and not focused or hovered, the border stays absent.

Figure 11.15 Maintaining the Share-button border when list is displayed

11.6.3 Animating the menu

Now that we've set our styles for both the open and closed states, let's animate the showing and hiding of the menu. We want the link list to expand from the left, as depicted in figure 11.16.

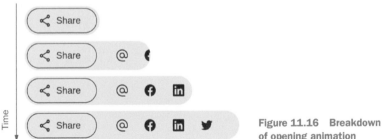

Figure 11.16 Breakdown of opening animation

When the menu closes, we'll want to perform the inverse of the opening animation, retracting the menu and hiding the link. We'll do the same for the magnification effect on the links, using a transition. We don't need to use keyframes because the animation is going to be performed only once (when the button is clicked) and we already have the two states defined.

We'll add the `transition` declaration to the menu as follows: `transition: width 250ms ease-in-out`. Again, we want to keep the transition snappy, so we give it a duration of 250 milliseconds.

After we add the transition, we realize that icons are becoming visible before they should. Figure 11.17 breaks down the effect.

Figure 11.17   Icons displaying too soon

Even if we change the transition to transition all properties instead of only `width`, the same problem occurs. The cause is overflow. When the menu is closed, we want the menu's overflow to be hidden; when it's open, we want it to be visible. But overflow can't be changed gradually, like width. It's either visible or it's not. There's no in-between state.

When opening the menu, we want to wait until the transition is done before we change `overflow` to `visible`. When we close, we want the overflow to be hidden immediately. This task is where we turn to JavaScript to support our CSS. We'll remove `overflow: visible` from our `.share_expanded .share__menu` class and handle adding it via JavaScript.

Listing 11.16 singles out the relevant JavaScript for handling the overflow. The magic lies in the `transitionstart` and `transitionend` event listeners. Attached to the menu, they listen for when the transition is triggered and when it's done performing the change. When the event happens, they trigger their functions to handle the overflow for the menu.

Listing 11.16   JavaScript for handling overflow

```
(() => {
  'use strict';

  let expanded = false;
  const container = document.getElementById('share');
```

```
      const menu = container.querySelector('menu');
    ...
      addTransitionListeners();
    ...
      function addTransitionListeners() {
        menu.addEventListener('transitionstart', handleAnimationStart);
        menu.addEventListener('transitionend', handleAnimationEnd);
      }
    ...
      function handleAnimationStart() {
        if (!expanded) { menu.style.overflow = 'hidden'; }
      }
    ...
      function handleAnimationEnd() {
        if (expanded) { menu.style.overflow = 'visible'; }
      }
    })()
```

If in the process of closing, hides the menu's overflow

Triggers when the transition starts

Triggers when the transition ends

If just opened, shows the overflow

NOTE As we mention earlier in the chapter, the JavaScript is included in the starter code. If you're following along, you don't need to edit the JavaScript; it should work.

The next listing shows the CSS that makes the animation work.

Listing 11.17 Updated CSS for open and close animation

```
.share__menu {
  display: flex;
  margin: 0;
  padding: 0;
  background: inherit;
  border-radius: inherit;
  width: 0;
  overflow: hidden;
  transition: width 250ms ease-in-out;
}
```

Adds the animation

With these last edits made to make the animation smooth, we've finished our animated social media share component. The final product is shown in figure 11.18.

Closed   Open

Figure 11.18 Final product

Summary

- We have several ways to organize CSS. Three common patterns are OOCSS, SMACSS, and BEM.
- Icons are subject to copyright, so follow brand guidelines when using social media icons.
- We can make elements displayed via Flexbox behave like inline-level elements by using `inline-flex`. `inline-flex` uses the same properties as `flex`.
- The position of an outline can be controlled via `outline-offset`.
- The `scale()` function allows us to grow or shrink an element proportionally.
- The `inherit` property value allows us to inherit values from the parent element that generally wouldn't be inherited.
- Transitions don't require keyframes but still allow us to animate CSS changes from one state to another.
- The `overflow` property allows us to control whether elements that extend beyond their container are displayed or hidden.
- When using JavaScript to extend our transitions' functionality, we can use the `ontransitionstart` and `ontransitionend` event listeners to trigger JavaScript change in response to the transition's life cycle.

Using preprocessors

This chapter covers

- CSS preprocessors
- Examples of how Sass extends CSS functionality

So far in this book, we've been writing all our styles using plain CSS. We can also use preprocessors, however. Each processor has its own syntax, and most preprocessors extend the existing CSS functionality. The most commonly used are

- Sass (https://sass-lang.com)
- Less (https://lesscss.org)
- Stylus (https://stylus-lang.com)

They were created to facilitate writing code that's easier to read and maintain as well as to add functionality that's not available in CSS. Styles written for use with preprocessors have their own syntax and must be built or compiled into CSS. Although some preprocessors provide browser-side compilation, the most common implementation is to preprocess the styles and serve the output CSS to the browser (http://mng.bz/Wzex).

The benefit of using a preprocessor is the added functionality it provides, examples of which we cover in this chapter. The drawback is that now we need a build step for our code. The choice of preprocessor is based on what functionality is needed for the project, the team's knowledge, and (if the project uses a framework) which frameworks are supported. For our project, we're going to choose based on popularity. When developers were surveyed about their sentiments regarding CSS preprocessors, the majority favored Sass (figure 12.1), so that's what we're going to use.

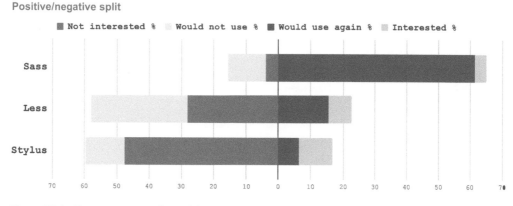

Figure 12.1 Preprocessor sentiment (data source http://mng.bz/8ry2)

12.1 Running the preprocessor

Our project consists of styling a how-to article—something we might see in a wiki or documentation (figure 12.2).

As in earlier chapters, the starting code is available at GitHub (http://mng.bz/EQnl) and CodePen (https://codepen.io/michaelgearon/pen/WNpNoGN). But running the project is going to be a little bit different. Because we're going to write our styles with Sass, which outputs the CSS rather than writing it directly, we'll need a build step. To run this project and code along with this chapter, you have two options:

- npm
- CodePen

NOTE *npm* (Node.js package manager) is a software library, manager, and installer. If you aren't familiar with npm, that's OK. You can run this project in CodePen, following the instructions in section 12.1.3.

12.1.1 Setup instructions for npm

Via the command line from the chapter-12 directory, install the dependencies using npm install; then start the processor using npm start. This command starts a watcher that will monitor changes in styles.scss (in the before and after directories) and output the styles.css and styles.map.css files.

The second file—styles.map.css—is a source map. Because the CSS was generated from another language, the source map allows the browser's developer tools to

Keeping it Sassy

Step 1

Lorem ipsum dolor sit amet, consectetur adipiscing elit. Sed porta erat nec ipsum volutpat ultrices. Pellentesque ac mi lobortis, tincidunt purus eu, gravida enim. Vestibulum pharetra a arcu ac suscipit. Ut et lorem dui. Donec non vehicula orci. Nunc non ornare mi, ac aliquam risus.

Success: You did it!

Ut maximus id erat et mollis. Aenean sit amet fringilla augue. Donec convallis vel nibh vitae porttitor. Phasellus elementum nibh at erat semper consectetur. Praesent convallis iaculis mauris, sit amet egestas nunc gravida in. Donec dapibus mattis nibh, sed iaculis libero blandit et.

Step 2

Aenean non lorem tincidunt, vulputate nibh et, convallis felis. Donec at tristique sem. Aenean id leo non lectus hendrerit sodales. Maecenas vulputate scelerisque dignissim. Integer purus nisl, blandit in odio a, gravida interdum velit. Etiam consectetur risus ante, vel pulvinar felis eleifend ut. Phasellus nec tellus vitae sem semper ultrices at et ligula.

Warning: Don't press the big red button

Proin pharetra, urna et sagittis lacinia, quam metus vulputate eros, ac congue quam leo suscipit est. Vestibulum ante ipsum primis in faucibus orci luctus et ultrices posuere cubilia curae; Vestibulum nec suscipit ipsum. Vestibulum dapibus, neque vel lacinia mattis, magna sapien hendrerit justo, sed laoreet sapien enim quis mauris.

Step 3

Nullam ut auctor nisi. Vestibulum pretium vitae erat et hendrerit. Donec velit ipsum, fringilla sed aliquam non, tincidunt a mauris. Mauris sit amet diam lacus. Donec gravida felis nec ligula ultricies, et molestie tellus tristique.

Error: Mistakes have been made

Vestibulum interdum eleifend suscipit. Nullam imperdiet dignissim nulla, et mattis erat dignissim ut. Proin dui felis, venenatis sit amet lacus at, commodo elementum dolor. Vestibulum et justo eu est pharetra pulvinar. Duis fermentum iaculis velit, in hendrerit metus efficitur vel. Fusce vitae mollis nisl. Fusce eu viverra erat. Vivamus nunc risus, consectetur at eros ac, bibendum viverra massa. Aliquam metus lacus, condimentum in ligula eget, molestie faucibus odio. Integer eros tellus, tristique non elementum eget, congue scelerisque quam.

Figure 12.2   **Finished project**

tell us where the piece of code originated in the preprocessed file (for this project, `styles.scss`).

12.1.2 *.sass versus .scss*

Although we're using Sass, our file extension is `.scss`. Sass has two syntaxes we can choose—indented and SCSS—and the file extension reflects the syntax.

INDENTED SYNTAX

Sometimes referred to as *Sass syntax, indented syntax* uses the `.sass` file extension. When writing rulesets using this syntax, we omit curly braces and semicolons, using tabs to describe the format of the document. The following listing shows two rules using indented syntax, the first handling margin and padding on the body text and the second changing the line height of the paragraphs.

Listing 12.1 Sass using indented syntax

```
body
    margin: 0
    padding: 20px


p
    line-height: 1.5
```

SCSS SYNTAX

The second syntax is SCSS, which uses the file extension `.scss`. We'll use that syntax in this project. *SCSS syntax* is a superset of CSS that allows us to use any valid CSS in addition to Sass features. The following listing shows the rules from listing 12.1 in SCSS syntax.

Listing 12.2 Sass using SCSS syntax

```
body {
  margin: 0;
  padding: 20px;
}

p {
  line-height: 1.5;
}
```

The code looks like CSS, which is exactly the point. In SCSS, we can write CSS the way we're used to writing it and have access to all the functionality Sass provides as well. Because of its similarity to CSS, and because it doesn't require developers to learn a new syntax, SCSS is the more popular of the two syntax options.

12.1.3 Setup instructions for CodePen

To set up the project for CodePen, follow these steps:

1 Go to https://codepen.io.
2 In a new pen, using the code in the `chapter-12/before` folder, copy the HTML inside the `body` element to the HTML panel.
3 Copy the starting styles in the `.scss` file to the CSS panel.
4 To make the panel use Sass with SCSS syntax instead of CSS, click the gear in the top-right corner of the CSS panel (figure 12.3).

Figure 12.3   Settings button

5 Choose SCSS from the CSS Preprocessor drop-down menu (figure 12.4).

Figure 12.4   CodePen CSS preprocessor settings

6 Click the green Save & Close button at the bottom of the Pen Settings dialog box.

12.1.4 Starting HTML and SCSS

Our project is composed of headers, paragraphs, links, and images (listing 12.3). Notice that in our head, we reference the CSS stylesheet, not the SCSS. The browser uses the compiled version.

Listing 12.3   Starting HTML

```html
<!DOCTYPE html>
<html lang="en">

<head>
  <title>Chapter 12: Pre-processors | Tiny CSS Projects</title>
  <meta charset="utf-8">
  <meta name="viewport" content="width=device-width, initial-scale=1">
  <link rel="stylesheet" href="styles.css">         ◁────  Links to the
</head>                                                     processed
                                                           CSS file
<body>
  <h1>Keeping it Sassy</h1>
  <h2>Step 1</h2>
  <img src="https://bit.ly/3VUzJ7g" alt="blue print">
  <p>
    Lorem ipsum dolor sit amet...
    <a href="">tincidunt purus</a>
    eu, gravida enim. Vestibulum...
  </p>                                           Green success
  <p class="success">You did it!</p>    ◁────    callout
  <p>Ut maximus id erat et mollis...</p>
  <h2>Step 2</h2>
  <img src="https://bit.ly/3F4vd0f" alt="crane">
  <p>Aenean non lorem tincidunt...</p>
  <p class="warning">Don't press the big red button</p>   ◁──   Orange
  <p>                                                            warning
    Proin pharetra, urna et sagittis lacinia...               callout
    <a href="">orci luctus</a>
    et ultrices posuere cubilia curae…
  </p>
  <h2>Step 3</h2>
  <img src="https://bit.ly/3N42oD1" alt="wrong way">
  <p>Nullam ut auctor nisi...</p>
  <p class="error">Mistakes have been made</p>   ◁────   Red error
  <p>Vestibulum interdum eleifend...</p>                 callout
</body>

</html>
```

Our starting styles set up our typography and constrain the content's width when the page gets wide, as shown in the following listing.

Listing 12.4   Starting SCSS

```scss
@import url('https://fonts.googleapis.com/css2?
⮕  family=Nunito:wght@300;400;500;800&display=swap');

body {
  font-family: 'Nunito', sans-serif;
  font-weight: 300;
```

```
  max-width: 72ch;
  margin: 2rem auto;
}

p { line-height: 1.5 }
```

So far, we're not using any of the extended functionality that Sass provides. As a matter of fact, if we look at the CSS output (listing 12.5), we notice that the file contents are the same except for the map reference at the bottom of the file. This comment tells the browser where to find the source map. Figure 12.5 shows our starting point.

> **NOTE**   If you're using CodePen, you can view the compiled CSS by clicking the down arrow next to the gear in the top-right corner of the CSS panel (refer to figure 12.3) and choosing View Compiled CSS from the drop-down menu.

Listing 12.5   Starting CSS output

```
@import url("https://fonts.googleapis.com/css2?
➥ family=Nunito:wght@300;400;500;800&display=swap");
body {
  font-family: "Nunito", sans-serif;
  font-weight: 300;
  max-width: 72ch;
  margin: 2rem auto;
}

p {
  line-height: 1.5;
}
                                                      Source map
                                                      reference
/*# sourceMappingURL=styles.css.map */   ◁┘
```

> **NOTE**   If you aren't seeing the CSS file being created and styles being applied, make sure that you're running the Sass watcher (npm start). When the watcher starts, let it run in the background; it updates the CSS file automatically when you save your changes in the SCSS file. You'll still need to refresh the browser manually.

Keeping it Sassy

Step 1

Lorem ipsum dolor sit amet, consectetur adipiscing elit. Sed porta erat nec ipsum volutpat ultrices. Pellentesque ac mi lobortis, tincidunt purus eu, gravida enim. Vestibulum pharetra a arcu ac suscipit. Ut et lorem dui. Donec non vehicula orci. Nunc non ornare mi, ac aliquam risus.

You did it!

Ut maximus id erat et mollis. Aenean ut amet fringilla augue. Donec convallis vel nibh vitae porttitor. Phasellus elementum nibh at erat semper consectetur. Praesent convallis iaculis mauris sit amet egestas nunc gravida in. Donec dapibus mattis nibh, sed iaculis libero blandit et.

Step 2

Aenean non lorem tincidunt, vulputate nibh et, convallis felis. Donec at tristique sem. Aenean id leo non lectus hendrerit sodales. Maecenas vulputate scelerisque dignissim. Integer purus nisl, blandit in odio a, gravida interdum velit. Etiam consectetur risus ante, vel pulvinar felis eleifend ut. Phasellus nec tellus vitae sem semper ultrices et et ligula.

Don't press the big red button

Proin pharetra, urna et sagittis lacinia, quam metus vulputate eros, ac congue quam leo suscipit est. Vestibulum ante ipsum primis in faucibus orci luctus et ultrices posuere cubilia curae. Vestibulum nec suscipit ipsum. Vestibulum dapibus, neque vel lacinia mattis, magna sapien hendrerit justo, sed laoreet sapien enim quis mauris.

Step 3

Nullam ut auctor nisl. Vestibulum pretium vitae erat et hendrerit. Donec velit ipsum, fringilla sed aliquam non, tincidunt a mauris. Mauris sit amet diam lacus. Donec gravida felis nec ligula ultrices, et molestie tellus tristique.

Mistakes have been made

Vestibulum interdum eleifend suscipit. Nullam imperdiet dignissim nulla, et mattis erat dignissim ut. Proin dui felis, venenatis id amet lacus at, commodo elementum dolor. Vestibulum et justo eu est pharetra pulvinar. Duis fermentum iaculis velit, in hendrerit metus efficitur vel. Fusce vitae mollis nisl. Fusce eu viverra erat. Vivamus nunc risus, consectetur at eros ac, bibendum viverra massa. Aliquam metus lacus, condimentum in ligula eget, molestie faucibus odio. Integer eros tellus, tristique non elementum eget, congue scelerisque quam.

Figure 12.5   **Starting point**

12.2 Sass variables

One reason why preprocessors became popular early on is that they had variables before browsers supported custom properties. Sass variables are quite distinct from CSS custom properties in that they have different syntax and function differently. Let's first look at the syntax. To create a variable, we start with a dollar sign ($) followed by the variable name, a colon (:), and then a value (figure 12.6).

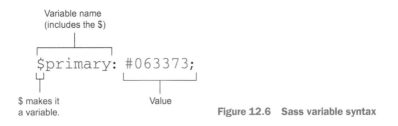

Figure 12.6 Sass variable syntax

In terms of functionality, Sass variables aren't aware of the Document Object Model (DOM) and don't understand cascading or inheritance. They're block-scoped: only properties within the curly braces they're defined in know about their existence. Therefore, the scenario presented in the following listing would throw an undefined variable error at compile time because the variable is defined and used in two different rules or blocks.

Listing 12.6 `$myColor` variable undefined in second rule

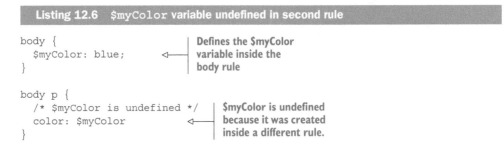

To prevent this problem, we can place our variables outside a rule, which would make them available to the entire document, as shown in the following listing.

Listing 12.7 Defining variables

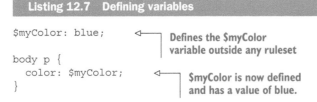

Unlike custom properties, which are dynamic, Sass variables are static. If we define a variable, use it, change its value, and then use it again, any property it was assigned to before the change will retain the original value, and those assigned after the change will have the new value. The examples shown in listings 12.8 and 12.9 make this situation a bit clearer. Note that the examples aren't part of our project; we present them here only to illustrate the concept. You can find the code on CodePen at https://codepen.io/martine-dowden/pen/QWxLjWy.

Listing 12.8   Custom properties versus variables (HTML)

```html
<p class="first">My first paragraph</p>
<p class="second">My second paragraph</p>
```

Listing 12.9   Custom properties versus variables (SCSS)

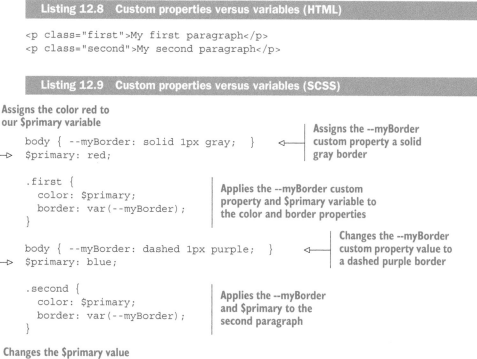

The first big difference between the custom properties and the variables is that we aren't required to have our variables inside a rule. Also, the border styles of both paragraphs are the same, but the color of the text is not (figure 12.7), even though both the custom property and the variable were reassigned between the first and second rule.

My first paragraph

My second paragraph

Figure 12.7   Example output

When we reassign the value of the custom property (the border), it's applied everywhere, whereas the color doesn't change retroactively; only the rule after the change is affected. The reason is that custom properties are dynamic and variables are static.

With this understanding, let's get back to our project and define some variables for the colors we'll use. At the top of the file, we'll define four color variables. Then we'll apply the primary color to all our headers, as shown in the following listing.

Listing 12.10   Color variables (SCSS)

```
@import url('https://fonts.googleapis.com/css2
   ?family=Nunito:wght@300;400;500;800&display=swap');

$primary: #063373;
$success: #747d10;
$warning: #fc9d03;
$error: #940a0a;

p { line-height: 1.5 }

h1, h2 { color: $primary; }
```

Blue ⟶ `$primary: #063373;`
`$success: #747d10;` ⟵ Green
`$warning: #fc9d03;` ⟵ Orange
Red ⟶ `$error: #940a0a;`

`h1, h2 { color: $primary; }` ⟵ Makes our headers blue

We place our variables at the beginning of our file and outside any rule, so that from that point on and inside any rule, we can have access to them. We notice in our CSS output (listing 12.11) that our variables aren't visible in the compiled CSS. But in the rule defining our header color, the place where we used one of our variables has been replaced by its value.

Listing 12.11   Heading-color CSS output

```
@import url("https://fonts.googleapis.com/css2
   ?family=Nunito:wght@300;400;500;800&display=swap");
body {
  font-family: "Nunito", sans-serif;
  font-weight: 300;
  max-width: 72ch;
  margin: 2rem auto;
}

p {
  line-height: 1.5;
}

h1, h2 {
  color: #063373;
}

/*# sourceMappingURL=styles.css.map */
```

Now our project headers look like figure 12.8. Let's style our images next.

Keeping it Sassy

Step 1

Figure 12.8   Updated header color

12.2.1 @extend

Sass gives us several new at-rules, two of which are `@extend` and `@include`. These rules allow us to build generic classes that we can reuse throughout our code. One way we can reuse classes in CSS is to have multiple selectors for a single rule, as we did when we styled our headers. Instead of creating two identical rules for each header (`<h1>` and `<h2>`), we created one rule and gave it two selectors: `h1, h2 { }`.

`@extend` allows us to create a base rule that we can point to from a different rule later. Then the selector will be added to the base rule's list of selectors. Let's use this technique to style our images and see it at work.

First, we create the base rule that will define the `height`, `width`, `object-fit`, and `margin` for our image. Because we have three images, and because we want to give each image a slightly different border radius and positioning, we point each image individually back to our `base-image` rule. The following listing shows how.

Listing 12.12 Extending image styles (SCSS)

```scss
.image-base {
  width: 300px;
  height: 300px;          Base
  object-fit: cover;      rule
  margin: 0 2rem;
}

img:first-of-type { @extend .image-base; }
img:nth-of-type(2) { @extend .image-base; }    Images extending
img:last-of-type { @extend .image-base; }      the base rule
```

The following listing shows the CSS output.

Listing 12.13 Extending image styles (CSS output)

```css
.image-base, img:last-of-type, img:nth-of-type(2), img:first-of-type {
  width: 300px;
  height: 300px;
  object-fit: cover;
  margin: 0 2rem;
}
```

By creating a base rule and then using `@extend`, we can create some defaults and apply them to any other selector without duplicating our CSS code. We can also keep all our code related to a selector in one rule. With our default image styles applied (figure 12.9), let's customize them individually.

Keeping it Sassy

Step 1

Lorem ipsum dolor sit amet, consectetur adipiscing elit. Sed porta erat nec ipsum volutpat ultrices. Pellentesque ac mi lobortis, tincidunt purus eu gravida enim. Vestibulum pharetra a arcu ac suscipit. Ut et lorem dui. Donec non vehicula erat. Nunc non ornare mi, ac aliquam risus.

You did it!

Ut maximus id erat et mollis. Aenean sit amet fringilla augue. Donec convallis vel nibh vitae porttitor. Phasellus elementum nibh at erat semper consectetur. Praesent convallis iaculis mauris, sit amet egestas nunc gravida in. Donec dapibus mattis nibh, sed iaculis libero blandit et.

Step 2

Aenean non lorem tincidunt, vulputate nibh et, convallis felis. Donec at tristique sem. Aenean id leo non lectus hendrerit sodales. Maecenas vulputate scelerisque dignissim. Integer purus nisl, blandit in odio a, gravida interdum velit. Etiam consectetur risus ante, vel pulvinar felis eleifend ut. Phasellus nec tellus vitae sem semper ultrices at et ligula.

Don't press the big red button

Proin pharetra, urna et sagittis lacinia, quam metus vulputate eros, ac congue quam leo suscipit est. Vestibulum ante ipsum primis in faucibus orci luctus et ultrices posuere cubilia curae. Vestibulum nec suscipit ipsum. Vestibulum dapibus, neque vel lacinia mattis, magna sapien hendrerit justo, sed laoreet sapien enim quis mauris.

Step 3

Nullam ut auctor nisi. Vestibulum pretium vitae erat et hendrerit. Donec velit ipsum, fringilla sed aliquam non, tincidunt a mauris. Mauris sit amet diam lacus. Donec gravida felis nec ligula ultricies et molestie tellus tristique.

Mistakes have been made

Vestibulum interdum eleifend suscipit. Nullam imperdiet dignissim nulla, et mattis erat dignissim ut. Proin dui felis, venenatis sit amet lacus et, commodo elementum dolor. Vestibulum et justo eu est pharetra pulvinar. Duis fermentum iaculis velit, in hendrerit metus efficitur vel. Fusce vitae mollis nisl. Fusce eu viverra erat. Vivamus nunc risus, consectetur at eros ac, bibendum viverra massa. Aliquam metus lacus, condimentum in ligula eget, molestie faucibus odio. Integer eros tellus, tristique non elementum eget, congue scelerisque quam.

Figure 12.9   Base image styles

12.3   *@mixin and @include*

We want to customize each image's `border-radius`, `position`, and `object-position`. To do this, we're going to use a mixin. *Mixins* allow us to generate declarations and rules. Like functions, they take parameters (although they're not mandatory) and return styles. Let's write one that will return our three declarations for each image. A mixin is an at-rule, so it starts with `@mixin` followed by the name we want to give it. Next, we add parentheses with any parameters we want to pass in. Finally, we add a set of curly braces, inside which we define the styles we want the mixin to return. Figure 12.10 shows the syntax.

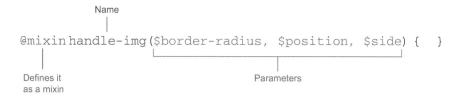

Name

@mixin handle-img ($border-radius, $position, $side) {   }

Defines it
as a mixin

Parameters

Figure 12.10   Mixin syntax

Notice that each parameter starts with a dollar sign. In Sass, the name of the parameter is defined the same way as a variable starting with $.

Inside the mixin, we assign these parameter values to properties, as shown in listing 12.14. We alter the border radius, float the image, and remove the margin on the side it is being floated to. Note that the mixin needs to be defined before it can be used, so it's common to place mixins at the beginning of the file.

Listing 12.14   Building the mixin (SCSS)

```scss
@mixin handle-img($border-radius, $position, $side) {
  border-radius: $border-radius;
  object-position: $position;
  float: $side;
  margin-#{$side}: 0;      ◁——  Interpolation
}                                (section 12.3.2)
```

At this point, we don't see a change in the project. We've defined the mixin but haven't used it yet. Before we apply it, let's take a closer look at some of its properties.

12.3.1 object-fit property

In our base rule, we set our object-fit property value to cover. The object-position property, which we also use in our mixin, works hand in hand with object-fit and determines the alignment of the image within its bounding box. Remember that cover makes the browser calculate the optimum size of the image based on the dimensions provided so that as much of the image that can be shown without distortion appears.

If the dimensions provided to the image don't have the same aspect ratio as the image, the excess is clipped. object-position changes where the image is positioned inside the container, allowing us to manipulate which part of the image is clipped when the ratios don't match (figure 12.11).

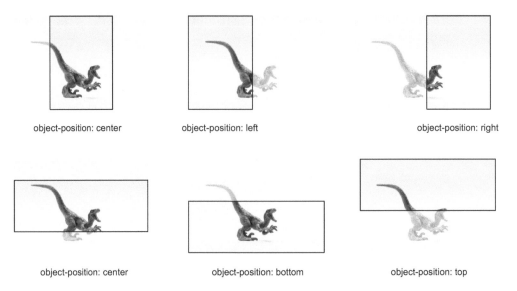

object-position: center   object-position: left   object-position: right

object-position: center   object-position: bottom   object-position: top

Figure 12.11   Visible vs. clipped portions of the image when using `object-position` **in conjunction with** `object-fit: cover`

12.3.2 *Interpolation*

Notice the syntax for the margin: `margin-#{$side}: 0;`. We added a hash (#) and curly braces around the variable. This syntax, called *interpolation,* allows us to insert a value into our parameter. It embeds the result of the expression inside the curly braces in our CSS, replacing the hash. If the value of `$side` is equal to `"left"`, for example, our declaration will compile to `margin-left: 0;`.

You may have encountered interpolation in JavaScript in the context of string interpolation in template literals: `` `margin-${side}` ``. In our project, we're trying to concatenate `margin-` and the value of the `$side` variable. Because `'margin-' + $side` isn't a valid property declaration, we use interpolation to insert the value.

12.3.3 *Using mixins*

Next, we're going to use our mixin in each image rule. To do that, we use `@include` followed by the mixin's name and, in parentheses, the parameters it requires (figure 12.12).

In all three image rules, we use `@include handle-img()` and pass in the `border-radius`, `object-position`, and `float` property values we want to use (listing 12.15).

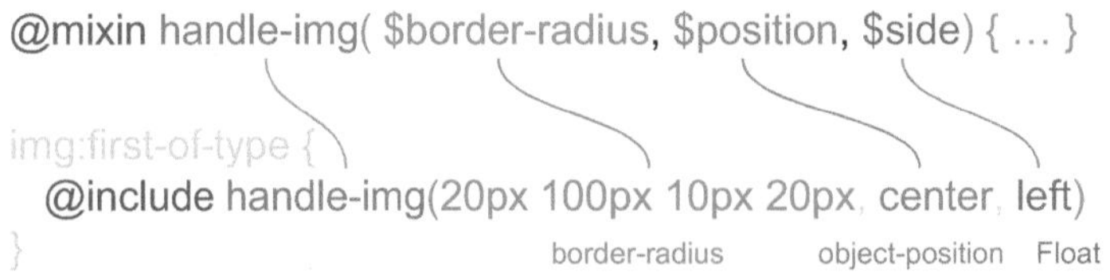

```
@mixin handle-img( $border-radius, $position, $side) { … }

img:first-of-type {
    @include handle-img(20px 100px 10px 20px, center, left)
                        border-radius      object-position  Float
}
```

Figure 12.12
`@mixin` **syntax**

All three images have rounded corners (the first parameter of our mixin). Our first and second image use the border-radius shorthand property, which we'll talk about in section 12.3.4.

Listing 12.15   Using the mixin (SCSS)

```scss
@mixin handle-img($border-radius, $position, $side) {
  border-radius: $border-radius;
  object-position: $position;
  float: $side;
  margin-#{$side}: 0;
}

img:first-of-type {
  @extend .image-base;
  @include handle-img(20px 100px 10px 20px, center, left);
}

img:nth-of-type(2) {
  @extend .image-base;
  @include handle-img(100px 20px 10px 20px, left top, right);
}

img:last-of-type {
  @extend .image-base;
  @include handle-img(50px, center, left);
}
```

In our output CSS, the mixin itself isn't there, but we have three new rules, one for each image, as shown in the following listing.

Listing 12.16   Using the mixin output (CSS)

Selectors added to the base class by using @extend

```css
.image-base, img:last-of-type, img:nth-of-type(2), img:first-of-type {
  width: 300px;
  height: 300px;
  object-fit: cover;
  margin: 0 2rem;
}

img:first-of-type {
  border-radius: 20px 100px 10px 20px;
  object-position: center;
  float: left;
  margin-left: 0;
}
```

Generated by using the mixin (@include)

```css
img:nth-of-type(2) {
  border-radius: 100px 20px 10px 20px;
  object-position: left top;
  float: right;
  margin-right: 0;
}
```

```
img:last-of-type {
  border-radius: 50px;
  object-position: center;
  float: left;
  margin-left: 0;
}
```

Generated by
using the mixin
(@include)

This output exposes the difference between using `@extend` and using a mixin (`@include`). When we extend a rule, Sass doesn't copy or generate code; it only adds the selector to the base. When we use a mixin, Sass generates code. If we're setting properties dynamically, we want to use a mixin. But if the property values are static, we want to extend; otherwise, we'd be copying those values every time we used the mixin, bloating our stylesheet. At this point, our project looks like figure 12.13.

Keeping it Sassy

Step 1

Lorem ipsum dolor sit amet, consectetur adipiscing elit. Sed porta erat nec ipsum volutpat ultrices. Pellentesque ac mi lobortis, tincidunt purus eu, gravida enim. Vestibulum pharetra a arcu ac suscipit. Ut et lorem dui. Donec non vehicula orci. Nunc non ornare mi, ac aliquam risus.

You did it!

Ut maximus id erat et mollis. Aenean sit amet fringilla augue. Donec convallis vel nibh vitae porttitor. Phasellus elementum nibh at erat semper consectetur. Praesent convallis iaculis mauris, sit amet egestas nunc gravida in. Donec dapibus mattis nibh, sed iaculis libero blandit et.

Step 2

Aenean non lorem tincidunt, vulputate nibh et. convallis felis. Donec at tristique sem. Aenean id leo non lectus hendrerit sodales. Maecenas vulputate scelerisque dignissim. Integer purus nisl, blandit in odio a, gravida interdum velit. Etiam consectetur risus ante, vel pulvinar felis eleifend ut. Phasellus nec tellus vitae sem semper ultrices at et ligula.

Don't press the big red button

Proin pharetra, urna et sagittis lacinia, quam metus vulputate eros, ac congue quam leo suscipit est. Vestibulum ante ipsum primis in faucibus orci luctus et ultrices posuere cubilia curae; Vestibulum nec suscipit ipsum. Vestibulum dapibus, neque vel lacinia mattis, magna sapien hendrerit justo, sed laoreet sapien enim quis mauris.

Step 3

Nullam ut auctor nisi. Vestibulum pretium vitae erat et hendrerit. Donec velit ipsum, fringilla sed aliquam non, tincidunt a mauris. Mauris sit amet diam lacus. Donec gravida felis nec ligula ultricies, et molestie tellus tristique.

Mistakes have been made

Vestibulum interdum eleifend suscipit. Nullam imperdiet dignissim nulla, et mattis erat dignissim ut. Proin dui felis, venenatis sit amet lacus at, commodo elementum dolor. Vestibulum et justo eu est pharetra pulvinar. Duis fermentum iaculis velit, in hendrerit metus efficitur vel. Fusce vitae mollis nisl. Fusce eu viverra erat. Vivamus nunc risus, consectetur at eros ac, bibendum viverra massa. Aliquam metus lacus, condimentum in ligula eget, molestie faucibus odio. Integer eros tellus, tristique non elementum eget, congue scelerisque quam.

Figure 12.13   Styled images

12.3.4 *border-radius shorthand*

For our first and second images, we're using the border-radius shorthand. The first image's generated CSS has a border-radius property value of 20px 100px 10px 20px. Just as we set different padding values for all four sides of an element in one declaration, border-radius allows us to use a similar syntax (figure 12.14). Each value defines the radius of the corner starting at top left and rotating clockwise.

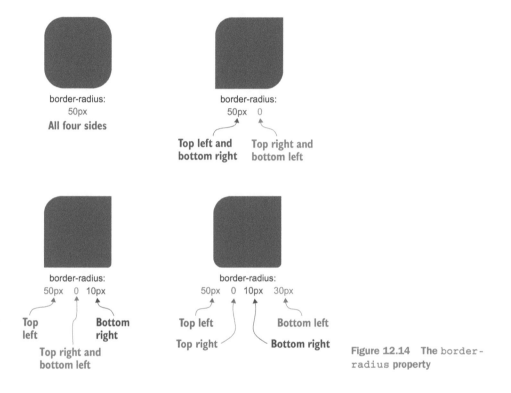

Figure 12.14 The border-radius property

Now that our images are styled, let's take a closer look at our text. In some paragraphs, we have links to style.

12.4 Nesting

One cool thing that Sass lets us do is nest rules. When we style links, we often write several rules so that we can handle the various states (link, visited, hover, focus, and so on). We can nest them together as shown in listing 12.17. Nesting our rules clearly shows the ancestor–descendant relationships in our code and keeps our rules grouped and organized.

To select the parent selector, we use an ampersand (&). In our rule, the parent rule is for the anchor element. Inside this rule, we need to reference the parent (a) to use with the :link, :visited, :hover, and :focus pseudo-classes, so we precede them with &.

We make all our anchor elements bold, make them blue by using our $primary variable, and edit the underline of our links from solid to dotted. On hover, we make the underline a dashed line. Finally, we make the focus underline a solid line. On focus, we also remove the default outline that exists in some browsers.

Listing 12.17   Nesting rules (SCSS)

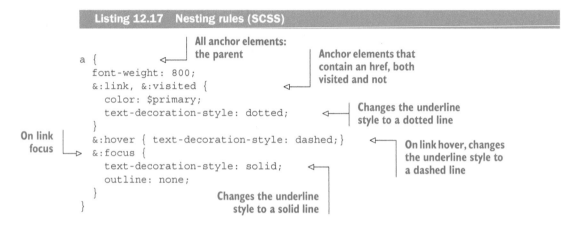

In our CSS output, shown in the following listing, our nested rule has been flattened, creating individual rules for the anchor element and each of its states. Now our links look like figure 12.15.

Listing 12.18   Nesting rules (CSS output)

```css
a {
  font-weight: 800;
}
a:link, a:visited {
  color: #063373;
  text-decoration-style: dotted;
}
a:hover {
  text-decoration-style: dashed;
}
a:focus {
  text-decoration-style: solid;
  outline: none;
}
```

> **NOTE** Nesting is a great way to keep our rules grouped and organized. But for every level of nesting, there is another level of specificity. In listing 12.17, we nest the hover and focus inside the anchor (a) rule. The selector in the output (listing 12.18) for the inner rules are more specific than the outer rule: a:hover is more specific than a. By nesting rules, we can easily end up creating

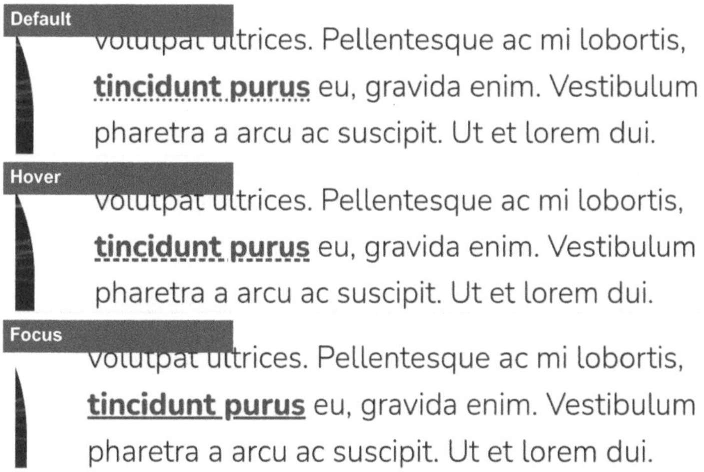

Figure 12.15 Styled links: (top to bottom) default, hover, and focus

overly specific rules, which decrease performance. We need to be on the lookout for excessive nesting in our code. If we notice that nesting becomes more than three levels deep, we should examine how our rules are nested and see whether some of the rules could be unnested.

With links styled, the next pieces of text we want to turn our attention to are the callout paragraphs.

12.5 @each

In our text, we have three callout paragraphs that have classes of `success`, `warning`, and `error`. As we did when we styled our images (section 12.4), we'll create a base rule and then extend it (listing 12.19). The rule defines the `border`, `border-radius`, and `padding` we want our callouts to have, and it includes the styles all three types have in common.

Listing 12.19 Callout base rule

```
.callout {
  border: solid 1px;
  border-radius: 4px;
  padding: .5rem 1rem;
}
```

Next, instead of writing individual rules for each callout type, we're going to create a map, a list of key-value pairs that we can iterate over to generate the rulesets. Because the differentiating factor of our callouts is the color, our key will be the type, and our value will be the color variable we defined at the beginning of this chapter. Our map, therefore, will be `$callouts: (success: $success, warning: $warning, error: $error);`. Figure 12.16 breaks down the syntax.

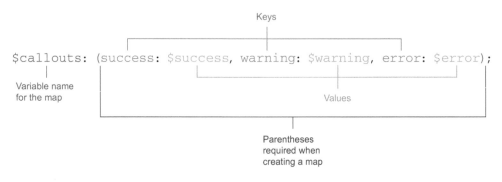

Figure 12.16 Sass map syntax

With the map created, we can loop over each key-value pair to generate our classes. For looping, we'll use `@each`. This at-rule iterates over all the items in a list or map in order, which is perfect for our use case. We'll add the following rule to our SCSS: `@each $type, $color in $callouts {}`. The first variable (`$type`) gives us access to the key, the second (`$color`) is the value of the key pair, and the last (`$callouts`) is the map we want to iterate over. We'll put the code to generate our rules inside the curly braces. To test our loop, we can add an `@debug` declaration inside the curly braces to check that our variable values are what we expect (listing 12.20).

> **NOTE** `@debug` is the Sass equivalent of JavaScript's `console.log()`. It allows us to print values to the terminal. Unfortunately, CodePen doesn't seem to have a way to expose Sass debug statements in its console. These statements won't show up in the browser's console, either. You'll be able to see the debug output only if you're running the project locally.

Listing 12.20   `@debug` statement inside our loop (SCSS)

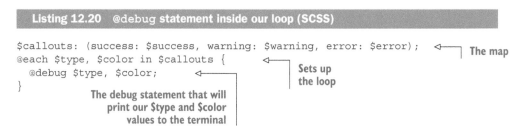

In the terminal where we have our Sass watcher running, the `@debug` statement outputs the file name, line number, the word *Debug*, and the values for our two variables (listing 12.21). Note that your line numbers may differ slightly from those displayed in the listing.

Listing 12.21   Output in terminal

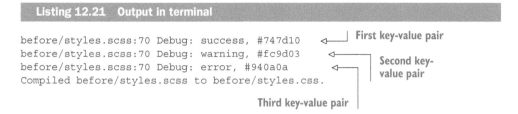

```
before/styles.scss:70 Debug: success, #747d10
before/styles.scss:70 Debug: warning, #fc9d03
before/styles.scss:70 Debug: error, #940a0a
Compiled before/styles.scss to before/styles.css.
```

First key-value pair

Second key-value pair

Third key-value pair

Now that we know our loop is working correctly, we can create rules for our callout types. In each ruleset, we extend our .callout base rule and add the correct border color for each type by using border-color. The value of the border-color property is the $color variable that comes from our @each loop. We mentioned earlier that Sass variables are static (section 12.2). As a result, the $color variable's value is reassigned for each key-value pair in the map, assigning the border-color correctly for each callout type.

Next, we add the type name before the paragraph by using the ::before pseudo element so that we have a visual indicator other than color telling the user what type of callout it is. Because the type value is lowercase in our map, we also use text-transform to capitalize it. Listing 12.22 shows our updated loop.

> **NOTE** Never use color alone to convey meaning. Some users, such as those who are color-blind, may have difficulty perceiving colors or may not be able to see them at all. In our case, the color conveys the type of callout, so we should include some other indicator (the text).

Listing 12.22   Adding to the loop (SCSS)

```scss
.callout {
  border: solid 1px;
  border-radius: 4px;
  padding: .5rem 1rem;
}


$callouts: (success: $success, warning: $warning, error: $error);
@each $type, $color in $callouts {
  @debug $type, $color;
  .#{$type} {                  ← Interpolation to create
    @extend .callout;            the class name
    border-color: $color;
    &::before {
      content: "#{$type}: ";   ← Interpolation to get
      text-transform: capitalize;  the type name in the
    }                              content
  }
}
```

As we did when we used interpolation to create a margin declaration in section 12.3.2, we use it here to create the class name and add the type to the content. By looping over the map, our @each rule creates three rules, one for each type. Each selector also gets added to the .callout rule via the @extend, as shown in the following listing.

Listing 12.23   Loop CSS output

```
.callout, .error, .warning, .success {
  border: solid 1px;
  border-radius: 4px;
  padding: 0.5rem 1rem;
}

.success {
  border-color: #747d10;
}
.success::before {
  content: "success: ";
  text-transform: capitalize;
}

.warning {
  border-color: #fc9d03;
}
.warning::before {
  content: "warning: ";
  text-transform: capitalize;
}

.error {
  border-color: #940a0a;
}
.error::before {
  content: "error: ";
  text-transform: capitalize;
}
```

All three class selectors (.error, .warning, .success) are added to the .callout base class.

Now our three callouts have colored borders (figure 12.17). But we still need to bold-face *Error:* in the error callout and add the background colors.

Pellentesque ac mi lobortis, **tincidunt purus** eu,
gravida enim. Vestibulum pharetra a arcu ac
suscipit. Ut et lorem dui. Donec non vehicula orci.
Nunc non ornare mi, ac aliquam risus.

Success: You did it!

Ut maximus id erat et mollis. Aenean sit amet
fringilla augue. Donec convallis vel nibh vitae
porttitor. Phasellus elementum nibh at erat semper
consectetur. Praesent convallis iaculis mauris, sit
amet egestas nunc gravida in. Donec dapibus mattis nibh, sed iaculis libero blandit et.

Step 2

Aenean non lorem tincidunt, vulputate nibh et,
convallis felis. Donec at tristique sem. Aenean id
leo non lectus hendrerit sodales. Maecenas
vulputate scelerisque dignissim. Integer purus nisl,
blandit in odio a, gravida interdum velit. Etiam
consectetur risus ante, vel pulvinar felis eleifend ut.
Phasellus nec tellus vitae sem semper ultrices at
et ligula.

Warning: Don't press the big red button

Proin pharetra, urna et sagittis lacinia, quam metus
vulputate eros, ac congue quam leo suscipit est.
Vestibulum ante ipsum primis in faucibus **orci luctus** et ultrices posuere cubilia curae; Vestibulum
nec suscipit ipsum. Vestibulum dapibus, neque vel lacinia mattis, magna sapien hendrerit justo,
sed laoreet sapien enim quis mauris.

Step 3

Nullam ut auctor nisi. Vestibulum pretium vitae
erat et hendrerit. Donec velit ipsum, fringilla sed
aliquam non, tincidunt a mauris. Mauris sit amet
diam lacus. Donec gravida felis nec ligula ultricies,
et molestie tellus tristique.

Error: Mistakes have been made

Vestibulum interdum eleifend suscipit. Nullam
imperdiet dignissim nulla, et mattis erat dignissim

Figure 12.17   Callout styles including colored borders

12.6   *Color functions*

We want the background colors for each callout to be significantly lighter than the
colors we currently have stored in our variables. To make working with colors easier,
Sass provides functions for manipulating colors. We're going to use `scale-color()`.
The `scale-color()` function is incredibly versatile and can be used to change the

amount of red, blue, and green in a color; change the saturation or opacity; and make a color lighter or darker (figure 12.18).

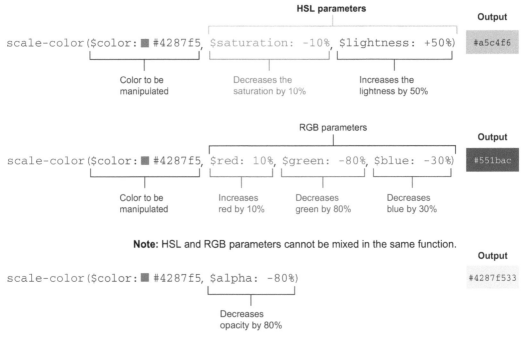

Figure 12.18 The `scale-color()` function

Worth noting is the fact that `scale-color()` operates with either HSL (hue, saturation, and lightness) or RGB (red, green, and blue) parameters; they can't be mixed. The alpha (transparency) parameter, however, can be used with either set of parameters. Also, parameters can be omitted. So if we want to change only the opacity, we need to pass only the initial color and the parameter(s) with which we want to manipulate the color.

For our backgrounds, we need to increase the lightness of the color, so we use HSL parameters. We don't need to change the saturation, so we'll omit the saturation parameter and pass in only the color and the amount by which we want to increase the lightness (`86%`), as shown in the following listing.

Listing 12.24   Adding the background color (SCSS)

```scss
$callouts: (success: $success, warning: $warning, error: $error);
@each $type, $color in $callouts {
  @debug $type, $color;
  .#{$type} {
    @extend .callout;
    background-color: scale-color($color, $lightness: +86%);
    border-color: $color;
```

> Increases the lightness of the color provided in the map by 86%

```
    &::before {
      content: "#{$type}: ";
      text-transform: capitalize;
    }
  }
}
```

The following listing shows the color generated by the scale-color() function in our
CSS output.

Listing 12.25   `scale-color()` function output (CSS)

```
.callout, .error, .warning, .success {
  border: solid 1px;
  border-radius: 4px;
  padding: 0.5rem 1rem;
}

.success {
  background-color: #f6f9d1;
  border-color: #747d10;
}
.success::before {
  content: "success: ";
  text-transform: capitalize;
}

.warning {
  background-color: #fff1dc;
  border-color: #fc9d03;
}
.warning::before {
  content: "warning: ";
  text-transform: capitalize;
}

.error {
  background-color: #fcd1d1;
  border-color: #940a0a;
}
.error::before {
  content: "error: ";
  text-transform: capitalize;
}
```

Now that we've added the background colors (figure 12.19), all we have left to do is
boldface *Error:* as part of the ::before content for the error callout.

12.7   @if and @else

Another set of at-rules that are available thanks to Sass are @if and @else, which control whether a block of code is evaluated and provide a fallback condition if the condition isn't met. We're going to use them inside our loop to boldface only the contents

of the ::before pseudo-element if the type of callout is error and increase the font weight to medium (500) for the others.

If you're used to JavaScript, a couple of gotchas can trip you up when evaluating equality in Sass, because Saas doesn't have truthy/falsy behaviors. Values are considered to be equal only if they have the same value and type. Also, Sass doesn't use the double pipe (||) or double ampersand (&&) but or and and for considering multiple conditions. The following listing shows examples of some of Sass's equality operators and what they resolve to.

Listing 12.26   Equalities (SCSS)

```
@debug '' == false;            // false        true, false, and null
@debug 'true' == true;         // false        are equal only to
@debug null == false;          // false        themselves.
@debug Verdana == 'Verdana';   // true
@debug 1cm == 10mm;            // true         Converted to the same
@debug 4 > 5 or 8 > 5;         // true         unit, they're equal in
@debug 4 > 5 and 8 > 5;        // false        size; therefore,
                                               they're equal.
Both values are
considered to
be strings.
```

To check that our $type variable is equal to 'error', our condition will be $type == 'error' coupled with @if and @else. Our rule looks like the following listing.

Listing 12.27   Conditionally boldfacing the callout type (SCSS)

```
$callouts: (success: $success, warning: $warning, error: $error);
@each $type, $color in $callouts {
  @debug $type, $color;
  .#{$type} {
    @extend .callout;
    background-color: scale-color($color, $lightness: +86%);
    border-color: $color;
    &::before {
      content: "#{$type}: ";                   The type is error;
      text-transform: capitalize;              therefore, we add a
      @if $type == 'error' {                   font width of 800.
        font-weight: 800;
      } @else {                                The type isn't error (it's either
        font-weight: 500;                      success or warning), so font-
      }                                        weight is set to 500.
    }
  }
}
```

The following listing shows that font weights have been added to each type in the CSS output.

Listing 12.28   Conditionally boldfacing the callout type (CSS output)

```css
.callout, .error, .warning, .success {
  border: solid 1px;
  border-radius: 4px;
  padding: 0.5rem 1rem;
}

.success {
  background-color: #f6f9d1;
  border-color: #747d10;
}
.success::before {
  content: "success: ";
  text-transform: capitalize;
  font-weight: 500;
}

.warning {
  background-color: #fff1dc;
  border-color: #fc9d03;
}
.warning::before {
  content: "warning: ";
  text-transform: capitalize;
  font-weight: 500;
}

.error {
  background-color: #fcd1d1;
  border-color: #940a0a;
}
.error::before {
  content: "error: ";
  text-transform: capitalize;
  font-weight: 800;
}
```

The text added as part of the `::before` pseudo-element has a `font-weight` of `500` for both `.success` and `.warning`. The `.error::before` rule, on the other hand, has a `font-weight` of `800`.

   With this last detail added, our project is complete. Figure 12.19 shows the final output.

12.8   Final thoughts

This chapter illustrates several things Saas lets us do that we can't do with CSS alone, but it covers only a small percentage of Saas's features and delves into only one preprocessor. Preprocessors can do much more; this chapter only scratches the surface. The takeaway is that preprocessors provide cool functionality that can make code more efficient to write and also more complex. They also require a build step and slightly more complicated setup.

Keeping it Sassy

Step 1

Lorem ipsum dolor sit amet, consectetur adipiscing elit. Sed porta erat nec ipsum volutpat ultrices. Pellentesque ac mi lobortis, **tincidunt purus** eu, gravida enim. Vestibulum pharetra a arcu ac suscipit. Ut et lorem dui. Donec non vehicula orci. Nunc non ornare mi, ac aliquam risus.

> **Success:** You did it!

Ut maximus id erat et mollis. Aenean sit amet fringilla augue. Donec convallis vel nibh vitae porttitor. Phasellus elementum nibh at erat semper consectetur. Praesent convallis iaculis mauris, sit amet egestas nunc gravida in. Donec dapibus mattis nibh, sed iaculis libero blandit et.

Step 2

Aenean non lorem tincidunt, vulputate nibh et, convallis felis. Donec at tristique sem. Aenean id leo non lectus hendrerit sodales. Maecenas vulputate scelerisque dignissim. Integer purus nisl, blandit in odio a, gravida interdum velit. Etiam consectetur risus ante, vel pulvinar felis eleifend ut. Phasellus nec tellus vitae sem semper ultrices at et ligula.

> **Warning:** Don't press the big red button

Proin pharetra, urna et sagittis lacinia, quam metus vulputate eros, ac congue quam leo suscipit est. Vestibulum ante ipsum primis in faucibus orci luctus et ultrices posuere cubilia curae; Vestibulum nec suscipit ipsum. Vestibulum dapibus, neque vel lacinia mattis, magna sapien hendrerit justo, sed laoreet sapien enim quis mauris.

Step 3

Nullam ut auctor nisi. Vestibulum pretium vitae erat et hendrerit. Donec velit ipsum, fringilla sed aliquam non, tincidunt a mauris. Mauris sit amet diam lacus. Donec gravida felis nec ligula ultricies, et molestie tellus tristique.

> **Error:** Mistakes have been made

Vestibulum interdum eleifend suscipit. Nullam imperdiet dignissim nulla, et mattis erat dignissim ut. Proin dui felis, venenatis sit amet lacus at, commodo elementum dolor. Vestibulum et justo eu est pharetra pulvinar. Duis fermentum iaculis velit, in hendrerit metus efficitur vel. Fusce vitae mollis nisl. Fusce eu viverra erat. Vivamus nunc risus, consectetur at eros ac, bibendum viverra massa. Aliquam metus lacus, condimentum in ligula eget, molestie faucibus odio. Integer eros tellus, tristique non elementum eget, congue scelerisque quam.

Figure 12.19   Finished project

Although we didn't dive into Less or Stylus, here are some questions that may help when you're choosing a preprocessor:

- Do I need a preprocessor?
- What functionality does the preprocessor need?
- How is using a preprocessor going to help the development of my project?
- If the project uses a user-interface framework or library, does it support one or more preprocessors? If so, which ones?
- What will having a preprocessor change about my build-and-deploy process because now the CSS needs to be built?
- What skills do my team members have, and which preprocessors are they familiar with?

Whether or not preprocessors are for you, the important thing to remember is that every project is different. Keep learning, exploring, and trying new things, and have some fun. Happy coding!

Summary

- Sass has two syntaxes: indented and SCSS.
- Variables and CSS custom properties work differently.
- Sass variables are block-scoped.
- `@extend` extends existing rules, whereas mixins generate new code.
- Mixins can take parameters.
- When used in conjunction with `object-fit: cover`, `object-position` helps position an image within its bound box when the image doesn't have the same aspect ratio as the dimensions it's given.
- Interpolation is used to embed the result of an expression, such as when creating rule names from variables.
- The `border-radius` property can take multiple values to assign different curvature to each corner of an element, starting from top left and rotating clockwise.
- Sass allows us to nest rules.
- We can use `@each` to loop over lists and maps.
- `@debug` allows us to print values in the terminal output.
- Sass provides functions such as `scale-color()` to manipulate and alter colors.
- `@if` and `@else` can be used to determine conditionally whether a block of code should be evaluated.

appendix

Working with vendor prefixes and feature flags

Probably one of the most frustrating aspects of CSS, especially when using new CSS syntax, is vendor prefixing. Each browser has a type of engine, which is referred to as the *vendor*. The purpose of the engine is to convert the code (HTML, CSS, and JavaScript) into what the end user sees and interacts with, such as a web page or application. There are three main browser engines:

- *Gecko* (also known as Quantum)—Used by the Firefox browser and maintained by Mozilla
- *WebKit*—Used by Safari and iOS Safari, and developed by Apple
- *Blink*—Used by Chrome, Microsoft Edge, and Opera, and maintained by Google

As a writer of CSS, you may find that some properties still require vendor prefixes, especially if you or the organization you work for supports old browser engines. The prefix comes before the CSS property. In total, there are four prefixes, listed in table A.1.

Table A.1 Vendor prefixes by browser

Prefix	Browser
-webkit-	Android, Chrome, iOS, Edge and Opera (newer versions), and Safari
-ms-	Internet Explorer and Edge (older versions)
-o-	Opera (older versions)
-moz-	Firefox

360

Although Chrome uses the Blink engine, it still uses the `-webkit-` prefix, as Chrome was built on WebKit. When Chrome moved to the Blink engine, it decided to stick with the `-webkit-` prefix rather than create a new one, to reduce confusion. As you'll see in this appendix, there's a move away from prefixes anyway.

When using prefixes, you should put the prefixed versions before the nonprefixed versions. The reason to include the nonprefixed version is that when the browser supports that property fully, it will use the nonprefixed version; then you can remove the prefix. An example of a CSS property that needs prefixing is `user-select`, if you use `none` as the value:

```
.prevent-selecting{
  -moz-user-select: none;
  -webkit-user-select: none;
  -ms-user-select: none;
  user-select: none;
}
```

The idea behind vendor prefixes is that you can try new CSS without breaking the experience while the new CSS is being standardized across browsers. We don't recommend putting out prefixed code live to users, however, as the way that browsers interpret that code can change.

There's a shift away from browser prefixes because they've led to partial implementations and bugs and have long confused developers. We often see stylesheets with prefixes that haven't been required for several years because the stylesheets haven't been updated or the developers aren't sure whether it's safe to remove the prefixes. Instead, there's a move toward feature flags, which users can control. When writing CSS, you'll find that some CSS properties still in use need browser prefixes. In this case, the prefix versions of the CSS property should come before the nonprefixed version.

Using browser developer tools

Chrome, Safari, Firefox, and other mainstream browsers have developer tools, which are perfect for editing and diagnosing problems, particularly if you're doing frontend development. You can edit your CSS within the browser and then copy and paste the styles to your project.

The tools and the way they're presented vary among browsers. Following are some useful features that are universal in the main browsers:

- *Elements panel*, where you can view and change the document object model (DOM) and CSS.
- *Console panel*, which highlights any errors loading assets such as the CSS, images, and other media items.
- *Network and performance panels*, which can vary among browsers. In Chrome, you use these panels to see how the web page is loading and find opportunities to improve the performance and efficiency of the page.

Each browser has its own documentation for developer tools, and this material is worth exploring as you develop your knowledge of CSS (table A.2).

Table A.2 Browser developer tools documentation

Browser	URL
Chrome	http://mng.bz/N2d2
Firefox	http://mng.bz/D489
Safari	https://developer.apple.com/safari/tools
Edge	http://mng.bz/lWEM

index

RELATED MANNING TITLES

Web Design Playground, Second Edition
by Paul McFedries

ISBN 9781633438323
400 pages *(estimated)*, $39.99
Fall 2023 *(estimated)*

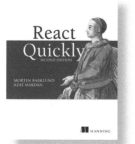

React Quickly, Second Edition
by Morten Barklund and Azat Mardan

ISBN 9781633439290
575 pages *(estimated)*, $59.99
Fall 2023 *(estimated)*

Testing Web APIs
by Mark Winteringham
Foreword by Janet Gregory and Lisa Crispin

ISBN 9781617299537
264 pages, $59.99
October 2022

Learn AI-Assisted Python Programming
by Daniel Zingaro and Leo Porter

ISBN 9781633437784
300 pages *(estimated)*, $49.99
Spring 2024 *(estimated)*

For ordering information, go to www.manning.com

 **MANNING**

Hands-on projects for learning your way

liveProjects are an exciting way to develop your skills that's just like learning on the job.

In a Manning liveProject, you tackle a real-world IT challenge and work out your own solutions. To make sure you succeed, you'll get 90 days of full and unlimited access to a hand-picked list of Manning book and video resources.

Here's how liveProject works:

- **Achievable milestones.** Each project is broken down into steps and sections so you can keep track of your progress.

- **Collaboration and advice.** Work with other liveProject participants through chat, working groups, and peer project reviews.

- **Compare your results.** See how your work shapes up against an expert implementation by the liveProject's creator.

- **Everything you need to succeed.** Datasets and carefully selected learning resources come bundled with every liveProject.

- **Build your portfolio.** All liveProjects teach skills that are in demand from industry. When you're finished, you'll have the satisfaction that comes with success and a real project to add to your portfolio.

Explore dozens of data, development, and cloud engineering liveProjects at www.manning.com!